# Laws

**Plato**

**Translated by Benjamin Jowett**

This book has been published by:

NuVision Publications, LLC
The future of digital publishing.

Contact: sales@nuvisionpublications.com

URL: http://www.nuvisionpublications.com

Publishing Date: 2006

ISBN# 1-59547-953-8

# Table of Contents

## Laws

# LAWS

## BOOK I.

PERSONS OF THE DIALOGUE: An Athenian Stranger, Cleinias (a Cretan), Megillus (a Lacedaemonian).

**ATHENIAN:** Tell me, Strangers, is a God or some man supposed to be the author of your laws?

**CLEINIAS:** A God, Stranger; in very truth a God: among us Cretans he is said to have been Zeus, but in Lacedaemon, whence our friend here comes, I believe they would say that Apollo is their lawgiver: would they not, Megillus?

**MEGILLUS:** Certainly.

**ATHENIAN:** And do you, Cleinias, believe, as Homer tells, that every ninth year Minos went to converse with his Olympian sire, and was inspired by him to make laws for your cities?

**CLEINIAS:** Yes, that is our tradition; and there was Rhadamanthus, a brother of his, with whose name you are familiar; he is reputed to have been the justest of men, and we Cretans are of opinion that he earned this reputation from his righteous administration of justice when he was alive.

**ATHENIAN:** Yes, and a noble reputation it was, worthy of a son of Zeus. As you and Megillus have been trained in these institutions, I dare say that you will not be unwilling to give an account of your government and laws; on our way we can pass the time pleasantly in talking about them, for I am told that the distance from Cnosus to the cave and temple of Zeus is considerable; and doubtless there are shady places under the lofty trees, which will protect us from this scorching sun. Being no longer young, we may often stop to rest beneath them, and get over the whole journey without difficulty, beguiling the time by conversation.

**CLEINIAS:** Yes, Stranger, and if we proceed onward we shall come to groves of cypresses, which are of rare height and beauty, and there are green meadows, in which we may repose and converse.

**ATHENIAN:** Very good.

**CLEINIAS:** Very good, indeed; and still better when we see them; let us move on cheerily.

**ATHENIAN:** I am willing--And first, I want to know why the law has ordained that you shall have common meals and gymnastic exercises, and wear arms.

**CLEINIAS:** I think, Stranger, that the aim of our institutions is easily intelligible to any one. Look at the character of our country: Crete is not like Thessaly, a large plain; and for this reason they have horsemen in Thessaly, and we have runners--the inequality of the ground in our country is more adapted to locomotion on foot; but then, if you have runners you must have light arms--no one can carry a heavy weight when running, and bows and arrows are convenient because they are light. Now all these regulations have been made with a view to war, and the legislator appears to me to have looked to this in all his arrangements:--the common meals, if I am not mistaken, were instituted by him for a similar reason, because he saw that while they are in the field the citizens are by the nature of the case compelled to take their meals together for the sake of mutual protection. He seems to me to have thought the world foolish in not understanding that all men are always at war with one another; and if in war there ought to be common meals and certain persons regularly appointed under others to protect an army, they should be continued in peace. For what men in general term peace would be said by him to be only a name; in reality every city is in a natural state of war with every other, not indeed proclaimed by heralds, but everlasting. And if you look closely, you will find that this was the intention of the Cretan legislator; all institutions, private as well as public, were arranged by him with a view to war; in giving them he was under the impression that no possessions or institutions are of any value to him who is defeated in battle; for all the good things of the conquered pass into the hands of the conquerors.

**ATHENIAN:** You appear to me, Stranger, to have been thoroughly trained in the Cretan institutions, and to be well informed about them; will you tell me a little more explicitly what is the principle of government which you would lay down? You seem to imagine that a well-governed state ought to be so ordered as to conquer all other states in war: am I right in supposing this to be your meaning?

**CLEINIAS:** Certainly; and our Lacedaemonian friend, if I am not mistaken, will agree with me.

**MEGILLUS:** Why, my good friend, how could any Lacedaemonian say anything else?

**ATHENIAN:** And is what you say applicable only to states, or also to villages?

**CLEINIAS:** To both alike.

**ATHENIAN:** The case is the same?

**CLEINIAS:** Yes.

**ATHENIAN:** And in the village will there be the same war of family against family, and of individual against individual?

**CLEINIAS:** The same.

**ATHENIAN:** And should each man conceive himself to be his own enemy:--what shall we say?

**CLEINIAS:** O Athenian Stranger--inhabitant of Attica I will not call you, for you seem to deserve rather to be named after the goddess herself, because you go back to first principles,--you have thrown a light upon the argument, and will now be better able to understand what I was just saying, --that all men are publicly one another's enemies, and each man privately his own.

(**ATHENIAN:** My good sir, what do you mean?)--

**CLEINIAS:**...Moreover, there is a victory and defeat--the first and best of victories, the lowest and worst of defeats--which each man gains or sustains at the hands, not of another, but of himself; this shows that there is a war against ourselves going on within every one of us.

**ATHENIAN:** Let us now reverse the order of the argument: Seeing that every individual is either his own superior or his own inferior, may we say that there is the same principle in the house, the village, and the state?

**CLEINIAS:** You mean that in each of them there is a principle of superiority or inferiority to self?

**ATHENIAN:** Yes.

**CLEINIAS:** You are quite right in asking the question, for there certainly is such a principle, and above all in states; and the state in which the better citizens win a victory over the mob and over the inferior classes may be truly said to be better than itself, and may be justly praised, where such a victory is gained, or censured in the opposite case.

**ATHENIAN:** Whether the better is ever really conquered by the worse, is a question which requires more discussion, and may be therefore left for the present. But I now quite understand your meaning when you say that citizens who are of the same race and live in the same cities may unjustly conspire, and having the superiority in numbers may overcome and enslave the few just; and when they prevail, the state may be truly called its own inferior and therefore bad; and when they are defeated, its own superior and therefore good.

**CLEINIAS:** Your remark, Stranger, is a paradox, and yet we cannot possibly deny it.

**ATHENIAN:** Here is another case for consideration;--in a family there may be several brothers, who are the offspring of a single pair; very possibly the majority of them may be unjust, and the just may be in a minority.

**CLEINIAS:** Very possibly.

**ATHENIAN:** And you and I ought not to raise a question of words as to whether this family and household are rightly said to be superior when they conquer, and inferior when they are conquered; for we are not now considering what may or may not be the proper or customary way of speaking, but we are considering the natural principles of right and wrong in laws.

**CLEINIAS:** What you say, Stranger, is most true.

**MEGILLUS:** Quite excellent, in my opinion, as far as we have gone.

**ATHENIAN:** Again; might there not be a judge over these brethren, of whom we were speaking?

**CLEINIAS:** Certainly.

**ATHENIAN:** Now, which would be the better judge--one who destroyed the bad and appointed the good to govern themselves; or one who, while allowing the good to govern, let the bad live, and made them voluntarily submit? Or third, I suppose, in the scale of excellence might be placed a judge, who, finding the family distracted, not only did not destroy any one, but reconciled them to one another for ever after, and gave them laws which they mutually observed, and was able to keep them friends.

**CLEINIAS:** The last would be by far the best sort of judge and legislator.

**ATHENIAN:** And yet the aim of all the laws which he gave would be the reverse of war.

**CLEINIAS:** Very true.

**ATHENIAN:** And will he who constitutes the state and orders the life of man have in view external war, or that kind of intestine war called civil, which no one, if he could prevent, would like to have occurring in his own state; and when occurring, every one would wish to be quit of as soon as possible?

**CLEINIAS:** He would have the latter chiefly in view.

**ATHENIAN:** And would he prefer that this civil war should be terminated by the destruction of one of the parties, and by the victory of the other, or that peace and friendship should be re-established, and that, being reconciled, they should give their attention to foreign enemies?

**CLEINIAS:** Every one would desire the latter in the case of his own state.

**ATHENIAN:** And would not that also be the desire of the legislator?

**CLEINIAS:** Certainly.

**ATHENIAN:** And would not every one always make laws for the sake of the best?

**CLEINIAS:** To be sure.

**ATHENIAN:** But war, whether external or civil, is not the best, and the need of either is to be deprecated; but peace with one another, and good will, are best. Nor is the victory of the state over itself to be regarded as a really good thing, but as a necessity; a man might as well say that the body was in the best state when sick and purged by medicine, forgetting that there is also a state of the body which needs no purge. And in like manner no one can be a true statesman, whether he aims at the happiness of the individual or state, who looks only, or first of all, to external warfare; nor will he ever be a sound legislator who orders peace for the sake of war, and not war for the sake of peace.

**CLEINIAS:** I suppose that there is truth, Stranger, in that remark of yours; and yet I am greatly mistaken if war is not the entire aim and object of our own institutions, and also of the Lacedaemonian.

**ATHENIAN:** I dare say; but there is no reason why we should rudely quarrel with one another about your legislators, instead of gently questioning them, seeing that both we and they are equally in earnest. Please follow me and the argument closely:--And first I will put forward Tyrtaeus, an Athenian by birth, but also a Spartan citizen, who of all men was most eager about war: Well, he says,

*'I sing not, I care not, about any man, even if he were the richest of men, and possessed every good (and then he gives a whole list of them), if he be not at all times a brave warrior.' I imagine that you, too,*

*must have heard his poems; our Lacedaemonian friend has probably heard more than enough of them.*

**MEGILLUS:** Very true.

**CLEINIAS:** And they have found their way from Lacedaemon to Crete.

**ATHENIAN:** Come now and let us all join in asking this question of Tyrtaeus: O most divine poet, we will say to him, the excellent praise which you have bestowed on those who excel in war sufficiently proves that you are wise and good, and I and Megillus and Cleinias of Cnosus do, as I believe, entirely agree with you. But we should like to be quite sure that we are speaking of the same men; tell us, then, do you agree with us in thinking that there are two kinds of war; or what would you say? A far inferior man to Tyrtaeus would have no difficulty in replying quite truly, that war is of two kinds,--one which is universally called civil war, and is, as we were just now saying, of all wars the worst; the other, as we should all admit, in which we fall out with other nations who are of a different race, is a far milder form of warfare.

**CLEINIAS:** Certainly, far milder.

**ATHENIAN:** Well, now, when you praise and blame war in this high-flown strain, whom are you praising or blaming, and to which kind of war are you referring? I suppose that you must mean foreign war, if I am to judge from expressions of yours in which you say that you abominate those *'Who refuse to look upon fields of blood, and will not draw near and strike at their enemies.'*

And we shall naturally go on to say to him,--You, Tyrtaeus, as it seems, praise those who distinguish themselves in external and foreign war; and he must admit this.

**CLEINIAS:** Evidently.

**ATHENIAN:** They are good; but we say that there are still better men whose virtue is displayed in the greatest of all battles. And we too have a poet whom we summon as a witness, Theognis, citizen of Megara in Sicily: *'Cyrnus,' he says, 'he who is faithful in a civil broil is worth his weight in gold and silver.'*

And such an one is far better, as we affirm, than the other in a more difficult kind of war, much in the same degree as justice and temperance and wisdom, when united with courage, are better than courage only; for a man cannot be faithful and good in civil strife without having all virtue. But in the war of which Tyrtaeus speaks, many a mercenary soldier will take his stand and be ready to die at his post, and yet they are generally and almost without exception insolent, unjust, violent men, and the most senseless of human beings. You will ask what the conclusion is, and what I am seeking to prove: I maintain that the divine legislator of Crete, like any other who is worthy of consideration, will always and above all things in making laws have regard to the greatest virtue; which, according to Theognis, is loyalty in the hour of danger, and may be truly called perfect justice. Whereas, that virtue which Tyrtaeus highly praises is well enough, and was praised by the poet at the right time, yet in place and dignity may be said to be only fourth rate (i.e., it ranks after justice, temperance, and wisdom.).

**CLEINIAS:** Stranger, we are degrading our inspired lawgiver to a rank which is far beneath him.

**ATHENIAN:** Nay, I think that we degrade not him but ourselves, if we imagine that Lycurgus and Minos laid down laws both in Lacedaemon and Crete mainly with a view to war.

**CLEINIAS:** What ought we to say then?

**ATHENIAN:** What truth and what justice require of us, if I am not mistaken, when speaking in behalf of divine excellence;--that the legislator when making his laws had in view not a part only, and this the lowest part of virtue, but all virtue, and that he devised classes of laws answering to the kinds of virtue; not in the way in which modern inventors of laws make the classes, for they only investigate and offer laws whenever a want is felt, and one man has a class of laws about allotments and heiresses, another about assaults; others about ten thousand other such matters. But we maintain that the right way of examining into laws is to proceed as we have now done, and I admired the spirit of your exposition; for you were quite right in beginning with virtue, and saying that this was the aim of the giver of the law, but I thought that you went wrong when you added that all his legislation had a view only to a part, and the least part of virtue, and this called forth my subsequent remarks. Will you allow me then to explain how I should have liked to have heard you expound the matter?

**CLEINIAS:** By all means.

**ATHENIAN:** You ought to have said, Stranger--The Cretan laws are with reason famous among the Hellenes; for they fulfil the object of laws, which is to make those who use them happy; and they confer every sort of good. Now goods are of two kinds: there are human and there are divine goods, and the human hang upon the divine; and the state which attains the greater, at the same time acquires the less, or, not having the greater, has neither. Of the lesser goods the first is health, the second beauty, the third strength, including swiftness in running and bodily agility generally, and the fourth is wealth, not the blind god (Pluto), but one who is keen of sight, if only he has wisdom for his companion. For wisdom is chief and leader of the divine class of goods, and next follows temperance; and from the union of these two with courage springs justice, and fourth in the scale of virtue is courage.

All these naturally take precedence of the other goods, and this is the order in which the legislator must place them, and after them he will enjoin the rest of his ordinances on the citizens with a view to these, the human looking to the divine, and the divine looking to their leader mind. Some of his ordinances will relate to contracts of marriage which they make one with another, and then to the procreation and education of children, both male and female; the duty of the lawgiver will be to take charge of his citizens, in youth and age, and at every time of life, and to give them punishments and rewards; and in reference to all their intercourse with one another, he ought to consider their pains and pleasures and desires, and the vehemence of all their passions; he should keep a watch over them, and blame and praise them rightly by the mouth of the laws themselves. Also with regard to anger and terror, and the other perturbations of the soul, which arise out of misfortune, and the deliverances from them which prosperity brings, and the experiences which come to men in diseases, or in war, or poverty, or the opposite of these; in all these states he should determine and teach what is the good and evil of the condition of each. In the next place, the legislator has to be careful how the citizens make their money and in what way they spend it, and to have an eye to their mutual contracts and dissolutions of contracts, whether voluntary or involuntary: he should see how they order all this, and consider where justice as well as injustice is found or is wanting in their several dealings with one another; and honour those who obey the law, and impose fixed penalties on those who disobey, until the round of civil life is ended, and the time has come for the consideration of the proper funeral rites and honours of the dead. And the lawgiver reviewing his work, will appoint guardians to preside over these things,--some who walk by intelligence, others by true opinion only, and then mind will bind together all his ordinances and show them to be in harmony with temperance and justice, and not with wealth or ambition. This is the spirit, Stranger, in which I was and am desirous that you should pursue the subject. And I want to know the nature of all these things, and how they are arranged in the laws of Zeus, as they are termed, and in those of the Pythian Apollo, which Minos and Lycurgus gave; and how the order of them is discovered to his eyes, who has experience in laws gained either by study or habit, although they are far from being self-evident to the rest of mankind like ourselves.

**CLEINIAS:** How shall we proceed, Stranger?

**ATHENIAN:** I think that we must begin again as before, and first consider the habit of courage; and then we will go on and discuss another and then another form of virtue, if you please. In this way we shall have a model of the whole; and with these and similar discourses we will beguile the way. And when we have gone through all the virtues, we will show, by the grace of God, that the institutions of which I was speaking look to virtue.

**MEGILLUS:** Very good; and suppose that you first criticize this praise of Zeus and the laws of Crete.

**ATHENIAN:** I will try to criticize you and myself, as well as him, for the argument is a common concern. Tell me,--were not first the syssitia, and secondly the gymnasia, invented by your legislator with a view to war?

**MEGILLUS:** Yes.

**ATHENIAN:** And what comes third, and what fourth? For that, I think, is the sort of enumeration which ought to be made of the remaining parts of virtue, no matter whether you call them parts or what their name is, provided the meaning is clear.

**MEGILLUS:** Then I, or any other Lacedaemonian, would reply that hunting is third in order.

**ATHENIAN:** Let us see if we can discover what comes fourth and fifth.

**MEGILLUS:** I think that I can get as far as the fourth head, which is the frequent endurance of pain, exhibited among us Spartans in certain hand-to- hand fights; also in stealing with the prospect of getting a good beating; there is, too, the so-called Crypteia, or secret service, in which wonderful endurance is shown,--our people wander over the whole country by day and by night, and even in winter have not a shoe to their foot, and are without beds to lie upon, and have to attend upon themselves. Marvellous, too, is the endurance which our citizens show in their naked exercises, contending against the violent summer heat; and there are many similar practices, to speak of which in detail would be endless.

**ATHENIAN:** Excellent, O Lacedaemonian Stranger. But how ought we to define courage? Is it to be regarded only as a combat against fears and pains, or also against desires and pleasures, and against flatteries; which exercise such a tremendous power, that they make the hearts even of respectable citizens to melt like wax?

**MEGILLUS:** I should say the latter.

**ATHENIAN:** In what preceded, as you will remember, our Cnosian friend was speaking of a man or a city being inferior to themselves:--Were you not, Cleinias?

**CLEINIAS:** I was.

**ATHENIAN:** Now, which is in the truest sense inferior, the man who is overcome by pleasure or by pain?

**CLEINIAS:** I should say the man who is overcome by pleasure; for all men deem him to be inferior in a more disgraceful sense, than the other who is overcome by pain.

**ATHENIAN:** But surely the lawgivers of Crete and Lacedaemon have not legislated for a courage which is lame of one leg, able only to meet attacks which come from the left, but impotent against the insidious flatteries which come from the right?

**CLEINIAS:** Able to meet both, I should say.

**ATHENIAN:** Then let me once more ask, what institutions have you in either of your states which give a taste of pleasures, and do not avoid them any more than they avoid pains; but which set a person in the midst of them, and compel or induce him by the prospect of reward to get the better of them? Where is an ordinance about pleasure similar to that about pain to be found in your laws? Tell me what there is of this nature among you:-- What is there which makes your citizen equally brave against pleasure and pain, conquering what they ought to conquer, and superior to the enemies who are most dangerous and nearest home?

**MEGILLUS:** I was able to tell you, Stranger, many laws which were directed against pain; but I do not know that I can point out any great or obvious examples of similar institutions which are concerned with pleasure; there are some lesser provisions, however, which I might mention.

**CLEINIAS:** Neither can I show anything of that sort which is at all equally prominent in the Cretan laws.

**ATHENIAN:** No wonder, my dear friends; and if, as is very likely, in our search after the true and good, one of us may have to censure the laws of the others, we must not be offended, but take kindly what another says.

**CLEINIAS:** You are quite right, Athenian Stranger, and we will do as you say.

**ATHENIAN:** At our time of life, Cleinias, there should be no feeling of irritation.

**CLEINIAS:** Certainly not.

**ATHENIAN:** I will not at present determine whether he who censures the Cretan or Lacedaemonian polities is right or wrong. But I believe that I can tell better than either of you what the many say about them. For assuming that you have reasonably good laws, one of the best of them will be the law forbidding any young men to enquire which of them are right or wrong; but with one mouth and one voice they must all agree that the laws are all good, for they came from God; and any one who says the contrary is not to be listened to. But an old man who remarks any defect in your laws may communicate his observation to a ruler or to an equal in years when no young man is present.

**CLEINIAS:** Exactly so, Stranger; and like a diviner, although not there at the time, you seem to me quite to have hit the meaning of the legislator, and to say what is most true.

**ATHENIAN:** As there are no young men present, and the legislator has given old men free licence, there will be no impropriety in our discussing these very matters now that we are alone.

**CLEINIAS:** True. And therefore you may be as free as you like in your censure of our laws, for there is no discredit in knowing what is wrong; he who receives what is said in a generous and friendly spirit will be all the better for it.

**ATHENIAN:** Very good; however, I am not going to say anything against your laws until to the best of my ability I have examined them, but I am going to raise doubts about them. For you are the only people known to us, whether Greek or barbarian, whom the legislator commanded to eschew all great pleasures and amusements and never to touch them; whereas in the matter of pains or fears which we have just been discussing, he thought that they who from infancy had always avoided pains and fears and sorrows, when they were compelled to face them would run away from those who were hardened in them, and would become their subjects. Now the legislator ought to have considered that this was equally true of pleasure; he should have said to himself, that if our citizens are from their youth upward unacquainted with the greatest pleasures, and unused to endure amid the temptations of pleasure, and are not disciplined to refrain from all things evil, the sweet feeling of pleasure will overcome them just as fear would overcome the former class; and in another, and even a worse manner, they will be the slaves of those who are able to endure amid pleasures, and have had the opportunity of enjoying them, they being often the worst of mankind. One half of their souls will be a slave, the other half free; and they will not be worthy to be called in the true sense men and freemen. Tell me whether you assent to my words?

**CLEINIAS:** On first hearing, what you say appears to be the truth; but to be hasty in coming to a conclusion about such important matters would be very childish and simple.

**ATHENIAN:** Suppose, Cleinias and Megillus, that we consider the virtue which follows next of those which we intended to discuss (for after courage comes temperance), what institutions shall we find relating to temperance, either in Crete or Lacedaemon, which, like your military institutions, differ from those of any ordinary state.

**MEGILLUS:** That is not an easy question to answer; still I should say that the common meals and gymnastic exercises have been excellently devised for the promotion both of temperance and courage.

**ATHENIAN:** There seems to be a difficulty, Stranger, with regard to states, in making words and facts coincide so that there can be no dispute about them. As in the human body, the regimen which does good in one way does harm in another; and we can hardly say that any one course of treatment is adapted to a particular constitution. Now the gymnasia and common meals do a great deal of good, and yet they are a source of evil in civil troubles; as is shown in the case of the Milesian, and Boeotian, and Thurian youth, among whom these institutions seem always to have had a tendency to degrade the ancient and natural custom of love below the level, not only of man, but of the beasts. The charge may be fairly brought against your cities above all others, and is true also of most other states which especially cultivate gymnastics. Whether such matters are to be regarded jestingly or seriously, I think that the pleasure is to be deemed natural which arises out of the intercourse between men and women; but that the intercourse of men with men, or of women with women, is contrary to nature, and that the bold attempt was originally due to unbridled lust. The Cretans are always accused of having invented the story of Ganymede and Zeus because they wanted to justify themselves in the enjoyment of unnatural pleasures by the practice of the god whom they believe to have been their lawgiver. Leaving the story, we may observe that any speculation about laws turns almost entirely on pleasure and pain, both in states and in individuals: these are two fountains which nature lets flow, and he who draws from them where and when, and as much as he ought, is happy; and this holds of men and animals--of individuals as well as states; and he who indulges in them ignorantly and at the wrong time, is the reverse of happy.

**MEGILLUS:** I admit, Stranger, that your words are well spoken, and I hardly know what to say in answer to you; but still I think that the Spartan lawgiver was quite right in forbidding pleasure. Of the Cretan laws, I shall leave the defence to my Cnosian friend. But the laws of Sparta, in as far as they relate to pleasure, appear to me to be the best in the world; for that which leads mankind in general into the wildest pleasure and licence, and every other folly, the law has clean driven out; and neither in the country nor in towns which are under the control of Sparta, will you find revelries and the many incitements of every kind of pleasure which accompany them; and any one who meets a drunken and disorderly person, will immediately have him most severely punished, and will not let him off on any pretence, not even at the time of a Dionysiac festival; although I have remarked that this may happen at your performances 'on the cart,' as they are called; and among our Tarentine colonists I have seen the whole city drunk at a Dionysiac festival; but nothing of the sort happens among us.

**ATHENIAN:** O Lacedaemonian Stranger, these festivities are praiseworthy where there is a spirit of endurance, but are very senseless when they are under no regulations. In order to retaliate, an Athenian has only to point out the licence which exists among your women. To all such accusations, whether they are brought against the Tarentines, or us, or you, there is one answer which exonerates the practice in question from impropriety. When a stranger expresses wonder at the singularity of what he sees, any inhabitant will naturally answer him:--Wonder not, O stranger; this is our custom, and you may very likely have some other custom about the same things. Now we are speaking, my friends, not about men in general, but about the merits and defects of the lawgivers themselves. Let us then discourse a little more at length about intoxication, which is a very important subject, and will seriously task the discrimination of the legislator. I am not speaking of drinking, or not drinking, wine at all, but of intoxication. Are we to follow the custom of the Scythians, and Persians, and Carthaginians, and Celts, and Iberians, and Thracians, who are all warlike nations, or that of your countrymen, for they, as you say, altogether abstain? But the Scythians and Thracians, both men and women, drink unmixed wine, which they pour on their garments, and this they think a happy and glorious institution. The Persians, again, are much given to other practices of luxury which you reject, but they have more moderation in them than the Thracians and Scythians.

**MEGILLUS:** O best of men, we have only to take arms into our hands, and we send all these nations flying before us.

**ATHENIAN:** Nay, my good friend, do not say that; there have been, as there always will be, flights and pursuits of which no account can be given, and therefore we cannot say that victory or defeat in battle affords more than a doubtful proof of the goodness or badness of institutions. For when the greater states conquer and enslave the lesser, as the Syracusans have done the Locrians, who appear to be the best-governed people in their part of the world, or as the Athenians have done the Ceans (and there are ten thousand other instances of the same sort of thing), all this is not to the point; let us endeavour rather to form a conclusion about each institution in itself and say nothing, at present, of victories and defeats. Let us only say that such and such a custom is honourable, and another not. And first permit me to tell you how good and bad are to be estimated in reference to these very matters.

**MEGILLUS:** How do you mean?

**ATHENIAN:** All those who are ready at a moment's notice to praise or censure any practice which is matter of discussion, seem to me to proceed in a wrong way. Let me give you an illustration of what I mean:--You may suppose a person to be praising wheat as a good kind of food, whereupon another person instantly blames wheat, without ever enquiring into its effect or use, or in what way, or to whom, or with what, or in what state and how, wheat is to be given. And that is just what we are doing in this discussion. At the very mention of the word intoxication, one side is ready with their praises and the other with their censures; which is absurd. For either side adduce their witnesses and approvers, and some of us think that we speak with authority because we have many witnesses; and others because they see those who abstain conquering in battle, and this again is disputed by us. Now I cannot say that I shall be satisfied, if we go on discussing each of the remaining laws in the same way. And about this very point of intoxication I should like to speak in another way, which I hold to be the right one; for if number is to be the criterion, are there not myriads upon myriads of nations ready to dispute the point with you, who are only two cities?

**MEGILLUS:** I shall gladly welcome any method of enquiry which is right.

**ATHENIAN:** Let me put the matter thus:--Suppose a person to praise the keeping of goats, and the creatures themselves as capital things to have, and then some one who had seen goats feeding without a goatherd in cultivated spots, and doing mischief, were to censure a goat or any other animal who has no keeper, or a bad keeper, would there be any sense or justice in such censure?

**MEGILLUS:** Certainly not.

**ATHENIAN:** Does a captain require only to have nautical knowledge in order to be a good captain, whether he is sea-sick or not? What do you say?

**MEGILLUS:** I say that he is not a good captain if, although he have nautical skill, he is liable to sea-sickness.

**ATHENIAN:** And what would you say of the commander of an army? Will he be able to command merely because he has military skill if he be a coward, who, when danger comes, is sick and drunk with fear?

**MEGILLUS:** Impossible.

**ATHENIAN:** And what if besides being a coward he has no skill?

**MEGILLUS:** He is a miserable fellow, not fit to be a commander of men, but only of old women.

**ATHENIAN:** And what would you say of some one who blames or praises any sort of meeting which is intended by nature to have a ruler, and is well enough when under his presidency? The critic, however, has never seen the society meeting together at an orderly feast under the control of a president, but always without a ruler or with a bad one:--

when observers of this class praise or blame such meetings, are we to suppose that what they say is of any value?

**MEGILLUS:** Certainly not, if they have never seen or been present at such a meeting when rightly ordered.

**ATHENIAN:** Reflect; may not banqueters and banquets be said to constitute a kind of meeting?

**MEGILLUS:** Of course.

**ATHENIAN:** And did any one ever see this sort of convivial meeting rightly ordered? Of course you two will answer that you have never seen them at all, because they are not customary or lawful in your country, but I have come across many of them in many different places, and moreover I have made enquiries about them wherever I went, as I may say, and never did I see or hear of anything of the kind which was carried on altogether rightly; in some few particulars they might be right, but in general they were utterly wrong.

**CLEINIAS:** What do you mean, Stranger, by this remark? Explain. For we, as you say, from our inexperience in such matters, might very likely not know, even if they came in our way, what was right or wrong in such societies.

**ATHENIAN:** Likely enough; then let me try to be your instructor: You would acknowledge, would you not, that in all gatherings of mankind, of whatever sort, there ought to be a leader?

**CLEINIAS:** Certainly I should.

**ATHENIAN:** And we were saying just now, that when men are at war the leader ought to be a brave man?

**CLEINIAS:** We were.

**ATHENIAN:** The brave man is less likely than the coward to be disturbed by fears?

**CLEINIAS:** That again is true.

**ATHENIAN:** And if there were a possibility of having a general of an army who was absolutely fearless and imperturbable, should we not by all means appoint him?

**CLEINIAS:** Assuredly.

**ATHENIAN:** Now, however, we are speaking not of a general who is to command an army, when foe meets foe in time of war, but of one who is to regulate meetings of another sort, when friend meets friend in time of peace.

**CLEINIAS:** True.

**ATHENIAN:** And that sort of meeting, if attended with drunkenness, is apt to be unquiet.

**CLEINIAS:** Certainly; the reverse of quiet.

**ATHENIAN:** In the first place, then, the revellers as well as the soldiers will require a ruler?

**CLEINIAS:** To be sure; no men more so.

**ATHENIAN:** And we ought, if possible, to provide them with a quiet ruler?

**CLEINIAS:** Of course.

**ATHENIAN:** And he should be a man who understands society; for his duty is to preserve the friendly feelings which exist among the company at the time, and to increase them for the future by his use of the occasion.

**CLEINIAS:** Very true.

**ATHENIAN:** Must we not appoint a sober man and a wise to be our master of the revels? For if the ruler of drinkers be himself young and drunken, and not over-wise, only by some special good fortune will he be saved from doing some great evil.

**CLEINIAS:** It will be by a singular good fortune that he is saved.

**ATHENIAN:** Now suppose such associations to be framed in the best way possible in states, and that some one blames the very fact of their existence--he may very likely be right. But if he blames a practice which he only sees very much mismanaged, he shows in the first place that he is not aware of the mismanagement, and also not aware that everything done in this way will turn out to be wrong, because done without the superintendence of a sober ruler. Do you not see that a drunken pilot or a drunken ruler of any sort will ruin ship, chariot, army--anything, in short, of which he has the direction?

**CLEINIAS:** The last remark is very true, Stranger; and I see quite clearly the advantage of an army having a good leader--he will give victory in war to his followers, which is a very great advantage; and so of other things. But I do not see any similar advantage which either individuals or states gain from the good management of a feast; and I want you to tell me what great good will be effected, supposing that this drinking ordinance is duly established.

**ATHENIAN:** If you mean to ask what great good accrues to the state from the right training of a single youth, or of a single chorus--when the question is put in that form, we cannot deny that the good is not very great in any particular instance. But if you ask what is the good of education in general, the answer is easy--that education makes good men, and that good men act nobly, and conquer their enemies in battle, because they are good. Education certainly gives victory, although victory sometimes produces forgetfulness of education; for many have grown insolent from victory in war, and this insolence has engendered in them innumerable evils; and many a victory has been and will be suicidal to the victors; but education is never suicidal.

**CLEINIAS:** You seem to imply, my friend, that convivial meetings, when rightly ordered, are an important element of education.

**ATHENIAN:** Certainly I do.

**CLEINIAS:** And can you show that what you have been saying is true?

**ATHENIAN:** To be absolutely sure of the truth of matters concerning which there are many opinions, is an attribute of the Gods not given to man, Stranger; but I shall be very happy to tell you what I think, especially as we are now proposing to enter on a discussion concerning laws and constitutions.

**CLEINIAS:** Your opinion, Stranger, about the questions which are now being raised, is precisely what we want to hear.

**ATHENIAN:** Very good; I will try to find a way of explaining my meaning, and you shall try to have the gift of understanding me. But first let me make an apology. The Athenian citizen is reputed among all the Hellenes to be a great talker, whereas Sparta is renowned for brevity, and the Cretans have more wit than words. Now I am afraid of appearing to elicit a very long discourse out of very small materials. For drinking indeed may appear to be a slight matter, and yet is one which cannot be rightly ordered according to nature, without correct principles of music; these are necessary to any clear or satisfactory treatment of the subject, and music again runs up into education generally, and there is much to be said about all this. What would you say then to leaving these matters for the present, and passing on to some other question of law?

**MEGILLUS:** O Athenian Stranger, let me tell you what perhaps you do not know, that our family is the proxenus of your state. I imagine that from their earliest youth all boys, when they are told that they are the proxeni of a particular state, feel kindly towards their second country; and this has certainly been my own feeling. I can well remember from the days of my boyhood, how, when any Lacedaemonians praised or blamed the Athenians, they used to say to me,--*'See, Megillus, how ill or how well,'* as the case might be, 'has your state treated us'; and having always had to fight your battles against detractors when I heard you assailed, I became warmly attached to you. And I always like to hear the Athenian tongue spoken; the common saying is quite true, that a good Athenian is more than ordinarily good, for he is the only man who is freely and genuinely good by the divine inspiration of his own nature, and is not manufactured. Therefore be assured that I shall like to hear you say whatever you have to say.

**CLEINIAS:** Yes, Stranger; and when you have heard me speak, say boldly what is in your thoughts. Let me remind you of a tie which unites you to Crete. You must have heard here the story of the prophet Epimenides, who was of my family, and came to Athens ten years before the Persian war, in accordance with the response of the Oracle, and offered certain sacrifices which the God commanded. The Athenians were at that time in dread of the Persian invasion; and he said that for ten years they would not come, and that when they came, they would go away again without accomplishing any of their objects, and would suffer more evil than they inflicted. At that time my forefathers formed ties of hospitality with you; thus ancient is the friendship which I and my parents have had for you.

**ATHENIAN:** You seem to be quite ready to listen; and I am also ready to perform as much as I can of an almost impossible task, which I will nevertheless attempt. At the outset of the discussion, let me define the nature and power of education; for this is the way by which our argument must travel onwards to the God Dionysus.

**CLEINIAS:** Let us proceed, if you please.

**ATHENIAN:** Well, then, if I tell you what are my notions of education, will you consider whether they satisfy you?

**CLEINIAS:** Let us hear.

**ATHENIAN:** According to my view, any one who would be good at anything must practise that thing from his youth upwards, both in sport and earnest, in its several branches: for example, he who is to be a good builder, should play at building children's houses; he who is to be a good husbandman, at tilling the ground; and those who have the care of their education should provide them when young with mimic tools. They should learn beforehand the knowledge which they will afterwards require for their art. For example, the future carpenter should learn to measure or apply the line in play; and the future warrior should learn riding, or some other exercise, for amusement, and the teacher should endeavour to direct the children's inclinations and pleasures, by the help of amusements, to their final aim in life. The most important part of education is right training in the nursery. The soul of the child in his play should be guided to the love of that sort of excellence in which when he grows up to manhood he will have to be perfected. Do you agree with me thus far?

**CLEINIAS:** Certainly.

**ATHENIAN:** Then let us not leave the meaning of education ambiguous or ill- defined. At present, when we speak in terms of praise or blame about the bringing-up of each person, we call one man educated and another uneducated, although the uneducated man may be sometimes very well educated for the calling of a retail trader, or of a captain of a ship, and the like. For we are not speaking of education in this narrower sense, but of that other education in virtue from youth upwards, which makes a man eagerly pursue the ideal perfection of citizenship, and teaches him how rightly to rule and how to obey. This is the only education which, upon our view, deserves the name; that other sort of training, which aims at the acquisition of wealth or bodily strength, or mere cleverness apart from intelligence and justice, is mean and illiberal, and is not worthy to be called education at all. But let us not quarrel with one another about a word, provided that the proposition which has just been granted hold good: to wit, that those who are rightly educated generally become good men. Neither must we cast a slight upon education, which is the first and fairest thing that the best of men can ever have, and which, though liable to take a wrong direction, is capable of reformation. And this work of reformation is the great business of every man while he lives.

**CLEINIAS:** Very true; and we entirely agree with you.

**ATHENIAN:** And we agreed before that they are good men who are able to rule themselves, and bad men who are not.

**CLEINIAS:** You are quite right.

**ATHENIAN:** Let me now proceed, if I can, to clear up the subject a little further by an illustration which I will offer you.

**CLEINIAS:** Proceed.

**ATHENIAN:** Do we not consider each of ourselves to be one?

**CLEINIAS:** We do.

**ATHENIAN:** And each one of us has in his bosom two counsellors, both foolish and also antagonistic; of which we call the one pleasure, and the other pain.

**CLEINIAS:** Exactly.

**ATHENIAN:** Also there are opinions about the future, which have the general name of expectations; and the specific name of fear, when the expectation is of pain; and of hope, when of pleasure; and further, there is reflection about the good or evil of them, and this, when embodied in a decree by the State, is called Law.

**CLEINIAS:** I am hardly able to follow you; proceed, however, as if I were.

**MEGILLUS:** I am in the like case.

**ATHENIAN:** Let us look at the matter thus: May we not conceive each of us living beings to be a puppet of the Gods, either their plaything only, or created with a purpose--which of the two we cannot certainly know? But we do know, that these affections in us are like cords and strings, which pull us different and opposite ways, and to opposite actions; and herein lies the difference between virtue and vice. According to the argument there is one among these cords which every man ought to grasp and never let go, but to pull with it against all the rest; and this is the sacred and golden cord of reason, called by us the common law of the State; there are others which are hard and of iron, but this one is soft because golden; and there are several other kinds. Now we ought always to cooperate with the lead of the best, which is law. For inasmuch as reason is beautiful and gentle, and not violent, her rule must needs have ministers in order to help the golden principle in vanquishing the other principles. And thus the moral of the tale about our being puppets will not have been lost, and the meaning of the expression 'superior or inferior to a man's self' will become clearer; and the individual, attaining to right reason in this matter of pulling the strings of the puppet, should live according to its rule; while the city, receiving the same from some god or from one who has knowledge of these things, should embody it in a law, to be her guide in her dealings with herself and with other states. In this way virtue and vice will be more clearly distinguished by us. And when they have become clearer, education and other institutions will in like manner become clearer; and in particular that question of convivial entertainment, which may seem, perhaps, to have been a very trifling matter, and to have taken a great many more words than were necessary.

**CLEINIAS:** Perhaps, however, the theme may turn out not to be unworthy of the length of discourse.

**ATHENIAN:** Very good; let us proceed with any enquiry which really bears on our present object.

**CLEINIAS:** Proceed.

**ATHENIAN:** Suppose that we give this puppet of ours drink,--what will be the effect on him?

**CLEINIAS:** Having what in view do you ask that question?

**ATHENIAN:** Nothing as yet; but I ask generally, when the puppet is brought to the drink, what sort of result is likely to follow. I will endeavour to explain my meaning more clearly: what I am now asking is this--Does the drinking of wine heighten and increase pleasures and pains, and passions and loves?

**CLEINIAS:** Very greatly.

**ATHENIAN:** And are perception and memory, and opinion and prudence, heightened and increased? Do not these qualities entirely desert a man if he becomes saturated with drink?

**CLEINIAS:** Yes, they entirely desert him.

**ATHENIAN:** Does he not return to the state of soul in which he was when a young child?

**CLEINIAS:** He does.

**ATHENIAN:** Then at that time he will have the least control over himself?

**CLEINIAS:** The least.

**ATHENIAN:** And will he not be in a most wretched plight?

**CLEINIAS:** Most wretched.

**ATHENIAN:** Then not only an old man but also a drunkard becomes a second time a child?

**CLEINIAS:** Well said, Stranger.

**ATHENIAN:** Is there any argument which will prove to us that we ought to encourage the taste for drinking instead of doing all we can to avoid it?

**CLEINIAS:** I suppose that there is; you at any rate, were just now saying that you were ready to maintain such a doctrine.

**ATHENIAN:** True, I was; and I am ready still, seeing that you have both declared that you are anxious to hear me.

**CLEINIAS:** To be sure we are, if only for the strangeness of the paradox, which asserts that a man ought of his own accord to plunge into utter degradation.

**ATHENIAN:** Are you speaking of the soul?

**CLEINIAS:** Yes.

**ATHENIAN:** And what would you say about the body, my friend? Are you not surprised at any one of his own accord bringing upon himself deformity, leanness, ugliness, decrepitude?

**CLEINIAS:** Certainly.

**ATHENIAN:** Yet when a man goes of his own accord to a doctor's shop, and takes medicine, is he not aware that soon, and for many days afterwards, he will be in a state of body which he would die rather than accept as the permanent condition of his life? Are not those who train in gymnasia, at first beginning reduced to a state of weakness?

**CLEINIAS:** Yes, all that is well known.

**ATHENIAN:** Also that they go of their own accord for the sake of the subsequent benefit?

**CLEINIAS:** Very good.

**ATHENIAN:** And we may conceive this to be true in the same way of other practices?

**CLEINIAS:** Certainly.

**ATHENIAN:** And the same view may be taken of the pastime of drinking wine, if we are right in supposing that the same good effect follows?

**CLEINIAS:** To be sure.

**ATHENIAN:** If such convivialities should turn out to have any advantage equal in importance to that of gymnastic, they are in their very nature to be preferred to mere bodily exercise, inasmuch as they have no accompaniment of pain.

**CLEINIAS:** True; but I hardly think that we shall be able to discover any such benefits to be derived from them.

**ATHENIAN:** That is just what we must endeavour to show. And let me ask you a question:--Do we not distinguish two kinds of fear, which are very different?

**CLEINIAS:** What are they?

**ATHENIAN:** There is the fear of expected evil.

**CLEINIAS:** Yes.

**ATHENIAN:** And there is the fear of an evil reputation; we are afraid of being thought evil, because we do or say some dishonourable thing, which fear we and all men term shame.

**CLEINIAS:** Certainly.

**ATHENIAN:** These are the two fears, as I called them; one of which is the opposite of pain and other fears, and the opposite also of the greatest and most numerous sort of pleasures.

**CLEINIAS:** Very true.

**ATHENIAN:** And does not the legislator and every one who is good for anything, hold this fear in the greatest honour? This is what he terms reverence, and the confidence which is the reverse of this he terms insolence; and the latter he always deems to be a very great evil both to individuals and to states.

**CLEINIAS:** True.

**ATHENIAN:** Does not this kind of fear preserve us in many important ways? What is there which so surely gives victory and safety in war? For there are two things which give victory--confidence before enemies, and fear of disgrace before friends.

**CLEINIAS:** There are.

**ATHENIAN:** Then each of us should be fearless and also fearful; and why we should be either has now been determined.

**CLEINIAS:** Certainly.

**ATHENIAN:** And when we want to make any one fearless, we and the law bring him face to face with many fears.

**CLEINIAS:** Clearly.

**ATHENIAN:** And when we want to make him rightly fearful, must we not introduce him to shameless pleasures, and train him to take up arms against them, and to overcome them? Or does this principle apply to courage only, and must he who would be perfect in valour fight against and overcome his own natural character,--since if he be unpractised and inexperienced in such conflicts, he will not be half the man which he might have been,--and are we to suppose, that with temperance it is otherwise, and that he who has never fought with the shameless and unrighteous temptations of his pleasures and lusts, and conquered them, in earnest and in play, by word, deed, and act, will still be perfectly temperate?

**CLEINIAS:** A most unlikely supposition.

**ATHENIAN:** Suppose that some God had given a fear-potion to men, and that the more a man drank of this the more he regarded himself at every draught as a child of misfortune, and that he feared everything happening or about to happen to him; and that at last the most courageous of men utterly lost his presence of mind for a time, and only came to himself again when he had slept off the influence of the draught.

**CLEINIAS:** But has such a draught, Stranger, ever really been known among men?

**ATHENIAN:** No; but, if there had been, might not such a draught have been of use to the legislator as a test of courage? Might we not go and say to him, 'O legislator, whether you are legislating for the Cretan, or for any other state, would you not like to have a touchstone of the courage and cowardice of your citizens?'

**CLEINIAS:** 'I should,' will be the answer of every one.

**ATHENIAN:** 'And you would rather have a touchstone in which there is no risk and no great danger than the reverse?'

**CLEINIAS:** In that proposition every one may safely agree.

**ATHENIAN:** 'And in order to make use of the draught, you would lead them amid these imaginary terrors, and prove them, when the affection of fear was working upon them, and compel them to be fearless, exhorting and admonishing them; and also honouring them, but dishonouring any one who will not be persuaded by you to be in all respects such as you command him; and if he underwent the trial well and manfully, you would let him go unscathed; but if ill, you would inflict a punishment upon him? Or would you abstain from using the potion altogether, although you have no reason for abstaining?'

**CLEINIAS:** He would be certain, Stranger, to use the potion.

**ATHENIAN:** This would be a mode of testing and training which would be wonderfully easy in comparison with those now in use, and might be applied to a single person, or to a few, or indeed to any number; and he would do well who provided himself with the potion only, rather than with any number of other things, whether he preferred to be by himself in solitude, and there contend with his fears, because he was ashamed to be seen by the eye of man until he was perfect; or trusting to the force of his own nature and habits, and believing that he had been already disciplined sufficiently, he did not hesitate to train himself in company with any number of others, and display his power in conquering the irresistible change effected by the draught--his virtue being such, that he never in any instance fell into any great unseemliness, but was always himself, and left off before he arrived at the last cup, fearing that he, like all other men, might be overcome by the potion.

**CLEINIAS:** Yes, Stranger, in that last case, too, he might equally show his self-control.

**ATHENIAN:** Let us return to the lawgiver, and say to him:--'Well, lawgiver, there is certainly no such fear-potion which man has either received from the Gods or himself discovered; for witchcraft has no place at our board. But is there any potion which might serve as a test of overboldness and excessive and indiscreet boasting?

**CLEINIAS:** I suppose that he will say, Yes,--meaning that wine is such a potion.

**ATHENIAN:** Is not the effect of this quite the opposite of the effect of the other? When a man drinks wine he begins to be better pleased with himself, and the more he drinks the more he is filled full of brave hopes, and conceit of his power, and at last the string of his tongue is loosened, and fancying himself wise, he is brimming over with lawlessness, and has no more fear or respect, and is ready to do or say anything.

**CLEINIAS:** I think that every one will admit the truth of your description.

**MEGILLUS:** Certainly.

**ATHENIAN:** Now, let us remember, as we were saying, that there are two things which should be cultivated in the soul: first, the greatest courage; secondly, the greatest fear--

**CLEINIAS:** Which you said to be characteristic of reverence, if I am not mistaken.

**ATHENIAN:** Thank you for reminding me. But now, as the habit of courage and fearlessness is to be trained amid fears, let us consider whether the opposite quality is not also to be trained among opposites.

**CLEINIAS:** That is probably the case.

**ATHENIAN:** There are times and seasons at which we are by nature more than commonly valiant and bold; now we ought to train ourselves on these occasions to be as free from impudence and shamelessness as possible, and to be afraid to say or suffer or do anything that is base.

**CLEINIAS:** True.

**ATHENIAN:** Are not the moments in which we are apt to be bold and shameless such as these?--when we are under the influence of anger, love, pride, ignorance, avarice, cowardice? or when wealth, beauty, strength, and all the intoxicating workings of pleasure madden us? What is better adapted than the festive use of wine, in the first place to test, and in the second place to train the character of a man, if care be taken in the use of it? What is there cheaper, or more innocent? For do but consider which is the greater risk:--Would you rather test a man of a morose and savage nature, which is the source of ten thousand acts of injustice, by making bargains with him at a risk to yourself, or by having him as a companion at the festival of Dionysus? Or would you, if you wanted to apply a touchstone to a man who is prone to love, entrust your wife, or your sons, or daughters to him, perilling your dearest interests in order to have a view of the condition of his soul? I might mention numberless cases, in which the advantage would be manifest of getting to know a character in sport, and without paying dearly for experience. And I do not believe that either a Cretan, or any other man, will doubt that such a test is a fair test, and safer, cheaper, and speedier than any other.

**CLEINIAS:** That is certainly true.

**ATHENIAN:** And this knowledge of the natures and habits of men's souls will be of the greatest use in that art which has the management of them; and that art, if I am not mistaken, is politics.

**CLEINIAS:** Exactly so.

# BOOK II.

**ATHENIAN:** And now we have to consider whether the insight into human nature is the only benefit derived from well-ordered potations, or whether there are not other advantages great and much to be desired. The argument seems to imply that there are. But how and in what way these are to be attained, will have to be considered attentively, or we may be entangled in error.

**CLEINIAS:** Proceed.

**ATHENIAN:** Let me once more recall our doctrine of right education; which, if I am not mistaken, depends on the due regulation of convivial intercourse.

**CLEINIAS:** You talk rather grandly.

**ATHENIAN:** Pleasure and pain I maintain to be the first perceptions of children, and I say that they are the forms under which virtue and vice are originally present to them. As to wisdom and true and fixed opinions, happy is the man who acquires them, even when declining in years; and we may say that he who possesses them, and the blessings which are contained in them, is a perfect man. Now I mean by education that training which is given by suitable habits to the first instincts of virtue in children;-- when pleasure, and friendship, and pain, and hatred, are rightly implanted in souls not yet capable of understanding the nature of them, and who find them, after they have attained reason, to be in harmony with her. This harmony of the soul, taken as a whole, is virtue; but the particular training in respect of pleasure and pain, which leads you always to hate what you ought to hate, and love what you ought to love from the beginning of life to the end, may be separated off; and, in my view, will be rightly called education.

**CLEINIAS:** I think, Stranger, that you are quite right in all that you have said and are saying about education.

**ATHENIAN:** I am glad to hear that you agree with me; for, indeed, the discipline of pleasure and pain which, when rightly ordered, is a principle of education, has been often relaxed and corrupted in human life. And the Gods, pitying the toils which our race is born to undergo, have appointed holy festivals, wherein men alternate rest with labour; and have given them the Muses and Apollo, the leader of the Muses, and Dionysus, to be companions in their revels, that they may improve their education by taking part in the festivals of the Gods, and with their help I should like to know whether a common saying is in our opinion true to nature or not. For men say that the young of all creatures cannot be quiet in their bodies or in their voices; they are always wanting to move and cry out; some leaping and skipping, and overflowing with sportiveness and delight at something, others uttering all sorts of cries. But, whereas the animals have no perception of order or disorder in their movements, that is, of rhythm or harmony, as they are called, to us, the Gods, who, as we say, have been appointed to be our companions in the dance, have given the pleasurable sense of harmony and rhythm; and so they stir us into life, and we follow them, joining hands together in dances and songs; and these they call choruses, which is a term naturally expressive of cheerfulness. Shall we begin, then, with the acknowledgment that education is first given through Apollo and the Muses? What do you say?

**CLEINIAS:** I assent.

**ATHENIAN:** And the uneducated is he who has not been trained in the chorus, and the educated is he who has been well trained?

**CLEINIAS:** Certainly.

**ATHENIAN:** And the chorus is made up of two parts, dance and song?

**CLEINIAS:** True.

**ATHENIAN:** Then he who is well educated will be able to sing and dance well?

**CLEINIAS:** I suppose that he will.

**ATHENIAN:** Let us see; what are we saying?

**CLEINIAS:** What?

**ATHENIAN:** He sings well and dances well; now must we add that he sings what is good and dances what is good?

**CLEINIAS:** Let us make the addition.

**ATHENIAN:** We will suppose that he knows the good to be good, and the bad to be bad, and makes use of them accordingly: which now is the better trained in dancing and music--he who is able to move his body and to use his voice in what is understood to be the right manner, but has no delight in good or hatred of evil; or he who is incorrect in gesture and voice, but is right in his sense of pleasure and pain, and welcomes what is good, and is offended at what is evil?

**CLEINIAS:** There is a great difference, Stranger, in the two kinds of education.

**ATHENIAN:** If we three know what is good in song and dance, then we truly know also who is educated and who is uneducated; but if not, then we certainly shall not know wherein lies the safeguard of education, and whether there is any or not.

**CLEINIAS:** True.

**ATHENIAN:** Let us follow the scent like hounds, and go in pursuit of beauty of figure, and melody, and song, and dance; if these escape us, there will be no use in talking about true education, whether Hellenic or barbarian.

**CLEINIAS:** Yes.

**ATHENIAN:** And what is beauty of figure, or beautiful melody? When a manly soul is in trouble, and when a cowardly soul is in similar case, are they likely to use the same figures and gestures, or to give utterance to the same sounds?

**CLEINIAS:** How can they, when the very colours of their faces differ?

**ATHENIAN:** Good, my friend; I may observe, however, in passing, that in music there certainly are figures and there are melodies: and music is concerned with harmony and rhythm, so that you may speak of a melody or figure having good rhythm or good harmony--the term is correct enough; but to speak metaphorically of a melody or figure having a 'good colour,' as the masters of choruses do, is not allowable, although you can speak of the melodies or figures of the brave and the coward, praising the one and censuring the other. And not to be tedious, let us say that the figures and melodies which are expressive of virtue of soul or body, or of images of virtue, are without exception good, and those which are expressive of vice are the reverse of good.

**CLEINIAS:** Your suggestion is excellent; and let us answer that these things are so.

**ATHENIAN:** Once more, are all of us equally delighted with every sort of dance?

**CLEINIAS:** Far otherwise.

**ATHENIAN:** What, then, leads us astray? Are beautiful things not the same to us all, or are they the same in themselves, but not in our opinion of them? For no one will admit that forms of vice in the dance are more beautiful than forms of virtue, or that he himself delights in the forms of vice, and others in a muse of another character. And yet most persons say, that the excellence of music is to give pleasure to our souls. But this is intolerable and blasphemous; there is, however, a much more plausible account of the delusion.

**CLEINIAS:** What?

**ATHENIAN:** The adaptation of art to the characters of men. Choric movements are imitations of manners occurring in various actions, fortunes, dispositions,--each particular is imitated, and those to whom the words, or songs, or dances are suited, either by nature or habit or both, cannot help feeling pleasure in them and applauding them, and calling them beautiful. But those whose natures, or ways, or habits are unsuited to them, cannot delight in them or applaud them, and they call them base. There are others, again, whose natures are right and their habits wrong, or whose habits are right and their natures wrong, and they praise one thing, but are pleased at another. For they say that all these imitations are pleasant, but not good. And in the presence of those whom they think wise, they are ashamed of dancing and singing in the baser manner, or of deliberately lending any countenance to such proceedings; and yet, they have a secret pleasure in them.

**CLEINIAS:** Very true.

**ATHENIAN:** And is any harm done to the lover of vicious dances or songs, or any good done to the approver of the opposite sort of pleasure?

**CLEINIAS:** I think that there is.

**ATHENIAN:** 'I think' is not the word, but I would say, rather, 'I am certain.' For must they not have the same effect as when a man associates with bad characters, whom he likes and approves rather than dislikes, and only censures playfully because he has a suspicion of his own badness? In that case, he who takes pleasure in them will surely become like those in whom he takes pleasure, even though he be ashamed to praise them. And what greater good or evil can any destiny ever make us undergo?

**CLEINIAS:** I know of none.

**ATHENIAN:** Then in a city which has good laws, or in future ages is to have them, bearing in mind the instruction and amusement which are given by music, can we suppose that the poets are to be allowed to teach in the dance anything which they themselves like, in the way of rhythm, or melody, or words, to the young children of any well-conditioned parents? Is the poet to train his choruses as he pleases, without reference to virtue or vice?

**CLEINIAS:** That is surely quite unreasonable, and is not to be thought of.

**ATHENIAN:** And yet he may do this in almost any state with the exception of Egypt.

**CLEINIAS:** And what are the laws about music and dancing in Egypt?

**ATHENIAN:** You will wonder when I tell you: Long ago they appear to have recognized the very principle of which we are now speaking--that their young citizens must be habituated to forms and strains of virtue. These they fixed, and exhibited the patterns of them in their temples; and no painter or artist is allowed to innovate upon them, or to leave the traditional forms and invent new ones. To this day, no alteration is allowed either in these arts, or in music at all. And you will find that their works of art are painted or moulded in the same forms which they had ten thousand years ago;--this is literally true and no exaggeration,--their ancient paintings and sculptures are not a whit better or worse than the work of to-day, but are made with just the same skill.

**CLEINIAS:** How extraordinary!

**ATHENIAN:** I should rather say, How statesmanlike, how worthy of a legislator! I know that other things in Egypt are not so well. But what I am telling you about music is true and deserving of consideration, because showing that a lawgiver may institute melodies which have a natural truth and correctness without any fear of failure. To do this, however, must be the work of God, or of a divine person; in Egypt they have a tradition that their ancient chants which have been preserved for so many ages are the composition of the Goddess Isis. And therefore, as I was saying, if a person can only find in any way the natural melodies, he may confidently embody them in a fixed and legal form. For the love of novelty which arises out of pleasure in the new and weariness of the old, has not strength enough to corrupt the consecrated song and dance, under the plea that they have become antiquated. At any rate, they are far from being corrupted in Egypt.

**CLEINIAS:** Your arguments seem to prove your point.

**ATHENIAN:** May we not confidently say that the true use of music and of choral festivities is as follows: We rejoice when we think that we prosper, and again we think that we prosper when we rejoice?

**CLEINIAS:** Exactly.

**ATHENIAN:** And when rejoicing in our good fortune, we are unable to be still?

**CLEINIAS:** True.

**ATHENIAN:** Our young men break forth into dancing and singing, and we who are their elders deem that we are fulfilling our part in life when we look on at them. Having lost our agility, we delight in their sports and merry- making, because we love to think of our former selves; and gladly institute contests for those who are able to awaken in us the memory of our youth.

**CLEINIAS:** Very true.

**ATHENIAN:** Is it altogether unmeaning to say, as the common people do about festivals, that he should be adjudged the wisest of men, and the winner of the palm, who gives us the greatest amount of pleasure and mirth? For on such occasions, and when mirth is the order of the day, ought not he to be honoured most, and, as I was saying, bear the palm, who gives most mirth to the greatest number? Now is this a true way of speaking or of acting?

**CLEINIAS:** Possibly.

**ATHENIAN:** But, my dear friend, let us distinguish between different cases, and not be hasty in forming a judgment: One way of considering the question will be to imagine a festival at which there are entertainments of all sorts, including gymnastic, musical, and equestrian contests: the citizens are assembled; prizes are offered, and proclamation is made that any one who likes may enter the lists, and that he is to bear the palm who gives the most pleasure to the spectators--there is to be no regulation about the manner how; but he who is most successful in giving pleasure is to be crowned victor, and deemed to be the pleasantest of the candidates: What is likely to be the result of such a proclamation?

**CLEINIAS:** In what respect?

**ATHENIAN:** There would be various exhibitions: one man, like Homer, will exhibit a rhapsody, another a performance on the lute; one will have a tragedy, and another a comedy. Nor would there be anything astonishing in some one imagining that he could gain the prize by exhibiting a puppet- show. Suppose these competitors to meet, and not these only, but innumerable others as well--can you tell me who ought to be the victor?

**CLEINIAS:** I do not see how any one can answer you, or pretend to know, unless he has heard with his own ears the several competitors; the question is absurd.

**ATHENIAN:** Well, then, if neither of you can answer, shall I answer this question which you deem so absurd?

**CLEINIAS:** By all means.

**ATHENIAN:** If very small children are to determine the question, they will decide for the puppet show.

**CLEINIAS:** Of course.

**ATHENIAN:** The older children will be advocates of comedy; educated women, and young men, and people in general, will favour tragedy.

**CLEINIAS:** Very likely.

**ATHENIAN:** And I believe that we old men would have the greatest pleasure in hearing a rhapsodist recite well the Iliad and Odyssey, or one of the Hesiodic poems, and would award the victory to him. But, who would really be the victor?--that is the question.

**CLEINIAS:** Yes.

**ATHENIAN:** Clearly you and I will have to declare that those whom we old men adjudge victors ought to win; for our ways are far and away better than any which at present exist anywhere in the world.

**CLEINIAS:** Certainly.

**ATHENIAN:** Thus far I too should agree with the many, that the excellence of music is to be measured by pleasure. But the pleasure must not be that of chance persons; the fairest music is that which delights the best and best educated, and especially that which delights the one man who is pre- eminent in virtue and education. And therefore the judges must be men of character, for they will require both wisdom and courage; the true judge must not draw his inspiration from the theatre, nor ought he to be unnerved by the clamour of the many and his own incapacity; nor again, knowing the truth, ought he through cowardice and unmanliness carelessly to deliver a lying judgment, with the very same lips which have just appealed to the Gods before he judged. He is sitting not as the disciple of the theatre, but, in his proper place, as their instructor, and he ought to be the enemy of all pandering to the pleasure of the spectators. The ancient and common custom of Hellas, which still prevails in Italy and Sicily, did certainly leave the judgment to the body of spectators, who determined the victor by show of hands. But this custom has been the destruction of the poets; for they are now in the habit of composing with a view to please the bad taste of their judges, and the result is that the spectators instruct themselves;--and also it has been the ruin of the theatre; they ought to be having characters put before them better than their own, and so receiving a higher pleasure, but now by their own act the opposite result follows. What inference is to be drawn from all this? Shall I tell you?

**CLEINIAS:** What?

**ATHENIAN:** The inference at which we arrive for the third or fourth time is, that education is the constraining and directing of youth towards that right reason, which the law affirms, and which the experience of the eldest and best has agreed to be truly right. In order, then, that the soul of the child may not be habituated to feel joy and sorrow in a manner at variance with the law, and those who obey the law, but may rather follow the law and rejoice and sorrow at the same things as the aged--in order, I say, to produce this effect, chants appear to have been invented, which really enchant, and are designed to implant that harmony of which we speak. And, because the mind of the child is incapable of enduring serious training, they are called plays and songs, and are performed in play; just as when men are sick and ailing in their bodies, their attendants give them wholesome diet in pleasant meats and drinks, but unwholesome diet in disagreeable things, in order that they may learn, as they ought, to like the one, and to dislike the other. And similarly the true legislator will persuade, and, if he cannot persuade, will compel the poet to express, as he ought, by fair and noble words, in his rhythms, the figures, and in his melodies, the music of temperate and brave and in every way good men.

**CLEINIAS:** But do you really imagine, Stranger, that this is the way in which poets generally compose in States at the present day? As far as I can observe, except among us and among the Lacedaemonians, there are no regulations like those of which you speak; in other places novelties are always being introduced in dancing and in music, generally not under the authority of any law, but at the instigation of lawless pleasures; and these pleasures are so far from being the same, as you describe the Egyptian to be, or having the same principles, that they are never the same.

**ATHENIAN:** Most true, Cleinias; and I daresay that I may have expressed myself obscurely, and so led you to imagine that I was speaking of some really existing state of things, whereas I was only saying what regulations I would like to have about music; and hence there occurred a misapprehension on your part. For when evils are far gone and irremediable, the task of censuring them is never pleasant, although at times necessary. But as we do not really differ, will you let me ask you whether you consider such institutions to be more prevalent among the Cretans and Lacedaemonians than among the other Hellenes?

**CLEINIAS:** Certainly they are.

**ATHENIAN:** And if they were extended to the other Hellenes, would it be an improvement on the present state of things?

**CLEINIAS:** A very great improvement, if the customs which prevail among them were such as prevail among us and the Lacedaemonians, and such as you were just now saying ought to prevail.

**ATHENIAN:** Let us see whether we understand one another:--Are not the principles of education and music which prevail among you as follows: you compel your poets to say that the good man, if he be temperate and just, is fortunate and happy; and this whether he be great and strong or small and weak, and whether he be rich or poor; and, on the other hand, if he have a wealth passing that of Cinyras or

Midas, and be unjust, he is wretched and lives in misery? As the poet says, and with truth: I sing not, I care not about him who accomplishes all noble things, not having justice; let him who 'draws near and stretches out his hand against his enemies be a just man.' But if he be unjust, I would not have him 'look calmly upon bloody death,' nor 'surpass in swiftness the Thracian Boreas;' and let no other thing that is called good ever be his. For the goods of which the many speak are not really good: first in the catalogue is placed health, beauty next, wealth third; and then innumerable others, as for example to have a keen eye or a quick ear, and in general to have all the senses perfect; or, again, to be a tyrant and do as you like; and the final consummation of happiness is to have acquired all these things, and when you have acquired them to become at once immortal. But you and I say, that while to the just and holy all these things are the best of possessions, to the unjust they are all, including even health, the greatest of evils. For in truth, to have sight, and hearing, and the use of the senses, or to live at all without justice and virtue, even though a man be rich in all the so-called goods of fortune, is the greatest of evils, if life be immortal; but not so great, if the bad man lives only a very short time. These are the truths which, if I am not mistaken, you will persuade or compel your poets to utter with suitable accompaniments of harmony and rhythm, and in these they must train up your youth. Am I not right? For I plainly declare that evils as they are termed are goods to the unjust, and only evils to the just, and that goods are truly good to the good, but evil to the evil. Let me ask again, Are you and I agreed about this?

**CLEINIAS:** I think that we partly agree and partly do not.

**ATHENIAN:** When a man has health and wealth and a tyranny which lasts, and when he is pre-eminent in strength and courage, and has the gift of immortality, and none of the so-called evils which counter-balance these goods, but only the injustice and insolence of his own nature--of such an one you are, I suspect, unwilling to believe that he is miserable rather than happy.

**CLEINIAS:** That is quite true.

**ATHENIAN:** Once more: Suppose that he be valiant and strong, and handsome and rich, and does throughout his whole life whatever he likes, still, if he be unrighteous and insolent, would not both of you agree that he will of necessity live basely? You will surely grant so much?

**CLEINIAS:** Certainly.

**ATHENIAN:** And an evil life too?

**CLEINIAS:** I am not equally disposed to grant that.

**ATHENIAN:** Will he not live painfully and to his own disadvantage?

**CLEINIAS:** How can I possibly say so?

**ATHENIAN:** How! Then may Heaven make us to be of one mind, for now we are of two. To me, dear Cleinias, the truth of what I am saying is as plain as the fact that Crete is an island. And, if I were a lawgiver, I would try to make the poets and all the citizens speak in this strain, and I would inflict the heaviest penalties on any one in all the land who should dare to say that there are bad men who lead pleasant lives, or that the profitable and gainful is one thing, and the just another; and there are many other matters about which I should make my citizens speak in a manner different from the Cretans and Lacedaemonians of this age, and I may say, indeed, from the world in general. For tell me, my good friends, by Zeus and Apollo tell me, if I were to ask these same Gods who were your legislators,--Is not the most just life also the pleasantest? or are there two lives, one of which is the justest and the other the pleasantest?--and they were to reply that there are two; and thereupon I proceeded to ask, (that would be the right way of pursuing the enquiry), Which are the happier--those who lead the justest, or those who lead the pleasantest life? and they replied, Those who lead the pleasantest--that would be a very strange answer, which I should not like to put into the mouth of the Gods. The words will come with more propriety from the lips of fathers and legislators, and therefore I will repeat my former questions to one of them, and suppose him to say again that he who leads the pleasantest life is the happiest. And to that I rejoin:--O my father, did you not wish me to live as happily as possible? And yet you also never ceased telling me that I should live as justly as possible. Now, here the giver of the rule, whether he be legislator or father, will be in a dilemma, and will in vain endeavour to be consistent with himself. But if he were to declare that the justest life is also the happiest, every one hearing him would enquire, if I am not mistaken, what is that good and noble principle in life which the law approves, and which is superior to pleasure. For what good can the just man have which is separated from pleasure? Shall we say that glory and fame, coming from Gods and men, though good and noble, are nevertheless unpleasant, and infamy pleasant? Certainly not, sweet legislator. Or shall we say that the not-doing of wrong and there being no wrong done is good and honourable, although there is no pleasure in it, and that the doing wrong is pleasant, but evil and base?

**CLEINIAS:** Impossible.

**ATHENIAN:** The view which identifies the pleasant and the pleasant and the just and the good and the noble has an excellent moral and religious tendency. And the opposite view is most at variance with the designs of the legislator, and is, in his opinion, infamous; for no one, if he can help, will be persuaded to do that which gives him more pain than pleasure. But as distant prospects are apt to make us dizzy, especially in childhood, the legislator will try to purge away the darkness and exhibit the truth; he will persuade the citizens, in some way or other, by customs and praises and words, that just and unjust are shadows only, and that injustice, which seems opposed to justice, when contemplated by the unjust and evil man appears pleasant and the just most unpleasant; but that from the just man's point of view, the very opposite is the appearance of both of them.

**CLEINIAS:** True.

**ATHENIAN:** And which may be supposed to be the truer judgment--that of the inferior or of the better soul?

**CLEINIAS:** Surely, that of the better soul.

**ATHENIAN:** Then the unjust life must not only be more base and depraved, but also more unpleasant than the just and holy life?

**CLEINIAS:** That seems to be implied in the present argument.

**ATHENIAN:** And even supposing this were otherwise, and not as the argument has proven, still the lawgiver, who is worth anything, if he ever ventures to tell a lie to the young for their good, could not invent a more useful lie than this, or one which will have a better effect in making them do what is right, not on compulsion but voluntarily.

**CLEINIAS:** Truth, Stranger, is a noble thing and a lasting, but a thing of which men are hard to be persuaded.

**ATHENIAN:** And yet the story of the Sidonian Cadmus, which is so improbable, has been readily believed, and also innumerable other tales.

**CLEINIAS:** What is that story?

**ATHENIAN:** The story of armed men springing up after the sowing of teeth, which the legislator may take as a proof that he can persuade the minds of the young of anything; so that he has only to reflect and find out what belief will be of the greatest public advantage, and then use all his efforts to make the whole community utter one and the same word in their songs and tales and discourses all their life long. But if you do not agree with me, there is no reason why you should not argue on the other side.

**CLEINIAS:** I do not see that any argument can fairly be raised by either of us against what you are now saying.

**ATHENIAN:** The next suggestion which I have to offer is, that all our three choruses shall sing to the young and tender souls of children, reciting in their strains all the noble thoughts of which we have already spoken, or are about to speak; and the sum of them shall be, that the life which is by the Gods deemed to be the happiest is also the best;--

we shall affirm this to be a most certain truth; and the minds of our young disciples will be more likely to receive these words of ours than any others which we might address to them.

**CLEINIAS:** I assent to what you say.

**ATHENIAN:** First will enter in their natural order the sacred choir composed of children, which is to sing lustily the heaven-taught lay to the whole city. Next will follow the choir of young men under the age of thirty, who will call upon the God Paean to testify to the truth of their words, and will pray him to be gracious to the youth and to turn their hearts. Thirdly, the choir of elder men, who are from thirty to sixty years of age, will also sing. There remain those who are too old to sing, and they will tell stories, illustrating the same virtues, as with the voice of an oracle.

**CLEINIAS:** Who are those who compose the third choir, Stranger? for I do not clearly understand what you mean to say about them.

**ATHENIAN:** And yet almost all that I have been saying has been said with a view to them.

**CLEINIAS:** Will you try to be a little plainer?

**ATHENIAN:** I was speaking at the commencement of our discourse, as you will remember, of the fiery nature of young creatures: I said that they were unable to keep quiet either in limb or voice, and that they called out and jumped about in a disorderly manner; and that no other animal attained to any perception of order, but man only. Now the order of motion is called rhythm, and the order of the voice, in which high and low are duly mingled, is called harmony; and both together are termed choric song. And I said that the Gods had pity on us, and gave us Apollo and the Muses to be our playfellows and leaders in the dance; and Dionysus, as I dare say that you will remember, was the third.

**CLEINIAS:** I quite remember.

**ATHENIAN:** Thus far I have spoken of the chorus of Apollo and the Muses, and I have still to speak of the remaining chorus, which is that of Dionysus.

**CLEINIAS:** How is that arranged? There is something strange, at any rate on first hearing, in a Dionysiac chorus of old men, if you really mean that those who are above thirty, and may be fifty, or from fifty to sixty years of age, are to dance in his honour.

**ATHENIAN:** Very true; and therefore it must be shown that there is good reason for the proposal.

**CLEINIAS:** Certainly.

**ATHENIAN:** Are we agreed thus far?

**CLEINIAS:** About what?

**ATHENIAN:** That every man and boy, slave and free, both sexes, and the whole city, should never cease charming themselves with the strains of which we have spoken; and that there should be every sort of change and variation of them in order to take away the effect of sameness, so that the singers may always receive pleasure from their hymns, and may never weary of them?

**CLEINIAS:** Every one will agree.

**ATHENIAN:** Where, then, will that best part of our city which, by reason of age and intelligence, has the greatest influence, sing these fairest of strains, which are to do so much good? Shall we be so foolish as to let them off who would give us the most beautiful and also the most useful of songs?

**CLEINIAS:** But, says the argument, we cannot let them off.

**ATHENIAN:** Then how can we carry out our purpose with decorum? Will this be the way?

**CLEINIAS:** What?

**ATHENIAN:** When a man is advancing in years, he is afraid and reluctant to sing;--he has no pleasure in his own performances; and if compulsion is used, he will be more and more ashamed, the older and more discreet he grows;--is not this true?

**CLEINIAS:** Certainly.

**ATHENIAN:** Well, and will he not be yet more ashamed if he has to stand up and sing in the theatre to a mixed audience?--and if moreover when he is required to do so, like the other choirs who contend for prizes, and have been trained under a singing master, he is pinched and hungry, he will certainly have a feeling of shame and discomfort which will make him very unwilling to exhibit.

**CLEINIAS:** No doubt.

**ATHENIAN:** How, then, shall we reassure him, and get him to sing? Shall we begin by enacting that boys shall not taste wine at all until they are eighteen years of age; we will tell them that fire must not be poured upon fire, whether in the body or in the soul, until they begin to go to work-- this is a precaution which has to be taken against the excitableness of youth;--afterwards they may taste wine in moderation up to the age of thirty, but while a man is young he should abstain altogether from intoxication and from excess of wine; when, at length, he has reached forty years, after dinner at a public mess, he may invite not only the other Gods, but Dionysus above all, to the mystery and festivity of the elder men, making use of the wine which he has given men to lighten the sourness of old age; that in age we may renew our youth, and forget our sorrows; and also in order that the nature of the soul, like iron melted in the fire, may become softer and so more impressible. In the first place, will not any one who is thus mellowed be more ready and less ashamed to sing--I do not say before a large audience, but before a moderate company; nor yet among strangers, but among his familiars, and, as we have often said, to chant, and to enchant?

**CLEINIAS:** He will be far more ready.

**ATHENIAN:** There will be no impropriety in our using such a method of persuading them to join with us in song.

**CLEINIAS:** None at all.

**ATHENIAN:** And what strain will they sing, and what muse will they hymn? The strain should clearly be one suitable to them.

**CLEINIAS:** Certainly.

**ATHENIAN:** And what strain is suitable for heroes? Shall they sing a choric strain?

**CLEINIAS:** Truly, Stranger, we of Crete and Lacedaemon know no strain other than that which we have learnt and been accustomed to sing in our chorus.

**ATHENIAN:** I dare say; for you have never acquired the knowledge of the most beautiful kind of song, in your military way of life, which is modelled after the camp, and is not like that of dwellers in cities; and you have your young men herding and feeding together like young colts. No one takes his own individual colt and drags him away from his fellows against his will, raging and foaming, and gives him a groom to attend to him alone, and trains and rubs him down privately, and gives him the qualities in education which will make him not only a good soldier, but also a governor of a state and of cities. Such an one, as we said at first, would be a greater warrior than he of whom Tyrtaeus sings; and he would honour courage everywhere, but always as the fourth, and not as the first part of virtue, either in individuals or states.

**CLEINIAS:** Once more, Stranger, I must complain that you depreciate our lawgivers.

**ATHENIAN:** Not intentionally, if at all, my good friend; but whither the argument leads, thither let us follow; for if there be indeed some strain of song more beautiful than that of the choruses or the public theatres, I should like to impart it to those who, as we say, are ashamed of these, and want to have the best.

**CLEINIAS:** Certainly.

**ATHENIAN:** When things have an accompanying charm, either the best thing in them is this very charm, or there is some rightness or utility possessed by them;--for example, I should say that eating and drinking, and the use of food in general, have an accompanying charm which we call pleasure; but that this rightness and utility is just the healthfulness of the things served up to us, which is their true rightness.

**CLEINIAS:** Just so.

**ATHENIAN:** Thus, too, I should say that learning has a certain accompanying charm which is the pleasure; but that the right and the profitable, the good and the noble, are qualities which the truth gives to it.

**CLEINIAS:** Exactly.

**ATHENIAN:** And so in the imitative arts--if they succeed in making likenesses, and are accompanied by pleasure, may not their works be said to have a charm?

**CLEINIAS:** Yes.

**ATHENIAN:** But equal proportions, whether of quality or quantity, and not pleasure, speaking generally, would give them truth or rightness.

**CLEINIAS:** Yes.

**ATHENIAN:** Then that only can be rightly judged by the standard of pleasure, which makes or furnishes no utility or truth or likeness, nor on the other hand is productive of any hurtful quality, but exists solely for the sake of the accompanying charm; and the term 'pleasure' is most appropriately applied to it when these other qualities are absent.

**CLEINIAS:** You are speaking of harmless pleasure, are you not?

**ATHENIAN:** Yes; and this I term amusement, when doing neither harm nor good in any degree worth speaking of.

**CLEINIAS:** Very true.

**ATHENIAN:** Then, if such be our principles, we must assert that imitation is not to be judged of by pleasure and false opinion; and this is true of all equality, for the equal is not equal or the symmetrical

symmetrical, because somebody thinks or likes something, but they are to be judged of by the standard of truth, and by no other whatever.

**CLEINIAS:** Quite true.

**ATHENIAN:** Do we not regard all music as representative and imitative?

**CLEINIAS:** Certainly.

**ATHENIAN:** Then, when any one says that music is to be judged of by pleasure, his doctrine cannot be admitted; and if there be any music of which pleasure is the criterion, such music is not to be sought out or deemed to have any real excellence, but only that other kind of music which is an imitation of the good.

**CLEINIAS:** Very true.

**ATHENIAN:** And those who seek for the best kind of song and music ought not to seek for that which is pleasant, but for that which is true; and the truth of imitation consists, as we were saying, in rendering the thing imitated according to quantity and quality.

**CLEINIAS:** Certainly.

**ATHENIAN:** And every one will admit that musical compositions are all imitative and representative. Will not poets and spectators and actors all agree in this?

**CLEINIAS:** They will.

**ATHENIAN:** Surely then he who would judge correctly must know what each composition is; for if he does not know what is the character and meaning of the piece, and what it represents, he will never discern whether the intention is true or false.

**CLEINIAS:** Certainly not.

**ATHENIAN:** And will he who does not know what is true be able to distinguish what is good and bad? My statement is not very clear; but perhaps you will understand me better if I put the matter in another way.

**CLEINIAS:** How?

**ATHENIAN:** There are ten thousand likenesses of objects of sight?

**CLEINIAS:** Yes.

**ATHENIAN:** And can he who does not know what the exact object is which is imitated, ever know whether the resemblance is truthfully executed? I mean, for example, whether a statue has the proportions of a body, and the true situation of the parts; what those proportions are, and how the parts fit into one another in due order; also their colours and conformations, or whether this is all confused in the execution: do you think that any one can know about this, who does not know what the animal is which has been imitated?

**CLEINIAS:** Impossible.

**ATHENIAN:** But even if we know that the thing pictured or sculptured is a man, who has received at the hand of the artist all his proper parts and colours and shapes, must we not also know whether the work is beautiful or in any respect deficient in beauty?

**CLEINIAS:** If this were not required, Stranger, we should all of us be judges of beauty.

**ATHENIAN:** Very true; and may we not say that in everything imitated, whether in drawing, music, or any other art, he who is to be a competent judge must possess three things;--he must know, in the first place, of what the imitation is; secondly, he must know that it is true; and thirdly, that it has been well executed in words and melodies and rhythms?

**CLEINIAS:** Certainly.

**ATHENIAN:** Then let us not faint in discussing the peculiar difficulty of music. Music is more celebrated than any other kind of imitation, and therefore requires the greatest care of them all. For if a man makes a mistake here, he may do himself the greatest injury by welcoming evil dispositions, and the mistake may be very difficult to discern, because the poets are artists very inferior in character to the Muses themselves, who would never fall into the monstrous error of assigning to the words of men the gestures and songs of women; nor after combining the melodies with the gestures of freemen would they add on the rhythms of slaves and men of the baser sort; nor, beginning with the rhythms and gestures of freemen, would they assign to them a melody or words which are of an opposite character; nor would they mix up the voices and sounds of animals and of men and instruments, and every other sort of noise, as if they were all one. But human poets are fond of introducing this sort of inconsistent mixture, and so make themselves ridiculous in the eyes of those who, as Orpheus says, 'are ripe for true pleasure.' The experienced see all this confusion, and yet the poets go on and make still further havoc by separating the rhythm and the figure of the dance from the melody, setting bare words to metre, and also separating the melody and the rhythm from the words, using the lyre or the flute alone. For when there are no words, it is very difficult to recognize the meaning of the harmony and rhythm, or to see that any worthy object is imitated by them. And we must acknowledge that all this sort of thing, which aims only at swiftness and smoothness and a brutish noise, and uses the flute and the lyre not as the mere accompaniments of the dance and song, is exceedingly coarse and tasteless. The use of either instrument, when unaccompanied, leads to every sort of irregularity and trickery. This is all rational enough. But we are considering not how our choristers, who are from thirty to fifty years of age, and may be over fifty, are not to use the Muses, but how they are to use them. And the considerations which we have urged seem to show in what way these fifty years' old choristers who are to sing, may be expected to be better trained. For they need to have a quick perception and knowledge of harmonies and rhythms; otherwise, how can they ever know whether a melody would be rightly sung to the Dorian mode, or to the rhythm which the poet has assigned to it?

**CLEINIAS:** Clearly they cannot.

**ATHENIAN:** The many are ridiculous in imagining that they know what is in proper harmony and rhythm, and what is not, when they can only be made to sing and step in rhythm by force; it never occurs to them that they are ignorant of what they are doing. Now every melody is right when it has suitable harmony and rhythm, and wrong when unsuitable.

**CLEINIAS:** That is most certain.

**ATHENIAN:** But can a man who does not know a thing, as we were saying, know that the thing is right?

**CLEINIAS:** Impossible.

**ATHENIAN:** Then now, as would appear, we are making the discovery that our newly-appointed choristers, whom we hereby invite and, although they are their own masters, compel to sing, must be educated to such an extent as to be able to follow the steps of the rhythm and the notes of the song, that they may know the harmonies and rhythms, and be able to select what are suitable for men of their age and character to sing; and may sing them, and have innocent pleasure from their own performance, and also lead younger men to welcome with dutiful delight good dispositions. Having such training, they will attain a more accurate knowledge than falls to the lot of the common people, or even of the poets themselves. For the poet need not know the third point, viz., whether the imitation is good or not, though he can hardly help knowing the laws of melody and rhythm. But the aged chorus must know all the three, that they may choose the best, and that which is nearest to the best; for otherwise they will never be able to charm the souls of young men in the way of virtue. And now the original design of the argument which was intended to bring eloquent aid to the Chorus of Dionysus, has been accomplished to the best of our ability, and let us see whether we were right:--I should imagine that a drinking assembly is likely to become more and more tumultuous as the drinking goes on: this, as we were saying at first, will certainly be the case.

**CLEINIAS:** Certainly.

**ATHENIAN:** Every man has a more than natural elevation; his heart is glad within him, and he will say anything and will be restrained by nobody at such a time; he fancies that he is able to rule over himself and all mankind.

**CLEINIAS:** Quite true.

**ATHENIAN:** Were we not saying that on such occasions the souls of the drinkers become like iron heated in the fire, and grow softer and younger, and are easily moulded by him who knows how to educate and fashion them, just as when they were young, and that this fashioner of them is the same who prescribed for them in the days of their youth, viz., the good legislator; and that he ought to enact laws of the banquet, which, when a man is confident, bold, and impudent, and unwilling to wait his turn and have his share of silence and speech, and drinking and music, will change his character into the opposite--such laws as will infuse into him a just and noble fear, which will take up arms at the approach of insolence, being that divine fear which we have called reverence and shame?

**CLEINIAS:** True.

**ATHENIAN:** And the guardians of these laws and fellow-workers with them are the calm and sober generals of the drinkers; and without their help there is greater difficulty in fighting against drink than in fighting against enemies when the commander of an army is not himself calm; and he who is unwilling to obey them and the commanders of Dionysiac feasts who are more than sixty years of age, shall suffer a disgrace as great as he who disobeys military leaders, or even greater.

**CLEINIAS:** Right.

**ATHENIAN:** If, then, drinking and amusement were regulated in this way, would not the companions of our revels be improved? they would part better friends than they were, and not, as now, enemies. Their whole intercourse would be regulated by law and observant of it, and the sober would be the leaders of the drunken.

**CLEINIAS:** I think so too, if drinking were regulated as you propose.

**ATHENIAN:** Let us not then simply censure the gift of Dionysus as bad and unfit to be received into the State. For wine has many excellences, and one pre-eminent one, about which there is a difficulty in speaking to the many, from a fear of their misconceiving and misunderstanding what is said.

**CLEINIAS:** To what do you refer?

**ATHENIAN:** There is a tradition or story, which has somehow crept about the world, that Dionysus was robbed of his wits by his stepmother Here, and that out of revenge he inspires Bacchic furies and dancing madnesses in others; for which reason he gave men wine. Such traditions concerning the Gods I leave to those who think that they may be safely uttered; I only know that no animal at birth is mature or perfect in intelligence; and in the intermediate period, in which he has not yet acquired his own proper sense, he rages and roars without rhyme or reason; and when he has once got on his legs he jumps about without rhyme or reason; and this, as you will remember, has been already said by us to be the origin of music and gymnastic.

**CLEINIAS:** To be sure, I remember.

**ATHENIAN:** And did we not say that the sense of harmony and rhythm sprang from this beginning among men, and that Apollo and the Muses and Dionysus were the Gods whom we had to thank for them?

**CLEINIAS:** Certainly.

**ATHENIAN:** The other story implied that wine was given man out of revenge, and in order to make him mad; but our present doctrine, on the contrary, is, that wine was given him as a balm, and in order to implant modesty in the soul, and health and strength in the body.

**CLEINIAS:** That, Stranger, is precisely what was said.

**ATHENIAN:** Then half the subject may now be considered to have been discussed; shall we proceed to the consideration of the other half?

**CLEINIAS:** What is the other half, and how do you divide the subject?

**ATHENIAN:** The whole choral art is also in our view the whole of education; and of this art, rhythms and harmonies form the part which has to do with the voice.

**CLEINIAS:** Yes.

**ATHENIAN:** The movement of the body has rhythm in common with the movement of the voice, but gesture is peculiar to it, whereas song is simply the movement of the voice.

**CLEINIAS:** Most true.

**ATHENIAN:** And the sound of the voice which reaches and educates the soul, we have ventured to term music.

**CLEINIAS:** We were right.

**ATHENIAN:** And the movement of the body, when regarded as an amusement, we termed dancing; but when extended and pursued with a view to the excellence of the body, this scientific training may be called gymnastic.

**CLEINIAS:** Exactly.

**ATHENIAN:** Music, which was one half of the choral art, may be said to have been completely discussed. Shall we proceed to the other half or not? What would you like?

**CLEINIAS:** My good friend, when you are talking with a Cretan and Lacedaemonian, and we have discussed music and not gymnastic, what answer are either of us likely to make to such an enquiry?

**ATHENIAN:** An answer is contained in your question; and I understand and accept what you say not only as an answer, but also as a command to proceed with gymnastic.

**CLEINIAS:** You quite understand me; do as you say.

**ATHENIAN:** I will; and there will not be any difficulty in speaking intelligibly to you about a subject with which both of you are far more familiar than with music.

**CLEINIAS:** There will not.

**ATHENIAN:** Is not the origin of gymnastics, too, to be sought in the tendency to rapid motion which exists in all animals; man, as we were saying, having attained the sense of rhythm, created and invented dancing; and melody arousing and awakening rhythm, both united formed the choral art?

**CLEINIAS:** Very true.

**ATHENIAN:** And one part of this subject has been already discussed by us, and there still remains another to be discussed?

**CLEINIAS:** Exactly.

**ATHENIAN:** I have first a final word to add to my discourse about drink, if you will allow me to do so.

**CLEINIAS:** What more have you to say?

**ATHENIAN:** I should say that if a city seriously means to adopt the practice of drinking under due regulation and with a view to the enforcement of temperance, and in like manner, and on the same principle, will allow of other pleasures, designing to gain the victory over them--in this way all of them may be used. But if the State makes drinking an amusement only, and whoever likes may drink whenever he likes, and with whom he likes, and add to this any other indulgences, I shall never agree or allow that this city or this man should practise drinking. I would go further than the Cretans and Lacedaemonians, and am disposed rather to the law of the Carthaginians, that no one while he is on a campaign should be allowed to taste wine at all, but that he should drink water during all that time, and that in the city no slave, male or female, should ever drink wine; and that no magistrates should drink during their year of office, nor should pilots of vessels or judges while on duty taste wine at all, nor any one who is going to hold a consultation about any matter of importance; nor in the day-time at all, unless in consequence of exercise or as medicine; nor again at night, when any one, either man or woman, is minded to get children. There are numberless other cases also in which those who have good sense and good laws ought not to drink wine, so that if what I say is true, no city will need many vineyards. Their husbandry and their way of life in general will follow an appointed order, and their cultivation of the vine will be the most limited and the least common of their employments. And this, Stranger, shall be the crown of my discourse about wine, if you agree.

**CLEINIAS:** Excellent: we agree.

# BOOK III.

**ATHENIAN:** Enough of this. And what, then, is to be regarded as the origin of government? Will not a man be able to judge of it best from a point of view in which he may behold the progress of states and their transitions to good or evil?

**CLEINIAS:** What do you mean?

**ATHENIAN:** I mean that he might watch them from the point of view of time, and observe the changes which take place in them during infinite ages.

**CLEINIAS:** How so?

**ATHENIAN:** Why, do you think that you can reckon the time which has elapsed since cities first existed and men were citizens of them?

**CLEINIAS:** Hardly.

**ATHENIAN:** But are sure that it must be vast and incalculable?

**CLEINIAS:** Certainly.

**ATHENIAN:** And have not thousands and thousands of cities come into being during this period and as many perished? And has not each of them had every form of government many times over, now growing larger, now smaller, and again improving or declining?

**CLEINIAS:** To be sure.

**ATHENIAN:** Let us endeavour to ascertain the cause of these changes; for that will probably explain the first origin and development of forms of government.

**CLEINIAS:** Very good. You shall endeavour to impart your thoughts to us, and we will make an effort to understand you.

**ATHENIAN:** Do you believe that there is any truth in ancient traditions?

**CLEINIAS:** What traditions?

**ATHENIAN:** The traditions about the many destructions of mankind which have been occasioned by deluges and pestilences, and in many other ways, and of the survival of a remnant?

**CLEINIAS:** Every one is disposed to believe them.

**ATHENIAN:** Let us consider one of them, that which was caused by the famous deluge.

**CLEINIAS:** What are we to observe about it?

**ATHENIAN:** I mean to say that those who then escaped would only be hill shepherds,--small sparks of the human race preserved on the tops of mountains.

**CLEINIAS:** Clearly.

**ATHENIAN:** Such survivors would necessarily be unacquainted with the arts and the various devices which are suggested to the dwellers in cities by interest or ambition, and with all the wrongs which they contrive against one another.

**CLEINIAS:** Very true.

**ATHENIAN:** Let us suppose, then, that the cities in the plain and on the sea-coast were utterly destroyed at that time.

**CLEINIAS:** Very good.

**ATHENIAN:** Would not all implements have then perished and every other excellent invention of political or any other sort of wisdom have utterly disappeared?

**CLEINIAS:** Why, yes, my friend; and if things had always continued as they are at present ordered, how could any discovery have ever been made even in the least particular? For it is evident that the arts were unknown during ten thousand times ten thousand years. And no more than a thousand or two thousand years have elapsed since the discoveries of Daedalus, Orpheus and Palamedes,--since Marsyas and Olympus invented music, and Amphion the lyre --not to speak of numberless other inventions which are but of yesterday.

**ATHENIAN:** Have you forgotten, Cleinias, the name of a friend who is really of yesterday?

**CLEINIAS:** I suppose that you mean Epimenides.

**ATHENIAN:** The same, my friend; he does indeed far overleap the heads of all mankind by his invention; for he carried out in practice, as you declare, what of old Hesiod (Works and Days) only preached.

**CLEINIAS:** Yes, according to our tradition.

**ATHENIAN:** After the great destruction, may we not suppose that the state of man was something of this sort:--In the beginning of things there was a fearful illimitable desert and a vast expanse of land; a herd or two of oxen would be the only survivors of the animal world; and there might be a few goats, these too hardly enough to maintain the shepherds who tended them?

**CLEINIAS:** True.

**ATHENIAN:** And of cities or governments or legislation, about which we are now talking, do you suppose that they could have any recollection at all?

**CLEINIAS:** None whatever.

**ATHENIAN:** And out of this state of things has there not sprung all that we now are and have: cities and governments, and arts and laws, and a great deal of vice and a great deal of virtue?

**CLEINIAS:** What do you mean?

**ATHENIAN:** Why, my good friend, how can we possibly suppose that those who knew nothing of all the good and evil of cities could have attained their full development, whether of virtue or of vice?

**CLEINIAS:** I understand your meaning, and you are quite right.

**ATHENIAN:** But, as time advanced and the race multiplied, the world came to be what the world is.

**CLEINIAS:** Very true.

**ATHENIAN:** Doubtless the change was not made all in a moment, but little by little, during a very long period of time.

**CLEINIAS:** A highly probable supposition.

**ATHENIAN:** At first, they would have a natural fear ringing in their ears which would prevent their descending from the heights into the plain.

**CLEINIAS:** Of course.

**ATHENIAN:** The fewness of the survivors at that time would have made them all the more desirous of seeing one another; but then the means of travelling either by land or sea had been almost entirely lost, as I may say, with the loss of the arts, and there was great difficulty in getting at one another; for iron and brass and all metals were jumbled together and had disappeared in the chaos; nor was there any possibility of extracting ore from them; and they had scarcely any means of felling timber. Even if you suppose that some implements might have been preserved in the mountains, they must quickly have worn out and vanished, and there would be no more of them until the art of metallurgy had again revived.

**CLEINIAS:** There could not have been.

**ATHENIAN:** In how many generations would this be attained?

**CLEINIAS:** Clearly, not for many generations.

**ATHENIAN:** During this period, and for some time afterwards, all the arts which require iron and brass and the like would disappear.

**CLEINIAS:** Certainly.

**ATHENIAN:** Faction and war would also have died out in those days, and for many reasons.

**CLEINIAS:** How would that be?

**ATHENIAN:** In the first place, the desolation of these primitive men would create in them a feeling of affection and goodwill towards one another; and, secondly, they would have no occasion to quarrel about their subsistence, for they would have pasture in abundance, except just at first, and in some particular cases; and from their pasture-land they would obtain the greater part of their food in a primitive age, having plenty of milk and flesh; moreover they would procure other food by the chase, not to be despised either in quantity or quality. They would also have abundance of clothing, and bedding, and dwellings, and utensils either capable of standing on the fire or not; for the plastic and weaving arts do not require any use of iron: and God has given these two arts to man in order to provide him with all such things, that, when reduced to the last extremity, the human race may still grow and increase. Hence in those days mankind were not very poor; nor was poverty a cause of difference among them; and rich they could not have been, having neither gold nor silver:-- such at that time was their condition. And the community which has neither poverty nor riches will always have the noblest principles; in it there is no insolence or injustice, nor, again, are there any contentions or envyings. And therefore they were good, and also because they were what is called simple-minded; and when they were told about good and evil, they in their simplicity believed what they heard to be very truth and practised it. No one had the wit to suspect another of a falsehood, as men do now; but what they heard about Gods and men they believed to be true, and lived accordingly; and therefore they were in all respects such as we have described them.

**CLEINIAS:** That quite accords with my views, and with those of my friend here.

**ATHENIAN:** Would not many generations living on in a simple manner, although ruder, perhaps, and more ignorant of the arts generally, and in particular of those of land or naval warfare, and likewise of other arts, termed in cities legal practices and party conflicts, and including all conceivable ways of hurting one another in word and deed;--although inferior to those who lived before the deluge, or to the men of our day in these respects, would they not, I say, be simpler and more manly, and also more temperate and altogether more just? The reason has been already explained.

**CLEINIAS:** Very true.

**ATHENIAN:** I should wish you to understand that what has preceded and what is about to follow, has been, and will be said, with the intention of explaining what need the men of that time had of laws, and who was their lawgiver.

**CLEINIAS:** And thus far what you have said has been very well said.

**ATHENIAN:** They could hardly have wanted lawgivers as yet; nothing of that sort was likely to have existed in their days, for they had no letters at this early period; they lived by habit and the customs of their ancestors, as they are called.

**CLEINIAS:** Probably.

**ATHENIAN:** But there was already existing a form of government which, if I am not mistaken, is generally termed a lordship, and this still remains in many places, both among Hellenes and barbarians, and is the government which is declared by Homer to have prevaile among the Cyclopes:--

*'They have neither councils nor judgments, but they dwell in hollow caves on the tops of high mountains, and every one gives law to his wife and children, and they do not busy themselves about one another.' (Odyss.)*

**CLEINIAS:** That seems to be a charming poet of yours; I have read some other verses of his, which are very clever; but I do not know much of him, for foreign poets are very little read among the Cretans.

**MEGILLUS:** But they are in Lacedaemon, and he appears to be the prince of them all; the manner of life, however, which he describes is not Spartan, but rather Ionian, and he seems quite to confirm what you are saying, when he traces up the ancient state of mankind by the help of tradition to barbarism.

**ATHENIAN:** Yes, he does confirm it; and we may accept his witness to the fact that such forms of government sometimes arise.

**CLEINIAS:** We may.

**ATHENIAN:** And were not such states composed of men who had been dispersed in single habitations and families by the poverty which attended the devastations; and did not the eldest then rule among them, because with them government originated in the authority of a father and a mother, whom, like a flock of birds, they followed, forming one troop under the patriarchal rule and sovereignty of their parents, which of all sovereignties is the most just?

**CLEINIAS:** Very true.

**ATHENIAN:** After this they came together in greater numbers, and increased the size of their cities, and betook themselves to husbandry, first of all at the foot of the mountains, and made enclosures of loose walls and works of defence, in order to keep off wild beasts; thus creating a single large and common habitation.

**CLEINIAS:** Yes; at least we may suppose so.

**ATHENIAN:** There is another thing which would probably happen.

**CLEINIAS:** What?

**ATHENIAN:** When these larger habitations grew up out of the lesser original ones, each of the lesser ones would survive in the larger; every family would be under the rule of the eldest, and, owing to their separation from one another, would have peculiar customs in things divine and human, which they would have received from their several parents who had educated them; and these customs would incline them to order, when the parents had the element of order in their nature, and to courage, when they had the element of courage. And they would naturally stamp upon their children, and upon their children's children, their own likings; and, as we are saying, they would find their way into the larger society, having already their own peculiar laws.

**CLEINIAS:** Certainly.

**ATHENIAN:** And every man surely likes his own laws best, and the laws of others not so well.

**CLEINIAS:** True.

**ATHENIAN:** Then now we seem to have stumbled upon the beginnings of legislation.

**CLEINIAS:** Exactly.

**ATHENIAN:** The next step will be that these persons who have met together, will select some arbiters, who will review the laws of all of them, and will publicly present such as they approve to the chiefs who lead the tribes, and who are in a manner their kings, allowing them to choose those which they think best. These persons will themselves be called legislators, and will appoint the magistrates, framing some sort of aristocracy, or perhaps monarchy, out of the dynasties or lordships, and in this altered state of the government they will live.

**CLEINIAS:** Yes, that would be the natural order of things.

**ATHENIAN:** Then, now let us speak of a third form of government, in which all other forms and conditions of polities and cities concur.

**CLEINIAS:** What is that?

**ATHENIAN:** The form which in fact Homer indicates as following the second. This third form arose when, as he says, Dardanus founded Dardania:--

*'For not as yet had the holy Ilium been built on the plain to be a city of speaking men; but they were still dwelling at the foot of many-fountained Ida.'*

For indeed, in these verses, and in what he said of the Cyclopes, he speaks the words of God and nature; for poets are a divine race, and often in their strains, by the aid of the Muses and the Graces, they attain truth.

**CLEINIAS:** Yes.

**ATHENIAN:** Then now let us proceed with the rest of our tale, which will probably be found to illustrate in some degree our proposed design:--Shall we do so?

**CLEINIAS:** By all means.

**ATHENIAN:** Ilium was built, when they descended from the mountain, in a large and fair plain, on a sort of low hill, watered by many rivers descending from Ida.

**CLEINIAS:** Such is the tradition.

**ATHENIAN:** And we must suppose this event to have taken place many ages after the deluge?

**ATHENIAN:** A marvellous forgetfulness of the former destruction would appear to have come over them, when they placed their town right under numerous streams flowing from the heights, trusting for their security to not very high hills, either.

**CLEINIAS:** There must have been a long interval, clearly.

**ATHENIAN:** And, as population increased, many other cities would begin to be inhabited.

**CLEINIAS:** Doubtless.

**ATHENIAN:** Those cities made war against Troy--by sea as well as land--for at that time men were ceasing to be afraid of the sea.

**CLEINIAS:** Clearly.

**ATHENIAN:** The Achaeans remained ten years, and overthrew Troy.

**CLEINIAS:** True.

**ATHENIAN:** And during the ten years in which the Achaeans were besieging Ilium, the homes of the besiegers were falling into an evil plight. Their youth revolted; and when the soldiers returned to their own cities and families, they did not receive them properly, and as they ought to have done, and numerous deaths, murders, exiles, were the consequence. The exiles came again, under a new name, no longer Achaeans, but Dorians,--a name which they derived from Dorieus; for it was he who gathered them together. The rest of the story is told by you Lacedaemonians as part of the history of Sparta.

**MEGILLUS:** To be sure.

**ATHENIAN:** Thus, after digressing from the original subject of laws into music and drinking-bouts, the argument has, providentially, come back to the same point, and presents to us another handle. For we have reached the settlement of Lacedaemon; which, as you truly say, is in laws and in institutions the sister of Crete. And we are all the better for the digression, because we have gone through various governments and settlements, and have been present at the foundation of a first, second, and third state, succeeding one another in infinite time. And now there appears on the horizon a fourth state or nation which was once in process of settlement and has continued settled to this day. If, out of all this, we are able to discern what is well or ill settled, and what laws are the salvation and what are the destruction of cities, and what changes would make a state happy, O Megillus and Cleinias, we may now begin again, unless we have some fault to find with the previous discussion.

**MEGILLUS:** If some God, Stranger, would promise us that our new enquiry about legislation would be as good and full as the present, I would go a great way to hear such another, and would think that a day as long as this --and we are now approaching the longest day of the year--was too short for the discussion.

**ATHENIAN:** Then I suppose that we must consider this subject?

**MEGILLUS:** Certainly.

**ATHENIAN:** Let us place ourselves in thought at the moment when Lacedaemon and Argos and Messene and the rest of the Peloponnesus were all in complete subjection, Megillus, to your ancestors; for afterwards, as the legend informs us, they divided their army into three portions, and settled three cities, Argos, Messene, Lacedaemon.

**MEGILLUS:** True.

**ATHENIAN:** Temenus was the king of Argos, Cresphontes of Messene, Procles and Eurysthenes of Lacedaemon.

**MEGILLUS:** Certainly.

**ATHENIAN:** To these kings all the men of that day made oath that they would assist them, if any one subverted their kingdom.

**MEGILLUS:** True.

**ATHENIAN:** But can a kingship be destroyed, or was any other form of government ever destroyed, by any but the rulers themselves? No indeed, by Zeus. Have we already forgotten what was said a little while ago?

**MEGILLUS:** No.

**ATHENIAN:** And may we not now further confirm what was then mentioned? For we have come upon facts which have brought us back again to the same principle; so that, in resuming the discussion, we shall not be enquiring about an empty theory, but about events which actually happened. The case was as follows:--Three royal heroes made oath to three cities which were under a kingly government, and the cities to the kings, that both rulers and subjects should govern and be governed according to the laws which were common to all of them: the rulers promised that as time and the race went forward they would not make their rule more arbitrary; and the subjects said that, if the rulers observed these conditions, they would never subvert or permit others to subvert those kingdoms; the kings were to assist kings and peoples when injured, and the peoples were to assist peoples and kings in like manner. Is not this the fact?

**MEGILLUS:** Yes.

**ATHENIAN:** And the three states to whom these laws were given, whether their kings or any others were the authors of them, had therefore the greatest security for the maintenance of their constitutions?

**MEGILLUS:** What security?

**ATHENIAN:** That the other two states were always to come to the rescue against a rebellious third.

**MEGILLUS:** True.

**ATHENIAN:** Many persons say that legislators ought to impose such laws as the mass of the people will be ready to receive; but this is just as if one were to command gymnastic masters or physicians to treat or cure their pupils or patients in an agreeable manner.

**MEGILLUS:** Exactly.

**ATHENIAN:** Whereas the physician may often be too happy if he can restore health, and make the body whole, without any very great infliction of pain.

**MEGILLUS:** Certainly.

**ATHENIAN:** There was also another advantage possessed by the men of that day, which greatly lightened the task of passing laws.

**MEGILLUS:** What advantage?

**ATHENIAN:** The legislators of that day, when they equalized property, escaped the great accusation which generally arises in legislation, if a person attempts to disturb the possession of land, or to abolish debts, because he sees that without this reform there can never be any real equality. Now, in general, when the legislator attempts to make a new settlement of such matters, every one meets him with the cry, that 'he is not to disturb vested interests,'--declaring with imprecations that he is introducing agrarian laws and cancelling of debts, until a man is at his wits' end; whereas no one could quarrel with the Dorians for distributing the land,--there was nothing to hinder them; and as for debts, they had none which were considerable or of old standing.

**MEGILLUS:** Very true.

**ATHENIAN:** But then, my good friends, why did the settlement and legislation of their country turn out so badly?

**MEGILLUS:** How do you mean; and why do you blame them?

**ATHENIAN:** There were three kingdoms, and of these, two quickly corrupted their original constitution and laws, and the only one which remained was the Spartan.

**MEGILLUS:** The question which you ask is not easily answered.

**ATHENIAN:** And yet must be answered when we are enquiring about laws, this being our old man's sober game of play, whereby we beguile the way, as I was saying when we first set out on our journey.

**MEGILLUS:** Certainly; and we must find out why this was.

**ATHENIAN:** What laws are more worthy of our attention than those which have regulated such cities? or what settlements of states are greater or more famous?

**MEGILLUS:** I know of none.

**ATHENIAN:** Can we doubt that your ancestors intended these institutions not only for the protection of Peloponnesus, but of all the Hellenes, in case they were attacked by the barbarian? For the inhabitants of the region about Ilium, when they provoked by their insolence the Trojan war, relied upon the power of the Assyrians and the Empire of Ninus, which still existed and had a great prestige; the people of those days fearing the united Assyrian Empire just as we now fear the Great King. And the second capture of Troy was a serious offence against them, because Troy was a portion of the Assyrian Empire. To meet the danger the single army was distributed between three cities by the royal brothers, sons of Heracles,-- a fair device, as it seemed, and a far better arrangement than the expedition against Troy. For, firstly, the people of that day had, as they thought, in the Heraclidae better leaders than the Pelopidae; in the next place, they considered that their army was superior in valour to that which went against Troy; for, although the latter conquered the Trojans, they were themselves conquered by the Heraclidae--Achaeans by Dorians. May we not suppose that this was the intention with which the men of those days framed the constitutions of their states?

**MEGILLUS:** Quite true.

**ATHENIAN:** And would not men who had shared with one another many dangers, and were governed by a single race of royal brothers, and had taken the advice of oracles, and in particular of the Delphian Apollo, be likely to think that such states would be firmly and lastingly established?

**MEGILLUS:** Of course they would.

**ATHENIAN:** Yet these institutions, of which such great expectations were entertained, seem to have all rapidly vanished away; with the exception, as I was saying, of that small part of them which existed in your land. And this third part has never to this day ceased warring against the two others; whereas, if the original idea had been carried out, and they had agreed to be one, their power would have been invincible in war.

**MEGILLUS:** No doubt.

**ATHENIAN:** But what was the ruin of this glorious confederacy? Here is a subject well worthy of consideration.

**MEGILLUS:** Certainly, no one will ever find more striking instances of laws or governments being the salvation or destruction of great and noble interests, than are here presented to his view.

**ATHENIAN:** Then now we seem to have happily arrived at a real and important question.

**MEGILLUS:** Very true.

**ATHENIAN:** Did you never remark, sage friend, that all men, and we ourselves at this moment, often fancy that they see some beautiful thing which might have effected wonders if any one had only known how to make a right use of it in some way; and yet this mode of looking at things may turn out after all to be a mistake, and not according to nature, either in our own case or in any other?

**MEGILLUS:** To what are you referring, and what do you mean?

**ATHENIAN:** I was thinking of my own admiration of the aforesaid Heracleid expedition, which was so noble, and might have had such wonderful results for the Hellenes, if only rightly used; and I was just laughing at myself.

**MEGILLUS:** But were you not right and wise in speaking as you did, and we in assenting to you?

**ATHENIAN:** Perhaps; and yet I cannot help observing that any one who sees anything great or powerful, immediately has the feeling that--'If the owner only knew how to use his great and noble possession, how happy would he be, and what great results would he achieve!'

**MEGILLUS:** And would he not be justified?

**ATHENIAN:** Reflect; in what point of view does this sort of praise appear just: First, in reference to the question in hand:--If the then commanders had known how to arrange their army properly, how would they have attained success? Would not this have been the way? They would have bound them all firmly together and preserved them for ever, giving them freedom and dominion at pleasure, combined with the power of doing in the whole world, Hellenic and barbarian, whatever they and their descendants desired. What other aim would they have had?

**MEGILLUS:** Very good.

**ATHENIAN:** Suppose any one were in the same way to express his admiration at the sight of great wealth or family honour, or the like, he would praise them under the idea that through them he would attain either all or the greater and chief part of what he desires.

**MEGILLUS:** He would.

**ATHENIAN:** Well, now, and does not the argument show that there is one common desire of all mankind?

**MEGILLUS:** What is it?

**ATHENIAN:** The desire which a man has, that all things, if possible,--at any rate, things human,--may come to pass in accordance with his soul's desire.

**MEGILLUS:** Certainly.

**ATHENIAN:** And having this desire always, and at every time of life, in youth, in manhood, in age, he cannot help always praying for the fulfilment of it.

**MEGILLUS:** No doubt.

**ATHENIAN:** And we join in the prayers of our friends, and ask for them what they ask for themselves.

**MEGILLUS:** We do.

**ATHENIAN:** Dear is the son to the father--the younger to the elder.

**MEGILLUS:** Of course.

**ATHENIAN:** And yet the son often prays to obtain things which the father prays that he may not obtain.

**MEGILLUS:** When the son is young and foolish, you mean?

**ATHENIAN:** Yes; or when the father, in the dotage of age or the heat of youth, having no sense of right and justice, prays with fervour, under the influence of feelings akin to those of Theseus when he cursed the unfortunate Hippolytus, do you imagine that the son, having a sense of right and justice, will join in his father's prayers?

**MEGILLUS:** I understand you to mean that a man should not desire or be in a hurry to have all things according to his wish, for his wish may be at variance with his reason. But every state and every individual ought to pray and strive for wisdom.

**ATHENIAN:** Yes; and I remember, and you will remember, what I said at first, that a statesman and legislator ought to ordain laws with a view to wisdom; while you were arguing that the good lawgiver ought to order all with a view to war. And to this I replied that there were four virtues, but that upon your view one of them only was the aim of legislation; whereas you ought to regard all virtue, and especially that which comes first, and is the leader of all the rest--I mean wisdom and mind and opinion, having affection and desire in their train. And now the argument returns to the same point, and I say once more, in jest if you like, or in earnest if you like, that the prayer of a fool is full of danger, being likely to end in the opposite of what he desires. And if you would rather receive my words in earnest, I am willing that you should; and you will find, I suspect, as I have said already, that not cowardice was the cause of the ruin of the Dorian kings and of their whole design, nor ignorance of military matters, either on the part of the rulers or of their subjects; but their misfortunes were due to their general degeneracy, and especially to their ignorance of the most important human affairs. That was then, and is still, and always will be the case, as I will endeavour, if you will allow me, to make out and demonstrate as well as I am able to you who are my friends, in the course of the argument.

**CLEINIAS:** Pray go on, Stranger;--compliments are troublesome, but we will show, not in word but in deed, how greatly we prize your words, for we will give them our best attention; and that is the way in which a freeman best shows his approval or disapproval.

**MEGILLUS:** Excellent, Cleinias; let us do as you say.

**CLEINIAS:** By all means, if Heaven wills. Go on.

**ATHENIAN:** Well, then, proceeding in the same train of thought, I say that the greatest ignorance was the ruin of the Dorian power, and that now, as then, ignorance is ruin. And if this be true, the legislator must endeavour to implant wisdom in states, and banish ignorance to the utmost of his power.

**CLEINIAS:** That is evident.

**ATHENIAN:** Then now consider what is really the greatest ignorance. I should like to know whether you and Megillus would agree with me in what I am about to say; for my opinion is--

**CLEINIAS:** What?

**ATHENIAN:** That the greatest ignorance is when a man hates that which he nevertheless thinks to be good and noble, and loves and embraces that which he knows to be unrighteous and evil. This disagreement between the sense of pleasure and the judgment of reason in the soul is, in my opinion, the worst ignorance; and also the greatest, because affecting the great mass of the human soul; for the principle which feels pleasure and pain in the individual is like the mass or populace in a state. And when the soul is opposed to knowledge, or opinion, or reason, which are her natural lords, that I call folly, just as in the state, when the multitude refuses to obey their rulers and the laws; or, again, in the individual, when fair reasonings have their habitation in the soul and yet do no good, but rather the reverse of good. All these cases I term the worst ignorance, whether in individuals or in states. You will understand, Stranger, that I am speaking of something which is very different from the ignorance of handicraftsmen.

**CLEINIAS:** Yes, my friend, we understand and agree.

**ATHENIAN:** Let us, then, in the first place declare and affirm that the citizen who does not know these things ought never to have any kind of authority entrusted to him: he must be stigmatized as ignorant, even though he be versed in calculation and skilled in all sorts of accomplishments, and feats of mental dexterity; and the opposite are to be called wise, even although, in the words of the proverb, they know neither how to read nor how to swim; and to them, as to men of sense, authority is to be committed. For, O my friends, how can there be the least shadow of wisdom when there is no harmony? There is none; but the noblest and greatest of harmonies may be truly said to be the greatest wisdom; and of this he is a partaker who lives according to reason; whereas he who is devoid of reason is the destroyer of his house and the very opposite of a saviour of the state: he is utterly ignorant of political wisdom. Let this, then, as I was saying, be laid down by us.

**CLEINIAS:** Let it be so laid down.

**ATHENIAN:** I suppose that there must be rulers and subjects in states?

**CLEINIAS:** Certainly.

**ATHENIAN:** And what are the principles on which men rule and obey in cities, whether great or small; and similarly in families? What are they, and how many in number? Is there not one claim of authority which is always just,--that of fathers and mothers and in general of progenitors to rule over their offspring?

**CLEINIAS:** There is.

**ATHENIAN:** Next follows the principle that the noble should rule over the ignoble; and, thirdly, that the elder should rule and the younger obey?

**CLEINIAS:** To be sure.

**ATHENIAN:** And, fourthly, that slaves should be ruled, and their masters rule?

**CLEINIAS:** Of course.

**ATHENIAN:** Fifthly, if I am not mistaken, comes the principle that the stronger shall rule, and the weaker be ruled?

**CLEINIAS:** That is a rule not to be disobeyed.

**ATHENIAN:** Yes, and a rule which prevails very widely among all creatures, and is according to nature, as the Theban poet Pindar once said; and the sixth principle, and the greatest of all, is, that the wise should lead and command, and the ignorant follow and obey; and yet, O thou most wise Pindar, as I should reply him, this surely is not contrary to nature, but according to nature, being the rule of law over willing subjects, and not a rule of compulsion.

**CLEINIAS:** Most true.

**ATHENIAN:** There is a seventh kind of rule which is awarded by lot, and is dear to the Gods and a token of good fortune: he on whom the lot falls is a ruler, and he who fails in obtaining the lot goes away and is the subject; and this we affirm to be quite just.

**CLEINIAS:** Certainly.

**ATHENIAN:** 'Then now,' as we say playfully to any of those who lightly undertake the making of laws, 'you see, legislator, the principles of government, how many they are, and that they are naturally opposed to each other. There we have discovered a fountain-head of seditions, to which you must attend. And, first, we will ask you to consider with us, how and in what respect the kings of Argos and Messene violated these our maxims, and ruined themselves and the great and famous Hellenic power of the olden time. Was it because they did not know how wisely Hesiod spoke when he said that the half is often more than the whole? His meaning was, that when to take the whole would be dangerous, and to take the half would be the safe and moderate course, then the moderate or better was more than the immoderate or worse.'

**CLEINIAS:** Very true.

**ATHENIAN:** And may we suppose this immoderate spirit to be more fatal when found among kings than when among peoples?

**CLEINIAS:** The probability is that ignorance will be a disorder especially prevalent among kings, because they lead a proud and luxurious life.

**ATHENIAN:** Is it not palpable that the chief aim of the kings of that time was to get the better of the established laws, and that they were not in harmony with the principles which they had agreed to observe by word and oath? This want of harmony may have had the appearance of wisdom, but was really, as we assert, the greatest ignorance, and utterly overthrew the whole empire by dissonance and harsh discord.

**CLEINIAS:** Very likely.

**ATHENIAN:** Good; and what measures ought the legislator to have then taken in order to avert this calamity? Truly there is no great wisdom in knowing, and no great difficulty in telling, after the evil has happened; but to have foreseen the remedy at the time would have taken a much wiser head than ours.

**MEGILLUS:** What do you mean?

**ATHENIAN:** Any one who looks at what has occurred with you Lacedaemonians, Megillus, may easily know and may easily say what ought to have been done at that time.

**MEGILLUS:** Speak a little more clearly.

**ATHENIAN:** Nothing can be clearer than the observation which I am about to make.

**MEGILLUS:** What is it?

**ATHENIAN:** That if any one gives too great a power to anything, too large a sail to a vessel, too much food to the body, too much authority to the mind, and does not observe the mean, everything is overthrown, and, in the wantonness of excess, runs in the one case to disorders, and in the other to injustice, which is the child of excess. I mean to say, my dear friends, that there is no soul of man, young and irresponsible, who will be able to sustain the temptation of arbitrary power--no one who will not, under such circumstances, become filled with folly, that worst of diseases, and be hated by his nearest and dearest friends: when this happens his kingdom is undermined, and all his power vanishes from him. And great legislators who know the mean should take heed of the danger. As far as we can guess at this distance of time, what happened was as follows:--

**MEGILLUS:** What?

**ATHENIAN:** A God, who watched over Sparta, seeing into the future, gave you two families of kings instead of one; and thus brought you more within the limits of moderation. In the next place, some human wisdom mingled with divine power, observing that the constitution of your government was still feverish and excited, tempered your inborn strength and pride of birth with the moderation which comes of age, making the power of your twenty-eight elders equal with that of the kings in the most important matters. But your third saviour, perceiving that your government was still swelling and foaming, and desirous to impose a curb upon it, instituted the Ephors, whose power he made to resemble that of magistrates elected by lot; and by this arrangement the kingly office, being compounded of the right elements and duly moderated, was preserved, and was the means of preserving all the rest. Since, if there had been only the original legislators, Temenus, Cresphontes, and their contemporaries, as far as they were concerned not even the portion of Aristodemus would have been preserved; for they had no proper experience in legislation, or they would surely not have imagined that oaths would moderate a youthful spirit invested with a power which might be converted into a tyranny. Now that God has instructed us what sort of government would have been or will be lasting, there is no wisdom, as I have already said, in judging after the event; there is no difficulty in learning from an example which has already occurred. But if any one could have foreseen all this at the time, and had been able to moderate the government of the three kingdoms and unite them into one, he might have saved all the excellent institutions which were then conceived; and no Persian or any other armament would have dared to attack us, or would have regarded Hellas as a power to be despised.

**CLEINIAS:** True.

**ATHENIAN:** There was small credit to us, Cleinias, in defeating them; and the discredit was, not that the conquerors did not win glorious victories both by land and sea, but what, in my opinion, brought discredit was, first of all, the circumstance that of the three cities one only fought on behalf of Hellas, and the two others were so utterly good for nothing that the one was waging a mighty war against Lacedaemon, and was thus preventing her from rendering assistance, while the city of Argos, which had the precedence at the time of the distribution, when asked to aid in repelling the barbarian, would not answer to the call, or give aid. Many things might be told about Hellas in connexion with that war which are far from honourable; nor, indeed, can we rightly say that Hellas repelled the invader; for the truth is, that unless the Athenians and Lacedaemonians, acting in concert, had warded off the impending yoke, all the tribes of Hellas would have been fused in a chaos of Hellenes mingling with one another, of barbarians mingling with Hellenes, and Hellenes with barbarians; just as nations who are now subject to the Persian power, owing to unnatural separations and combinations of them, are dispersed and scattered, and live miserably. These, Cleinias and Megillus, are the reproaches which we have to make against statesmen and legislators, as they are called, past and present, if we would analyse the causes of their failure, and find out what else might have been done. We said, for instance, just now, that there ought to be no great and unmixed powers; and this was under the idea that a state ought to be free and wise and harmonious, and that a legislator ought to legislate with a view to this end. Nor is there any reason to be surprised at our continually proposing aims for the legislator which appear not to be always the same; but we should consider when we say that temperance is to be the aim, or wisdom is to be the aim, or friendship is to be the aim, that all these aims are really the same; and if so, a variety in the modes of expression ought not to disturb us.

**CLEINIAS:** Let us resume the argument in that spirit. And now, speaking of friendship and wisdom and freedom, I wish that you would tell me at what, in your opinion, the legislator should aim.

**ATHENIAN:** Hear me, then: there are two mother forms of states from which the rest may be truly said to be derived; and one of them may be called monarchy and the other democracy: the Persians have the highest form of the one, and we of the other; almost all the rest, as I was saying, are variations of these. Now, if you are to have liberty and the combination of friendship with wisdom, you must have both these forms of government in a measure; the argument emphatically declares that no city can be well governed which is not made up of both.

**CLEINIAS:** Impossible.

**ATHENIAN:** Neither the one, if it be exclusively and excessively attached to monarchy, nor the other, if it be similarly attached to freedom, observes moderation; but your states, the Laconian and Cretan, have more of it; and the same was the case with the Athenians and Persians of old time, but now they have less. Shall I tell you why?

**CLEINIAS:** By all means, if it will tend to elucidate our subject.

**ATHENIAN:** Hear, then:--There was a time when the Persians had more of the state which is a mean between slavery and freedom. In the reign of Cyrus they were freemen and also lords of many others: the rulers gave a share of freedom to the subjects, and being treated as equals, the soldiers were on better terms with their generals, and showed themselves more ready in the hour of danger. And if there was any wise man among them, who was able to give good counsel, he imparted his wisdom to the public; for the king was not jealous, but allowed him full liberty of speech, and gave honour to those who could advise him in any matter. And the nation waxed in all respects, because there was freedom and friendship and communion of mind among them.

**CLEINIAS:** That certainly appears to have been the case.

**ATHENIAN:** How, then, was this advantage lost under Cambyses, and again recovered under Darius? Shall I try to divine?

**CLEINIAS:** The enquiry, no doubt, has a bearing upon our subject.

**ATHENIAN:** I imagine that Cyrus, though a great and patriotic general, had never given his mind to education, and never attended to the order of his household.

**CLEINIAS:** What makes you say so?

**ATHENIAN:** I think that from his youth upwards he was a soldier, and entrusted the education of his children to the women; and they brought them up from their childhood as the favourites of fortune, who were blessed already, and needed no more blessings. They thought that they were happy enough, and that no one should be allowed to oppose them in any way, and they compelled every one to praise all that they said or did. This was how they brought them up.

**CLEINIAS:** A splendid education truly!

**ATHENIAN:** Such an one as women were likely to give them, and especially princesses who had recently grown rich, and in the absence of the men, too, who were occupied in wars and dangers, and had no time to look after them.

**CLEINIAS:** What would you expect?

**ATHENIAN:** Their father had possessions of cattle and sheep, and many herds of men and other animals, but he did not consider that those to whom he was about to make them over were not trained in his own calling, which was Persian; for the Persians are shepherds--sons of a rugged land, which is a stern mother, and well fitted to produce a sturdy race able to live in the open air and go without sleep, and also to fight, if fighting is required. He did not observe that his sons were trained differently; through the so-called blessing of being royal they were educated in the Median fashion by women and eunuchs, which led to their becoming such as people do become when they are brought up unreproved. And so, after the death of Cyrus, his sons, in the fulness of luxury and licence, took the kingdom, and first one slew the other because he could not endure a rival; and, afterwards, the slayer himself, mad with wine and brutality, lost his kingdom through the Medes and the Eunuch, as they called him, who despised the folly of Cambyses.

**CLEINIAS:** So runs the tale, and such probably were the facts.

**ATHENIAN:** Yes; and the tradition says, that the empire came back to the Persians, through Darius and the seven chiefs.

**CLEINIAS:** True.

**ATHENIAN:** Let us note the rest of the story. Observe, that Darius was not the son of a king, and had not received a luxurious education. When he came to the throne, being one of the seven, he divided the country into seven portions, and of this arrangement there are some shadowy traces still remaining; he made laws upon the principle of introducing universal equality in the order of the state, and he embodied in his laws the settlement of the tribute which Cyrus promised,--thus creating a feeling of friendship and community among all the Persians, and attaching the people to him with money and gifts. Hence his armies cheerfully acquired for him countries as large as those which Cyrus had left behind him. Darius was succeeded by his son Xerxes; and he again was brought up in the royal and luxurious fashion. Might we not most justly say: 'O Darius, how came you to bring up Xerxes in the same way in which Cyrus brought up Cambyses, and not to see his fatal mistake?' For Xerxes, being the creation of the same education, met with much the same fortune as Cambyses; and from that time until now there has never been a really great king among the Persians, although they are all called Great. And their degeneracy is not to be attributed to chance, as I maintain; the reason is rather the evil life which is generally led by the sons of very rich and royal persons; for never will boy or man, young or old, excel in virtue, who has been thus educated. And this, I say, is what the legislator has to consider, and what at the present moment has to be considered by us. Justly may you, O Lacedaemonians, be praised, in that you do not give special honour or a special education to wealth rather than to poverty, or to a royal rather than to a private station, where the divine and inspired lawgiver has not originally commanded them to be given. For no man ought to have pre- eminent honour in a state because he surpasses others in wealth, any more than because he is swift of foot or fair or strong, unless he have some virtue in him; nor even if he have virtue, unless he have this particular virtue of temperance.

**MEGILLUS:** What do you mean, Stranger?

**ATHENIAN:** I suppose that courage is a part of virtue?

**MEGILLUS:** To be sure.

**ATHENIAN:** Then, now hear and judge for yourself:--Would you like to have for a fellow-lodger or neighbour a very courageous man, who had no control over himself?

**MEGILLUS:** Heaven forbid!

**ATHENIAN:** Or an artist, who was clever in his profession, but a rogue?

**MEGILLUS:** Certainly not.

**ATHENIAN:** And surely justice does not grow apart from temperance?

**MEGILLUS:** Impossible.

**ATHENIAN:** Any more than our pattern wise man, whom we exhibited as having his pleasures and pains in accordance with and corresponding to true reason, can be intemperate?

**MEGILLUS:** No.

**ATHENIAN:** There is a further consideration relating to the due and undue award of honours in states.

**MEGILLUS:** What is it?

**ATHENIAN:** I should like to know whether temperance without the other virtues, existing alone in the soul of man, is rightly to be praised or blamed?

**MEGILLUS:** I cannot tell.

**ATHENIAN:** And that is the best answer; for whichever alternative you had chosen, I think that you would have gone wrong.

**MEGILLUS:** I am fortunate.

**ATHENIAN:** Very good; a quality, which is a mere appendage of things which can be praised or blamed, does not deserve an expression of opinion, but is best passed over in silence.

**MEGILLUS:** You are speaking of temperance?

**ATHENIAN:** Yes; but of the other virtues, that which having this appendage is also most beneficial, will be most deserving of honour, and next that which is beneficial in the next degree; and so each of them will be rightly honoured according to a regular order.

**MEGILLUS:** True.

**ATHENIAN:** And ought not the legislator to determine these classes?

**MEGILLUS:** Certainly he should.

**ATHENIAN:** Suppose that we leave to him the arrangement of details. But the general division of laws according to their importance into a first and second and third class, we who are lovers of law may make ourselves.

**MEGILLUS:** Very good.

**ATHENIAN:** We maintain, then, that a State which would be safe and happy, as far as the nature of man allows, must and ought to distribute honour and dishonour in the right way. And the right way is to place the goods of the soul first and highest in the scale, always assuming temperance to be the condition of them; and to assign the second place to the goods of the body; and the third place to money and property. And if any legislator or state departs from this rule by giving money the place of honour, or in any way preferring that which is really last, may we not say, that he or the state is doing an unholy and unpatriotic thing?

**MEGILLUS:** Yes; let that be plainly declared.

**ATHENIAN:** The consideration of the Persian governments led us thus far to enlarge. We remarked that the Persians grew worse and worse. And we affirm the reason of this to have been, that they too much diminished the freedom of the people, and introduced too much of despotism, and so destroyed friendship and community of feeling. And when there is an end of these, no longer do the governors govern on behalf of their subjects or of the people, but on behalf of themselves; and if they think that they can gain ever so small an advantage for themselves, they devastate cities, and send fire and desolation among friendly races. And as they hate ruthlessly and horribly, so are they hated; and when they want the people to fight for them, they find no community of feeling or willingness to risk their lives on their behalf; their untold myriads are useless to them on the field of battle, and they think that their salvation depends on the employment of mercenaries and strangers whom they hire, as if they were in want of more men. And they cannot help being stupid, since they proclaim by their actions that the ordinary distinctions of right and wrong which are made in a state are a trifle, when compared with gold and silver.

**MEGILLUS:** Quite true.

**ATHENIAN:** And now enough of the Persians, and their present mal-administration of their government, which is owing to the excess of slavery and despotism among them.

**MEGILLUS:** Good.

**ATHENIAN:** Next, we must pass in review the government of Attica in like manner, and from this show that entire freedom and the absence of all superior authority is not by any means so good as government by others when properly limited, which was our ancient Athenian constitution at the time when the Persians made their attack on Hellas, or, speaking more correctly, on the whole continent of Europe. There were four classes, arranged according to a property census, and reverence was our queen and mistress, and made us willing to live in obedience to the laws which then prevailed. Also the vastness of the Persian armament, both by sea and on land, caused a helpless terror, which made us more and more the servants of our rulers and of the laws; and for all these reasons an exceeding harmony prevailed among us. About ten years before the naval engagement at Salamis, Datis came, leading a Persian host by command of Darius, which was expressly directed against the Athenians and Eretrians, having orders to carry them away captive; and these orders he was to execute under pain of death. Now Datis and his myriads soon became complete masters of Eretria, and he sent a fearful report to Athens that no Eretrian had escaped him; for the soldiers of Datis had joined hands and netted the whole of Eretria. And this report, whether well or ill founded, was terrible to all the Hellenes, and above all to the Athenians, and they dispatched embassies in all directions, but no one was willing to come to their relief, with the exception of the Lacedaemonians; and they, either because they were detained by the Messenian war, which was then going on, or for some other reason of which we are not told, came a day too late for the battle of Marathon. After a while, the news arrived of mighty preparations being made, and innumerable threats came from the king. Then, as time went on, a rumour reached us that Darius had died, and that his son, who was young and hot-headed, had come to the throne and was persisting in his design. The Athenians were under the impression that the whole expedition was directed against them, in consequence of the battle of Marathon; and hearing of the bridge over the Hellespont, and the canal of Athos, and the host of ships, considering that there was no salvation for them either by land or by sea, for there was no one to help them, and remembering that in the first expedition, when the Persians destroyed Eretria, no one came to their help, or would risk the danger of an alliance with them, they thought that this would happen again, at least on land; nor, when they looked to the sea, could they descry any hope of salvation; for they were attacked by a thousand vessels and more. One chance of safety remained, slight indeed and desperate, but their only one. They saw that on the former occasion they had gained a seemingly impossible victory, and borne up by this hope, they found that their only refuge was in themselves and in the Gods. All these things created in them the spirit of friendship; there was the fear of the moment, and there was that higher fear, which they had acquired by obedience to their ancient laws, and which I have several times in the preceding discourse called reverence, of which the good man ought to be a willing servant, and of which the coward is independent and fearless. If this fear had not possessed them, they would never have met the enemy, or defended their temples and sepulchres and their country, and everything that was near and dear to them, as they did; but little by little they would have been all scattered and dispersed.

**MEGILLUS:** Your words, Athenian, are quite true, and worthy of yourself and of your country.

**ATHENIAN:** They are true, Megillus; and to you, who have inherited the virtues of your ancestors, I may properly speak of the actions of that day. And I would wish you and Cleinias to consider whether my words have not also a bearing on legislation; for I am not discoursing only for the pleasure of talking, but for the argument's sake. Please to remark that the experience both of ourselves and the Persians was, in a certain sense, the same; for as they led their people into utter servitude, so we too led ours into all freedom. And now, how shall we proceed? for I would like you to observe that our previous arguments have good deal to say for themselves.

**MEGILLUS:** True; but I wish that you would give us a fuller explanation.

**ATHENIAN:** I will. Under the ancient laws, my friends, the people was not as now the master, but rather the willing servant of the laws.

**MEGILLUS:** What laws do you mean?

**ATHENIAN:** In the first place, let us speak of the laws about music,--that is to say, such music as then existed--in order that we may trace the growth of the excess of freedom from the beginning. Now music was early divided among us into certain kinds and manners. One sort consisted of prayers to the Gods, which were called hymns; and there was another and opposite sort called lamentations, and another termed paeans, and another, celebrating the birth of Dionysus, called, I believe, 'dithyrambs.' And they used the actual word 'laws,' or nomoi, for another kind of song; and to this they added the term 'citharoedic.' All these and others were duly distinguished, nor were the performers allowed to confuse one style of music with another. And the authority which determined and gave judgment, and punished the disobedient, was not expressed in a hiss, nor in the most unmusical shouts of the multitude, as in our days, nor in applause and clapping of hands. But the directors of public instruction insisted that the spectators should listen in silence to the end; and boys and their tutors, and the multitude in general, were kept quiet by a hint from a stick. Such was the good order which the multitude were willing to observe; they would never have dared to give judgment by noisy cries. And then, as time went on, the poets themselves introduced the reign of vulgar and lawless innovation. They were men of genius, but they had no perception of what is just and lawful in music; raging like Bacchanals and possessed with inordinate delights--mingling lamentations with hymns, and paeans with dithyrambs; imitating the sounds of the flute on the lyre, and making one general confusion; ignorantly affirming that music has no truth, and, whether good or bad, can only be judged of rightly by the pleasure of the hearer. And by composing such licentious works, and adding to them words as licentious, they have inspired the multitude with lawlessness and boldness, and made them fancy that they can judge for themselves about melody and song. And in this way the theatres from being mute have become vocal, as though they had understanding of good and bad in music and poetry; and instead of an aristocracy, an evil sort of theatrocracy has grown up. For if the democracy which judged had only consisted of educated persons, no fatal harm would have been done; but in music there first arose the universal conceit of omniscience and general lawlessness;--freedom came following afterwards, and men, fancying that they knew what they did not know, had no longer any fear, and the absence of fear begets shamelessness. For what is this shamelessness, which is so evil a thing, but the insolent refusal to regard the opinion of the better by reason of an over-daring sort of liberty?

**MEGILLUS:** Very true.

**ATHENIAN:** Consequent upon this freedom comes the other freedom, of disobedience to rulers; and then the attempt to escape the control and exhortation of father, mother, elders, and when near the end, the control of the laws also; and at the very end there is the contempt of oaths and pledges, and no regard at all for the Gods,--herein they exhibit and imitate the old so-called Titanic nature, and come to the same point as the Titans when they rebelled against God, leading a life of endless evils. But why have I said all this? I ask, because the argument ought to be pulled up from time to time, and not be allowed to run away, but held with bit and bridle, and then we shall not, as the proverb says, fall off our ass. Let us then once more ask the question, To what end has all this been said?

**MEGILLUS:** Very good.

**ATHENIAN:** This, then, has been said for the sake--

**MEGILLUS:** Of what?

**ATHENIAN:** We were maintaining that the lawgiver ought to have three things in view: first, that the city for which he legislates should be free; and secondly, be at unity with herself; and thirdly, should have understanding; --these were our principles, were they not?

**MEGILLUS:** Certainly.

**ATHENIAN:** With a view to this we selected two kinds of government, the one the most despotic, and the other the most free; and now we are considering which of them is the right form: we took a mean in both cases, of despotism in the one, and of liberty in the other, and we saw that in a mean they attained their perfection; but that when they were carried to the extreme of either, slavery or licence, neither party were the gainers.

**MEGILLUS:** Very true.

**ATHENIAN:** And that was our reason for considering the settlement of the Dorian army, and of the city built by Dardanus at the foot of the mountains, and the removal of cities to the seashore, and of our mention of the first men, who were the survivors of the deluge. And all that was previously said about music and drinking, and what preceded, was said with the view of seeing how a state might be best administered, and how an individual might best order his own life. And now, Megillus and Cleinias, how can we put to the proof the value of our words?

**CLEINIAS:** Stranger, I think that I see how a proof of their value may be obtained. This discussion of ours appears to me to have been singularly fortunate, and just what I at this moment want; most auspiciously have you and my friend Megillus come in my way. For I will tell you what has happened to me; and I regard the coincidence as a sort of omen. The greater part of Crete is going to send out a colony, and they have entrusted the management of the affair to the Cnosians; and the Cnosian government to me and nine others. And they desire us to give them any laws which we please, whether taken from the Cretan model or from any other; and they do not mind about their being foreign if they are better. Grant me then this favour, which will also be a gain to yourselves:--Let us make a selection from what has been said, and then let us imagine a State of which we will suppose ourselves to be the original founders. Thus we shall proceed with our enquiry, and, at the same time, I may have the use of the framework which you are constructing, for the city which is in contemplation.

**ATHENIAN:** Good news, Cleinias; if Megillus has no objection, you may be sure that I will do all in my power to please you.

**CLEINIAS:** Thank you.

**MEGILLUS:** And so will I.

**CLEINIAS:** Excellent; and now let us begin to frame the State.

# BOOK IV.

**ATHENIAN:** And now, what will this city be? I do not mean to ask what is or will hereafter be the name of the place; that may be determined by the accident of locality or of the original settlement--a river or fountain, or some local deity may give the sanction of a name to the newly-founded city; but I do want to know what the situation is, whether maritime or inland.

**CLEINIAS:** I should imagine, Stranger, that the city of which we are speaking is about eighty stadia distant from the sea.

**ATHENIAN:** And are there harbours on the seaboard?

**CLEINIAS:** Excellent harbours, Stranger; there could not be better.

**ATHENIAN:** Alas! what a prospect! And is the surrounding country productive, or in need of importations?

**CLEINIAS:** Hardly in need of anything.

**ATHENIAN:** And is there any neighbouring State?

**CLEINIAS:** None whatever, and that is the reason for selecting the place; in days of old, there was a migration of the inhabitants, and the region has been deserted from time immemorial.

**ATHENIAN:** And has the place a fair proportion of hill, and plain, and wood?

**CLEINIAS:** Like the rest of Crete in that.

**ATHENIAN:** You mean to say that there is more rock than plain?

**CLEINIAS:** Exactly.

**ATHENIAN:** Then there is some hope that your citizens may be virtuous: had you been on the sea, and well provided with harbours, and an importing rather than a producing country, some mighty saviour would have been needed, and lawgivers more than mortal, if you were ever to have a chance of preserving your state from degeneracy and discordance of manners. But there is comfort in the eighty stadia; although the sea is too near, especially if, as you say, the harbours are so good. Still we may be content. The sea is pleasant enough as a daily companion, but has indeed also a bitter and brackish quality; filling the streets with merchants and shopkeepers, and begetting in the souls of men uncertain and unfaithful ways--making the state unfriendly and unfaithful both to her own citizens, and also to other nations. There is a consolation, therefore, in the country producing all things at home; and yet, owing to the ruggedness of the soil, not providing anything in great abundance. Had there been abundance, there might have been a great export trade, and a great return of gold and silver; which, as we may safely affirm, has the most fatal results on a State whose aim is the attainment of just and noble sentiments: this was said by us, if you remember, in the previous discussion.

**CLEINIAS:** I remember, and am of opinion that we both were and are in the right.

**ATHENIAN:** Well, but let me ask, how is the country supplied with timber for ship-building?

**CLEINIAS:** There is no fir of any consequence, nor pine, and not much cypress; and you will find very little stone-pine or plane-wood, which shipwrights always require for the interior of ships.

**ATHENIAN:** These are also natural advantages.

**CLEINIAS:** Why so?

**ATHENIAN:** Because no city ought to be easily able to imitate its enemies in what is mischievous.

**CLEINIAS:** How does that bear upon any of the matters of which we have been speaking?

**ATHENIAN:** Remember, my good friend, what I said at first about the Cretan laws, that they looked to one thing only, and this, as you both agreed, was war; and I replied that such laws, in so far as they tended to promote virtue, were good; but in that they regarded a part only, and not the whole of virtue, I disapproved of them. And now I hope that you in your turn will follow and watch me if I legislate with a view to anything but virtue, or with a view to a part of virtue only. For I consider that the true lawgiver, like an archer, aims only at that on which some eternal beauty is always attending, and dismisses everything else, whether wealth or any other benefit, when separated from virtue. I was saying that the imitation of enemies was a bad thing; and I was thinking of a case in which a maritime people are harassed by enemies, as the Athenians were by Minos (I do not speak from any desire to recall past grievances); but he, as we know, was a great naval potentate, who compelled the inhabitants of Attica to pay him a cruel tribute; and in those days they had no ships of war as they now have, nor was the country filled with ship-timber, and therefore they could not readily build them. Hence they could not learn how to imitate their enemy at sea, and in this way, becoming sailors themselves, directly repel their enemies. Better for them to have lost many times over the seven youths, than that heavy-armed and stationary troops should have been turned into sailors, and accustomed to be often leaping on shore, and again to come running back to their ships; or should have fancied that there was no disgrace in not awaiting the attack of an enemy and dying boldly; and that there were good reasons, and plenty of them, for a man throwing away his arms, and betaking himself to flight,--which is not dishonourable, as people say, at certain times. This is the language of naval warfare, and is anything but worthy of extraordinary praise. For we should not teach bad habits, least of all to the best part of the citizens. You may learn the evil of such a practice from Homer, by whom Odysseus is introduced, rebuking Agamemnon, because he desires to draw down the ships to the sea at a time when the Achaeans are hard pressed by the Trojans,--he gets angry with him, and says:

*'Who, at a time when the battle is in full cry, biddest to drag the well-benched ships into the sea, that the prayers of the Trojans may be accomplished yet more, and high ruin fall upon us. For the Achaeans will not maintain the battle, when the ships are drawn into the sea, but they will look behind and will cease from strife; in that the counsel which you give will prove injurious.'*

You see that he quite knew triremes on the sea, in the neighbourhood of fighting men, to be an evil;--lions might be trained in that way to fly from a herd of deer. Moreover, naval powers which owe their safety to ships, do not give honour to that sort of warlike excellence which is most deserving of it. For he who owes his safety to the pilot and the captain, and the oarsman, and all sorts of rather inferior persons, cannot rightly give honour to whom honour is due. But how can a state be in a right condition which cannot justly award honour?

**CLEINIAS:** It is hardly possible, I admit; and yet, Stranger, we Cretans are in the habit of saying that the battle of Salamis was the salvation of Hellas.

**ATHENIAN:** Why, yes; and that is an opinion which is widely spread both among Hellenes and barbarians. But Megillus and I say rather, that the battle of Marathon was the beginning, and the battle of Plataea the completion, of the great deliverance, and that these battles by land made the Hellenes better; whereas the sea-fights of Salamis and Artemisium--for I may as well put them both together--made them no better, if I may say so without offence about the battles which helped to save us. And in estimating the goodness of a state, we regard both the situation of the country and the order of the laws, considering that the mere preservation and continuance of life is not the most honourable thing for men, as the vulgar think, but the continuance of the best life, while we live; and that again, if I am not mistaken, is a remark which has been made already.

**CLEINIAS:** Yes.

**ATHENIAN:** Then we have only to ask, whether we are taking the course which we acknowledge to be the best for the settlement and legislation of states.

**CLEINIAS:** The best by far.

**ATHENIAN:** And now let me proceed to another question: Who are to be the colonists? May any one come out of all Crete; and is the idea that the population in the several states is too numerous for the means of subsistence? For I suppose that you are not going to send out a general invitation to any Hellene who likes to come. And yet I observe that to your country settlers have come from Argos and Aegina and other parts of Hellas. Tell me, then, whence do you draw your recruits in the present enterprise?

**CLEINIAS:** They will come from all Crete; and of other Hellenes, Peloponnesians will be most acceptable. For, as you truly observe, there are Cretans of Argive descent; and the race of Cretans which has the highest character at the present day is the Gortynian, and this has come from Gortys in the Peloponnesus.

**ATHENIAN:** Cities find colonization in some respects easier if the colonists are one race, which like a swarm of bees is sent out from a single country, either when friends leave friends, owing to some pressure of population or other similar necessity, or when a portion of a state is driven by factions to emigrate. And there have been whole cities which have taken flight when utterly conquered by a superior power in war. This, however, which is in one way an advantage to the colonist or legislator, in another point of view creates a difficulty. There is an element of friendship in the community of race, and language, and laws, and in common temples and rites of worship; but colonies which are of this homogeneous sort are apt to kick against any laws or any form of constitution differing from that which they had at home; and although the badness of their own laws may have been the cause of the factions which prevailed among them, yet from the force of habit they would fain preserve the very customs which were their ruin, and the leader of the colony, who is their legislator, finds them troublesome and rebellious. On the other hand, the conflux of several populations might be more disposed to listen to new laws; but then, to make them combine and pull together, as they say of horses, is a most difficult task, and the work of years. And yet there is nothing which tends more to the improvement of mankind than legislation and colonization.

**CLEINIAS:** No doubt; but I should like to know why you say so.

**ATHENIAN:** My good friend, I am afraid that the course of my speculations is leading me to say something depreciatory of legislators; but if the word be to the purpose, there can be no harm. And yet, why am I disquieted, for I believe that the same principle applies equally to all human things?

**CLEINIAS:** To what are you referring?

**ATHENIAN:** I was going to say that man never legislates, but accidents of all sorts, which legislate for us in all sorts of ways. The violence of war and the hard necessity of poverty are constantly overturning governments and changing laws. And the power of disease has often caused innovations in the state, when there have been pestilences, or when there has been a succession of bad seasons continuing during many years. Any one who sees all this, naturally rushes to the conclusion of which I was speaking, that no mortal legislates in anything, but that in human affairs chance is almost everything. And this may be said of the arts of the sailor, and the pilot, and the physician, and the general, and may seem to be well said; and yet there is another thing which may be said with equal truth of all of them.

**CLEINIAS:** What is it?

**ATHENIAN:** That God governs all things, and that chance and opportunity co- operate with Him in the government of human affairs. There is, however, a third and less extreme view, that art should be there also; for I should say that in a storm there must surely be a great advantage in having the aid of the pilot's art. You would agree?

**CLEINIAS:** Yes.

**ATHENIAN:** And does not a like principle apply to legislation as well as to other things: even supposing all the conditions to be favourable which are needed for the happiness of the state, yet the true legislator must from time to time appear on the scene?

**CLEINIAS:** Most true.

**ATHENIAN:** In each case the artist would be able to pray rightly for certain conditions, and if these were granted by fortune, he would then only require to exercise his art?

**CLEINIAS:** Certainly.

**ATHENIAN:** And all the other artists just now mentioned, if they were bidden to offer up each their special prayer, would do so?

**CLEINIAS:** Of course.

**ATHENIAN:** And the legislator would do likewise?

**CLEINIAS:** I believe that he would.

**ATHENIAN:** 'Come, legislator,' we will say to him; 'what are the conditions which you require in a state before you can organize it?' How ought he to answer this question? Shall I give his answer?

**CLEINIAS:** Yes.

**ATHENIAN:** He will say--'Give me a state which is governed by a tyrant, and let the tyrant be young and have a good memory; let him be quick at learning, and of a courageous and noble nature; let him have that quality which, as I said before, is the inseparable companion of all the other parts of virtue, if there is to be any good in them.'

**CLEINIAS:** I suppose, Megillus, that this companion virtue of which the Stranger speaks, must be temperance?

**ATHENIAN:** Yes, Cleinias, temperance in the vulgar sense; not that which in the forced and exaggerated language of some philosophers is called prudence, but that which is the natural gift of children and animals, of whom some live continently and others incontinently, but when isolated, was, as we said, hardly worth reckoning in the catalogue of goods. I think that you must understand my meaning.

**CLEINIAS:** Certainly.

**ATHENIAN:** Then our tyrant must have this as well as the other qualities, if the state is to acquire in the best manner and in the shortest time the form of government which is most conducive to happiness; for there neither is nor ever will be a better or speedier way of establishing a polity than by a tyranny.

**CLEINIAS:** By what possible arguments, Stranger, can any man persuade himself of such a monstrous doctrine?

**ATHENIAN:** There is surely no difficulty in seeing, Cleinias, what is in accordance with the order of nature?

**CLEINIAS:** You would assume, as you say, a tyrant who was young, temperate, quick at learning, having a good memory, courageous, of a noble nature?

**ATHENIAN:** Yes; and you must add fortunate; and his good fortune must be that he is the contemporary of a great legislator, and that some happy chance brings them together. When this has been accomplished, God has done all that he ever does for a state which he desires to be eminently prosperous; He has done second best for a state in which there are two such rulers, and third best for a state in which there are three. The difficulty increases with the increase, and diminishes with the diminution of the number.

**CLEINIAS:** You mean to say, I suppose, that the best government is produced from a tyranny, and originates in a good lawgiver and an orderly tyrant, and that the change from such a tyranny into a perfect form of government takes place most easily; less easily when from an oligarchy; and, in the third degree, from a democracy: is not that your meaning?

**ATHENIAN:** Not so; I mean rather to say that the change is best made out of a tyranny; and secondly, out of a monarchy; and thirdly, out of some sort of democracy: fourth, in the capacity for improvement, comes oligarchy, which has the greatest difficulty in admitting of such a change, because the government is in the hands of a number of potentates. I am supposing that the legislator is by nature of the true sort, and that his strength is united with that of the chief men of the state; and when the ruling element is numerically small, and at the same time very strong, as in a tyranny, there the change is likely to be easiest and most rapid.

**CLEINIAS:** How? I do not understand.

**ATHENIAN:** And yet I have repeated what I am saying a good many times; but I suppose that you have never seen a city which is under a tyranny?

**CLEINIAS:** No, and I cannot say that I have any great desire to see one.

**ATHENIAN:** And yet, where there is a tyranny, you might certainly see that of which I am now speaking.

**CLEINIAS:** What do you mean?

**ATHENIAN:** I mean that you might see how, without trouble and in no very long period of time, the tyrant, if he wishes, can change the manners of a state: he has only to go in the direction of virtue or of vice, whichever he prefers, he himself indicating by his example the lines of conduct, praising and rewarding some actions and reproving others, and degrading those who disobey.

**CLEINIAS:** But how can we imagine that the citizens in general will at once follow the example set to them; and how can he have this power both of persuading and of compelling them?

**ATHENIAN:** Let no one, my friends, persuade us that there is any quicker and easier way in which states change their laws than when the rulers lead: such changes never have, nor ever will, come to pass in any other way. The real impossibility or difficulty is of another sort, and is rarely surmounted in the course of ages; but when once it is surmounted, ten thousand or rather all blessings follow.

**CLEINIAS:** Of what are you speaking?

**ATHENIAN:** The difficulty is to find the divine love of temperate and just institutions existing in any powerful forms of government, whether in a monarchy or oligarchy of wealth or of birth. You might as well hope to reproduce the character of Nestor, who is said to have excelled all men in the power of speech, and yet more in his temperance. This, however, according to the tradition, was in the times of Troy; in our own days there is nothing of the sort; but if such an one either has or ever shall come into being, or is now among us, blessed is he and blessed are they who hear the wise words that flow from his lips. And this may be said of power in general: When the supreme power in man coincides with the greatest wisdom and temperance, then the best laws and the best constitution come into being; but in no other way. And let what I have been saying be regarded as a kind of sacred legend or oracle, and let this be our proof that, in one point of view, there may be a difficulty for a city to have good laws, but that there is another point of view in which nothing can be easier or sooner effected, granting our supposition.

**CLEINIAS:** How do you mean?

**ATHENIAN:** Let us try to amuse ourselves, old boys as we are, by moulding in words the laws which are suitable to your state.

**CLEINIAS:** Let us proceed without delay.

**ATHENIAN:** Then let us invoke God at the settlement of our state; may He hear and be propitious to us, and come and set in order the State and the laws!

**CLEINIAS:** May He come!

**ATHENIAN:** But what form of polity are we going to give the city?

**CLEINIAS:** Tell us what you mean a little more clearly. Do you mean some form of democracy, or oligarchy, or aristocracy, or monarchy? For we cannot suppose that you would include tyranny.

**ATHENIAN:** Which of you will first tell me to which of these classes his own government is to be referred?

**MEGILLUS:** Ought I to answer first, since I am the elder?

**CLEINIAS:** Perhaps you should.

**MEGILLUS:** And yet, Stranger, I perceive that I cannot say, without more thought, what I should call the government of Lacedaemon, for it seems to me to be like a tyranny,--the power of our Ephors is marvellously tyrannical; and sometimes it appears to me to be of all cities the most democratical; and who can reasonably deny that it is an aristocracy? We have also a monarchy which is held for life, and is said by all mankind, and not by ourselves only, to be the most ancient of all monarchies; and, therefore, when asked on a sudden, I cannot precisely say which form of government the Spartan is.

**CLEINIAS:** I am in the same difficulty, Megillus; for I do not feel confident that the polity of Cnosus is any of these.

**ATHENIAN:** The reason is, my excellent friends, that you really have polities, but the states of which we were just now speaking are merely aggregations of men dwelling in cities who are the subjects and servants of a part of their own state, and each of them is named after the dominant power; they are not polities at all. But if states are to be named after their rulers, the true state ought to be called by the name of the God who rules over wise men.

**CLEINIAS:** And who is this God?

**ATHENIAN:** May I still make use of fable to some extent, in the hope that I may be better able to answer your question: shall I?

**CLEINIAS:** By all means.

**ATHENIAN:** In the primeval world, and a long while before the cities came into being whose settlements we have described, there is said to have been in the time of Cronos a blessed rule and life, of which the best-ordered of existing states is a copy.

**CLEINIAS:** It will be very necessary to hear about that.

**ATHENIAN:** I quite agree with you; and therefore I have introduced the subject.

**CLEINIAS:** Most appropriately; and since the tale is to the point, you will do well in giving us the whole story.

**ATHENIAN:** I will do as you suggest. There is a tradition of the happy life of mankind in days when all things were spontaneous and abundant. And of this the reason is said to have been as follows:--Cronos knew what we ourselves were declaring, that no human nature invested with supreme power is able to order human affairs and not overflow with insolence and wrong. Which reflection led him to appoint not men but demigods, who are of a higher and more divine race, to be the kings and rulers of our cities; he did as we do with flocks of sheep and other tame animals. For we do not appoint oxen to be the lords of oxen, or goats of goats; but we ourselves are a superior race, and rule over them. In like manner God, in His love of mankind, placed over us the demons, who are a superior race, and they with great ease and pleasure to themselves, and no less to us, taking care of us and giving us peace and reverence and order and justice never failing, made the tribes of men happy and united. And this tradition, which is true, declares that cities of which some mortal man and not God is the ruler, have no escape from evils and toils. Still we must do all that we can to imitate the life which is said to have existed in the days of Cronos, and, as far as the principle of immortality dwells in us, to that we must hearken, both in private and public life, and regulate our cities and houses according to law, meaning by the very term 'law,' the distribution of mind. But if either a single person or an oligarchy or a democracy has a soul eager after pleasures and desires--wanting to be filled with them, yet retaining none of them, and perpetually afflicted with an endless and insatiable disorder; and this evil spirit, having first trampled the laws under foot, becomes the master either of a state or of an individual,--then, as I was saying, salvation is hopeless. And now, Cleinias, we have to consider whether you will or will not accept this tale of mine.

**CLEINIAS:** Certainly we will.

**ATHENIAN:** You are aware,--are you not?--that there are often said to be as many forms of laws as there are of governments, and of the latter we have already mentioned all those which are commonly recognized. Now you must regard this as a matter of first-rate importance. For what is to be the standard of just and unjust, is once more the point at issue. Men say that the law ought not to regard either military virtue, or virtue in general, but only the interests and power and preservation of the established form of government; this is thought by them to be the best way of expressing the natural definition of justice.

**CLEINIAS:** How?

**ATHENIAN:** Justice is said by them to be the interest of the stronger .

**CLEINIAS:** Speak plainer.

**ATHENIAN:** I will:--*'Surely,'* they say, *'the governing power makes whatever laws have authority in any state'?*

**CLEINIAS:** True.

**ATHENIAN:** *'Well,'* they would add, *'and do you suppose that tyranny or democracy, or any other conquering power, does not make the continuance of the power which is possessed by them the first or principal object of their laws'?*

**CLEINIAS:** How can they have any other?

**ATHENIAN:** *'And whoever transgresses these laws is punished as an evil-doer by the legislator, who calls the laws just'?*

**CLEINIAS:** Naturally.

**ATHENIAN:** *'This, then, is always the mode and fashion in which justice exists.'*

**CLEINIAS:** Certainly, if they are correct in their view.

**ATHENIAN:** Why, yes, this is one of those false principles of government to which we were referring.

**CLEINIAS:** Which do you mean?

**ATHENIAN:** Those which we were examining when we spoke of who ought to govern whom. Did we not arrive at the conclusion that parents ought to govern their children, and the elder the younger, and the noble the ignoble? And there were many other principles, if you remember, and they were not always consistent. One principle was this very principle of might, and we said that Pindar considered violence natural and justified it.

**CLEINIAS:** Yes; I remember.

**ATHENIAN:** Consider, then, to whom our state is to be entrusted. For there is a thing which has occurred times without number in states--

**CLEINIAS:** What thing?

**ATHENIAN:** That when there has been a contest for power, those who gain the upper hand so entirely monopolize the government, as to refuse all share to the defeated party and their descendants--they live watching one another, the ruling class being in perpetual fear that some one who has a recollection of former wrongs will come into power and rise up against them. Now, according to our view, such governments are not polities at all, nor are laws right which are passed for the good of particular classes and not for the good of the whole state. States which have such laws are not polities but parties, and their notions of justice are simply unmeaning. I say this, because I am going to assert that we must not entrust the government in your state to any one because he is rich, or because he possesses any other advantage, such as strength, or stature, or again birth: but he who is most obedient to the laws of the state, he shall win the palm; and to him who is victorious in the first degree shall be given the highest office and chief ministry of the gods; and the second to him who bears the second palm; and on a similar principle shall all the other offices be assigned to those who come next in order. And when I call the rulers servants or ministers of the law, I give them this name not for the sake of novelty, but because I certainly believe that upon such service or ministry depends the well- or ill-being of the state. For that state in which the law is subject and has no authority, I perceive to be on the highway to ruin; but I see that the state in which the law is above the rulers, and the rulers are the inferiors of the law, has salvation, and every blessing which the Gods can confer.

**CLEINIAS:** Truly, Stranger, you see with the keen vision of age.

**ATHENIAN:** Why, yes; every man when he is young has that sort of vision dullest, and when he is old keenest.

**CLEINIAS:** Very true.

**ATHENIAN:** And now, what is to be the next step? May we not suppose the colonists to have arrived, and proceed to make our speech to them?

**CLEINIAS:** Certainly.

**ATHENIAN:** *'Friends,'* we say to them,--*'God, as the old tradition declares, holding in his hand the beginning, middle, and end of all that is, travels according to His nature in a straight line towards the accomplishment of His end. Justice always accompanies Him, and is the punisher of those who fall short of the divine law. To justice, he who would be happy holds fast, and follows in her company with all humility and order; but he who is lifted up with pride, or elated by wealth or rank, or beauty, who is young and foolish, and has a soul hot with insolence, and thinks that he has no need of any guide or ruler, but is able himself to be the guide of others, he, I say, is left deserted of God; and being thus deserted, he takes to him others who are like himself, and dances about, throwing all things into confusion, and many think that he is a great man, but in a short time he pays a penalty which justice cannot but approve, and is utterly destroyed, and his family and city with him. Wherefore, seeing that human things are thus ordered, what should a wise man do or think, or not do or think'?*

**CLEINIAS:** Every man ought to make up his mind that he will be one of the followers of God; there can be no doubt of that.

**ATHENIAN:** Then what life is agreeable to God, and becoming in His followers? One only, expressed once for all in the old saying that 'like agrees with like, with measure measure,' but things which have no measure agree neither with themselves nor with the things which have. Now God ought to be to us the measure of all things, and not man, as men commonly say (Protagoras): the words are far more true of Him. And he who would be dear to God must, as far as is possible, be like Him and such as He is. Wherefore the temperate man is the friend of God, for he is like Him; and the intemperate man is unlike Him, and different from Him, and unjust. And the same applies to other things; and this is the conclusion, which is also the noblest and truest of all sayings,--that for the good man to offer sacrifice to the Gods, and hold converse with them by means of prayers and offerings and every kind of service, is the noblest and best of all things, and also the most conducive to a happy life, and very fit and meet. But with the bad man, the opposite of this is true: for the bad man has an impure soul, whereas the good is pure; and from one who is polluted, neither a good man nor God can without impropriety receive gifts. Wherefore the unholy do only waste their much service upon the Gods, but when offered by any holy man, such service is most acceptable to them. This is the mark at which we ought to aim. But what weapons shall we use, and how shall we direct them? In the first place, we affirm that next after the Olympian Gods and the Gods of the State, honour should be given to the Gods below; they should receive everything in even numbers, and of the second choice, and ill omen, while the odd numbers, and the first choice, and the things of lucky omen, are given to the Gods above, by him who would rightly hit the mark of piety. Next to these Gods, a wise man will do service to the demons or spirits, and then to the heroes, and after them will follow the private and ancestral Gods, who are worshipped as the law prescribes in the places which are sacred to them. Next comes the honour of living parents, to whom, as is meet, we have to pay the first and greatest and oldest of all debts, considering that all which a man has belongs to those who gave him birth and brought him up, and that he must do all that he can to minister to them, first, in his property, secondly, in his person, and thirdly, in his soul, in return for the endless care and travail which they bestowed upon him of old, in the days of his infancy, and which he is now to pay back to them when they are old and in the extremity of their need. And all his life long he ought never to utter, or to have uttered, an unbecoming word to them; for of light and fleeting words the penalty is most severe; Nemesis, the messenger of justice, is appointed to watch over all such matters. When they are angry and want to satisfy their feelings in word or deed, he should give way to them; for a father who thinks that he has been wronged by his son may be reasonably expected to be very angry. At their death, the most moderate funeral is best, neither exceeding the customary expense, nor yet falling short of the honour which has been usually shown by the former generation to their parents. And let a man not forget to pay the yearly tribute of respect to the dead, honouring them chiefly by omitting nothing that conduces to a perpetual remembrance of them, and giving a reasonable portion of his fortune to the dead. Doing this, and living after this manner, we shall receive our reward from the Gods and those who are above us (i.e. the demons); and we shall spend our days for the most part in good hope. And how a man ought to order what relates to his descendants and his kindred and friends and fellow-citizens, and the rites of hospitality taught by Heaven, and the intercourse which arises out of all these duties, with a view to the embellishment and orderly regulation of his own life--these things, I say, the laws, as we proceed with them, will accomplish, partly persuading, and partly when natures do not yield to the persuasion of custom, chastising them by might and right, and will thus render our state, if the Gods co-operate with us, prosperous and happy. But of what has to be said, and must be said by the legislator who is of my way of thinking, and yet, if said in the form of law, would be out of place--of this I think that he may give a sample for the instruction of himself and of those for whom he is legislating;

and then when, as far as he is able, he has gone through all the preliminaries, he may proceed to the work of legislation. Now, what will be the form of such prefaces? There may be a difficulty in including or describing them all under a single form, but I think that we may get some notion of them if we can guarantee one thing.

**CLEINIAS:** What is that?

**ATHENIAN:** I should wish the citizens to be as readily persuaded to virtue as possible; this will surely be the aim of the legislator in all his laws.

**CLEINIAS:** Certainly.

**ATHENIAN:** The proposal appears to me to be of some value; and I think that a person will listen with more gentleness and good-will to the precepts addressed to him by the legislator, when his soul is not altogether unprepared to receive them. Even a little done in the way of conciliation gains his ear, and is always worth having. For there is no great inclination or readiness on the part of mankind to be made as good, or as quickly good, as possible. The case of the many proves the wisdom of Hesiod, who says that the road to wickedness is smooth and can be travelled without perspiring, because it is so very short:

*'But before virtue the immortal Gods have placed the sweat of labour, and long and steep is the way thither, and rugged at first; but when you have reached the top, although difficult before, it is then easy.' (Works and Days.)*

**CLEINIAS:** Yes; and he certainly speaks well.

**ATHENIAN:** Very true: and now let me tell you the effect which the preceding discourse has had upon me.

**CLEINIAS:** Proceed.

**ATHENIAN:** Suppose that we have a little conversation with the legislator, and say to him--*'O, legislator, speak; if you know what we ought to say and do, you can surely tell.'*

**CLEINIAS:** Of course he can.

**ATHENIAN:** *'Did we not hear you just now saying, that the legislator ought not to allow the poets to do what they liked? For that they would not know in which of their words they went against the laws, to the hurt of the state.'*

**CLEINIAS:** That is true.

**ATHENIAN:** May we not fairly make answer to him on behalf of the poets?

**CLEINIAS:** What answer shall we make to him?

**ATHENIAN:** That the poet, according to the tradition which has ever prevailed among us, and is accepted of all men, when he sits down on the tripod of the muse, is not in his right mind; like a fountain, he allows to flow out freely whatever comes in, and his art being imitative, he is often compelled to represent men of opposite dispositions, and thus to contradict himself; neither can he tell whether there is more truth in one thing that he has said than in another. This is not the case in a law; the legislator must give not two rules about the same thing, but one only. Take an example from what you have just been saying. Of three kinds of funerals, there is one which is too extravagant, another is too niggardly, the third in a mean; and you choose and approve and order the last without qualification. But if I had an extremely rich wife, and she bade me bury her and describe her burial in a poem, I should praise the extravagant sort; and a poor miserly man, who had not much money to spend, would approve of the niggardly; and the man of moderate means, who was himself moderate, would praise a moderate funeral. Now you in the capacity of legislator must not barely say 'a moderate funeral,' but you must define what moderation is, and how much; unless you are definite, you must not suppose that you are speaking a language that can become law.

**CLEINIAS:** Certainly not.

**ATHENIAN:** And is our legislator to have no preface to his laws, but to say at once Do this, avoid that--and then holding the penalty in terrorem, to go on to another law; offering never a word of advice or exhortation to those for whom he is legislating, after the manner of some doctors? For of doctors, as I may remind you, some have a gentler, others a ruder method of cure; and as children ask the doctor to be gentle with them, so we will ask the legislator to cure our disorders with the gentlest remedies. What I mean to say is, that besides doctors there are doctors' servants, who are also styled doctors.

**CLEINIAS:** Very true.

**ATHENIAN:** And whether they are slaves or freemen makes no difference; they acquire their knowledge of medicine by obeying and observing their masters; empirically and not according to the natural way of learning, as the manner of freemen is, who have learned scientifically themselves the art which they impart scientifically to their pupils. You are aware that there are these two classes of doctors?

**CLEINIAS:** To be sure.

**ATHENIAN:** And did you ever observe that there are two classes of patients in states, slaves and freemen; and the slave doctors run about and cure the slaves, or wait for them in the dispensaries--practitioners of this sort never talk to their patients individually, or let them talk about their own individual complaints? The slave doctor prescribes what mere experience suggests, as if he had exact knowledge; and when he has given his orders, like a tyrant, he rushes off with equal assurance to some other servant who is ill; and so he relieves the master of the house of the care of his invalid slaves. But the other doctor, who is a freeman, attends and practices upon freemen; and he carries his enquiries far back, and goes into the nature of the disorder; he enters into discourse with the patient and with his friends, and is at once getting information from the sick man, and also instructing him as far as he is able, and he will not prescribe for him until he has first convinced him; at last, when he has brought the patient more and more under his persuasive influences and set him on the road to health, he attempts to effect a cure. Now which is the better way of proceeding in a physician and in a trainer? Is he the better who accomplishes his ends in a double way, or he who works in one way, and that the ruder and inferior?

**CLEINIAS:** I should say, Stranger, that the double way is far better.

**ATHENIAN:** Should you like to see an example of the double and single method in legislation?

**CLEINIAS:** Certainly I should.

**ATHENIAN:** What will be our first law? Will not the legislator, observing the order of nature, begin by making regulations for states about births?

**CLEINIAS:** He will.

**ATHENIAN:** In all states the birth of children goes back to the connexion of marriage?

**CLEINIAS:** Very true.

**ATHENIAN:** And, according to the true order, the laws relating to marriage should be those which are first determined in every state?

**CLEINIAS:** Quite so.

**ATHENIAN:** Then let me first give the law of marriage in a simple form; it may run as follows:--A man shall marry between the ages of thirty and thirty-five, or, if he does not, he shall pay such and such a fine, or shall suffer the loss of such and such privileges. This would be the simple law about marriage. The double law would run thus:--A man shall marry between the ages of thirty and thirty-five, considering that in a manner the human race naturally partakes of immortality, which every man is by nature inclined to desire to the utmost; for the desire of every man that he may become famous, and not lie in the grave without a name, is only the love of continuance. Now mankind are coeval with all time, and are ever following, and will ever follow, the course of time; and so they are immortal, because they leave children's children behind them, and partake of immortality in the unity of generation. And for a man voluntarily to deprive himself of this gift, as he deliberately does who will not have a wife or children, is impiety. He who obeys the law shall be free, and shall pay no fine; but he who is disobedient, and does not marry, when he has arrived at the age of thirty-five, shall pay a yearly fine of a certain amount, in order that he may not imagine his celibacy to bring ease and profit to him; and he shall not share in the honours which the young men in the state give to the aged. Comparing now the two forms of the law, you will be able to arrive at a judgment about any other laws--whether they should be double in length even when shortest, because they have to persuade as well as threaten, or whether they shall only threaten and be of half the length.

**MEGILLUS:** The shorter form, Stranger, would be more in accordance with Lacedaemonian custom; although, for my own part, if any one were to ask me which I myself prefer in the state, I should certainly determine in favour of the longer; and I would have every law made after the same pattern, if I had to choose. But I think that Cleinias is the person to be consulted, for his is the state which is going to use these laws.

**CLEINIAS:** Thank you, Megillus.

**ATHENIAN:** Whether, in the abstract, words are to be many or few, is a very foolish question; the best form, and not the shortest, is to be approved; nor is length at all to be regarded. Of the two forms of law which have been recited, the one is not only twice as good in practical usefulness as the other, but the case is like that of the two kinds of doctors, which I was just now mentioning. And yet legislators never appear to have considered that they have two instruments which they might use in legislation--persuasion and force; for in dealing with the rude and uneducated multitude, they use the one only as far as they can; they do not mingle persuasion with coercion, but employ force pure and simple. Moreover, there is a third point, sweet friends, which ought to be, and never is, regarded in our existing laws.

**CLEINIAS:** What is it?

**ATHENIAN:** A point arising out of our previous discussion, which comes into my mind in some mysterious way. All this time, from early dawn until noon, have we been talking about laws in this charming retreat: now we are going to promulgate our laws, and what has preceded was only the prelude of them. Why do I mention this? For this reason:--Because all discourses and vocal exercises have preludes and overtures, which are a sort of artistic beginnings intended to help the strain which is to be performed; lyric measures and music of every other kind have preludes framed with wonderful care. But of the truer and higher strain of law and politics, no one has ever yet uttered any prelude, or composed or published any, as though there was no such thing in nature. Whereas our present discussion seems to me to imply that there is;--these double laws, of which we were speaking, are not exactly double, but they are in two parts, the law and the prelude of the law. The arbitrary command, which was compared to the commands of doctors, whom we described as of the meaner sort, was the law pure and simple; and that which preceded, and was described by our friend here as being hortatory only, was, although in fact, an exhortation, likewise analogous to the preamble of a discourse. For I imagine that all this language of conciliation, which the legislator has been uttering in the preface of the law, was intended to create good-will in the person whom he addressed, in order that, by reason of this good-will, he might more intelligently receive his command, that is to say, the law. And therefore, in my way of speaking, this is more rightly described as the preamble than as the matter of the law. And I must further proceed to observe, that to all his laws, and to each separately, the legislator should prefix a preamble; he should remember how great will be the difference between them, according as they have, or have not, such preambles, as in the case already given.

**CLEINIAS:** The lawgiver, if he asks my opinion, will certainly legislate in the form which you advise.

**ATHENIAN:** I think that you are right, Cleinias, in affirming that all laws have preambles, and that throughout the whole of this work of legislation every single law should have a suitable preamble at the beginning; for that which is to follow is most important, and it makes all the difference whether we clearly remember the preambles or not. Yet we should be wrong in requiring that all laws, small and great alike, should have preambles of the same kind, any more than all songs or speeches; although they may be natural to all, they are not always necessary, and whether they are to be employed or not has in each case to be left to the judgment of the speaker or the musician, or, in the present instance, of the lawgiver.

**CLEINIAS:** That I think is most true. And now, Stranger, without delay let us return to the argument, and, as people say in play, make a second and better beginning, if you please, with the principles which we have been laying down, which we never thought of regarding as a preamble before, but of which we may now make a preamble, and not merely consider them to be chance topics of discourse. Let us acknowledge, then, that we have a preamble. About the honour of the Gods and the respect of parents, enough has been already said; and we may proceed to the topics which follow next in order, until the preamble is deemed by you to be complete; and after that you shall go through the laws themselves.

**ATHENIAN:** I understand you to mean that we have made a sufficient preamble about Gods and demigods, and about parents living or dead; and now you would have us bring the rest of the subject into the light of day?

**CLEINIAS:** Exactly.

**ATHENIAN:** After this, as is meet and for the interest of us all, I the speaker, and you the listeners, will try to estimate all that relates to the souls and bodies and properties of the citizens, as regards both their occupations and amusements, and thus arrive, as far as in us lies, at the nature of education. These then are the topics which follow next in order.

**CLEINIAS:** Very good.

# BOOK V.

**ATHENIAN:** Listen, all ye who have just now heard the laws about Gods, and about our dear forefathers:--Of all the things which a man has, next to the Gods, his soul is the most divine and most truly his own. Now in every man there are two parts: the better and superior, which rules, and the worse and inferior, which serves; and the ruling part of him is always to be preferred to the subject. Wherefore I am right in bidding every one next to the Gods, who are our masters, and those who in order follow them (i.e. the demons), to honour his own soul, which every one seems to honour, but no one honours as he ought; for honour is a divine good, and no evil thing is honourable; and he who thinks that he can honour the soul by word or gift, or any sort of compliance, without making her in any way better, seems to honour her, but honours her not at all. For example, every man, from his very boyhood, fancies that he is able to know everything, and thinks that he honours his soul by praising her, and he is very ready to let her do whatever she may like. But I mean to say that in acting thus he injures his soul, and is far from honouring her; whereas, in our opinion, he ought to honour her as second only to the Gods. Again, when a man thinks that others are to be blamed, and not himself, for the errors which he has committed from time to time, and the many and great evils which befell him in consequence, and is always fancying himself to be exempt and innocent, he is under the idea that he is honouring his soul; whereas the very reverse is the fact, for he is really injuring her. And when, disregarding the word and approval of the legislator, he indulges in pleasure, then again he is far from honouring her; he only dishonours her, and fills her full of evil and remorse; or when he does not endure to the end the labours and fears and sorrows and pains which the legislator approves, but gives way before them, then, by yielding, he does not honour the soul, but by all such conduct he makes her to be dishonourable; nor when he thinks that life at any price is a good, does he honour her, but yet once more he dishonours her; for the soul having a notion that the world below is all evil, he yields to her, and does not resist and teach or convince her that, for aught she knows, the world of the Gods below, instead of being evil, may be the greatest of all goods. Again, when any one prefers beauty to virtue, what is this but the real and utter dishonour of the soul? For such a preference implies that the body is more honourable than the soul; and this is false, for there is nothing of earthly birth which is more honourable than the heavenly, and he who thinks otherwise of the soul has no idea how greatly he undervalues this wonderful possession; nor, again, when a person is willing, or not unwilling, to acquire dishonest gains, does he then honour his soul with gifts--far otherwise; he sells her glory and honour for a small piece of gold; but all the gold which is under or upon the earth is not enough to give in exchange for virtue. In a word, I may say that he who does not estimate the base and evil, the good and noble, according to the standard of the legislator, and abstain in every possible way from the one and practise the other to the utmost of his power, does not know that in all these respects he is most foully and disgracefully abusing his soul, which is the divinest part of man; for no one, as I may say, ever considers that which is declared to be the greatest penalty of evil-doing--namely, to grow into the likeness of bad men, and growing like them to fly from the conversation of the good, and be cut off from them, and cleave to and follow after the company of the bad. And he who is joined to them must do and suffer what such men by nature do and say to one another,--a suffering which is not justice but retribution; for justice and the just are noble, whereas retribution is the suffering which waits upon injustice; and whether a man escape or endure this, he is miserable,--in the former case, because he is not cured; while in the latter, he perishes in order that the rest of mankind may be saved.

Speaking generally, our glory is to follow the better and improve the inferior, which is susceptible of improvement, as far as this is possible. And of all human possessions, the soul is by nature most inclined to avoid the evil, and track out and find the chief good; which when a man has found, he should take up his abode with it during the remainder of his life. Wherefore the soul also is second (or next to God) in honour; and third, as every one will perceive, comes the honour of the body in natural order. Having determined this, we have next to consider that there is a natural honour of the body, and that of honours some are true and some are counterfeit. To decide which are which is the business of the legislator; and he, I suspect, would intimate that they are as follows:--Honour is not to be given to the fair body, or to the strong or the swift or the tall, or to the healthy body (although many may think otherwise), any more than to their opposites; but the mean states of all these habits are by far the safest and most moderate; for the one extreme makes the soul braggart and insolent, and the other, illiberal and base; and money, and property, and distinction all go to the same tune. The excess of any of these things is apt to be a source of hatreds and divisions among states and individuals; and the defect of them is commonly a cause of slavery. And, therefore, I would not have any one fond of heaping up riches for the sake of his children, in order that he may leave them as rich as possible. For the possession of great wealth is of no use, either to them or to the state. The condition of youth which is free from flattery, and at the same time not in need of the necessaries of life, is the best and most harmonious of all, being in accord and agreement with our nature, and making life to be most entirely free from sorrow. Let parents, then, bequeath to their children not a heap of riches, but the spirit of reverence. We, indeed, fancy that they will inherit reverence from us, if we rebuke them when they show a want of reverence. But this quality is not really imparted to them by the present style of admonition, which only tells them that the young ought always to be reverential. A sensible legislator will rather exhort the elders to reverence the younger, and above all to take heed that no young man sees or hears one of themselves doing or saying anything disgraceful; for where old men have no shame, there young men will most certainly be devoid of reverence. The best way of training the young is to train yourself at the same time; not to admonish them, but to be always carrying out your own admonitions in practice. He who honours his kindred, and reveres those who share in the same Gods and are of the same blood and family, may fairly expect that the Gods who preside over generation will be propitious to him, and will quicken his seed. And he who deems the services which his friends and acquaintances do for him, greater and more important than they themselves deem them, and his own favours to them less than theirs to him, will have their good-will in the intercourse of life. And surely in his relations to the state and his fellow citizens, he is by far the best, who rather than the Olympic or any other victory of peace or war, desires to win the palm of obedience to the laws of his country, and who, of all mankind, is the person reputed to have obeyed them best through life. In his relations to strangers, a man should consider that a contract is a most holy thing, and that all concerns and wrongs of strangers are more directly dependent on the protection of God, than wrongs done to citizens; for the stranger, having no kindred and friends, is more to be pitied by Gods and men. Wherefore, also, he who is most able to avenge him is most zealous in his cause; and he who is most able is the genius and the god of the stranger, who follow in the train of Zeus, the god of strangers. And for this reason, he who has a spark of caution in him, will do his best to pass through life without sinning against the stranger. And of offences committed, whether against strangers or fellow-countrymen, that against suppliants is the greatest. For the God who witnessed to the agreement made with the suppliant, becomes in a special manner the guardian of the sufferer; and he will certainly not suffer unavenged.

Thus we have fairly described the manner in which a man is to act about his parents, and himself, and his own affairs; and in relation to the state, and his friends, and kindred, both in what concerns his own countrymen, and in what concerns the stranger. We will now consider what manner of man he must be who would best pass through life in respect of those other things which are not matters of law, but of praise and blame only; in which praise and blame educate a man, and make him more tractable and amenable to the laws which are about to be imposed.

Truth is the beginning of every good thing, both to Gods and men; and he who would be blessed and happy, should be from the first a partaker of the truth, that he may live a true man as long as possible, for then he can be trusted; but he is not to be trusted who loves voluntary falsehood, and he who loves involuntary falsehood is a fool. Neither condition is enviable, for the untrustworthy and ignorant has no friend, and as time advances he becomes known, and lays up in store for himself isolation in crabbed age when life is on the wane: so that, whether his children or friends are alive or not, he is equally solitary.--Worthy of honour is he who does no injustice, and of more than twofold honour, if he not only does no injustice himself, but hinders others from doing any; the first may count as one man, the second is worth many men, because he informs the rulers of the injustice of others. And yet more highly to be esteemed is he who co- operates with the rulers in correcting the citizens as far as he can--he shall be proclaimed the great and perfect citizen, and bear away the palm of virtue. The same praise may be given about temperance and wisdom, and all other goods which may be imparted to others, as well as acquired by a man for himself; he who imparts them shall be honoured as the man of men, and he who is willing, yet is not able, may be allowed the second place; but he who is jealous and will not, if he can help, allow others to partake in a friendly way of any good, is deserving of blame: the good, however, which he has, is not to be undervalued by us because it is possessed by him, but must be acquired by us also to the utmost of our power. Let every man, then, freely strive for the prize of virtue, and let there be no envy. For the unenvious nature increases the greatness of states--he himself contends in the race, blasting the fair fame of no man; but the envious, who thinks that he ought to get the better by defaming others, is less energetic himself in the pursuit of true virtue, and reduces his rivals to despair by his unjust slanders of them. And so he makes the whole city to enter the arena untrained in the practice of virtue, and diminishes her glory as far as in him lies. Now every man should be valiant, but he should also be gentle. From the cruel, or hardly curable, or altogether incurable acts of injustice done to him by others, a man can only escape by fighting and defending himself and conquering, and by never ceasing to punish them; and no man who is not of a noble spirit is able to accomplish this. As to the actions of those who do evil, but whose evil is curable, in the first place, let us remember that the unjust man is not unjust of his own free will. For no man of his own free will would choose to possess the greatest of evils, and least of all in the most honourable part of himself. And the soul, as we said, is of a truth deemed by all men the most honourable. In the soul, then, which is the most honourable part of him, no one, if he could help, would admit, or allow to continue the greatest of evils. The unrighteous and vicious are always to be pitied in any case; and one can afford to forgive as well as pity him who is curable, and refrain and calm one's anger, not getting into a passion, like a woman, and nursing ill-feeling. But upon him who is incapable of reformation and wholly evil, the vials of our wrath should be poured out; wherefore I say that good men ought, when occasion demands, to be both gentle and passionate.

Of all evils the greatest is one which in the souls of most men is innate, and which a man is always excusing in himself and never correcting; I mean, what is expressed in the saying that 'Every man by nature is and ought to be his own friend.' Whereas the excessive love of self is in reality the source to each man of all offences; for the lover is blinded about the beloved, so that he judges wrongly of the just, the good, and the honourable, and thinks that he ought always to prefer himself to the truth. But he who would be a great man ought to regard, not himself or his interests, but what is just, whether the just act be his own or that of another. Through a similar error men are induced to fancy that their own ignorance is wisdom, and thus we who may be truly said to know nothing, think that we know all things; and because we will not let others act for us in what we do not know, we are compelled to act amiss ourselves. Wherefore let every man avoid excess of self-love, and condescend to follow a better man than himself, not allowing any false shame to stand in the way. There are also minor precepts which are often repeated, and are quite as useful; a man should recollect them and remind himself of them. For when a stream is flowing out, there should be water flowing in too; and recollection flows in while wisdom is departing. Therefore I say that a man should refrain from excess either of laughter or tears, and should exhort his neighbour to do the same; he should veil his immoderate sorrow or joy, and seek to behave with propriety, whether the genius of his good fortune remains with him, or whether at the crisis of his fate, when he seems to be mounting high and steep places, the Gods oppose him in some of his enterprises. Still he may ever hope, in the case of good men, that whatever afflictions are to befall them in the future God will lessen, and that present evils He will change for the better; and as to the goods which are the opposite of these evils, he will not doubt that they will be added to them, and that they will be fortunate. Such should be men's hopes, and such should be the exhortations with which they admonish one another, never losing an opportunity, but on every occasion distinctly reminding themselves and others of all these things, both in jest and earnest.

Enough has now been said of divine matters, both as touching the practices which men ought to follow, and as to the sort of persons who they ought severally to be. But of human things we have not as yet spoken, and we must; for to men we are discoursing and not to Gods. Pleasures and pains and desires are a part of human nature, and on them every mortal being must of necessity hang and depend with the most eager interest. And therefore we must praise the noblest life, not only as the fairest in appearance, but as being one which, if a man will only taste, and not, while still in his youth, desert for another, he will find to surpass also in the very thing which we all of us desire,--I mean in having a greater amount of pleasure and less of pain during the whole of life. And this will be plain, if a man has a true taste of them, as will be quickly and clearly seen. But what is a true taste? That we have to learn from the argument--the point being what is according to nature, and what is not according to nature. One life must be compared with another, the more pleasurable with the more painful, after this manner:--We desire to have pleasure, but we neither desire nor choose pain; and the neutral state we are ready to take in exchange, not for pleasure but for pain; and we also wish for less pain and greater pleasure, but less pleasure and greater pain we do not wish for; and an equal balance of either we cannot venture to assert that we should desire. And all these differ or do not differ severally in number and magnitude and intensity and equality, and in the opposites of these when regarded as objects of choice, in relation to desire. And such being the necessary order of things, we wish for that life in which there are many great and intense elements of pleasure and pain, and in which the pleasures are in excess, and do not wish for that in which the opposites exceed; nor, again, do we wish for that in which the elements of either are small and few and feeble, and the pains exceed. And when, as I said before, there is a balance of pleasure and pain in life, this is to be regarded by us as the balanced life; while other lives are preferred by us because they exceed in what we like, or are rejected by us because they exceed in what we dislike. All the lives of men may be regarded by us as bound up in these, and we must also consider what sort of lives we by nature desire. And if we wish for any others, I say that we desire them only through some ignorance and inexperience of the lives which actually exist.

Now, what lives are they, and how many in which, having searched out and beheld the objects of will and desire and their opposites, and making of them a law, choosing, I say, the dear and the pleasant and the best and noblest, a man may live in the happiest way possible? Let us say that the temperate life is one kind of life, and the rational another, and the courageous another, and the healthful another; and to these four let us oppose four other lives--the foolish, the cowardly, the intemperate, the diseased. He who knows the temperate life will describe it as in all things gentle, having gentle pains and gentle pleasures, and placid desires and loves not insane; whereas the intemperate life is impetuous in all things, and has violent pains and pleasures, and vehement and stinging desires, and loves utterly insane; and in the temperate life the pleasures exceed the pains, but in the intemperate life the pains exceed the pleasures in greatness and number and frequency. Hence one of the two lives is naturally and necessarily more pleasant and the other more painful, and he who would live pleasantly cannot possibly choose to live intemperately. And if this is true, the inference clearly is that no man is voluntarily intemperate; but that the whole multitude of men lack temperance in their lives, either from ignorance, or from want of self- control, or both. And the same holds of the diseased and healthy life; they both have pleasures and pains, but in health the pleasure exceeds the pain, and in sickness the pain exceeds the pleasure. Now our intention in choosing the lives is not that the painful should exceed, but the life in which pain is exceeded by pleasure we have determined to be the more pleasant life. And we should say that the temperate life has the elements both of pleasure and pain fewer and smaller and less frequent than the intemperate, and the wise life than the foolish life, and the life of courage than the life of cowardice; one of each pair exceeding in pleasure and the other in pain, the courageous surpassing the cowardly, and the wise exceeding the foolish. And so the one class of lives exceeds the other class in pleasure; the temperate and courageous and wise and healthy exceed the cowardly and foolish and intemperate and diseased lives; and generally speaking, that which has any virtue, whether of body or soul, is pleasanter than the vicious life, and far superior in beauty and rectitude and excellence and reputation, and causes him who lives accordingly to be infinitely happier than the opposite.

Enough of the preamble; and now the laws should follow; or, to speak more correctly, an outline of them. As, then, in the case of a web or any other tissue, the warp and the woof cannot be made of the same materials, but the warp is necessarily superior as being stronger, and having a certain character of firmness, whereas the woof is softer and has a proper degree of elasticity;--in a similar manner those who are to hold great offices in states, should be distinguished truly in each case from those who have been but slenderly proven by education. Let us suppose that there are two parts in the constitution of a state--one the creation of offices, the other the laws which are assigned to them to administer.

But, before all this, comes the following consideration:--The shepherd or herdsman, or breeder of horses or the like, when he has received his animals will not begin to train them until he has first purified them in a manner which befits a community of animals; he will divide the healthy and unhealthy, and the good breed and the bad breed, and will send away the unhealthy and badly bred to other herds, and tend the rest, reflecting that his labours will be vain and have no effect, either on the souls or bodies of those whom nature and ill nurture have corrupted, and that they will involve in destruction the pure and healthy nature and being of every other animal, if he should neglect to purify them. Now the case of other animals is not so important--they are only worth introducing for the sake of illustration; but what relates to man is of the highest importance; and the legislator should make enquiries, and indicate what is proper for each one in the way of purification and of any other procedure. Take, for example, the purification of a city--there are many kinds of purification, some easier and others more difficult; and some of them, and the best and most difficult of them, the legislator, if he be also a despot, may be able to effect; but the legislator, who, not being a despot, sets up a new government and laws, even if he attempt the mildest of purgations, may think himself happy if he can complete his work. The best kind of purification is painful, like similar cures in medicine, involving righteous punishment and inflicting death or exile in the last resort. For in this way we commonly dispose of great sinners who are incurable, and are the greatest injury of the whole state. But the milder form of purification is as follows:--when men who have nothing, and are in want of food, show a disposition to follow their leaders in an attack on the property of the rich--these, who are the natural plague of the state, are sent away by the legislator in a friendly spirit as far as he is able; and this dismissal of them is euphemistically termed a colony. And every legislator should contrive to do this at once. Our present case, however, is peculiar. For there is no need to devise any colony or purifying separation under the circumstances in which we are placed. But as, when many streams flow together from many sources, whether springs or mountain torrents, into a single lake, we ought to attend and take care that the confluent waters should be perfectly clear, and in order to effect this, should pump and draw off and divert impurities, so in every political arrangement there may be trouble and danger. But, seeing that we are now only discoursing and not acting, let our selection be supposed to be completed, and the desired purity attained. Touching evil men, who want to join and be citizens of our state, after we have tested them by every sort of persuasion and for a sufficient time, we will prevent them from coming; but the good we will to the utmost of our ability receive as friends with open arms.

Another piece of good fortune must not be forgotten, which, as we were saying, the Heraclid colony had, and which is also ours,--that we have escaped division of land and the abolition of debts; for these are always a source of dangerous contention, and a city which is driven by necessity to legislate upon such matters can neither allow the old ways to continue, nor yet venture to alter them. We must have recourse to prayers, so to speak, and hope that a slight change may be cautiously effected in a length of time. And such a change can be accomplished by those who have abundance of land, and having also many debtors, are willing, in a kindly spirit, to share with those who are in want, sometimes remitting and sometimes giving, holding fast in a path of moderation, and deeming poverty to be the increase of a man's desires and not the diminution of his property. For this is the great beginning of salvation to a state, and upon this lasting basis may be erected afterwards whatever political order is suitable under the circumstances; but if the change be based upon an unsound principle, the future administration of the country will be full of difficulties. That is a danger which, as I am saying, is escaped by us, and yet we had better say how, if we had not escaped, we might have escaped; and we may venture now to assert that no other way of escape, whether narrow or broad, can be devised but freedom from avarice and a sense of justice--upon this rock our city shall be built; for there ought to be no disputes among citizens about property. If there are quarrels of long standing among them, no legislator of any degree of sense will proceed a step in the arrangement of the state until they are settled. But that they to whom God has given, as He has to us, to be the founders of a new state as yet free from enmity--that they should create themselves enmities by their mode of distributing lands and houses, would be superhuman folly and wickedness.

How then can we rightly order the distribution of the land? In the first place, the number of the citizens has to be determined, and also the number and size of the divisions into which they will have to be formed; and the land and the houses will then have to be apportioned by us as fairly as we can. The number of citizens can only be estimated satisfactorily in relation to the territory and the neighbouring states. The territory must be sufficient to maintain a certain number of inhabitants in a moderate way of life--more than this is not required; and the number of citizens should be sufficient to defend themselves against the injustice of their neighbours, and also to give them the power of rendering efficient aid to their neighbours when they are wronged. After having taken a survey of their's and their neighbours' territory, we will determine the limits of them in fact as well as in theory. And now, let us proceed to legislate with a view to perfecting the form and outline of our state. The number of our citizens shall be 5040--this will be a convenient number; and these shall be owners of the land and protectors of the allotment. The houses and the land will be divided in the same way, so that every man may correspond to a lot. Let the whole number be first divided into two parts, and then into three; and the number is further capable of being divided into four or five parts, or any number of parts up to ten. Every legislator ought to know so much arithmetic as to be able to tell what number is most likely to be useful to all cities; and we are going to take that number which contains the greatest and most regular and unbroken series of divisions. The whole of number has every possible division, and the number 5040 can be divided by exactly fifty-nine divisors, and ten of these proceed without interval from one to ten: this will furnish numbers for war and peace, and for all contracts and dealings, including taxes and divisions of the land. These properties of number should be ascertained at leisure by those who are bound by law to know them; for they are true, and should be proclaimed at the foundation of the city, with a view to use. Whether the legislator is establishing a new state or restoring an old and decayed one, in respect of Gods and temples,--the temples which are to be built in each city, and the Gods or demi-gods after whom they are to be called,--if he be a man of sense, he will make no change in anything which the oracle of Delphi, or Dodona, or the God Ammon, or any ancient tradition has sanctioned in whatever manner, whether by apparitions or reputed inspiration of Heaven, in obedience to which mankind have established sacrifices in connexion with mystic rites, either originating on the spot, or derived from Tyrrhenia or Cyprus or some other place, and on the strength of which traditions they have consecrated oracles and images, and altars and temples, and portioned out a sacred domain for each of them. The least part of all these ought not to be disturbed by the legislator; but he should assign to the several districts some God, or demi-god, or hero, and, in the distribution of the soil, should give to these first their chosen domain and all things fitting, that the inhabitants of the several districts may meet at fixed times, and that they may readily supply their various wants, and entertain one another with sacrifices, and become friends and acquaintances; for there is no greater good in a state than that the citizens should be known to one another. When not light but darkness and ignorance of each other's characters prevails among them, no one will receive the honour of which he is deserving, or the power or the justice to which he is fairly entitled: wherefore, in every state, above all things, every man should take heed that he have no deceit in him, but that he be always true and simple; and that no deceitful person take any advantage of him.

The next move in our pastime of legislation, like the withdrawal of the stone from the holy line in the game of draughts, being an unusual one, will probably excite wonder when mentioned for the first time. And yet, if a man will only reflect and weigh the matter with care, he will see that our city is ordered in a manner which, if not the best, is the second best. Perhaps also some one may not approve this form, because he thinks that such a constitution is ill adapted to a legislator who has not despotic power. The truth is, that there are three forms of government, the best, the second and the third best, which we may just mention, and then leave the selection to the ruler of the settlement. Following this method in the present instance, let us speak of the states which are respectively first, second, and third in excellence, and then we will leave the choice to Cleinias now, or to any one else who may hereafter have to make a similar choice among constitutions, and may desire to give to his state some feature which is congenial to him and which he approves in his own country.

The first and highest form of the state and of the government and of the law is that in which there prevails most widely the ancient saying, that 'Friends have all things in common.' Whether there is anywhere now, or will ever be, this communion of women and children and of property, in which the private and individual is altogether banished from life, and things which are by nature private, such as eyes and ears and hands, have become common, and in some way see and hear and act in common, and all men express praise and blame and feel joy and sorrow on the same occasions, and whatever laws there are unite the city to the utmost,-- whether all this is possible or not, I say that no man, acting upon any other principle, will ever constitute a state which will be truer or better or more exalted in virtue. Whether such a state is governed by Gods or sons of Gods, one, or more than one, happy are the men who, living after this manner, dwell there; and therefore to this we are to look for the pattern of the state, and to cling to this, and to seek with all our might for one which is like this. The state which we have now in hand, when created, will be nearest to immortality and the only one which takes the second place; and after that, by the grace of God, we will complete the third one. And we will begin by speaking of the nature and origin of the second.

Let the citizens at once distribute their land and houses, and not till the land in common, since a community of goods goes beyond their proposed origin, and nurture, and education. But in making the distribution, let the several possessors feel that their particular lots also belong to the whole city; and seeing that the earth is their parent, let them tend her more carefully than children do their mother. For she is a goddess and their queen, and they are her mortal subjects. Such also are the feelings which they ought to entertain to the Gods and demi-gods of the country. And in order that the distribution may always remain, they ought to consider further that the present number of families should be always retained, and neither increased nor diminished. This may be secured for the whole city in the following manner:--Let the possessor of a lot leave the one of his children who is his best beloved, and one only, to be the heir of his dwelling, and his successor in the duty of ministering to the Gods, the state and the family, as well the living members of it as those who are departed when he comes into the inheritance; but of his other children, if he have more than one, he shall give the females in marriage according to the law to be hereafter enacted, and the males he shall distribute as sons to those citizens who have no children, and are disposed to receive them; or if there should be none such, and particular individuals have too many children, male or female, or too few, as in the case of barrenness--in all these cases let the highest and most honourable magistracy created by us judge and determine what is to be done with the redundant or deficient, and devise a means that the number of 5040 houses shall always remain the same. There are many ways of regulating numbers; for they in whom generation is affluent may be made to refrain, and, on the other hand, special care may be taken to increase the number of births by rewards and stigmas, or we may meet the evil by the elder men giving advice and administering rebuke to the younger--in this way the object may be attained. And if after all there be very great difficulty about the equal preservation of the 5040 houses, and there be an excess of citizens, owing to the too great love of those who live together, and we are at our wits' end, there is still the old device often mentioned by us of sending out a colony, which will part friends with us, and be composed of suitable persons. If, on the other hand, there come a wave bearing a deluge of disease, or a plague of war, and the inhabitants become much fewer than the appointed number by reason of bereavement, we ought not to introduce citizens of spurious birth and education, if this can be avoided; but even God is said not to be able to fight against necessity.

Wherefore let us suppose this 'high argument' of ours to address us in the following terms:--Best of men, cease not to honour according to nature similarity and equality and sameness and agreement, as regards number and every good and noble quality. And, above all, observe the aforesaid number 5040 throughout life; in the second place, do not disparage the small and modest proportions of the inheritances which you received in the distribution, by buying and selling them to one another. For then neither will the God who gave you the lot be your friend, nor will the legislator; and indeed the law declares to the disobedient that these are the terms upon which he may or may not take the lot. In the first place, the earth as he is informed is sacred to the Gods; and in the next place, priests and priestesses will offer up prayers over a first, and second, and even a third sacrifice, that he who buys or sells the houses or lands which he has received, may suffer the punishment which he deserves; and these their prayers they shall write down in the temples, on tablets of cypress-wood, for the instruction of posterity. Moreover they will set a watch over all these things, that they may be observed;--the magistracy which has the sharpest eyes shall keep watch that any infringement of these commands may be discovered and punished as offences both against the law and the God. How great is the benefit of such an ordinance to all those cities, which obey and are administered accordingly, no bad man can ever know, as the old proverb says; but only a man of experience and good habits. For in such an order of things there will not be much opportunity for making money; no man either ought, or indeed will be allowed, to exercise any ignoble occupation, of which the vulgarity is a matter of reproach to a freeman, and should never want to acquire riches by any such means.

Further, the law enjoins that no private man shall be allowed to possess gold and silver, but only coin for daily use, which is almost necessary in dealing with artisans, and for payment of hirelings, whether slaves or immigrants, by all those persons who require the use of them. Wherefore our citizens, as we say, should have a coin passing current among themselves, but not accepted among the rest of mankind; with a view, however, to expeditions and journeys to other lands,--for embassies, or for any other occasion which may arise of sending out a herald, the state must also possess a common Hellenic currency. If a private person is ever obliged to go abroad, let him have the consent of the magistrates and go; and if when he returns he has any foreign money remaining, let him give the surplus back to the treasury, and receive a corresponding sum in the local currency. And if he is discovered to appropriate it, let it be confiscated, and let him who knows and does not inform be subject to curse and dishonour equally him who brought the money, and also to a fine not less in amount than the foreign money which has been brought back. In marrying and giving in marriage, no one shall give or receive any dowry at all; and no one shall deposit money with another whom he does not trust as a friend, nor shall he lend money upon interest; and the borrower should be under no obligation to repay either capital or interest. That these principles are best, any one may see who compares them with the first principle and intention of a state. The intention, as we affirm, of a reasonable statesman, is not what the many declare to be the object of a good legislator, namely, that the state for the true interests of which he is advising should be as great and as rich as possible, and should possess gold and silver, and have the greatest empire by sea and land;--this they imagine to be the real object of legislation, at the same time adding, inconsistently, that the true legislator desires to have the city the best and happiest possible. But they do not see that some of these things are possible, and some of them are impossible; and he who orders the state will desire what is possible, and will not indulge in vain wishes or attempts to accomplish that which is impossible. The citizen must indeed be happy and good, and the legislator will seek to make him so; but very rich and very good at the same time he cannot be, not, at least, in the sense in which the many speak of riches. For they mean by 'the rich' the few who have the most valuable possessions, although the owner of them may quite well be a rogue. And if this is true, I can never assent to the doctrine that the rich man will be happy--he must be good as well as rich. And good in a high degree, and rich in a high degree at the same time, he cannot be. Some one will ask, why not? And we shall answer--Because acquisitions which come from sources which are just and unjust indifferently, are more than double those which come from just sources only; and the sums which are expended neither honourably nor disgracefully, are only half as great as those which are expended honourably and on honourable purposes. Thus, if the one acquires double and spends half, the other who is in the opposite case and is a good man cannot possibly be wealthier than he. The first--I am speaking of the saver and not of the spender--is not always bad; he may indeed in some cases be utterly bad, but, as I was saying, a good man he never is. For he who receives money unjustly as well as justly, and spends neither nor unjustly, will be a rich man if he be also thrifty. On the other hand, the utterly bad is in general profligate, and therefore very poor; while he who spends on noble objects, and acquires wealth by just means only, can hardly be remarkable for riches, any more than he can be very poor. Our statement, then, is true, that the very rich are not good, and, if they are not good, they are not happy. But the intention of our laws was, that the citizens should be as happy as may be, and as friendly as possible to one another. And men who are always at law with one another, and amongst whom there are many wrongs done, can never be friends to one another, but only those among whom crimes and lawsuits are few and slight. Therefore we say that gold and silver ought not to be allowed in the city, nor much of the vulgar sort of trade which is carried on by lending money, or rearing the meaner kinds of live stock; but only the produce of agriculture, and only so much of this as will not compel us in pursuing it to neglect that for the sake of which riches exist--I mean, soul and body, which without gymnastics, and without education, will never be worth anything; and therefore, as we have said not once but many times, the care of riches should have the last place in our thoughts. For there are in all three things about which every man has an interest; and the interest about money, when rightly regarded, is the third and lowest of them: midway comes the interest of the body; and, first of all, that of the soul; and the state which we are describing will have been rightly constituted if it ordains honours according to this scale. But if, in any of the laws which have been ordained, health has been preferred to temperance, or wealth to health and temperate habits, that law must clearly be wrong. Wherefore, also, the legislator ought often to impress upon himself the question--'What do I want?' and 'Do I attain my aim, or do I miss the mark?' In this way, and in this way only, he may acquit himself and free others from the work of legislation.

Let the allottee then hold his lot upon the conditions which we have mentioned.

It would be well that every man should come to the colony having all things equal; but seeing that this is not possible, and one man will have greater possessions than another, for many reasons and in particular in order to preserve equality in special crises of the state, qualifications of property must be unequal, in order that offices and contributions and distributions may be proportioned to the value of each person's wealth, and not solely to the virtue of his ancestors or himself, nor yet to the strength and beauty of his person, but also to the measure of his wealth or poverty; and so by a law of inequality, which will be in proportion to his wealth, he will receive honours and offices as equally as possible, and there will be no quarrels and disputes. To which end there should be four different standards appointed according to the amount of property: there should be a first and a second and a third and a fourth class, in which the citizens will be placed, and they will be called by these or similar names: they may continue in the same rank, or pass into another in any individual case, on becoming richer from being poorer, or poorer from being richer. The form of law which I should propose as the natural sequel would be as follows:--In a state which is desirous of being saved from the greatest of all plagues--not faction, but rather distraction;--there should exist among the citizens neither extreme poverty, nor, again, excess of wealth, for both are productive of both these evils. Now the legislator should determine what is to be the limit of poverty or wealth. Let the limit of poverty be the value of the lot; this ought to be preserved, and no ruler, nor any one else who aspires after a reputation for virtue, will allow the lot to be impaired in any case. This the legislator gives as a measure, and he will permit a man to acquire double or triple, or as much as four times the amount of this. But if a person have yet greater riches, whether he has found them, or they have been given to him, or he has made them in business, or has acquired by any stroke of fortune that which is in excess of the measure, if he give back the surplus to the state, and to the Gods who are the patrons of the state, he shall suffer no penalty or loss of reputation; but if he disobeys this our law, any one who likes may inform against him and receive half the value of the excess, and the delinquent shall pay a sum equal to the excess out of his own property, and the other half of the excess shall belong to the Gods. And let every possession of every man, with the exception of the lot, be publicly registered before the magistrates whom the law appoints, so that all suits about money may be easy and quite simple.

The next thing to be noted is, that the city should be placed as nearly as possible in the centre of the country; we should choose a place which possesses what is suitable for a city, and this may easily be imagined and described. Then we will divide the city into twelve portions, first founding temples to Hestia, to Zeus and to Athene, in a spot which we will call the Acropolis, and surround with a circular wall, making the division of the entire city and country radiate from this point. The twelve portions shall be equalized by the provision that those which are of good land shall be smaller, while those of inferior quality shall be larger. The number of the lots shall be 5040, and each of them shall be divided into two, and every allotment shall be composed of two such sections; one of land near the city, the other of land which is at a distance. This arrangement shall be carried out in the following manner: The section which is near the city shall be added to that which is on the borders, and form one lot, and the portion which is next nearest shall be added to the portion which is next farthest; and so of the rest. Moreover, in the two sections of the lots the same principle of equalization of the soil ought to be maintained; the badness and goodness shall be compensated by more and less. And the legislator shall divide the citizens into twelve parts, and arrange the rest of their property, as far as possible, so as to form twelve equal parts; and there shall be a registration of all. After this they shall assign twelve lots to twelve Gods, and call them by their names, and dedicate to each God their several portions, and call the tribes after them. And they shall distribute the twelve divisions of the city in the same way in which they divided the country; and every man shall have two habitations, one in the centre of the country, and the other at the extremity. Enough of the manner of settlement.

Now we ought by all means to consider that there can never be such a happy concurrence of circumstances as we have described; neither can all things coincide as they are wanted. Men who will not take offence at such a mode of living together, and will endure all their life long to have their property fixed at a moderate limit, and to beget children in accordance with our ordinances, and will allow themselves to be deprived of gold and other things which the legislator, as is evident from these enactments, will certainly forbid them; and will endure, further, the situation of the land with the city in the middle and dwellings round about;--all this is as if the legislator were telling his dreams, or making a city and citizens of wax. There is truth in these objections, and therefore every one should take to heart what I am going to say. Once more, then, the legislator shall appear and address us:--'O my friends,' he will say to us, 'do not suppose me ignorant that there is a certain degree of truth in your words; but I am of opinion that, in matters which are not present but future, he who exhibits a pattern of that at which he aims, should in nothing fall short of the fairest and truest; and that if he finds any part of this work impossible of execution he should avoid and not execute it, but he should contrive to carry out that which is nearest and most akin to it; you must allow the legislator to perfect his design, and when it is perfected, you should join with him in considering what part of his legislation is expedient and what will arouse opposition; for surely the artist who is to be deemed worthy of any regard at all, ought always to make his work self- consistent.'

Having determined that there is to be a distribution into twelve parts, let us now see in what way this may be accomplished. There is no difficulty in perceiving that the twelve parts admit of the greatest number of divisions of that which they include, or in seeing the other numbers which are consequent upon them, and are produced out of them up to 5040; wherefore the law ought to order phratries and demes and villages, and also military ranks and movements, as well as coins and measures, dry and liquid, and weights, so as to be commensurable and agreeable to one another. Nor should we fear the appearance of minuteness, if the law commands that all the vessels which a man possesses should have a common measure, when we consider generally that the divisions and variations of numbers have a use in respect of all the variations of which they are susceptible, both in themselves and as measures of height and depth, and in all sounds, and in motions, as well those which proceed in a straight direction, upwards or downwards, as in those which go round and round. The legislator is to consider all these things and to bid the citizens, as far as possible, not to lose sight of numerical order; for no single instrument of youthful education has such mighty power, both as regards domestic economy and politics, and in the arts, as the study of arithmetic. Above all, arithmetic stirs up him who is by nature sleepy and dull, and makes him quick to learn, retentive, shrewd, and aided by art divine he makes progress quite beyond his natural powers. All such things, if only the legislator, by other laws and institutions, can banish meanness and covetousness from the souls of men, so that they can use them properly and to their own good, will be excellent and suitable instruments of education. But if he cannot, he will unintentionally create in them, instead of wisdom, the habit of craft, which evil tendency may be observed in the Egyptians and Phoenicians, and many other races, through the general vulgarity of their pursuits and acquisitions, whether some unworthy legislator of theirs has been the cause, or some impediment of chance or nature. For we must not fail to observe, O Megillus and Cleinias, that there is a difference in places, and that some beget better men and others worse; and we must legislate accordingly. Some places are subject to strange and fatal influences by reason of diverse winds and violent heats, some by reason of waters; or, again, from the character of the food given by the earth, which not only affects the bodies of men for good or evil, but produces similar results in their souls. And in all such qualities those spots excel in which there is a divine inspiration, and in which the demigods have their appointed lots, and are propitious, not adverse, to the settlers in them. To all these matters the legislator, if he have any sense in him, will attend as far as man can, and frame his laws accordingly. And this is what you, Cleinias, must do, and to matters of this kind you must turn your mind since you are going to colonize a new country.

**CLEINIAS:** Your words, Athenian Stranger, are excellent, and I will do as you say.

# BOOK VI.

**ATHENIAN:** And now having made an end of the preliminaries we will proceed to the appointment of magistracies.

**CLEINIAS:** Very good.

**ATHENIAN:** In the ordering of a state there are two parts: first, the number of the magistracies, and the mode of establishing them; and, secondly, when they have been established, laws again will have to be provided for each of them, suitable in nature and number. But before electing the magistrates let us stop a little and say a word in season about the election of them.

**CLEINIAS:** What have you got to say?

**ATHENIAN:** This is what I have to say;--every one can see, that although the work of legislation is a most important matter, yet if a well-ordered city superadd to good laws unsuitable offices, not only will there be no use in having the good laws,--not only will they be ridiculous and useless, but the greatest political injury and evil will accrue from them.

**CLEINIAS:** Of course.

**ATHENIAN:** Then now, my friend, let us observe what will happen in the constitution of out intended state. In the first place, you will acknowledge that those who are duly appointed to magisterial power, and their families, should severally have given satisfactory proof of what they are, from youth upward until the time of election; in the next place, those who are to elect should have been trained in habits of law, and be well educated, that they may have a right judgment, and may be able to select or reject men whom they approve or disapprove, as they are worthy of either. But how can we imagine that those who are brought together for the first time, and are strangers to one another, and also uneducated, will avoid making mistakes in the choice of magistrates?

**CLEINIAS:** Impossible.

**ATHENIAN:** The matter is serious, and excuses will not serve the turn. I will tell you, then, what you and I will have to do, since you, as you tell me, with nine others, have offered to settle the new state on behalf of the people of Crete, and I am to help you by the invention of the present romance. I certainly should not like to leave the tale wandering all over the world without a head;--a headless monster is such a hideous thing.

**CLEINIAS:** Excellent, Stranger.

**ATHENIAN:** Yes; and I will be as good as my word.

**CLEINIAS:** Let us by all means do as you propose.

**ATHENIAN:** That we will, by the grace of God, if old age will only permit us.

**CLEINIAS:** But God will be gracious.

**ATHENIAN:** Yes; and under his guidance let us consider a further point.

**CLEINIAS:** What is it?

**ATHENIAN:** Let us remember what a courageously mad and daring creation this our city is.

**CLEINIAS:** What had you in your mind when you said that?

**ATHENIAN:** I had in my mind the free and easy manner in which we are ordaining that the inexperienced colonists shall receive our laws. Now a man need not be very wise, Cleinias, in order to see that no one can easily receive laws at their first imposition. But if we could anyhow wait until those who have been imbued with them from childhood, and have been nurtured in them, and become habituated to them, take their part in the public elections of the state; I say, if this could be accomplished, and rightly accomplished by any way or contrivance--then, I think that there would be very little danger, at the end of the time, of a state thus trained not being permanent.

**CLEINIAS:** A reasonable supposition.

**ATHENIAN:** Then let us consider if we can find any way out of the difficulty; for I maintain, Cleinias, that the Cnosians, above all the other Cretans, should not be satisfied with barely discharging their duty to the colony, but they ought to take the utmost pains to establish the offices which are first created by them in the best and surest manner. Above all, this applies to the selection of the guardians of the law, who must be chosen first of all, and with the greatest care; the others are of less importance.

**CLEINIAS:** What method can we devise of electing them?

**ATHENIAN:** This will be the method:--Sons of the Cretans, I shall say to them, inasmuch as the Cnosians have precedence over the other states, they should, in common with those who join this settlement, choose a body of thirty-seven in all, nineteen of them being taken from the settlers, and the remainder from the citizens of Cnosus. Of these latter the Cnosians shall make a present to your colony, and you yourself shall be one of the eighteen, and shall become a citizen of the new state; and if you and they cannot be persuaded to go, the Cnosians may fairly use a little violence in order to make you.

**CLEINIAS:** But why, Stranger, do not you and Megillus take a part in our new city?

**ATHENIAN:** O, Cleinias, Athens is proud, and Sparta too; and they are both a long way off. But you and likewise the other colonists are conveniently situated as you describe. I have been speaking of the way in which the new citizens may be best managed under present circumstances; but in after- ages, if the city continues to exist, let the election be on this wise. All who are horse or foot soldiers, or have seen military service at the proper ages when they were severally fitted for it, shall share in the election of magistrates; and the election shall be held in whatever temple the state deems most venerable, and every one shall carry his vote to the altar of the God, writing down on a tablet the name of the person for whom he votes, and his father's name, and his tribe, and ward; and at the side he shall write his own name in like manner. Any one who pleases may take away any tablet which he does not think properly filled up, and exhibit it in the Agora for a period of not less than thirty days. The tablets which are judged to be first, to the number of 300, shall be shown by the magistrates to the whole city, and the citizens shall in like manner select from these the candidates whom they prefer; and this second selection, to the number of 100, shall be again exhibited to the citizens; in the third, let any one who pleases select whom he pleases out of the 100, walking through the parts of victims, and let them choose for magistrates and proclaim the seven-and-thirty who have the greatest number of votes. But who, Cleinias and Megillus, will order for us in the colony all this matter of the magistrates, and the scrutinies of them? If we reflect, we shall see that cities which are in process of construction like ours must have some such persons, who cannot possibly be elected before there are any magistrates; and yet they must be elected in some way, and they are not to be inferior men, but the best possible. For as the proverb says, 'a good beginning is half the business'; and 'to have begun well' is praised by all, and in my opinion is a great deal more than half the business, and has never been praised by any one enough.

**CLEINIAS:** That is very true.

**ATHENIAN:** Then let us recognize the difficulty, and make clear to our own minds how the beginning is to be accomplished. There is only one proposal which I have to offer, and that is one which, under our circumstances, is both necessary and expedient.

**CLEINIAS:** What is it?

**ATHENIAN:** I maintain that this colony of ours has a father and mother, who are no other than the colonizing state. Well I know that many colonies have been, and will be, at enmity with their parents. But in early days the child, as in a family, loves and is beloved; even if there come a time later when the tie is broken, still, while he is in want of education, he naturally loves his parents and is beloved by them, and flies to his relatives for protection, and finds in them his only natural allies in time of need; and this parental feeling already exists in the Cnosians, as is shown by their care of the new city; and there is a similar feeling on the part of the young city towards Cnosus. And I repeat what I was saying--for there is no harm in repeating a good thing--that the Cnosians should take a common interest in all these matters, and choose, as far as they can, the eldest and best of the colonists, to the number of not less than a hundred; and let there be another hundred of the Cnosians themselves. These, I say, on their arrival, should have a joint care that the magistrates should be appointed according to law, and that when they are appointed they should undergo a scrutiny. When this has been effected, the Cnosians shall return home, and the new city do the best she can for her own preservation and happiness. I would have the seven-and-thirty now, and in all future time, chosen to fulfil the following duties:--Let them, in the first place, be the guardians of the law; and, secondly, of the registers in which each one registers before the magistrate the amount of his property, excepting four minae which are allowed to citizens of the first class, three allowed to the second, two to the third, and a single mina to the fourth. And if any one, despising the laws for the sake of gain, be found to possess anything more which has not been registered, let all that he has in excess be confiscated, and let him be liable to a suit which shall be the reverse of honourable or fortunate. And let any one who will, indict him on the charge of loving base gains, and proceed against him before the guardians of the law. And if he be cast, let him lose his share of the public possessions, and when there is any public distribution, let him have nothing but his original lot; and let him be written down a condemned man as long as he lives, in some place in which any one who pleases can read about his offences. The guardian of the law shall not hold office longer than twenty years, and shall not be less than fifty years of age when he is elected; or if he is elected when he is sixty years of age, he shall hold office for ten years only; and upon the same principle, he must not imagine that he will be permitted to hold such an important office as that of guardian of the laws after he is seventy years of age, if he live so long.

These are the three first ordinances about the guardians of the law; as the work of legislation progresses, each law in turn will assign to them their further duties. And now we may proceed in order to speak of the election of other officers; for generals have to be elected, and these again must have their ministers, commanders, and colonels of horse, and commanders of brigades of foot, who would be more rightly called by their popular name of brigadiers. The guardians of the law shall propose as generals men who are natives of the city, and a selection from the candidates proposed shall be made by those who are or have been of the age for military service. And if one who is not proposed is thought by somebody to be better than one who is, let him name whom he prefers in the place of whom, and make oath that he is better, and propose him; and whichever of them is approved by vote shall be admitted to the final selection; and the three who have the greatest number of votes shall be appointed generals, and superintendents of military affairs, after previously undergoing a scrutiny, like the guardians of the law. And let the generals thus elected propose twelve brigadiers, one for each tribe; and there shall be a right of counter-proposal as in the case of the generals, and the voting and decision shall take place in the same way. Until the prytanes and council are elected, the guardians of the law shall convene the assembly in some holy spot which is suitable to the purpose, placing the hoplites by themselves, and the cavalry by themselves, and in a third division all the rest of the army. All are to vote for the generals (and for the colonels of horse), but the brigadiers are to be voted for only by those who carry shields (i.e. the hoplites). Let the body of cavalry choose phylarchs for the generals; but captains of light troops, or archers, or any other division of the army, shall be appointed by the generals for themselves. There only remains the appointment of officers of cavalry: these shall be proposed by the same persons who proposed the generals, and the election and the counter- proposal of other candidates shall be arranged in the same way as in the case of the generals, and let the cavalry vote and the infantry look on at the election; the two who have the greatest number of votes shall be the leaders of all the horse. Disputes about the voting may be raised once or twice; but if the dispute be raised a third time, the officers who preside at the several elections shall decide.

The council shall consist of 30 x 12 members--360 will be a convenient number for sub-division. If we divide the whole number into four parts of ninety each, we get ninety counsellors for each class. First, all the citizens shall select candidates from the first class; they shall be compelled to vote, and, if they do not, shall be duly fined. When the candidates have been selected, some one shall mark them down; this shall be the business of the first day. And on the following day, candidates shall be selected from the second class in the same manner and under the same conditions as on the previous day; and on the third day a selection shall be made from the third class, at which every one may, if he likes vote, and the three first classes shall be compelled to vote; but the fourth and lowest class shall be under no compulsion, and any member of this class who does not vote shall not be punished. On the fourth day candidates shall be selected from the fourth and smallest class; they shall be selected by all, but he who is of the fourth class shall suffer no penalty, nor he who is of the third, if he be not willing to vote; but he who is of the first or second class, if he does not vote shall be punished;--he who is of the second class shall pay a fine of triple the amount which was exacted at first, and he who is of the first class quadruple. On the fifth day the rulers shall bring out the names noted down, for all the citizens to see, and every man shall choose out of them, under pain, if he do not, of suffering the first penalty; and when they have chosen 180 out of each of the classes, they shall choose one-half of them by lot, who shall undergo a scrutiny:--These are to form the council for the year.

The mode of election which has been described is in a mean between monarchy and democracy, and such a mean the state ought always to observe; for servants and masters never can be friends, nor good and bad, merely because they are declared to have equal privileges. For to unequals equals become unequal, if they are not harmonised by measure; and both by reason of equality, and by reason of inequality, cities are filled with seditions. The old saying, that 'equality makes friendship,' is happy and also true; but there is obscurity and confusion as to what sort of equality is meant. For there are two equalities which are called by the same name, but are in reality in many ways almost the opposite of one another; one of them may be introduced without difficulty, by any state or any legislator in the distribution of honours: this is the rule of measure, weight, and number, which regulates and apportions them. But there is another equality, of a better and higher kind, which is not so easily recognized. This is the judgment of Zeus; among men it avails but little; that little, however, is the source of the greatest good to individuals and states. For it gives to the greater more, and to the inferior less and in proportion to the nature of each; and, above all, greater honour always to the greater virtue, and to the less less; and to either in proportion to their respective measure of virtue and education. And this is justice, and is ever the true principle of states, at which we ought to aim, and according to this rule order the new city which is now being founded, and any other city which may be hereafter founded. To this the legislator should look,--not to the interests of tyrants one or more, or to the power of the people, but to justice always; which, as I was saying, is the distribution of natural equality among unequals in each case. But there are times at which every state is compelled to use the words, 'just,' 'equal,' in a secondary sense, in the hope of escaping in some degree from factions. For equity and indulgence are infractions of the perfect and strict rule of justice. And this is the reason why we are obliged to use the equality of the lot, in order to avoid the discontent of the people; and so we invoke God and fortune in our prayers, and beg that they themselves will direct the lot with a view to supreme justice. And therefore, although we are compelled to use both equalities, we should use that into which the element of chance enters as seldom as possible.

Thus, O my friends, and for the reasons given, should a state act which would endure and be saved. But as a ship sailing on the sea has to be watched night and day, in like manner a city also is sailing on a sea of politics, and is liable to all sorts of insidious assaults; and therefore from morning to night, and from night to morning, rulers must join hands with rulers, and watchers with watchers, receiving and giving up their trust in a perpetual succession. Now a multitude can never fulfil a duty of this sort with anything like energy. Moreover, the greater number of the senators will have to be left during the greater part of the year to order their concerns at their own homes. They will therefore have to be arranged in twelve portions, answering to the twelve months, and furnish guardians of the state, each portion for a single month. Their business is to be at hand and receive any foreigner or citizen who comes to them, whether to give information, or to put one of those questions, to which, when asked by other cities, a city should give an answer, and to which, if she ask them herself, she should receive an answer; or again, when there is a likelihood of internal commotions, which are always liable to happen in some form or other, they will, if they can, prevent their occurring; or if they have already occurred, will lose no time in making them known to the city, and healing the evil. Wherefore, also, this which is the presiding body of the state ought always to have the control of their assemblies, and of the dissolutions of them, ordinary as well as extraordinary. All this is to be ordered by the twelfth part of the council, which is always to keep watch together with the other officers of the state during one portion of the year, and to rest during the remaining eleven portions.

Thus will the city be fairly ordered. And now, who is to have the superintendence of the country, and what shall be the arrangement? Seeing that the whole city and the entire country have been both of them divided into twelve portions, ought there not to be appointed superintendents of the streets of the city, and of the houses, and buildings, and harbours, and the agora, and fountains, and sacred domains, and temples, and the like?

**CLEINIAS:** To be sure there ought.

**ATHENIAN:** Let us assume, then, that there ought to be servants of the temples, and priests and priestesses. There must also be superintendents of roads and buildings, who will have a care of men, that they may do no harm, and also of beasts, both within the enclosure and in the suburbs. Three kinds of officers will thus have to be appointed, in order that the city may be suitably provided according to her needs. Those who have the care of the city shall be called wardens of the city; and those who have the care of the agora shall be called wardens of the agora; and those who have the care of the temples shall be called priests. Those who hold hereditary offices as priests or priestesses, shall not be disturbed; but if there be few or none such, as is probable at the foundation of a new city, priests and priestesses shall be appointed to be servants of the Gods who have no servants. Some of our officers shall be elected, and others appointed by lot, those who are of the people and those who are not of the people mingling in a friendly manner in every place and city, that the state may be as far as possible of one mind. The officers of the temples shall be appointed by lot; in this way their election will be committed to God, that He may do what is agreeable to Him. And he who obtains a lot shall undergo a scrutiny, first, as to whether he is sound of body and of legitimate birth; and in the second place, in order to show that he is of a perfectly pure family, not stained with homicide or any similar impiety in his own person, and also that his father and mother have led a similar unstained life. Now the laws about all divine things should be brought from Delphi, and interpreters appointed, under whose direction they should be used. The tenure of the priesthood should always be for a year and no longer; and he who will duly execute the sacred office, according to the laws of religion, must be not less than sixty years of age--the laws shall be the same about priestesses. As for the interpreters, they shall be appointed thus:--Let the twelve tribes be distributed into groups of four, and let each group select four, one out of each tribe within the group, three times; and let the three who have the greatest number of votes (out of the twelve appointed by each group), after undergoing a scrutiny, nine in all, be sent to Delphi, in order that the God may return one out of each triad; their age shall be the same as that of the priests, and the scrutiny of them shall be conducted in the same manner; let them be interpreters for life, and when any one dies let the four tribes select another from the tribe of the deceased. Moreover, besides priests and interpreters, there must be treasurers, who will take charge of the property of the several temples, and of the sacred domains, and shall have authority over the produce and the letting of them; and three of them shall be chosen from the highest classes for the greater temples, and two for the lesser, and one for the least of all; the manner of their election and the scrutiny of them shall be the same as that of the generals. This shall be the order of the temples.

Let everything have a guard as far as possible. Let the defence of the city be commited to the generals, and taxiarchs, and hipparchs, and phylarchs, and prytanes, and the wardens of the city, and of the agora, when the election of them has been completed. The defence of the country shall be provided for as follows:--The entire land has been already distributed into twelve as nearly as possible equal parts, and let the tribe allotted to a division provide annually for it five wardens of the country and commanders of the watch; and let each body of five have the power of selecting twelve others out of the youth of their own tribe,-- these shall be not less than twenty-five years of age, and not more than thirty. And let there be allotted to them severally every month the various districts, in order that they may all acquire knowledge and experience of the whole country. The term of service for commanders and for watchers shall continue during two years. After having had their stations allotted to them, they will go from place to place in regular order, making their round from left to right as their commanders direct them; (when I speak of going to the right, I mean that they are to go to the east). And at the commencement of the second year, in order that as many as possible of the guards may not only get a knowledge of the country at any one season of the year, but may also have experience of the manner in which different places are affected at different seasons of the year, their then commanders shall lead them again towards the left, from place to place in succession, until they have completed the second year. In the third year other wardens of the country shall be chosen and commanders of the watch, five for each division, who are to be the superintendents of the bands of twelve. While on service at each station, their attention shall be directed to the following points:--In the first place, they shall see that the country is well protected against enemies; they shall trench and dig wherever this is required, and, as far as they can, they shall by fortifications keep off the evil-disposed, in order to prevent them from doing any harm to the country or the property; they shall use the beasts of burden and the labourers whom they find on the spot these will be their instruments whom they will superintend, taking them, as far as possible, at the times when they are not engaged in their regular business. They shall make every part of the country inaccessible to enemies, and as accessible as possible to friends; there shall be ways for man and beasts of burden and for cattle, and they shall take care to have them always as smooth as they can; and shall provide against the rains doing harm instead of good to the land, when they come down from the mountains into the hollow dells; and shall keep in the overflow by the help of works and ditches, in order that the valleys, receiving and drinking up the rain from heaven, and providing fountains and streams in the fields and regions which lie underneath, may furnish even to the dry places plenty of good water. The fountains of water, whether of rivers or of springs, shall be ornamented with plantations and buildings for beauty; and let them bring together the streams in subterraneous channels, and make all things plenteous; and if there be a sacred grove or dedicated precinct in the neighbourhood, they shall conduct the water to the actual temples of the Gods, and so beautify them at all seasons of the year. Everywhere in such places the youth shall make gymnasia for themselves, and warm baths for the aged, placing by them abundance of dry wood, for the benefit of those labouring under disease--there the weary frame of the rustic, worn with toil, will receive a kindly welcome, far better than he would at the hands of a not over-wise doctor.

The building of these and the like works will be useful and ornamental; they will provide a pleasing amusement, but they will be a serious employment too; for the sixty wardens will have to guard their several divisions, not only with a view to enemies, but also with an eye to professing friends. When a quarrel arises among neighbours or citizens, and any one whether slave or freeman wrongs another, let the five wardens decide small matters on their own authority; but where the charge against another relates to greater matters, the seventeen composed of the fives and twelves, shall determine any charges which one man brings against another, not involving more than three minae. Every judge and magistrate shall be liable to give an account of his conduct in office, except those who, like kings, have the final decision. Moreover, as regards the aforesaid wardens of the country, if they do any wrong to those of whom they have the care, whether by imposing upon them unequal tasks, or by taking the produce of the soil or implements of husbandry without their consent; also if they receive anything in the way of a bribe, or decide suits unjustly, or if they yield to the influences of flattery, let them be publicly dishonoured; and in regard to any other wrong which they do to the inhabitants of the country, if the question be of a mina, let them submit to the decision of the villagers in the neighbourhood; but in suits of greater amount, or in case of lesser, if they refuse to submit, trusting that their monthly removal into another part of the country will enable them to escape--in such cases the injured party may bring his suit in the common court, and if he obtain a verdict he may exact from the defendant, who refused to submit, a double penalty.

The wardens and the overseers of the country, while on their two years' service, shall have common meals at their several stations, and shall all live together; and he who is absent from the common meal, or sleeps out, if only for one day or night, unless by order of his commanders, or by reason of absolute necessity, if the five denounce him and inscribe his name in the agora as not having kept his guard, let him be deemed to have betrayed the city, as far as lay in his power, and let him be disgraced and beaten with impunity by any one who meets him and is willing to punish him. If any of the commanders is guilty of such an irregularity, the whole company of sixty shall see to it, and he who is cognisant of the offence, and does not bring the offender to trial, shall be amenable to the same laws as the younger offender himself, and shall pay a heavier fine, and be incapable of ever commanding the young. The guardians of the law are to be careful inspectors of these matters, and shall either prevent or punish offenders. Every man should remember the universal rule, that he who is not a good servant will not be a good master; a man should pride himself more upon serving well than upon commanding well: first upon serving the laws, which is also the service of the Gods; in the second place, upon having served ancient and honourable men in the days of his youth. Furthermore, during the two years in which any one is a warden of the country, his daily food ought to be of a simple and humble kind. When the twelve have been chosen, let them and the five meet together, and determine that they will be their own servants, and, like servants, will not have other slaves and servants for their own use, neither will they use those of the villagers and husbandmen for their private advantage, but for the public service only; and in general they should make up their minds to live independently by themselves, servants of each other and of themselves. Further, at all seasons of the year, summer and winter alike, let them be under arms and survey minutely the whole country; thus they will at once keep guard, and at the same time acquire a perfect knowledge of every locality. There can be no more important kind of information than the exact knowledge of a man's own country; and for this as well as for more general reasons of pleasure and advantage, hunting with dogs and other kinds of sports should be pursued by the young. The service to whom this is committed may be called the secret police or wardens of the country; the name does not much signify, but every one who has the safety of the state at heart will use his utmost diligence in this service.

After the wardens of the country, we have to speak of the election of wardens of the agora and of the city. The wardens of the country were sixty in number, and the wardens of the city will be three, and will divide the twelve parts of the city into three; like the former, they shall have care of the ways, and of the different high roads which lead out of the country into the city, and of the buildings, that they may be all made according to law;--also of the waters, which the guardians of the supply preserve and convey to them, care being taken that they may reach the fountains pure and abundant, and be both an ornament and a benefit to the city. These also should be men of influence, and at leisure to take care of the public interest. Let every man propose as warden of the city any one whom he likes out of the highest class, and when the vote has been given on them, and the number is reduced to the six who have the greatest number of votes, let the electing officers choose by lot three out of the six, and when they have undergone a scrutiny let them hold office according to the laws laid down for them. Next, let the wardens of the agora be elected in like manner, out of the first and second class, five in number: ten are to be first elected, and out of the ten five are to be chosen by lot, as in the election of the wardens of the city:--these when they have undergone a scrutiny are to be declared magistrates. Every one shall vote for every one, and he who will not vote, if he be informed against before the magistrates, shall be fined fifty drachmae, and shall also be deemed a bad citizen. Let any one who likes go to the assembly and to the general council; it shall be compulsory to go on citizens of the first and second class, and they shall pay a fine of ten drachmae if they be found not answering to their names at the assembly. But the third and fourth class shall be under no compulsion, and shall be let off without a fine, unless the magistrates have commanded all to be present, in consequence of some urgent necessity. The wardens of the agora shall observe the order appointed by law for the agora, and shall have the charge of the temples and fountains which are in the agora; and they shall see that no one injures anything, and punish him who does, with stripes and bonds, if he be a slave or stranger; but if he be a citizen who misbehaves in this way, they shall have the power themselves of inflicting a fine upon him to the amount of a hundred drachmae, or with the consent of the wardens of the city up to double that amount. And let the wardens of the city have a similar power of imposing punishments and fines in their own department; and let them impose fines by their own department; and let them impose fines by their own authority, up to a mina, or up to two minae with the consent of the wardens of the agora.

In the next place, it will be proper to appoint directors of music and gymnastic, two kinds of each--of the one kind the business will be education, of the other, the superintendence of contests. In speaking of education, the law means to speak of those who have the care of order and instruction in gymnasia and schools, and of the going to school, and of school buildings for boys and girls; and in speaking of contests, the law refers to the judges of gymnastics and of music; these again are divided into two classes, the one having to do with music, the other with gymnastics; and the same who judge of the gymnastic contests of men, shall judge of horses; but in music there shall be one set of judges of solo singing, and of imitation--I mean of rhapsodists, players on the harp, the flute and the like, and another who shall judge of choral song. First of all, we must choose directors for the choruses of boys, and men, and maidens, whom they shall follow in the amusement of the dance, and for our other musical arrangements;--one director will be enough for the choruses, and he should be not less than forty years of age. One director will also be enough to introduce the solo singers, and to give judgment on the competitors, and he ought not to be less than thirty years of age. The director and manager of the choruses shall be elected after the following manner:--Let any persons who commonly take an interest in such matters go to the meeting, and be fined if they do not go (the guardians of the law shall judge of their fault), but those who have no interest shall not be compelled. The elector shall propose as director some one who understands music, and he in the scrutiny may be challenged on the one part by those who say he has no skill, and defended on the other hand by those who say that he has. Ten are to be elected by vote, and he of the ten who is chosen by lot shall undergo a scrutiny, and lead the choruses for a year according to law. And in like manner the competitor who wins the lot shall be leader of the solo and concert music for that year; and he who is thus elected shall deliver the award to the judges. In the next place, we have to choose judges in the contests of horses and of men; these shall be selected from the third and also from the second class of citizens, and three first classes shall be compelled to go to the election, but the lowest may stay away with impunity; and let there be three elected by lot out of the twenty who have been chosen previously, and they must also have the vote and approval of the examiners. But if any one is rejected in the scrutiny at any ballot or decision, others shall be chosen in the same manner, and undergo a similar scrutiny.

There remains the minister of the education of youth, male and female; he too will rule according to law; one such minister will be sufficient, and he must be fifty years old, and have children lawfully begotten, both boys and girls by preference, at any rate, one or the other. He who is elected, and he who is the elector, should consider that of all the great offices of state this is the greatest; for the first shoot of any plant, if it makes a good start towards the attainment of its natural excellence, has the greatest effect on its maturity; and this is not only true of plants, but of animals wild and tame, and also of men. Man, as we say, is a tame or civilized animal; nevertheless, he requires proper instruction and a fortunate nature, and then of all animals he becomes the most divine and most civilized; but if he be insufficiently or ill educated he is the most savage of earthly creatures. Wherefore the legislator ought not to allow the education of children to become a secondary or accidental matter. In the first place, he who would be rightly provident about them, should begin by taking care that he is elected, who of all the citizens is in every way best; him the legislator shall do his utmost to appoint guardian and superintendent. To this end all the magistrates, with the exception of the council and prytanes, shall go to the temple of Apollo, and elect by ballot him of the guardians of the law whom they severally think will be the best superintendent of education. And he who has the greatest number of votes, after he has undergone a scrutiny at the hands of all the magistrates who have been his electors, with the exception of the guardians of the law,--shall hold office for five years; and in the sixth year let another be chosen in like manner to fill his office.

If any one dies while he is holding a public office, and more than thirty days before his term of office expires, let those whose business it is elect another to the office in the same manner as before. And if any one who is entrusted with orphans dies, let the relations both on the father's and mother's side, who are residing at home, including cousins, appoint another guardian within ten days, or be fined a drachma a day for neglect to do so.

A city which has no regular courts of law ceases to be a city; and again, if a judge is silent and says no more in preliminary proceedings than the litigants, as is the case in arbitrations, he will never be able to decide justly; wherefore a multitude of judges will not easily judge well, nor a few if they are bad. The point in dispute between the parties should be made clear; and time, and deliberation, and repeated examination, greatly tend to clear up doubts. For this reason, he who goes to law with another, should go first of all to his neighbours and friends who know best the questions at issue. And if he be unable to obtain from them a satisfactory decision, let him have recourse to another court; and if the two courts cannot settle the matter, let a third put an end to the suit.

Now the establishment of courts of justice may be regarded as a choice of magistrates, for every magistrate must also be a judge of some things; and the judge, though he be not a magistrate, yet in certain respects is a very important magistrate on the day on which he is determining a suit. Regarding then the judges also as magistrates, let us say who are fit to be judges, and of what they are to be judges, and how many of them are to judge in each suit. Let that be the supreme tribunal which the litigants appoint in common for themselves, choosing certain persons by agreement. And let there be two other tribunals: one for private causes, when a citizen accuses another of wronging him and wishes to get a decision; the other for public causes, in which some citizen is of opinion that the public has been wronged by an individual, and is willing to vindicate the common interests. And we must not forget to mention how the judges are to be qualified, and who they are to be. In the first place, let there be a tribunal open to all private persons who are trying causes one against another for the third time, and let this be composed as follows:--All the officers of state, as well annual as those holding office for a longer period, when the new year is about to commence, in the month following after the summer solstice, on the last day but one of the year, shall meet in some temple, and calling God to witness, shall dedicate one judge from every magistracy to be their first-fruits, choosing in each office him who seems to them to be the best, and whom they deem likely to decide the causes of his fellow-citizens during the ensuing year in the best and holiest manner. And when the election is completed, a scrutiny shall be held in the presence of the electors themselves, and if any one be rejected another shall be chosen in the same manner. Those who have undergone the scrutiny shall judge the causes of those who have declined the inferior courts, and shall give their vote openly. The councillors and other magistrates who have elected them shall be required to be hearers and spectators of the causes; and any one else may be present who pleases. If one man charges another with having intentionally decided wrong, let him go to the guardians of the law and lay his accusation before them, and he who is found guilty in such a case shall pay damages to the injured party equal to half the injury; but if he shall appear to deserve a greater penalty, the judges shall determine what additional punishment he shall suffer, and how much more he ought to pay to the public treasury, and to the party who brought the suit.

In the judgment of offences against the state, the people ought to participate, for when any one wrongs the state all are wronged, and may reasonably complain if they are not allowed to share in the decision. Such causes ought to originate with the people, and the ought also to have the final decision of them, but the trial of them shall take place before three of the highest magistrates, upon whom the plaintiff and the defendant shall agree; and if they are not able to come to an agreement themselves, the council shall choose one of the two proposed. And in private suits, too, as far as is possible, all should have a share; for he who has no share in the administration of justice, is apt to imagine that he has no share in the state at all. And for this reason there shall be a court of law in every tribe, and the judges shall be chosen by lot;--they shall give their decisions at once, and shall be inaccessible to entreaties. The final judgment shall rest with that court which, as we maintain, has been established in the most incorruptible form of which human things admit: this shall be the court established for those who are unable to get rid of their suits either in the courts of neighbours or of the tribes.

Thus much of the courts of law, which, as I was saying, cannot be precisely defined either as being or not being offices; a superficial sketch has been given of them, in which some things have been told and others omitted. For the right place of an exact statement of the laws respecting suits, under their several heads, will be at the end of the body of legislation;--let us then expect them at the end. Hitherto our legislation has been chiefly occupied with the appointment of offices. Perfect unity and exactness, extending to the whole and every particular of political administration, cannot be attained to the full, until the discussion shall have a beginning, middle, and end, and is complete in every part. At present we have reached the election of magistrates, and this may be regarded as a sufficient termination of what preceded. And now there need no longer be any delay or hesitation in beginning the work of legislation.

**CLEINIAS:** I like what you have said, Stranger; and I particularly like your manner of tacking on the beginning of your new discourse to the end of the former one.

**ATHENIAN:** Thus far, then, the old men's rational pastime has gone off well.

**CLEINIAS:** You mean, I suppose, their serious and noble pursuit?

**ATHENIAN:** Perhaps; but I should like to know whether you and I are agreed about a certain thing.

**CLEINIAS:** About what thing?

**ATHENIAN:** You know the endless labour which painters expend upon their pictures--they are always putting in or taking out colours, or whatever be the term which artists employ; they seem as if they would never cease touching up their works, which are always being made brighter and more beautiful.

**CLEINIAS:** I know something of these matters from report, although I have never had any great acquaintance with the art.

**ATHENIAN:** No matter; we may make use of the illustration notwithstanding: --Suppose that some one had a mind to paint a figure in the most beautiful manner, in the hope that his work instead of losing would always improve as time went on--do you not see that being a mortal, unless he leaves some one to succeed him who will correct the flaws which time may introduce, and be able to add what is left imperfect through the defect of the artist, and who will further brighten up and improve the picture, all his great labour will last but a short time?

**CLEINIAS:** True.

**ATHENIAN:** And is not the aim of the legislator similar? First, he desires that his laws should be written down with all possible exactness; in the second place, as time goes on and he has made an actual trial of his decrees, will he not find omissions? Do you imagine that there ever was a legislator so foolish as not to know that many things are necessarily omitted, which some one coming after him must correct, if the constitution and the order of government is not to deteriorate, but to improve in the state which he has established?

**CLEINIAS:** Assuredly, that is the sort of thing which every one would desire.

**ATHENIAN:** And if any one possesses any means of accomplishing this by word or deed, or has any way great or small by which he can teach a person to understand how he can maintain and amend the laws, he should finish what he has to say, and not leave the work incomplete.

**CLEINIAS:** By all means.

**ATHENIAN:** And is not this what you and I have to do at the present moment?

**CLEINIAS:** What have we to do?

**ATHENIAN:** As we are about to legislate and have chosen our guardians of the law, and are ourselves in the evening of life, and they as compared with us are young men, we ought not only to legislate for them, but to endeavour to make them not only guardians of the law but legislators themselves, as far as this is possible.

**CLEINIAS:** Certainly; if we can.

**ATHENIAN:** At any rate, we must do our best.

**CLEINIAS:** Of course.

**ATHENIAN:** We will say to them--O friends and saviours of our laws, in laying down any law, there are many particulars which we shall omit, and this cannot be helped; at the same time, we will do our utmost to describe what is important, and will give an outline which you shall fill up. And I will explain on what principle you are to act. Megillus and Cleinias and I have often spoken to one another touching these matters, and we are of opinion that we have spoken well. And we hope that you will be of the same mind with us, and become our disciples, and keep in view the things which in our united opinion the legislator and guardian of the law ought to keep in view. There was one main point about which we were agreed--that a man's whole energies throughout life should be devoted to the acquisition of the virtue proper to a man, whether this was to be gained by study, or habit, or some mode of acquisition, or desire, or opinion, or knowledge--and this applies equally to men and women, old and young--the aim of all should always be such as I have described; anything which may be an impediment, the good man ought to show that he utterly disregards. And if at last necessity plainly compels him to be an outlaw from his native land, rather than bow his neck to the yoke of slavery and be ruled by inferiors, and he has to fly, an exile he must be and endure all such trials, rather than accept another form of government, which is likely to make men worse. These are our original principles; and do you now, fixing your eyes upon the standard of what a man and a citizen ought or ought not to be, praise and blame the laws--blame those which have not this power of making the citizen better, but embrace those which have; and with gladness receive and live in them; bidding a long farewell to other institutions which aim at goods, as they are termed, of a different kind.

Let us proceed to another class of laws, beginning with their foundation in religion. And we must first return to the number 5040--the entire number had, and has, a great many convenient divisions, and the number of the tribes which was a twelfth part of the whole, being correctly formed by 21 x 20 (5040/(21 x 20), i.e., 5040/420 = 12), also has them. And not only is the whole number divisible by twelve, but also the number of each tribe is divisible by twelve. Now every portion should be regarded by us as a sacred gift of Heaven, corresponding to the months and to the revolution of the universe. Every city has a guiding and sacred principle given by nature, but in some the division or distribution has been more right than in others, and has been more sacred and fortunate. In our opinion, nothing can be more right than the selection of the number 5040, which may be divided by all numbers from one to twelve with the single exception of eleven, and that admits of a very easy correction; for if, turning to the dividend (5040), we deduct two families, the defect in the division is cured. And the truth of this may be easily proved when we have leisure. But for the present, trusting to the mere assertion of this principle, let us divide the state; and assigning to each portion some God or son of a God, let us give them altars and sacred rites, and at the altars let us hold assemblies for sacrifice twice in the month--twelve assemblies for the tribes, and twelve for the city, according to their divisions; the first in honour of the Gods and divine things, and the second to promote friendship and 'better acquaintance,' as the phrase is, and every sort of good fellowship with one another. For people must be acquainted with those into whose families and whom they marry and with those to whom they give in marriage; in such matters, as far as possible, a man should deem it all important to avoid a mistake, and with this serious purpose let games be instituted in which youths and maidens shall dance together, seeing one another and being seen naked, at a proper age, and on a suitable occasion, not transgressing the rules of modesty.

The directors of choruses will be the superintendents and regulators of these games, and they, together with the guardians of the law, will legislate in any matters which we have omitted; for, as we said, where there are numerous and minute details, the legislator must leave out something. And the annual officers who have experience, and know what is wanted, must make arrangements and improvements year by year, until such enactments and provisions are sufficiently determined. A ten years' experience of sacrifices and dances, if extending to all particulars, will be quite sufficient; and if the legislator be alive they shall communicate with him, but if he be dead then the several officers shall refer the omissions which come under their notice to the guardians of the law, and correct them, until all is perfect; and from that time there shall be no more change, and they shall establish and use the new laws with the others which the legislator originally gave them, and of which they are never, if they can help, to change aught; or, if some necessity overtakes them, the magistrates must be called into counsel, and the whole people, and they must go to all the oracles of the Gods; and if they are all agreed, in that case they may make the change, but if they are not agreed, by no manner of means, and any one who dissents shall prevail, as the law ordains.

Whenever any one over twenty-five years of age, having seen and been seen by others, believes himself to have found a marriage connexion which is to his mind, and suitable for the procreation of children, let him marry if he be still under the age of five-and-thirty years; but let him first hear how he ought to seek after what is suitable and appropriate. For, as Cleinias says, every law should have a suitable prelude.

**CLEINIAS:** You recollect at the right moment, Stranger, and do not miss the opportunity which the argument affords of saying a word in season.

**ATHENIAN:** I thank you. We will say to him who is born of good parents--O my son, you ought to make such a marriage as wise men would approve. Now they would advise you neither to avoid a poor marriage, nor specially to desire a rich one; but if other things are equal, always to honour inferiors, and with them to form connexions;--this will be for the benefit of the city and of the families which are united; for the equable and symmetrical tends infinitely more to virtue than the unmixed. And he who is conscious of being too headstrong, and carried away more than is fitting in all his actions, ought to desire to become the relation of orderly parents; and he who is of the opposite temper ought to seek the opposite alliance. Let there be one word concerning all marriages:--Every man shall follow, not after the marriage which is most pleasing to himself, but after that which is most beneficial to the state. For somehow every one is by nature prone to that which is likest to himself, and in this way the whole city becomes unequal in property and in disposition; and hence there arise in most states the very results which we least desire to happen. Now, to add to the law an express provision, not only that the rich man shall not marry into the rich family, nor the powerful into the family of the powerful, but that the slower natures shall be compelled to enter into marriage with the quicker, and the quicker with the slower, may awaken anger as well as laughter in the minds of many; for there is a difficulty in perceiving that the city ought to be well mingled like a cup, in which the maddening wine is hot and fiery, but when chastened by a soberer God, receives a fair associate and becomes an excellent and temperate drink. Yet in marriage no one is able to see that the same result occurs. Wherefore also the law must let alone such matters, but we should try to charm the spirits of men into believing the equability of their children's disposition to be of more importance than equality in excessive fortune when they marry; and him who is too desirous of making a rich marriage we should endeavour to turn aside by reproaches, not, however, by any compulsion of written law.

Let this then be our exhortation concerning marriage, and let us remember what was said before--that a man should cling to immortality, and leave behind him children's children to be the servants of God in his place for ever. All this and much more may be truly said by way of prelude about the duty of marriage. But if a man will not listen, and remains unsocial and alien among his fellow-citizens, and is still unmarried at thirty-five years of age, let him pay a yearly fine;--he who of the highest class shall pay a fine of a hundred drachmae, and he who is of the second class a fine of seventy drachmae; the third class shall pay sixty drachmae, and the fourth thirty drachmae, and let the money be sacred to Here; he who does not pay the fine annually shall owe ten times the sum, which the treasurer of the goddess shall exact; and if he fails in doing so, let him be answerable and give an account of the money at his audit. He who refuses to marry shall be thus punished in money, and also be deprived of all honour which the younger show to the elder; let no young man voluntarily obey him, and, if he attempt to punish any one, let every one come to the rescue and defend the injured person, and he who is present and does not come to the rescue, shall be pronounced by the law to be a coward and a bad citizen. Of the marriage portion I have already spoken; and again I say for the instruction of poor men that he who neither gives nor receives a dowry on account of poverty, has a compensation; for the citizens of our state are provided with the necessaries of life, and wives will be less likely to be insolent, and husbands to be mean and subservient to them on account of property. And he who obeys this law will do a noble action; but he who will not obey, and gives or receives more than fifty drachmae as the price of the marriage garments if he be of the lowest, or more than a mina, or a mina-and-a-half, if he be of the third or second classes, or two minae if he be of the highest class, shall owe to the public treasury a similar sum, and that which is given or received shall be sacred to Here and Zeus; and let the treasurers of these Gods exact the money, as was said before about the unmarried--that the treasurers of Here were to exact the money, or pay the fine themselves.

The betrothal by a father shall be valid in the first degree, that by a grandfather in the second degree, and in the third degree, betrothal by brothers who have the same father; but if there are none of these alive, the betrothal by a mother shall be valid in like manner; in cases of unexampled fatality, the next of kin and the guardians shall have authority. What are to be the rites before marriages, or any other sacred acts, relating either to future, present, or past marriages, shall be referred to the interpreters; and he who follows their advice may be satisfied. Touching the marriage festival, they shall assemble not more than five male and five female friends of both families; and a like number of members of the family of either sex, and no man shall spend more than his means will allow; he who is of the richest class may spend a mina,--he who is of the second, half a mina, and in the same proportion as the census of each decreases: all men shall praise him who is obedient to the law; but he who is disobedient shall be punished by the guardians of the law as a man wanting in true taste, and uninstructed in the laws of bridal song. Drunkenness is always improper, except at the festivals of the God who gave wine; and peculiarly dangerous, when a man is engaged in the business of marriage; at such a crisis of their lives a bride and bridegroom ought to have all their wits about them--they ought to take care that their offspring may be born of reasonable beings; for on what day or night Heaven will give them increase, who can say? Moreover, they ought not to begetting children when their bodies are dissipated by intoxication, but their offspring should be compact and solid, quiet and compounded properly; whereas the drunkard is all abroad in all his actions, and beside himself both in body and soul. Wherefore, also, the drunken man is bad and unsteady in sowing the seed of increase, and is likely to beget offspring who will be unstable and untrustworthy, and cannot be expected to walk straight either in body or mind. Hence during the whole year and all his life long, and especially while he is begetting children, he ought to take care and not intentionally do what is injurious to health, or what involves insolence and wrong; for he cannot help leaving the impression of himself on the souls and bodies of his offspring, and he begets children in every way inferior. And especially on the day and night of marriage should a man abstain from such things. For the beginning, which is also a God dwelling in man, preserves all things, if it meet with proper respect from each individual. He who marries is further to consider, that one of the two houses in the lot is the nest and nursery of his young, and there he is to marry and make a home for himself and bring up his children, going away from his father and mother. For in friendships there must be some degree of desire, in order to cement and bind together diversities of character; but excessive intercourse not having the desire which is created by time, insensibly dissolves friendships from a feeling of satiety; wherefore a man and his wife shall leave to his and her father and mother their own dwelling-places, and themselves go as to a colony and dwell there, and visit and be visited by their parents; and they shall beget and bring up children, handing on the torch of life from one generation to another, and worshipping the Gods according to law for ever.

In the next place, we have to consider what sort of property will be most convenient. There is no difficulty either in understanding or acquiring most kinds of property, but there is great difficulty in what relates to slaves. And the reason is, that we speak about them in a way which is right and which is not right; for what we say about our slaves is consistent and also inconsistent with our practice about them.

**MEGILLUS:** I do not understand, Stranger, what you mean.

**ATHENIAN:** I am not surprised, Megillus, for the state of the Helots among the Lacedaemonians is of all Hellenic forms of slavery the most controverted and disputed about, some approving and some condemning it; there is less dispute about the slavery which exists among the Heracleots, who have subjugated the Mariandynians, and about the Thessalian Penestae. Looking at these and the like examples, what ought we to do concerning property in slaves? I made a remark, in passing, which naturally elicited a question about my meaning from you. It was this:--We know that all would agree that we should have the best and most attached slaves whom we can get. For many a man has found his slaves better in every way than brethren or sons, and many times they have saved the lives and property of their masters and their whole house--such tales are well known.

**MEGILLUS:** To be sure.

**ATHENIAN:** But may we not also say that the soul of the slave is utterly corrupt, and that no man of sense ought to trust them? And the wisest of our poets, speaking of Zeus, says:

*'Far-seeing Zeus takes away half the understanding of men whom the day of slavery subdues.'*

Different persons have got these two different notions of slaves in their minds--some of them utterly distrust their servants, and, as if they were wild beasts, chastise them with goads and whips, and make their souls three times, or rather many times, as slavish as they were before;--and others do just the opposite.

**MEGILLUS:** True.

**CLEINIAS:** Then what are we to do in our own country, Stranger, seeing that there are such differences in the treatment of slaves by their owners?

**ATHENIAN:** Well, Cleinias, there can be no doubt that man is a troublesome animal, and therefore he is not very manageable, nor likely to become so, when you attempt to introduce the necessary division of slave, and freeman, and master.

**CLEINIAS:** That is obvious.

**ATHENIAN:** He is a troublesome piece of goods, as has been often shown by the frequent revolts of the Messenians, and the great mischiefs which happen in states having many slaves who speak the same language, and the numerous robberies and lawless life of the Italian banditti, as they are called. A man who considers all this is fairly at a loss. Two remedies alone remain to us,--not to have the slaves of the same country, nor if possible, speaking the same language; in this way they will more easily be held in subjection: secondly, we should tend them carefully, not only out of regard to them, but yet more out of respect to ourselves. And the right treatment of slaves is to behave properly to them, and to do to them, if possible, even more justice than to those who are our equals; for he who naturally and genuinely reverences justice, and hates injustice, is discovered in his dealings with any class of men to whom he can easily be unjust. And he who in regard to the natures and actions of his slaves is undefiled by impiety and injustice, will best sow the seeds of virtue in them; and this may be truly said of every master, and tyrant, and of every other having authority in relation to his inferiors. Slaves ought to be punished as they deserve, and not admonished as if they were freemen, which will only make them conceited. The language used to a servant ought always to be that of a command and we ought not to jest with them, whether they are males or females--this is a foolish way which many people have of setting up their slaves, and making the life of servitude more disagreeable both for them and for their masters.

**CLEINIAS:** True.

**ATHENIAN:** Now that each of the citizens is provided, as far as possible, with a sufficient number of suitable slaves who can help him in what he has to do, we may next proceed to describe their dwellings.

**CLEINIAS:** Very good.

**ATHENIAN:** The city being new and hitherto uninhabited, care ought to be taken of all the buildings, and the manner of building each of them, and also of the temples and walls. These, Cleinias, were matters which properly came before the marriages;--but, as we are only talking, there is no objection to changing the order. If, however, our plan of legislation is ever to take effect, then the house shall precede the marriage if God so will, and afterwards we will come to the regulations about marriage; but at present we are only describing these matters in a general outline.

**CLEINIAS:** Quite true.

**ATHENIAN:** The temples are to be placed all round the agora, and the whole city built on the heights in a circle, for the sake of defence and for the sake of purity. Near the temples are to be placed buildings for the magistrates and the courts of law; in these plaintiff and defendant will receive their due, and the places will be regarded as most holy, partly because they have to do with holy things: and partly because they are the dwelling-places of holy Gods: and in them will be held the courts in which cases of homicide and other trials of capital offences may fitly take place. As to the walls, Megillus, I agree with Sparta in thinking that they should be allowed to sleep in the earth, and that we should not attempt to disinter them; there is a poetical saying, which is finely expressed, that 'walls ought to be of steel and iron, and not of earth;' besides, how ridiculous of us to be sending out our young men annually into the country to dig and to trench, and to keep off the enemy by fortifications, under the idea that they are not to be allowed to set foot in our territory, and then, that we should surround ourselves with a wall, which, in the first place, is by no means conducive to the health of cities, and is also apt to produce a certain effeminacy in the minds of the inhabitants, inviting men to run thither instead of repelling their enemies, and leading them to imagine that their safety is due not to their keeping guard day and night, but that when they are protected by walls and gates, then they may sleep in safety; as if they were not meant to labour, and did not know that true repose comes from labour, and that disgraceful indolence and a careless temper of mind is only the renewal of trouble. But if men must have walls, the private houses ought to be so arranged from the first that the whole city may be one wall, having all the houses capable of defence by reason of their uniformity and equality towards the streets. The form of the city being that of a single dwelling will have an agreeable aspect, and being easily guarded will be infinitely better for security. Until the original building is completed, these should be the principal objects of the inhabitants; and the wardens of the city should superintend the work, and should impose a fine on him who is negligent; and in all that relates to the city they should have a care of cleanliness, and not allow a private person to encroach upon any public property either by buildings or excavations. Further, they ought to take care that the rains from heaven flow off easily, and of any other matters which may have to be administered either within or without the city. The guardians of the law shall pass any further enactments which their experience may show to be necessary, and supply any other points in which the law may be deficient. And now that these matters, and the buildings about the agora, and the gymnasia, and places of instruction, and theatres, are all ready and waiting for scholars and spectators, let us proceed to the subjects which follow marriage in the order of legislation.

**CLEINIAS:** By all means.

**ATHENIAN:** Assuming that marriages exist already, Cleinias, the mode of life during the year after marriage, before children are born, will follow next in order. In what way bride and bridegroom ought to live in a city which is to be superior to other cities, is a matter not at all easy for us to determine. There have been many difficulties already, but this will be the greatest of them, and the most disagreeable to the many. Still I cannot but say what appears to me to be right and true, Cleinias.

**CLEINIAS:** Certainly.

**ATHENIAN:** He who imagines that he can give laws for the public conduct of states, while he leaves the private life of citizens wholly to take care of itself; who thinks that individuals may pass the day as they please, and that there is no necessity of order in all things; he, I say, who gives up the control of their private lives, and supposes that they will conform to law in their common and public life, is making a great mistake. Why have I made this remark? Why, because I am going to enact that the bridegrooms should live at the common tables, just as they did before marriage. This was a singularity when first enacted by the legislator in your parts of the world, Megillus and Cleinias, as I should suppose, on the occasion of some war or other similar danger, which caused the passing of the law, and which would be likely to occur in thinly-peopled places, and in times of pressure. But when men had once tried and been accustomed to a common table, experience showed that the institution greatly conduced to security; and in some such manner the custom of having common tables arose among you.

**CLEINIAS:** Likely enough.

**ATHENIAN:** I said that there may have been singularity and danger in imposing such a custom at first, but that now there is not the same difficulty. There is, however, another institution which is the natural sequel to this, and would be excellent, if it existed anywhere, but at present it does not. The institution of which I am about to speak is not easily described or executed; and would be like the legislator 'combing wool into the fire,' as people say, or performing any other impossible and useless feat.

**CLEINIAS:** What is the cause, Stranger, of this extreme hesitation?

**ATHENIAN:** You shall hear without any fruitless loss of time. That which has law and order in a state is the cause of every good, but that which is disordered or ill-ordered is often the ruin of that which is well-ordered; and at this point the argument is now waiting. For with you, Cleinias and Megillus, the common tables of men are, as I said, a heaven-born and admirable institution, but you are mistaken in leaving the women unregulated by law. They have no similar institution of public tables in the light of day, and just that part of the human race which is by nature prone to secrecy and stealth on account of their weakness--I mean the female sex--has been left without regulation by the legislator, which is a great mistake. And, in consequence of this neglect, many things have grown lax among you, which might have been far better, if they had been only regulated by law; for the neglect of regulations about women may not only be regarded as a neglect of half the entire matter, but in proportion as woman's nature is inferior to that of men in capacity for virtue, in that degree the consequence of such neglect is more than twice as important. The careful consideration of this matter, and the arranging and ordering on a common principle of all our institutions relating both to men and women, greatly conduces to the happiness of the state. But at present, such is the unfortunate condition of mankind, that no man of sense will even venture to speak of common tables in places and cities in which they have never been established at all; and how can any one avoid being utterly ridiculous, who attempts to compel women to show in public how much they eat and drink? There is nothing at which the sex is more likely to take offence. For women are accustomed to creep into dark places, and when dragged out into the light they will exert their utmost powers of resistance, and be far too much for the legislator. And therefore, as I said before, in most places they will not endure to have the truth spoken without raising a tremendous outcry, but in this state perhaps they may. And if we may assume that our whole discussion about the state has not been mere idle talk, I should like to prove to you, if you will consent to listen, that this institution is good and proper; but if you had rather not, I will refrain.

**CLEINIAS:** There is nothing which we should both of us like better, Stranger, than to hear what you have to say.

**ATHENIAN:** Very good; and you must not be surprised if I go back a little, for we have plenty of leisure, and there is nothing to prevent us from considering in every point of view the subject of law.

**CLEINIAS:** True.

**ATHENIAN:** Then let us return once more to what we were saying at first. Every man should understand that the human race either had no beginning at all, and will never have an end, but always will be and has been; or that it began an immense while ago.

**CLEINIAS:** Certainly.

**ATHENIAN:** Well, and have there not been constitutions and destructions of states, and all sorts of pursuits both orderly and disorderly, and diverse desires of meats and drinks always, and in all the world, and all sorts of changes of the seasons in which animals may be expected to have undergone innumerable transformations of themselves?

**CLEINIAS:** No doubt.

**ATHENIAN:** And may we not suppose that vines appeared, which had previously no existence, and also olives, and the gifts of Demeter and her daughter, of which one Triptolemus was the minister, and that, before these existed, animals took to devouring each other as they do still?

**CLEINIAS:** True.

**ATHENIAN:** Again, the practice of men sacrificing one another still exists among many nations; while, on the other hand, we hear of other human beings who did not even venture to taste the flesh of a cow and had no animal sacrifices, but only cakes and fruits dipped in honey, and similar pure offerings, but no flesh of animals; from these they abstained under the idea that they ought not to eat them, and might not stain the altars of the Gods with blood. For in those days men are said to have lived a sort of Orphic life, having the use of all lifeless things, but abstaining from all living things.

**CLEINIAS:** Such has been the constant tradition, and is very likely true.

**ATHENIAN:** Some one might say to us, What is the drift of all this?

**CLEINIAS:** A very pertinent question, Stranger.

**ATHENIAN:** And therefore I will endeavour, Cleinias, if I can, to draw the natural inference.

**CLEINIAS:** Proceed.

**ATHENIAN:** I see that among men all things depend upon three wants and desires, of which the end is virtue, if they are rightly led by them, or the opposite if wrongly. Now these are eating and drinking, which begin at birth--every animal has a natural desire for them, and is violently excited, and rebels against him who says that he must not satisfy all his pleasures and appetites, and get rid of all the corresponding pains--and the third and greatest and sharpest want and desire breaks out last, and is the fire of sexual lust, which kindles in men every species of wantonness and madness. And these three disorders we must endeavour to master by the three great principles of fear and law and right reason; turning them away from that which is called pleasantest to the best, using the Muses and the Gods who preside over contests to extinguish their increase and influx.

But to return:--After marriage let us speak of the birth of children, and after their birth of their nurture and education. In the course of discussion the several laws will be perfected, and we shall at last arrive at the common tables. Whether such associations are to be confined to men, or extended to women also, we shall see better when we approach and take a nearer view of them; and we may then determine what previous institutions are required and will have to precede them. As I said before, we shall see them more in detail, and shall be better able to lay down the laws which are proper or suited to them.

**CLEINIAS:** Very true.

**ATHENIAN:** Let us keep in mind the words which have now been spoken; for hereafter there may be need of them.

**CLEINIAS:** What do you bid us keep in mind?

**ATHENIAN:** That which we comprehended under the three words--first, eating, secondly, drinking, thirdly, the excitement of love.

**CLEINIAS:** We shall be sure to remember, Stranger.

**ATHENIAN:** Very good. Then let us now proceed to marriage, and teach persons in what way they shall beget children, threatening them, if they disobey, with the terrors of the law.

**CLEINIAS:** What do you mean?

**ATHENIAN:** The bride and bridegroom should consider that they are to produce for the state the best and fairest specimens of children which they can. Now all men who are associated in any action always succeed when they attend and give their mind to what they are doing, but when they do not give their mind or have no mind, they fail; wherefore let the bridegroom give his mind to the bride and to the begetting of children, and the bride in like manner give her mind to the bridegroom, and particularly at the time when their children are not yet born. And let the women whom we have chosen be the overseers of such matters, and let them in whatever number, large or small, and at whatever time the magistrates may command, assemble every day in the temple of Eileithyia during a third part of the day, and being there assembled, let them inform one another of any one whom they see, whether man or woman, of those who are begetting children, disregarding the ordinances given at the time when the nuptial sacrifices and ceremonies were performed. Let the begetting of children and the supervision of those who are begetting them continue ten years and no longer, during the time when marriage is fruitful. But if any continue without children up to this time, let them take counsel with their kindred and with the women holding the office of overseer and be divorced for their mutual benefit. If, however, any dispute arises about what is proper and for the interest of either party, they shall choose ten of the guardians of the law and abide by their permission and appointment. The women who preside over these matters shall enter into the houses of the young, and partly by admonitions and partly by threats make them give over their folly and error: if they persist, let the women go and tell the guardians of the law, and the guardians shall prevent them. But if they too cannot prevent them, they shall bring the matter before the people; and let them write up their names and make oath that they cannot reform such and such an one; and let him who is thus written up, if he cannot in a court of law convict those who have inscribed his name, be deprived of the privileges of a citizen in the following respects:--let him not go to weddings nor to the thanksgivings after the birth of children; and if he go, let any one who pleases strike him with impunity; and let the same regulations hold about women: let not a woman be allowed to appear abroad, or receive honour, or go to nuptial and birthday festivals, if she in like manner be written up as acting disorderly and cannot obtain a verdict. And if, when they themselves have done begetting children according to the law, a man or woman have connexion with another man or woman who are still begetting children, let the same penalties be inflicted upon them as upon those who are still having a family; and when the time for procreation has passed let the man or woman who refrains in such matters be held in esteem, and let those who do not refrain be held in the contrary of esteem--that is to say, disesteem. Now, if the greater part of mankind behave modestly, the enactments of law may be left to slumber; but, if they are disorderly, the enactments having been passed, let them be carried into execution. To every man the first year is the beginning of life, and the time of birth ought to be written down in the temples of their fathers as the beginning of existence to every child, whether boy or girl. Let every phratria have inscribed on a whited wall the names of the successive archons by whom the years are reckoned. And near to them let the living members of the phratria be inscribed, and when they depart life let them be erased. The limit of marriageable ages for a woman shall be from sixteen to twenty years at the longest,--for a man, from thirty to thirty-five years; and let a woman hold office at forty, and a man at thirty years. Let a man go out to war from twenty to sixty years, and for a woman, if there appear any need to make use of her in military service, let the time of service be after she shall have brought forth children up to fifty years of age; and let regard be had to what is possible and suitable to each.

# BOOK VII.

And now, assuming children of both sexes to have been born, it will be proper for us to consider, in the next place, their nurture and education; this cannot be left altogether unnoticed, and yet may be thought a subject fitted rather for precept and admonition than for law. In private life there are many little things, not always apparent, arising out of the pleasures and pains and desires of individuals, which run counter to the intention of the legislator, and make the characters of the citizens various and dissimilar:--this is an evil in states; for by reason of their smallness and frequent occurrence, there would be an unseemliness and want of propriety in making them penal by law; and if made penal, they are the destruction of the written law because mankind get the habit of frequently transgressing the law in small matters. The result is that you cannot legislate about them, and still less can you be silent. I speak somewhat darkly, but I shall endeavour also to bring my wares into the light of day, for I acknowledge that at present there is a want of clearness in what I am saying.

**CLEINIAS:** Very true.

**ATHENIAN**: Am I not right in maintaining that a good education is that which tends most to the improvement of mind and body?

**CLEINIAS:** Undoubtedly.

**ATHENIAN:** And nothing can be plainer than that the fairest bodies are those which grow up from infancy in the best and straightest manner?

**CLEINIAS:** Certainly.

**ATHENIAN:** And do we not further observe that the first shoot of every living thing is by far the greatest and fullest? Many will even contend that a man at twenty-five does not reach twice the height which he attained at five.

**CLEINIAS:** True.

**ATHENIAN:** Well, and is not rapid growth without proper and abundant exercise the source endless evils in the body?

**CLEINIAS:** Yes.

**ATHENIAN:** And the body should have the most exercise when it receives most nourishment?

**CLEINIAS:** But, Stranger, are we to impose this great amount of exercise upon newly-born infants?

**ATHENIAN:** Nay, rather on the bodies of infants still unborn.

**CLEINIAS:** What do you mean, my good sir? In the process of gestation?

**ATHENIAN:** Exactly. I am not at all surprised that you have never heard of this very peculiar sort of gymnastic applied to such little creatures, which, although strange, I will endeavour to explain to you.

**CLEINIAS:** By all means.

**ATHENIAN:** The practice is more easy for us to understand than for you, by reason of certain amusements which are carried to excess by us at Athens. Not only boys, but often older persons, are in the habit of keeping quails and cocks, which they train to fight one another. And they are far from thinking that the contests in which they stir them up to fight with one another are sufficient exercise; for, in addition to this, they carry them about tucked beneath their armpits, holding the smaller birds in their hands, the larger under their arms, and go for a walk of a great many miles for the sake of health, that is to say, not their own health, but the health of the birds; whereby they prove to any intelligent person, that all bodies are benefited by shakings and movements, when they are moved without weariness, whether the motion proceeds from themselves, or is caused by a swing, or at sea, or on horseback, or by other bodies in whatever way moving, and that thus gaining the mastery over food and drink, they are able to impart beauty and health and strength. But admitting all this, what follows? Shall we make a ridiculous law that the pregnant woman shall walk about and fashion the embryo within as we fashion wax before it hardens, and after birth swathe the infant for two years? Suppose that we compel nurses, under penalty of a legal fine, to be always carrying the children somewhere or other, either to the temples, or into the country, or to their relations' houses, until they are well able to stand, and to take care that their limbs are not distorted by leaning on them when they are too young,--they should continue to carry them until the infant has completed its third year; the nurses should be strong, and there should be more than one of them. Shall these be our rules, and shall we impose a penalty for the neglect of them? No, no; the penalty of which we were speaking will fall upon our own heads more than enough.

**CLEINIAS:** What penalty?

**ATHENIAN:** Ridicule, and the difficulty of getting the feminine and servant-like dispositions of the nurses to comply.

**CLEINIAS:** Then why was there any need to speak of the matter at all?

**ATHENIAN:** The reason is, that masters and freemen in states, when they hear of it, are very likely to arrive at a true conviction that without due regulation of private life in cities, stability in the laying down of laws is hardly to be expected; and he who makes this reflection may himself adopt the laws just now mentioned, and, adopting them, may order his house and state well and be happy.

**CLEINIAS:** Likely enough.

**ATHENIAN:** And therefore let us proceed with our legislation until we have determined the exercises which are suited to the souls of young children, in the same manner in which we have begun to go through the rules relating to their bodies.

**CLEINIAS:** By all means.

**ATHENIAN:** Let us assume, then, as a first principle in relation both to the body and soul of very young creatures, that nursing and moving about by day and night is good for them all, and that the younger they are, the more they will need it; infants should live, if that were possible, as if they were always rocking at sea. This is the lesson which we may gather from the experience of nurses, and likewise from the use of the remedy of motion in the rites of the Corybantes; for when mothers want their restless children to go to sleep they do not employ rest, but, on the contrary, motion--rocking them in their arms; nor do they give them silence, but they sing to them and lap them in sweet strains; and the Bacchic women are cured of their frenzy in the same manner by the use of the dance and of music.

**CLEINIAS:** Well, Stranger, and what is the reason of this?

**ATHENIAN:** The reason is obvious.

**CLEINIAS:** What?

**ATHENIAN:** The affection both of the Bacchantes and of the children is an emotion of fear, which springs out of an evil habit of the soul. And when some one applies external agitation to affections of this sort, the motion coming from without gets the better of the terrible and violent internal one, and produces a peace and calm in the soul, and quiets the restless palpitation of the heart, which is a thing much to be desired, sending the children to sleep, and making the Bacchantes, although they remain awake, to dance to the pipe with the help of the Gods to whom they offer acceptable sacrifices, and producing in them a sound mind, which takes the place of their frenzy. And, to express what I mean in a word, there is a good deal to be said in favour of this treatment.

**CLEINIAS:** Certainly.

**ATHENIAN:** But if fear has such a power we ought to infer from these facts, that every soul which from youth upward has been familiar with fears, will be made more liable to fear, and every one will allow that this is the way to form a habit of cowardice and not of courage.

**CLEINIAS:** No doubt.

**ATHENIAN:** And, on the other hand, the habit of overcoming, from our youth upwards, the fears and terrors which beset us, may be said to be an exercise of courage.

**CLEINIAS:** True.

**ATHENIAN:** And we may say that the use of exercise and motion in the earliest years of life greatly contributes to create a part of virtue in the soul.

**CLEINIAS:** Quite true.

**ATHENIAN:** Further, a cheerful temper, or the reverse, may be regarded as having much to do with high spirit on the one hand, or with cowardice on the other.

**CLEINIAS:** To be sure.

**ATHENIAN:** Then now we must endeavour to show how and to what extent we may, if we please, without difficulty implant either character in the young.

**CLEINIAS:** Certainly.

**ATHENIAN:** There is a common opinion, that luxury makes the disposition of youth discontented and irascible and vehemently excited by trifles; that on the other hand excessive and savage servitude makes men mean and abject, and haters of their kind, and therefore makes them undesirable associates.

**CLEINIAS:** But how must the state educate those who do not as yet understand the language of the country, and are therefore incapable of appreciating any sort of instruction?

**ATHENIAN:** I will tell you how:--Every animal that is born is wont to utter some cry, and this is especially the case with man, and he is also affected with the inclination to weep more than any other animal.

**CLEINIAS:** Quite true.

**ATHENIAN:** Do not nurses, when they want to know what an infant desires, judge by these signs?--when anything is brought to the infant and he is silent, then he is supposed to be pleased, but, when he weeps and cries out, then he is not pleased. For tears and cries are the inauspicious signs by which children show what they love and hate. Now the time which is thus spent is no less than three years, and is a very considerable portion of life to be passed ill or well.

**CLEINIAS:** True.

**ATHENIAN:** Does not the discontented and ungracious nature appear to you to be full of lamentations and sorrows more than a good man ought to be?

**CLEINIAS:** Certainly.

**ATHENIAN:** Well, but if during these three years every possible care were taken that our nursling should have as little of sorrow and fear, and in general of pain as was possible, might we not expect in early childhood to make his soul more gentle and cheerful?

**CLEINIAS:** To be sure, Stranger--more especially if we could procure him a variety of pleasures.

**ATHENIAN:** There I can no longer agree, Cleinias: you amaze me. To bring him up in such a way would be his utter ruin; for the beginning is always the most critical part of education. Let us see whether I am right.

**CLEINIAS:** Proceed.

**ATHENIAN:** The point about which you and I differ is of great importance, and I hope that you, Megillus, will help to decide between us. For I maintain that the true life should neither seek for pleasures, nor, on the other hand, entirely avoid pains, but should embrace the middle state, which I just spoke of as gentle and benign, and is a state which we by some divine presage and inspiration rightly ascribe to God. Now, I say, he among men, too, who would be divine ought to pursue after this mean habit--he should not rush headlong into pleasures, for he will not be free from pains; nor should we allow any one, young or old, male or female, to be thus given any more than ourselves, and least of all the newly-born infant, for in infancy more than at any other time the character is engrained by habit. Nay, more, if I were not afraid of appearing to be ridiculous, I would say that a woman during her year of pregnancy should of all women be most carefully tended, and kept from violent or excessive pleasures and pains, and should at that time cultivate gentleness and benevolence and kindness.

**CLEINIAS:** You need not ask Megillus, Stranger, which of us has most truly spoken; for I myself agree that all men ought to avoid the life of unmingled pain or pleasure, and pursue always a middle course. And having spoken well, may I add that you have been well answered?

**ATHENIAN:** Very good, Cleinias; and now let us all three consider a further point.

**CLEINIAS:** What is it?

**ATHENIAN:** That all the matters which we are now describing are commonly called by the general name of unwritten customs, and what are termed the laws of our ancestors are all of similar nature. And the reflection which lately arose in our minds, that we can neither call these things laws, nor yet leave them unmentioned, is justified; for they are the bonds of the whole state, and come in between the written laws which are or are hereafter to be laid down; they are just ancestral customs of great antiquity, which, if they are rightly ordered and made habitual, shield and preserve the previously existing written law; but if they depart from right and fall into disorder, then they are like the props of builders which slip away out of their place and cause a universal ruin--one part drags another down, and the fair super-structure falls because the old foundations are undermined. Reflecting upon this, Cleinias, you ought to bind together the new state in every possible way, omitting nothing, whether great or small, of what are called laws or manners or pursuits, for by these means a city is bound together, and all these things are only lasting when they depend upon one another; and, therefore, we must not wonder if we find that many apparently trifling customs or usages come pouring in and lengthening out our laws.

**CLEINIAS:** Very true: we are disposed to agree with you.

**ATHENIAN:** Up to the age of three years, whether of boy or girl, if a person strictly carries out our previous regulations and makes them a principal aim, he will do much for the advantage of the young creatures. But at three, four, five, and even six years the childish nature will require sports; now is the time to get rid of self-will in him, punishing him, but not so as to disgrace him. We were saying about slaves, that we ought neither to add insult to punishment so as to anger them, nor yet to leave them unpunished lest they become self-willed; and a like rule is to be observed in the case of the free-born. Children at that age have certain natural modes of amusement which they find out for themselves when they meet. And all the children who are between the ages of three and six ought to meet at the temples of the villages, the several families of a village uniting on one spot. The nurses are to see that the children behave properly and orderly,--they themselves and all their companies are to be under the control of twelve matrons, one for each company, who are annually selected to inspect them from the women previously mentioned, (i.e. the women who have authority over marriage), whom the guardians of the law appoint. These matrons shall be chosen by the women who have authority over marriage, one out of each tribe; all are to be of the same age; and let each of them, as soon as she is appointed, hold office and go to the temples every day, punishing all offenders, male or female, who are slaves or strangers, by the help of some of the public slaves; but if any citizen disputes the punishment, let her bring him before the wardens of the city; or, if there be no dispute, let her punish him herself. After the age of six years the time has arrived for the separation of the sexes, --let boys live with boys, and girls in like manner with girls. Now they must begin to learn--the boys going to teachers of horsemanship and the use of the bow, the javelin, and sling, and the girls too, if they do not object, at any rate until they know how to manage these weapons, and especially how to handle heavy arms; for I may note, that the practice which now prevails is almost universally misunderstood.

**CLEINIAS:** In what respect?

**ATHENIAN:** In that the right and left hand are supposed to be by nature differently suited for our various uses of them; whereas no difference is found in the use of the feet and the lower limbs; but in the use of the hands we are, as it were, maimed by the folly of nurses and mothers; for although our several limbs are by nature balanced, we create a difference in them by bad habit. In some cases this is of no consequence, as, for example, when we hold the lyre in the left hand, and the plectrum in the right, but it is downright folly to make the same distinction in other cases. The custom of the Scythians proves our error; for they not only hold the bow from them with the left hand and draw the arrow to them with their right, but use either hand for both purposes. And there are many similar examples in charioteering and other things, from which we may learn that those who make the left side weaker than the right act contrary to nature. In the case of the plectrum, which is of horn only, and similar instruments, as I was saying, it is of no consequence, but makes a great difference, and may be of very great importance to the warrior who has to use iron weapons, bows and javelins, and the like; above all, when in heavy armour, he has to fight against heavy armour. And there is a very great difference between one who has learnt and one who has not, and between one who has been trained in gymnastic exercises and one who has not been. For as he who is perfectly skilled in the Pancratium or boxing or wrestling, is not unable to fight from his left side, and does not limp and draggle in confusion when his opponent makes him change his position, so in heavy- armed fighting, and in all other things, if I am not mistaken, the like holds--he who has these double powers of attack and defence ought not in any case to leave them either unused or untrained, if he can help; and if a person had the nature of Geryon or Briareus he ought to be able with his hundred hands to throw a hundred darts. Now, the magistrates, male and female, should see to all these things, the women superintending the nursing and amusements of the children, and the men superintending their education, that all of them, boys and girls alike, may be sound hand and foot, and may not, if they can help, spoil the gifts of nature by bad habits.

Education has two branches,--one of gymnastic, which is concerned with the body, and the other of music, which is designed for the improvement of the soul. And gymnastic has also two branches--dancing and wrestling; and one sort of dancing imitates musical recitation, and aims at preserving dignity and freedom, the other aims at producing health, agility, and beauty in the limbs and parts of the body, giving the proper flexion and extension to each of them, a harmonious motion being diffused everywhere, and forming a suitable accompaniment to the dance. As regards wrestling, the tricks which Antaeus and Cercyon devised in their systems out of a vain spirit of competition, or the tricks of boxing which Epeius or Amycus invented, are useless and unsuitable for war, and do not deserve to have much said about them; but the art of wrestling erect and keeping free the neck and hands and sides, working with energy and constancy, with a composed strength, and for the sake of health--these are always useful, and are not to be neglected, but to be enjoined alike on masters and scholars, when we reach that part of legislation; and we will desire the one to give their instructions freely, and the others to receive them thankfully. Nor, again, must we omit suitable imitations of war in our choruses; here in Crete you have the armed dances of the Curetes, and the Lacedaemonians have those of the Dioscuri. And our virgin lady, delighting in the amusement of the dance, thought it not fit to amuse herself with empty hands; she must be clothed in a complete suit of armour, and in this attire go through the dance; and youths and maidens should in every respect imitate her, esteeming highly the favour of the Goddess, both with a view to the necessities of war, and to festive occasions: it will be right also for the boys, until such time as they go out to war, to make processions and supplications to all the Gods in goodly array, armed and on horseback, in dances and marches, fast or slow, offering up prayers to the Gods and to the sons of Gods; and also engaging in contests and preludes of contests, if at all, with these objects: For these sorts of exercises, and no others, are useful both in peace and war, and are beneficial alike to states and to private houses. But other labours and sports and exercises of the body are unworthy of freemen, O Megillus and Cleinias.

I have now completely described the kind of gymnastic which I said at first ought to be described; if you know of any better, will you communicate your thoughts?

**CLEINIAS:** It is not easy, Stranger, to put aside these principles of gymnastic and wrestling and to enunciate better ones.

**ATHENIAN:** Now we must say what has yet to be said about the gifts of the Muses and of Apollo: before, we fancied that we had said all, and that gymnastic alone remained; but now we see clearly what points have been omitted, and should be first proclaimed; of these, then, let us proceed to speak.

**CLEINIAS:** By all means.

**ATHENIAN:** Let me tell you once more--although you have heard me say the same before--that caution must be always exercised, both by the speaker and by the hearer, about anything that is very singular and unusual. For my tale is one which many a man would be afraid to tell, and yet I have a confidence which makes me go on.

**CLEINIAS:** What have you to say, Stranger?

**ATHENIAN:** I say that in states generally no one has observed that the plays of childhood have a great deal to do with the permanence or want of permanence in legislation. For when plays are ordered with a view to children having the same plays, and amusing themselves after the same manner, and finding delight in the same playthings, the more solemn institutions of the state are allowed to remain undisturbed. Whereas if sports are disturbed, and innovations are made in them, and they constantly change, and the young never speak of their having the same likings, or the same established notions of good and bad taste, either in the bearing of their bodies or in their dress, but he who devises something new and out of the way in figures and colours and the like is held in special honour, we may truly say that no greater evil can happen in a state; for he who changes the sports is secretly changing the manners of the young, and making the old to be dishonoured among them and the new to be honoured. And I affirm that there is nothing which is a greater injury to all states than saying or thinking thus. Will you hear me tell how great I deem the evil to be?

**CLEINIAS:** You mean the evil of blaming antiquity in states?

**ATHENIAN:** Exactly.

**CLEINIAS:** If you are speaking of that, you will find in us hearers who are disposed to receive what you say not unfavourably but most favourably.

**ATHENIAN:** I should expect so.

**CLEINIAS:** Proceed.

**ATHENIAN:** Well, then, let us give all the greater heed to one another's words. The argument affirms that any change whatever except from evil is the most dangerous of all things; this is true in the case of the seasons and of the winds, in the management of our bodies and the habits of our minds--true of all things except, as I said before, of the bad. He who looks at the constitution of individuals accustomed to eat any sort of meat, or drink any drink, or to do any work which they can get, may see that they are at first disordered by them, but afterwards, as time goes on, their bodies grow adapted to them, and they learn to know and like variety, and have good health and enjoyment of life; and if ever afterwards they are confined again to a superior diet, at first they are troubled with disorders, and with difficulty become habituated to their new food. A similar principle we may imagine to hold good about the minds of men and the natures of their souls. For when they have been brought up in certain laws, which by some Divine Providence have remained unchanged during long ages, so that no one has any memory or tradition of their ever having been otherwise than they are, then every one is afraid and ashamed to change that which is established. The legislator must somehow find a way of implanting this reverence for antiquity, and I would propose the following way:--People are apt to fancy, as I was saying before, that when the plays of children are altered they are merely plays, not seeing that the most serious and detrimental consequences arise out of the change; and they readily comply with the child's wishes instead of deterring him, not considering that these children who make innovations in their games, when they grow up to be men, will be different from the last generation of children, and, being different, will desire a different sort of life, and under the influence of this desire will want other institutions and laws; and no one of them reflects that there will follow what I just now called the greatest of evils to states. Changes in bodily fashions are no such serious evils, but frequent changes in the praise and censure of manners are the greatest of evils, and require the utmost prevision.

**CLEINIAS:** To be sure.

**ATHENIAN:** And now do we still hold to our former assertion, that rhythms and music in general are imitations of good and evil characters in men? What say you?

**CLEINIAS:** That is the only doctrine which we can admit.

**ATHENIAN:** Must we not, then, try in every possible way to prevent our youth from even desiring to imitate new modes either in dance or song? nor must any one be allowed to offer them varieties of pleasures.

**CLEINIAS:** Most true.

**ATHENIAN:** Can any of us imagine a better mode of effecting this object than that of the Egyptians?

**CLEINIAS:** What is their method?

**ATHENIAN:** To consecrate every sort of dance or melody. First we should ordain festivals,--calculating for the year what they ought to be, and at what time, and in honour of what Gods, sons of Gods, and heroes they ought to be celebrated; and, in the next place, what hymns ought to be sung at the several sacrifices, and with what dances the particular festival is to be honoured. This has to be arranged at first by certain persons, and, when arranged, the whole assembly of the citizens are to offer sacrifices and libations to the Fates and all the other Gods, and to consecrate the several odes to Gods and heroes: and if any one offers any other hymns or dances to any one of the Gods, the priests and priestesses, acting in concert with the guardians of the law, shall, with the sanction of religion and the law, exclude him, and he who is excluded, if he do not submit, shall be liable all his life long to have a suit of impiety brought against him by any one who likes.

**CLEINIAS:** Very good.

**ATHENIAN:** In the consideration of this subject, let us remember what is due to ourselves.

**CLEINIAS:** To what are you referring?

**ATHENIAN:** I mean that any young man, and much more any old one, when he sees or hears anything strange or unaccustomed, does not at once run to embrace the paradox, but he stands considering, like a person who is at a place where three paths meet, and does not very well know his way--he may be alone or he may be walking with others, and he will say to himself and them, 'Which is the way?' and will not move forward until he is satisfied that he is going right. And this is what we must do in the present instance:--A strange discussion on the subject of law has arisen, which requires the utmost consideration, and we should not at our age be too ready to speak about such great matters, or be confident that we can say anything certain all in a moment.

**CLEINIAS:** Most true.

**ATHENIAN:** Then we will allow time for reflection, and decide when we have given the subject sufficient consideration. But that we may not be hindered from completing the natural arrangement of our laws, let us proceed to the conclusion of them in due order; for very possibly, if God will, the exposition of them, when completed, may throw light on our present perplexity.

**CLEINIAS:** Excellent, Stranger; let us do as you propose.

**ATHENIAN:** Let us then affirm the paradox that strains of music are our laws (nomoi), and this latter being the name which the ancients gave to lyric songs, they probably would not have very much objected to our proposed application of the word. Some one, either asleep or awake, must have had a dreamy suspicion of their nature. And let our decree be as follows:--No one in singing or dancing shall offend against public and consecrated models, and the general fashion among the youth, any more than he would offend against any other law. And he who observes this law shall be blameless; but he who is disobedient, as I was saying, shall be punished by the guardians of the laws, and by the priests and priestesses. Suppose that we imagine this to be our law.

**CLEINIAS:** Very good.

**ATHENIAN:** Can any one who makes such laws escape ridicule? Let us see. I think that our only safety will be in first framing certain models for composers. One of these models shall be as follows:--If when a sacrifice is going on, and the victims are being burnt according to law,--if, I say, any one who may be a son or brother, standing by another at the altar and over the victims, horribly blasphemes, will not his words inspire despondency and evil omens and forebodings in the mind of his father and of his other kinsmen?

**CLEINIAS:** Of course.

**ATHENIAN:** And this is just what takes place in almost all our cities. A magistrate offers a public sacrifice, and there come in not one but many choruses, who take up a position a little way from the altar, and from time to time pour forth all sorts of horrible blasphemies on the sacred rites, exciting the souls of the audience with words and rhythms and melodies most sorrowful to hear; and he who at the moment when the city is offering sacrifice makes the citizens weep most, carries away the palm of victory. Now, ought we not to forbid such strains as these? And if ever our citizens must hear such lamentations, then on some unblest and inauspicious day let there be choruses of foreign and hired minstrels, like those hirelings who accompany the departed at funerals with barbarous Carian chants. That is the sort of thing which will be appropriate if we have such strains at all; and let the apparel of the singers be, not circlets and ornaments of gold, but the reverse. Enough of all this. I will simply ask once more whether we shall lay down as one of our principles of song-

**CLEINIAS:** What?

**ATHENIAN:** That we should avoid every word of evil omen; let that kind of song which is of good omen be heard everywhere and always in our state. I need hardly ask again, but shall assume that you agree with me.

**CLEINIAS:** By all means; that law is approved by the suffrages of us all.

**ATHENIAN:** But what shall be our next musical law or type? Ought not prayers to be offered up to the Gods when we sacrifice?

**CLEINIAS:** Certainly.

**ATHENIAN:** And our third law, if I am not mistaken, will be to the effect that our poets, understanding prayers to be requests which we make to the Gods, will take especial heed that they do not by mistake ask for evil instead of good. To make such a prayer would surely be too ridiculous.

**CLEINIAS:** Very true.

**ATHENIAN:** Were we not a little while ago quite convinced that no silver or golden Plutus should dwell in our state?

**CLEINIAS:** To be sure.

**ATHENIAN:** And what has it been the object of our argument to show? Did we not imply that the poets are not always quite capable of knowing what is good or evil? And if one of them utters a mistaken prayer in song or words, he will make our citizens pray for the opposite of what is good in matters of the highest import; than which, as I was saying, there can be few greater mistakes. Shall we then propose as one of our laws and models relating to the Muses--

**CLEINIAS:** What?--will you explain the law more precisely?

**ATHENIAN:** Shall we make a law that the poet shall compose nothing contrary to the ideas of the lawful, or just, or beautiful, or good, which are allowed in the state? nor shall he be permitted to communicate his compositions to any private individuals, until he shall have shown them to the appointed judges and the guardians of the law, and they are satisfied with them. As to the persons whom we appoint to be our legislators about music and as to the director of education, these have been already indicated. Once more then, as I have asked more than once, shall this be our third law, and type, and model--What do you say?

**CLEINIAS:** Let it be so, by all means.

**ATHENIAN:** Then it will be proper to have hymns and praises of the God, intermingled with prayers; and after the Gods prayers and praises should be offered in like manner to demigods and heroes, suitable to their several characters.

**CLEINIAS:** Certainly.

**ATHENIAN:** In the next place there will be no objection to a law, that citizens who are departed and have done good and energetic deeds, either with their souls or with their bodies, and have been obedient to the laws, should receive eulogies; this will be very fitting.

**CLEINIAS:** Quite true.

**ATHENIAN:** But to honour with hymns and panegyrics those who are still alive is not safe; a man should run his course, and make a fair ending, and then we will praise him; and let praise be given equally to women as well as men who have been distinguished in virtue. The order of songs and dances shall be as follows:--There are many ancient musical compositions and dances which are excellent, and from these the newly-founded city may freely select what is proper and suitable;

and they shall choose judges of not less than fifty years of age, who shall make the selection, and any of the old poems which they deem sufficient they shall include; any that are deficient or altogether unsuitable, they shall either utterly throw aside, or examine and amend, taking into their counsel poets and musicians, and making use of their poetical genius; but explaining to them the wishes of the legislator in order that they may regulate dancing, music, and all choral strains, according to the mind of the judges; and not allowing them to indulge, except in some few matters, their individual pleasures and fancies. Now the irregular strain of music is always made ten thousand times better by attaining to law and order, and rejecting the honeyed Muse --not however that we mean wholly to exclude pleasure, which is the characteristic of all music. And if a man be brought up from childhood to the age of discretion and maturity in the use of the orderly and severe music, when he hears the opposite he detests it, and calls it illiberal; but if trained in the sweet and vulgar music, he deems the severer kind cold and displeasing. So that, as I was saying before, while he who hears them gains no more pleasure from the one than from the other, the one has the advantage of making those who are trained in it better men, whereas the other makes them worse.

**CLEINIAS:** Very true.

**ATHENIAN:** Again, we must distinguish and determine on some general principle what songs are suitable to women, and what to men, and must assign to them their proper melodies and rhythms. It is shocking for a whole harmony to be inharmonical, or for a rhythm to be unrhythmical, and this will happen when the melody is inappropriate to them. And therefore the legislator must assign to these also their forms. Now both sexes have melodies and rhythms which of necessity belong to them; and those of women are clearly enough indicated by their natural difference. The grand, and that which tends to courage, may be fairly called manly; but that which inclines to moderation and temperance, may be declared both in law and in ordinary speech to be the more womanly quality. This, then, will be the general order of them.

Let us now speak of the manner of teaching and imparting them, and the persons to whom, and the time when, they are severally to be imparted. As the shipwright first lays down the lines of the keel, and thus, as it were, draws the ship in outline, so do I seek to distinguish the patterns of life, and lay down their keels according to the nature of different men's souls; seeking truly to consider by what means, and in what ways, we may go through the voyage of life best. Now human affairs are hardly worth considering in earnest, and yet we must be in earnest about them,--a sad necessity constrains us. And having got thus far, there will be a fitness in our completing the matter, if we can only find some suitable method of doing so. But what do I mean? Some one may ask this very question, and quite rightly, too.

**CLEINIAS:** Certainly.

**ATHENIAN:** I say that about serious matters a man should be serious, and about a matter which is not serious he should not be serious; and that God is the natural and worthy object of our most serious and blessed endeavours, for man, as I said before, is made to be the plaything of God, and this, truly considered, is the best of him; wherefore also every man and woman should walk seriously, and pass life in the noblest of pastimes, and be of another mind from what they are at present.

**CLEINIAS:** In what respect?

**ATHENIAN:** At present they think that their serious pursuits should be for the sake of their sports, for they deem war a serious pursuit, which must be managed well for the sake of peace; but the truth is, that there neither is, nor has been, nor ever will be, either amusement or instruction in any degree worth speaking of in war, which is nevertheless deemed by us to be the most serious of our pursuits. And therefore, as we say, every one of us should live the life of peace as long and as well as he can. And what is the right way of living? Are we to live in sports always? If so, in what kind of sports? We ought to live sacrificing, and singing, and dancing, and then a man will be able to propitiate the Gods, and to defend himself against his enemies and conquer them in battle. The type of song or dance by which he will propitiate them has been described, and the paths along which he is to proceed have been cut for him. He will go forward in the spirit of the poet (Homer, Odyss.):--

'Telemachus, some things thou wilt thyself find in thy heart, but other things God will suggest; for I deem that thou wast not born or brought up without the will of the Gods.'

And this ought to be the view of our alumni; they ought to think that what has been said is enough for them, and that any other things their Genius and God will suggest to them--he will tell them to whom, and when, and to what Gods severally they are to sacrifice and perform dances, and how they may propitiate the deities, and live according to the appointment of nature; being for the most part puppets, but having some little share of reality.

**MEGILLUS:** You have a low opinion of mankind, Stranger.

**ATHENIAN:** Nay, Megillus, be not amazed, but forgive me:--I was comparing them with the Gods; and under that feeling I spoke. Let us grant, if you wish, that the human race is not to be despised, but is worthy of some consideration.

Next follow the buildings for gymnasia and schools open to all; these are to be in three places in the midst of the city; and outside the city and in the surrounding country, also in three places, there shall be schools for horse exercise, and large grounds arranged with a view to archery and the throwing of missiles, at which young men may learn and practise. Of these mention has already been made, and if the mention be not sufficiently explicit, let us speak further of them and embody them in laws. In these several schools let there be dwellings for teachers, who shall be brought from foreign parts by pay, and let them teach those who attend the schools the art of war and the art of music, and the children shall come not only if their parents please, but if they do not please; there shall be compulsory education, as the saying is, of all and sundry, as far this is possible; and the pupils shall be regarded as belonging to the state rather than to their parents. My law would apply to females as well as males; they shall both go through the same exercises. I assert without fear of contradiction that gymnastic and horsemanship are as suitable to women as to men. Of the truth of this I am persuaded from ancient tradition, and at the present day there are said to be countless myriads of women in the neighbourhood of the Black Sea, called Sauromatides, who not only ride on horseback like men, but have enjoined upon them the use of bows and other weapons equally with the men. And I further affirm, that if these things are possible, nothing can be more absurd than the practice which prevails in our own country, of men and women not following the same pursuits with all their strength and with one mind, for thus the state, instead of being a whole, is reduced to a half, but has the same imposts to pay and the same toils to undergo; and what can be a greater mistake for any legislator to make than this?

**CLEINIAS:** Very true; yet much of what has been asserted by us, Stranger, is contrary to the custom of states; still, in saying that the discourse should be allowed to proceed, and that when the discussion is completed, we should choose what seems best, you spoke very properly, and I now feel compunction for what I have said. Tell me, then, what you would next wish to say.

**ATHENIAN:** I should wish to say, Cleinias, as I said before, that if the possibility of these things were not sufficiently proven in fact, then there might be an objection to the argument, but the fact being as I have said, he who rejects the law must find some other ground of objection; and, failing this, our exhortation will still hold good, nor will any one deny that women ought to share as far as possible in education and in other ways with men. For consider;--if women do not share in their whole life with men, then they must have some other order of life.

**CLEINIAS:** Certainly.

**ATHENIAN:** And what arrangement of life to be found anywhere is preferable to this community which we are now assigning to them? Shall we prefer that which is adopted by the Thracians and many other races who use their women to till the ground and to be shepherds of their herds and flocks, and to minister to them like slaves?--Or shall we do as we and people in our part of the world do--getting together, as the phrase is, all our goods and chattels into one dwelling, we entrust them to our women, who are the stewards of them, and who also preside over the shuttles and the whole art of spinning? Or shall we take a middle course, as in Lacedaemon, Megillus --letting the girls share in gymnastic and music, while the grown-up women, no longer employed in spinning wool, are hard at work weaving the web of life, which will be no cheap or mean employment, and in the duty of serving and taking care of the household and bringing up children, in which they will observe a sort of mean, not participating in the toils of war; and if there were any necessity that they should fight for their city and families, unlike the Amazons, they would be unable to take part in archery or any other skilled use of missiles, nor could they, after the example of the Goddess, carry shield or spear, or stand up nobly for their country when it was being destroyed, and strike terror into their enemies, if only because they were seen in regular order? Living as they do, they would never dare at all to imitate the Sauromatides, who, when compared with ordinary women, would appear to be like men. Let him who will, praise your legislators, but I must say what I think. The legislator ought to be whole and perfect, and not half a man only; he ought not to let the female sex live softly and waste money and have no order of life, while he takes the utmost care of the male sex, and leaves half of life only blest with happiness, when he might have made the whole state happy.

**MEGILLUS:** What shall we do, Cleinias? Shall we allow a stranger to run down Sparta in this fashion?

**CLEINIAS:** Yes; for as we have given him liberty of speech we must let him go on until we have perfected the work of legislation.

**MEGILLUS:** Very true.

**ATHENIAN:** Then now I may proceed?

**CLEINIAS:** By all means.

**ATHENIAN:** What will be the manner of life among men who may be supposed to have their food and clothing provided for them in moderation, and who have entrusted the practice of the arts to others, and whose husbandry committed to slaves paying a part of the produce, brings them a return sufficient for men living temperately; who, moreover, have common tables in which the men are placed apart, and near them are the common tables of their families, of their daughters and mothers, which day by day, the officers, male and female, are to inspect--they shall see to the behaviour of the company, and so dismiss them; after which the presiding magistrate and his attendants shall honour with libations those Gods to whom that day and night are dedicated, and then go home? To men whose lives are thus ordered, is there no work remaining to be done which is necessary and fitting, but shall each one of them live fattening like a beast? Such a life is neither just nor honourable, nor can he who lives it fail of meeting his due; and the due reward of the idle fatted beast is that he should be torn in pieces by some other valiant beast whose fatness is worn down by brave deeds and toil. These regulations, if we duly consider them, will never be exactly carried into execution under present circumstances, nor as long as women and children and houses and all other things are the private property of individuals; but if we can attain the second-best form of polity, we shall be very well off. And to men living under this second polity there remains a work to be accomplished which is far from being small or insignificant, but is the greatest of all works, and ordained by the appointment of righteous law. For the life which may be truly said to be concerned with the virtue of body and soul is twice, or more than twice, as full of toil and trouble as the pursuit after Pythian and Olympic victories, which debars a man from every employment of life. For there ought to be no bye-work interfering with the greater work of providing the necessary exercise and nourishment for the body, and instruction and education for the soul. Night and day are not long enough for the accomplishment of their perfection and consummation; and therefore to this end all freemen ought to arrange the way in which they will spend their time during the whole course of the day, from morning till evening and from evening till the morning of the next sunrise. There may seem to be some impropriety in the legislator determining minutely the numberless details of the management of the house, including such particulars as the duty of wakefulness in those who are to be perpetual watchmen of the whole city; for that any citizen should continue during the whole of any night in sleep, instead of being seen by all his servants, always the first to awake and get up--this, whether the regulation is to be called a law or only a practice, should be deemed base and unworthy of a freeman; also that the mistress of the house should be awakened by her handmaidens instead of herself first awakening them, is what the slaves, male and female, and the serving-boys, and, if that were possible, everybody and everything in the house should regard as base. If they rise early, they may all of them do much of their public and of their household business, as magistrates in the city, and masters and mistresses in their private houses, before the sun is up. Much sleep is not required by nature, either for our souls or bodies, or for the actions which they perform. For no one who is asleep is good for anything, any more than if he were dead; but he of us who has the most regard for life and reason keeps awake as long he can, reserving only so much time for sleep as is expedient for health; and much sleep is not required, if the habit of moderation be once rightly formed. Magistrates in states who keep awake at night are terrible to the bad, whether enemies or citizens, and are honoured and reverenced by the just and temperate, and are useful to themselves and to the whole state.

A night which is passed in such a manner, in addition to all the above-mentioned advantages, infuses a sort of courage into the minds of the citizens. When the day breaks, the time has arrived for youth to go to their schoolmasters. Now neither sheep nor any other animals can live without a shepherd, nor can children be left without tutors, or slaves without masters. And of all animals the boy is the most unmanageable, inasmuch as he has the fountain of reason in him not yet regulated; he is the most insidious, sharp-witted, and insubordinate of animals. Wherefore he must be bound with many bridles; in the first place, when he gets away from mothers and nurses, he must be under the management of tutors on account of his childishness and foolishness; then, again, being a freeman, he must be controlled by teachers, no matter what they teach, and by studies; but he is also a slave, and in that regard any freeman who comes in his way may punish him and his tutor and his instructor, if any of them does anything wrong; and he who comes across him and does not inflict upon him the punishment which he deserves, shall incur the greatest disgrace; and let the guardian of the law, who is the director of education, see to him who coming in the way of the offences which we have mentioned, does not chastise them when he ought, or chastises them in a way which he ought not; let him keep a sharp look-out, and take especial care of the training of our children, directing their natures, and always turning them to good according to the law.

But how can our law sufficiently train the director of education himself; for as yet all has been imperfect, and nothing has been said either clear or satisfactory? Now, as far as possible, the law ought to leave nothing to him, but to explain everything, that he may be an interpreter and tutor to others. About dances and music and choral strains, I have already spoken both to the character of the selection of them, and the manner in which they are to be amended and consecrated. But we have not as yet spoken, O illustrious guardian of education, of the manner in which your pupils are to use those strains which are written in prose, although you have been informed what martial strains they are to learn and practise; what relates in the first place to the learning of letters, and secondly, to the lyre, and also to calculation, which, as we were saying, is needful for them all to learn, and any other things which are required with a view to war and the management of house and city, and, looking to the same object, what is useful in the revolutions of the heavenly bodies--the stars and sun and moon, and the various regulations about these matters which are necessary for the whole state--I am speaking of the arrangements of days in periods of months, and of months in years, which are to be observed, in order that seasons and sacrifices and festivals may have their regular and natural order, and keep the city alive and awake, the Gods receiving the honours due to them, and men having a better understanding about them: all these things, O my friend, have not yet been sufficiently declared to you by the legislator. Attend, then, to what I am now going to say:--We were telling you, in the first place, that you were not sufficiently informed about letters, and the objection was to this effect,--that you were never told whether he who was meant to be a respectable citizen should apply himself in detail to that sort of learning, or not apply himself at all; and the same remark holds good of the study of the lyre. But now we say that he ought to attend to them. A fair time for a boy of ten years old to spend in letters is three years; the age of thirteen is the proper time for him to begin to handle the lyre, and he may continue at this for another three years, neither more nor less, and whether his father or himself like or dislike the study, he is not to be allowed to spend more or less time in learning music than the law allows. And let him who disobeys the law be deprived of those youthful honours of which we shall hereafter speak. Hear, however, first of all, what the young ought to learn in the early years of life, and what their instructors ought to teach them. They ought to be occupied with their letters until they are to read and write; but the acquisition of perfect beauty or quickness in writing, if nature has not stimulated them to acquire these accomplishments in the given number of years, they should let alone. And as to the learning of compositions committed to writing which are not set to the lyre, whether metrical or without rhythmical divisions, compositions in prose, as they are termed, having no rhythm or harmony--seeing how dangerous are the writings handed down to us by many writers of this class--what will you do with them, O most excellent guardians of the law? or how can the lawgiver rightly direct you about them? I believe that he will be in great difficulty.

**CLEINIAS:** What troubles you, Stranger? and why are you so perplexed in your mind?

**ATHENIAN:** You naturally ask, Cleinias, and to you and Megillus, who are my partners in the work of legislation, I must state the more difficult as well as the easier parts of the task.

**CLEINIAS:** To what do you refer in this instance?

**ATHENIAN:** I will tell you. There is a difficulty in opposing many myriads of mouths.

**CLEINIAS:** Well, and have we not already opposed the popular voice in many important enactments?

**ATHENIAN:** That is quite true; and you mean to imply that the road which we are taking may be disagreeable to some but is agreeable to as many others, or if not to as many, at any rate to persons not inferior to the others, and in company with them you bid me, at whatever risk, to proceed along the path of legislation which has opened out of our present discourse, and to be of good cheer, and not to faint.

**CLEINIAS:** Certainly.

**ATHENIAN:** And I do not faint; I say, indeed, that we have a great many poets writing in hexameter, trimeter, and all sorts of measures--some who are serious, others who aim only at raising a laugh--and all mankind declare that the youth who are rightly educated should be brought up in them and saturated with them; some insist that they should be constantly hearing them read aloud, and always learning them, so as to get by heart entire poets; while others select choice passages and long speeches, and make compendiums of them, saying that these ought to be committed to memory, if a man is to be made good and wise by experience and learning of many things. And you want me now to tell them plainly in what they are right and in what they are wrong.

**CLEINIAS:** Yes, I do.

**ATHENIAN:** But how can I in one word rightly comprehend all of them? I am of opinion, and, if I am not mistaken, there is a general agreement, that every one of these poets has said many things well and many things the reverse of well; and if this be true, then I do affirm that much learning is dangerous to youth.

**CLEINIAS:** How would you advise the guardian of the law to act?

**ATHENIAN:** In what respect?

**CLEINIAS:** I mean to what pattern should he look as his guide in permitting the young to learn some things and forbidding them to learn others. Do not shrink from answering.

**ATHENIAN:** My good Cleinias, I rather think that I am fortunate.

**CLEINIAS:** How so?

**ATHENIAN:** I think that I am not wholly in want of a pattern, for when I consider the words which we have spoken from early dawn until now, and which, as I believe, have been inspired by Heaven, they appear to me to be quite like a poem. When I reflected upon all these words of ours, I naturally felt pleasure, for of all the discourses which I have ever learnt or heard, either in poetry or prose, this seemed to me to be the justest, and most suitable for young men to hear; I cannot imagine any better pattern than this which the guardian of the law who is also the director of education can have. He cannot do better than advise the teachers to teach the young these words and any which are of a like nature, if he should happen to find them, either in poetry or prose, or if he come across unwritten discourses akin to ours, he should certainly preserve them, and commit them to writing. And, first of all, he shall constrain the teachers themselves to learn and approve them, and any of them who will not, shall not be employed by him, but those whom he finds agreeing in his judgment, he shall make use of and shall commit to them the instruction and education of youth. And here and on this wise let my fanciful tale about letters and teachers of letters come to an end.

**CLEINIAS:** I do not think, Stranger, that we have wandered out of the proposed limits of the argument; but whether we are right or not in our whole conception, I cannot be very certain.

**ATHENIAN:** The truth, Cleinias, may be expected to become clearer when, as we have often said, we arrive at the end of the whole discussion about laws.

**CLEINIAS:** Yes.

**ATHENIAN:** And now that we have done with the teacher of letters, the teacher of the lyre has to receive orders from us.

**CLEINIAS:** Certainly.

**ATHENIAN:** I think that we have only to recollect our previous discussions, and we shall be able to give suitable regulations touching all this part of instruction and education to the teachers of the lyre.

**CLEINIAS:** To what do you refer?

**ATHENIAN:** We were saying, if I remember rightly, that the sixty-year-old choristers of Dionysus were to be specially quick in their perceptions of rhythm and musical composition, that they might be able to distinguish good and bad imitation, that is to say, the imitation of the good or bad soul when under the influence of passion, rejecting the one and displaying the other in hymns and songs, charming the souls of youth, and inviting them to follow and attain virtue by the way of imitation.

**CLEINIAS:** Very true.

**ATHENIAN:** And with this view, the teacher and the learner ought to use the sounds of the lyre, because its notes are pure, the player who teaches and his pupil rendering note for note in unison; but complexity, and variation of notes, when the strings give one sound and the poet or composer of the melody gives another,--also when they make concords and harmonies in which lesser and greater intervals, slow and quick, or high and low notes, are combined,--or, again, when they make complex variations of rhythms, which they adapt to the notes of the lyre,--all that sort of thing is not suited to those who have to acquire a speedy and useful knowledge of music in three years; for opposite principles are confusing, and create a difficulty in learning, and our young men should learn quickly, and their mere necessary acquirements are not few or trifling, as will be shown in due course. Let the director of education attend to the principles concerning music which we are laying down. As to the songs and words themselves which the masters of choruses are to teach and the character of them, they have been already described by us, and are the same which, when consecrated and adapted to the different festivals, we said were to benefit cities by affording them an innocent amusement.

**CLEINIAS:** That, again, is true.

**ATHENIAN:** Then let him who has been elected a director of music receive these rules from us as containing the very truth; and may he prosper in his office! Let us now proceed to lay down other rules in addition to the preceding about dancing and gymnastic exercise in general. Having said what remained to be said about the teaching of music, let us speak in like manner about gymnastic. For boys and girls ought to learn to dance and practise gymnastic exercises--ought they not?

**CLEINIAS:** Yes.

**ATHENIAN:** Then the boys ought to have dancing masters, and the girls dancing mistresses to exercise them.

**CLEINIAS:** Very good.

**ATHENIAN:** Then once more let us summon him who has the chief concern in the business, the superintendent of youth (i.e. the director of education); he will have plenty to do, if he is to have the charge of music and gymnastic.

**CLEINIAS:** But how will an old man be able to attend to such great charges?

**ATHENIAN:** O my friend, there will be no difficulty, for the law has already given and will give him permission to select as his assistants in this charge any citizens, male or female, whom he desires; and he will know whom he ought to choose, and will be anxious not to make a mistake, from a due sense of responsibility, and from a consciousness of the importance of his office, and also because he will consider that if young men have been and are well brought up, then all things go swimmingly, but if not, it is not meet to say, nor do we say, what will follow, lest the regarders of omens should take alarm about our infant state. Many things have been said by us about dancing and about gymnastic movements in general; for we include under gymnastics all military exercises, such as archery, and all hurling of weapons, and the use of the light shield, and all fighting with heavy arms, and military evolutions, and movements of armies, and encampings, and all that relates to horsemanship. Of all these things there ought to be public teachers, receiving pay from the state, and their pupils should be the men and boys in the state, and also the girls and women, who are to know all these things. While they are yet girls they should have practised dancing in arms and the whole art of fighting--when grown-up women, they should apply themselves to evolutions and tactics, and the mode of grounding and taking up arms; if for no other reason, yet in case the whole military force should have to leave the city and carry on operations of war outside, that those who will have to guard the young and the rest of the city may be equal to the task; and, on the other hand, when enemies, whether barbarian or Hellenic, come from without with mighty force and make a violent assault upon them, and thus compel them to fight for the possession of the city, which is far from being an impossibility, great would be the disgrace to the state, if the women had been so miserably trained that they could not fight for their young, as birds will, against any creature however strong, and die or undergo any danger, but must instantly rush to the temples and crowd at the altars and shrines, and bring upon human nature the reproach, that of all animals man is the most cowardly!

**CLEINIAS:** Such a want of education, Stranger, is certainly an unseemly thing to happen in a state, as well as a great misfortune.

**ATHENIAN:** Suppose that we carry our law to the extent of saying that women ought not to neglect military matters, but that all citizens, male and female alike, shall attend to them?

**CLEINIAS:** I quite agree.

**ATHENIAN:** Of wrestling we have spoken in part, but of what I should call the most important part we have not spoken, and cannot easily speak without showing at the same time by gesture as well as in word what we mean; when word and action combine, and not till then, we shall explain clearly what has been said, pointing out that of all movements wrestling is most akin to the military art, and is to be pursued for the sake of this, and not this for the sake of wrestling.

**CLEINIAS:** Excellent.

**ATHENIAN:** Enough of wrestling; we will now proceed to speak of other movements of the body. Such motion may be in general called dancing, and is of two kinds: one of nobler figures, imitating the honourable, the other of the more ignoble figures, imitating the mean; and of both these there are two further subdivisions. Of the serious, one kind is of those engaged in war and vehement action, and is the exercise of a noble person and a manly heart; the other exhibits a temperate soul in the enjoyment of prosperity and modest pleasures, and may be truly called and is the dance of peace. The warrior dance is different from the peaceful one, and may be rightly termed Pyrrhic; this imitates the modes of avoiding blows and missiles by dropping or giving way, or springing aside, or rising up or falling down; also the opposite postures which are those of action, as, for example, the imitation of archery and the hurling of javelins, and of all sorts of blows. And when the imitation is of brave bodies and souls, and the action is direct and muscular, giving for the most part a straight movement to the limbs of the body--that, I say, is the true sort; but the opposite is not right. In the dance of peace what we have to consider is whether a man bears himself naturally and gracefully, and after the manner of men who duly conform to the law. But before proceeding I must distinguish the dancing about which there is any doubt, from that about which there is no doubt. Which is the doubtful kind, and how are the two to be distinguished? There are dances of the Bacchic sort, both those in which, as they say, they imitate drunken men, and which are named after the Nymphs, and Pan, and Silenuses, and Satyrs; and also those in which purifications are made or mysteries celebrated,--all this sort of dancing cannot be rightly defined as having either a peaceful or a warlike character, or indeed as having any meaning whatever and may, I think, be most truly described as distinct from the warlike dance, and distinct from the peaceful, and not suited for a city at all. There let it lie; and so leaving it to lie, we will proceed to the dances of war and peace, for with these we are undoubtedly concerned. Now the unwarlike muse, which honours in dance the Gods and the sons of the Gods, is entirely associated with the consciousness of prosperity; this class may be subdivided into two lesser classes, of which one is expressive of an escape from some labour or danger into good, and has greater pleasures, the other expressive of preservation and increase of former good, in which the pleasure is less exciting;--in all these cases, every man when the pleasure is greater, moves his body more, and less when the pleasure is less; and, again, if he be more orderly and has learned courage from discipline he moves less, but if he be a coward, and has no training or self-control, he makes greater and more violent movements, and in general when he is speaking or singing he is not altogether able to keep his body still; and so out of the imitation of words in gestures the whole art of dancing has arisen. And in these various kinds of imitation one man moves in an orderly, another in a disorderly manner; and as the ancients may be observed to have given many names which are according to nature and deserving of praise, so there is an excellent one which they have given to the dances of men who in their times of prosperity are moderate in their pleasures--the giver of names, whoever he was, assigned to them a very true, and poetical, and rational name, when he called them Emmeleiai, or dances of order, thus establishing two kinds of dances of the nobler sort, the dance of war which he called the Pyrrhic, and the dance of peace which he called Emmeleia, or the dance of order; giving to each their appropriate and becoming name. These things the legislator should indicate in general outline, and the guardian of the law should enquire into them and search them out, combining dancing with music, and assigning to the several sacrificial feasts that which is suitable to them; and when he has consecrated all of them in due order, he shall for the future change nothing, whether of dance or song. Thenceforward the city and the citizens shall continue to have the same pleasures, themselves being as far as possible alike, and shall live well and happily.

I have described the dances which are appropriate to noble bodies and generous souls. But it is necessary also to consider and know uncomely persons and thoughts, and those which are intended to produce laughter in comedy, and have a comic character in respect of style, song, and dance, and of the imitations which these afford. For serious things cannot be understood without laughable things, nor opposites at all without opposites, if a man is really to have intelligence of either; but he cannot carry out both in action, if he is to have any degree of virtue. And for this very reason he should learn them both, in order that he may not in ignorance do or say anything which is ridiculous and out of place--he should command slaves and hired strangers to imitate such things, but he should never take any serious interest in them himself, nor should any freeman or freewoman be discovered taking pains to learn them; and there should always be some element of novelty in the imitation. Let these then be laid down, both in law and in our discourse, as the regulations of laughable amusements which are generally called comedy. And, if any of the serious poets, as they are termed, who write tragedy, come to us and say-- 'O strangers, may we go to your city and country or may we not, and shall we bring with us our poetry--what is your will about these matters?'--how shall we answer the divine men? I think that our answer should be as follows:--Best of strangers, we will say to them, we also according to our ability are tragic poets, and our tragedy is the best and noblest; for our whole state is an imitation of the best and noblest life, which we affirm to be indeed the very truth of tragedy. You are poets and we are poets, both makers of the same strains, rivals and antagonists in the noblest of dramas, which true law can alone perfect, as our hope is. Do not then suppose that we shall all in a moment allow you to erect your stage in the agora, or introduce the fair voices of your actors, speaking above our own, and permit you to harangue our women and children, and the common people, about our institutions, in language other than our own, and very often the opposite of our own. For a state would be mad which gave you this licence, until the magistrates had determined whether your poetry might be recited, and was fit for publication or not. Wherefore, O ye sons and scions of the softer Muses, first of all show your songs to the magistrates, and let them compare them with our own, and if they are the same or better we will give you a chorus; but if not, then, my friends, we cannot. Let these, then, be the customs ordained by law about all dances and the teaching of them, and let matters relating to slaves be separated from those relating to masters, if you do not object.

**CLEINIAS:** We can have no hesitation in assenting when you put the matter thus.

**ATHENIAN:** There still remain three studies suitable for freemen. Arithmetic is one of them; the measurement of length, surface, and depth is the second; and the third has to do with the revolutions of the stars in relation to one another. Not every one has need to toil through all these things in a strictly scientific manner, but only a few, and who they are to be we will hereafter indicate at the end, which will be the proper place; not to know what is necessary for mankind in general, and what is the truth, is disgraceful to every one: and yet to enter into these matters minutely is neither easy, nor at all possible for every one; but there is something in them which is necessary and cannot be set aside, and probably he who made the proverb about God originally had this in view when he said, that 'not even God himself can fight against necessity;'--he meant, if I am not mistaken, divine necessity; for as to the human necessities of which the many speak, when they talk in this manner, nothing can be more ridiculous than such an application of the words.

**CLEINIAS:** And what necessities of knowledge are there, Stranger, which are divine and not human?

**ATHENIAN:** I conceive them to be those of which he who has no use nor any knowledge at all cannot be a God, or demi-god, or hero to mankind, or able to take any serious thought or charge of them. And very unlike a divine man would he be, who is unable to count one, two, three, or to distinguish odd and even numbers, or is unable to count at all, or reckon night and day, and who is totally unacquainted with the revolution of the sun and moon, and the other stars. There would be great folly in supposing that all these are not necessary parts of knowledge to him who intends to know anything about the highest kinds of knowledge; but which these are, and how many there are of them, and when they are to be learned, and what is to be learned together and what apart, and the whole correlation of them, must be rightly apprehended first; and these leading the way we may proceed to the other parts of knowledge. For so necessity grounded in nature constrains us, against which we say that no God contends, or ever will contend.

**CLEINIAS:** I think, Stranger, that what you have now said is very true and agreeable to nature.

**ATHENIAN:** Yes, Cleinias, that is so. But it is difficult for the legislator to begin with these studies; at a more convenient time we will make regulations for them.

**CLEINIAS:** You seem, Stranger, to be afraid of our habitual ignorance of the subject: there is no reason why that should prevent you from speaking out.

**ATHENIAN:** I certainly am afraid of the difficulties to which you allude, but I am still more afraid of those who apply themselves to this sort of knowledge, and apply themselves badly. For entire ignorance is not so terrible or extreme an evil, and is far from being the greatest of all; too much cleverness and too much learning, accompanied with an ill bringing up, are far more fatal.
**CLEINIAS:** True.

**ATHENIAN:** All freemen, I conceive, should learn as much of these branches of knowledge as every child in Egypt is taught when he learns the alphabet. In that country arithmetical games have been invented for the use of mere children, which they learn as a pleasure and amusement. They have to distribute apples and garlands, using the same number sometimes for a larger and sometimes for a lesser number of persons; and they arrange pugilists and wrestlers as they pair together by lot or remain over, and show how their turns come in natural order. Another mode of amusing them is to distribute vessels, sometimes of gold, brass, silver, and the like, intermixed with one another, sometimes of one metal only; as I was saying they adapt to their amusement the numbers in common use, and in this way make more intelligible to their pupils the arrangements and movements of armies and expeditions, in the management of a household they make people more useful to themselves, and more wide awake; and again in measurements of things which have length, and breadth, and depth, they free us from that natural ignorance of all these things which is so ludicrous and disgraceful.

**CLEINIAS:** What kind of ignorance do you mean?

**ATHENIAN:** O my dear Cleinias, I, like yourself, have late in life heard with amazement of our ignorance in these matters; to me we appear to be more like pigs than men, and I am quite ashamed, not only of myself, but of all Hellenes.

**CLEINIAS:** About what? Say, Stranger, what you mean.

**ATHENIAN:** I will; or rather I will show you my meaning by a question, and do you please to answer me: You know, I suppose, what length is?

**CLEINIAS:** Certainly.

**ATHENIAN:** And what breadth is?

**CLEINIAS:** To be sure.

**ATHENIAN:** And you know that these are two distinct things, and that there is a third thing called depth?

**CLEINIAS:** Of course.

**ATHENIAN:** And do not all these seem to you to be commensurable with themselves?

**CLEINIAS:** Yes.

**ATHENIAN:** That is to say, length is naturally commensurable with length, and breadth with breadth, and depth in like manner with depth?

**CLEINIAS:** Undoubtedly.

**ATHENIAN:** But if some things are commensurable and others wholly incommensurable, and you think that all things are commensurable, what is your position in regard to them?

**CLEINIAS:** Clearly, far from good.

**ATHENIAN:** Concerning length and breadth when compared with depth, or breadth and length when compared with one another, are not all the Hellenes agreed that these are commensurable with one another in some way?

**CLEINIAS:** Quite true.

**ATHENIAN:** But if they are absolutely incommensurable, and yet all of us regard them as commensurable, have we not reason to be ashamed of our compatriots; and might we not say to them:--O ye best of Hellenes, is not this one of the things of which we were saying that not to know them is disgraceful, and of which to have a bare knowledge only is no great distinction?

**CLEINIAS:** Certainly.

**ATHENIAN:** And there are other things akin to these, in which there spring up other errors of the same family.

**CLEINIAS:** What are they?

**ATHENIAN:** The natures of commensurable and incommensurable quantities in their relation to one another. A man who is good for anything ought to be able, when he thinks, to distinguish them; and different persons should compete with one another in asking questions, which will be a far better and more graceful way of passing their time than the old man's game of draughts.

**CLEINIAS:** I dare say; and these pastimes are not so very unlike a game of draughts.

**ATHENIAN:** And these, as I maintain, Cleinias, are the studies which our youth ought to learn, for they are innocent and not difficult; the learning of them will be an amusement, and they will benefit the state. If any one is of another mind, let him say what he has to say.

**CLEINIAS:** Certainly.

**ATHENIAN:** Then if these studies are such as we maintain, we will include them; if not, they shall be excluded.

**CLEINIAS:** Assuredly: but may we not now, Stranger, prescribe these studies as necessary, and so fill up the lacunae of our laws?

**ATHENIAN:** They shall be regarded as pledges which may be hereafter redeemed and removed from our state, if they do not please either us who give them, or you who accept them.

**CLEINIAS:** A fair condition.

**ATHENIAN:** Next let us see whether we are or are not willing that the study of astronomy shall be proposed for our youth.

**CLEINIAS:** Proceed.

**ATHENIAN:** Here occurs a strange phenomenon, which certainly cannot in any point of view be tolerated.

**CLEINIAS:** To what are you referring?

**ATHENIAN:** Men say that we ought not to enquire into the supreme God and the nature of the universe, nor busy ourselves in searching out the causes of things, and that such enquiries are impious; whereas the very opposite is the truth.

**CLEINIAS:** What do you mean?

**ATHENIAN:** Perhaps what I am saying may seem paradoxical, and at variance with the usual language of age. But when any one has any good and true notion which is for the advantage of the state and in every way acceptable to God, he cannot abstain from expressing it.

**CLEINIAS:** Your words are reasonable enough; but shall we find any good or true notion about the stars?

**ATHENIAN:** My good friends, at this hour all of us Hellenes tell lies, if I may use such an expression, about those great Gods, the Sun and the Moon.

**CLEINIAS:** Lies of what nature?

**ATHENIAN:** We say that they and divers other stars do not keep the same path, and we call them planets or wanderers.

**CLEINIAS:** Very true, Stranger; and in the course of my life I have often myself seen the morning star and the evening star and divers others not moving in their accustomed course, but wandering out of their path in all manner of ways, and I have seen the sun and moon doing what we all know that they do.

**ATHENIAN:** Just so, Megillus and Cleinias; and I maintain that our citizens and our youth ought to learn about the nature of the Gods in heaven, so far as to be able to offer sacrifices and pray to them in pious language, and not to blaspheme about them.

**CLEINIAS:** There you are right, if such a knowledge be only attainable; and if we are wrong in our mode of speaking now, and can be better instructed and learn to use better language, then I quite agree with you that such a degree of knowledge as will enable us to speak rightly should be acquired by us. And now do you try to explain to us your whole meaning, and we, on our part, will endeavour to understand you.

**ATHENIAN:** There is some difficulty in understanding my meaning, but not a very great one, nor will any great length of time be required. And of this I am myself a proof; for I did not know these things long ago, nor in the days of my youth, and yet I can explain them to you in a brief space of time; whereas if they had been difficult I could certainly never have explained them all, old as I am, to old men like yourselves.

**CLEINIAS:** True; but what is this study which you describe as wonderful and fitting for youth to learn, but of which we are ignorant? Try and explain the nature of it to us as clearly as you can.

**ATHENIAN:** I will. For, O my good friends, that other doctrine about the wandering of the sun and the moon and the other stars is not the truth, but the very reverse of the truth. Each of them moves in the same path--not in many paths, but in one only, which is circular, and the varieties are only apparent. Nor are we right in supposing that the swiftest of them is the slowest, nor conversely, that the slowest is the quickest. And if what I say is true, only just imagine that we had a similar notion about horses running at Olympia, or about men who ran in the long course, and that we addressed the swiftest as the slowest and the slowest as the swiftest, and sang the praises of the vanquished as though he were the victor,--in that case our praises would not be true, nor very agreeable to the runners, though they be but men; and now, to commit the same error about the Gods which would have been ludicrous and erroneous in the case of men,--is not that ludicrous and erroneous?

**CLEINIAS:** Worse than ludicrous, I should say.

**ATHENIAN:** At all events, the Gods cannot like us to be spreading a false report of them.

**CLEINIAS:** Most true, if such is the fact.

**ATHENIAN:** And if we can show that such is really the fact, then all these matters ought to be learned so far as is necessary for the avoidance of impiety; but if we cannot, they may be let alone, and let this be our decision.

**CLEINIAS:** Very good.

**ATHENIAN:** Enough of laws relating to education and learning. But hunting and similar pursuits in like manner claim our attention. For the legislator appears to have a duty imposed upon him which goes beyond mere legislation. There is something over and above law which lies in a region between admonition and law, and has several times occurred to us in the course of discussion; for example, in the education of very young children there were things, as we maintain, which are not to be defined, and to regard them as matters of positive law is a great absurdity. Now, our laws and the whole constitution of our state having been thus delineated, the praise of the virtuous citizen is not complete when he is described as the person who serves the laws best and obeys them most, but the higher form of praise is that which describes him as the good citizen who passes through life undefiled and is obedient to the words of the legislator, both when he is giving laws and when he assigns praise and blame. This is the truest word that can be spoken in praise of a citizen; and the true legislator ought not only to write his laws, but also to interweave with them all such things as seem to him honourable and dishonourable. And the perfect citizen ought to seek to strengthen these no less than the principles of law which are sanctioned by punishments. I will adduce an example which will clear up my meaning, and will be a sort of witness to my words. Hunting is of wide extent, and has a name under which many things are included, for there is a hunting of creatures in the water, and of creatures in the air, and there is a great deal of hunting of land animals of all kinds, and not of wild beasts only. The hunting after man is also worthy of consideration; there is the hunting after him in war, and there is often a hunting after him in the way of friendship, which is praised and also blamed; and there is thieving, and the hunting which is practised by robbers, and that of armies against armies. Now the legislator, in laying down laws about hunting, can neither abstain from noting these things, nor can he make threatening ordinances which will assign rules and penalties about all of them. What is he to do? He will have to praise and blame hunting with a view to the exercise and pursuits of youth. And, on the other hand, the young man must listen obediently; neither pleasure nor pain should hinder him, and he should regard as his standard of action the praises and injunctions of the legislator rather than the punishments which he imposes by law. This being premised, there will follow next in order moderate praise and censure of hunting; the praise being assigned to that kind which will make the souls of young men better, and the censure to that which has the opposite effect. And now let us address young men in the form of a prayer for their welfare: O friends, we will say to them, may no desire or love of hunting in the sea, or of angling or of catching the creatures in the waters, ever take possession of you, either when you are awake or when you are asleep, by hook or with weels, which latter is a very lazy contrivance; and let not any desire of catching men and of piracy by sea enter into your souls and make you cruel and lawless hunters. And as to the desire of thieving in town or country, may it never enter into your most passing thoughts; nor let the insidious fancy of catching birds, which is hardly worthy of freemen, come into the head of any youth. There remains therefore for our athletes only the hunting and catching of land animals, of which the one sort is called hunting by night, in which the hunters sleep in turn and are lazy; this is not to be commended any more than that which has intervals of rest, in which the wild strength of beasts is subdued by nets and snares, and not by the victory of a laborious spirit. Thus, only the best kind of hunting is allowed at all--that of quadrupeds, which is carried on with horses and dogs and men's own persons, and they get the victory over the animals by running them down and striking them and hurling at them, those who have a care of godlike manhood taking them with their own hands. The praise and blame which is assigned to all these things has now been declared; and let the law be as follows:-- Let no one hinder these who verily are sacred hunters from following the chase wherever and whithersoever they will; but the hunter by night, who trusts to his nets and gins, shall not be allowed to hunt anywhere. The fowler in the mountains and waste places shall be permitted, but on cultivated ground and on consecrated wilds he shall not be permitted; and any one who meets him may stop him. As to the hunter in waters, he may hunt anywhere except in harbours or sacred streams or marshes or pools, provided only that he do not pollute the water with poisonous juices. And now we may say that all our enactments about education are complete.

**CLEINIAS:** Very good.

# BOOK VIII.

**ATHENIAN:** Next, with the help of the Delphian oracle, we have to institute festivals and make laws about them, and to determine what sacrifices will be for the good of the city, and to what Gods they shall be offered; but when they shall be offered, and how often, may be partly regulated by us.

**CLEINIAS:** The number--yes.

**ATHENIAN:** Then we will first determine the number; and let the whole number be 365--one for every day,--so that one magistrate at least will sacrifice daily to some God or demi-god on behalf of the city, and the citizens, and their possessions. And the interpreters, and priests, and priestesses, and prophets shall meet, and, in company with the guardians of the law, ordain those things which the legislator of necessity omits; and I may remark that they are the very persons who ought to take note of what is omitted. The law will say that there are twelve feasts dedicated to the twelve Gods, after whom the several tribes are named; and that to each of them they shall sacrifice every month, and appoint choruses, and musical and gymnastic contests, assigning them so as to suit the Gods and seasons of the year. And they shall have festivals for women, distinguishing those which ought to be separated from the men's festivals, and those which ought not. Further, they shall not confuse the infernal deities and their rites with the Gods who are termed heavenly and their rites, but shall separate them, giving to Pluto his own in the twelfth month, which is sacred to him, according to the law. To such a deity warlike men should entertain no aversion, but they should honour him as being always the best friend of man. For the connexion of soul and body is no way better than the dissolution of them, as I am ready to maintain quite seriously. Moreover, those who would regulate these matters rightly should consider, that our city among existing cities has no fellow, either in respect of leisure or command and of the necessaries of life, and that like an individual she ought to live happily. And those who would live happily should in the first place do no wrong to one another, and ought not themselves to be wronged by others; to attain the first is not difficult, but there is great difficulty in acquiring the power of not being wronged. No man can be perfectly secure against wrong, unless he has become perfectly good; and cities are like individuals in this, for a city if good has a life of peace, but if evil, a life of war within and without. Wherefore the citizens ought to practise war--not in time of war, but rather while they are at peace. And every city which has any sense, should take the field at least for one day in every month; and for more if the magistrates think fit, having no regard to winter cold or summer heat; and they should go out en masse, including their wives and their children, when the magistrates determine to lead forth the whole people, or in separate portions when summoned by them; and they should always provide that there should be games and sacrificial feasts, and they should have tournaments, imitating in as lively a manner as they can real battles. And they should distribute prizes of victory and valour to the competitors, passing censures and encomiums on one another according to the characters which they bear in the contests and their whole life, honouring him who seems to be the best, and blaming him who is the opposite. And let poets celebrate the victors,--not however every poet, but only one who in the first place is not less than fifty years of age; nor should he be one who, although he may have musical and poetical gifts, has never in his life done any noble or illustrious action; but those who are themselves good and also honourable in the state, creators of noble actions--let their poems be sung, even though they be not very musical. And let the judgment of them rest with the instructor of youth (i.e. the director of education) and the other guardians of the laws, who shall give them this privilege, and they alone shall be free to sing; but the rest of the world shall not have this liberty. Nor shall any one dare to sing a song which has not been approved by the judgment of the guardians of the laws, not even if his strain be sweeter than the songs of Thamyras and Orpheus; but only such poems as have been judged sacred and dedicated to the Gods, and such as are the works of good men, in which praise of blame has been awarded and which have been deemed to fulfil their design fairly.

The regulations about war, and about liberty of speech in poetry, ought to apply equally to men and women. The legislator may be supposed to argue the question in his own mind:--Who are my citizens for whom I have set in order the city? Are they not competitors in the greatest of all contests, and have they not innumerable rivals? To be sure, will be the natural reply. Well, but if we were training boxers, or pancratiasts, or any other sort of athletes, would they never meet until the hour of contest arrived; and should we do nothing to prepare ourselves previously by daily practice? Surely, if we were boxers, we should have been learning to fight for many days before, and exercising ourselves in imitating all those blows and wards which we were intending to use in the hour of conflict; and in order that we might come as near to reality as possible, instead of cestuses we should put on boxing gloves, that the blows and the wards might be practised by us to the utmost of our power. And if there were a lack of competitors, the ridicule of fools would not deter us from hanging up a lifeless image and practising at that. Or if we had no adversary at all, animate or inanimate, should we not venture in the dearth of antagonists to spar by ourselves? In what other manner could we ever study the art of self-defence?

**CLEINIAS:** The way which you mention, Stranger, would be the only way.

**ATHENIAN:** And shall the warriors of our city, who are destined when occasion calls to enter the greatest of all contests, and to fight for their lives, and their children, and their property, and the whole city, be worse prepared than boxers? And will the legislator, because he is afraid that their practising with one another may appear to some ridiculous, abstain from commanding them to go out and fight; will he not ordain that soldiers shall perform lesser exercises without arms every day, making dancing and all gymnastic tend to this end; and also will he not require that they shall practise some gymnastic exercises, greater as well as lesser, as often as every month; and that they shall have contests one with another in every part of the country, seizing upon posts and lying in ambush, and imitating in every respect the reality of war; fighting with boxing-gloves and hurling javelins, and using weapons somewhat dangerous, and as nearly as possible like the true ones, in order that the sport may not be altogether without fear, but may have terrors and to a certain degree show the man who has and who has not courage; and that the honour and dishonour which are assigned to them respectively, may prepare the whole city for the true conflict of life? If any one dies in these mimic contests, the homicide is involuntary, and we will make the slayer, when he has been purified according to law, to be pure of blood, considering that if a few men should die, others as good as they will be born; but that if fear is dead, then the citizens will never find a test of superior and inferior natures, which is a far greater evil to the state than the loss of a few.

**CLEINIAS:** We are quite agreed, Stranger, that we should legislate about such things, and that the whole state should practise them.

**ATHENIAN:** And what is the reason that dances and contests of this sort hardly ever exist in states, at least not to any extent worth speaking of? Is this due to the ignorance of mankind and their legislators?

**CLEINIAS:** Perhaps.

**ATHENIAN:** Certainly not, sweet Cleinias; there are two causes, which are quite enough to account for the deficiency.

**CLEINIAS:** What are they?

**ATHENIAN:** One cause is the love of wealth, which wholly absorbs men, and never for a moment allows them to think of anything but their own private possessions; on this the soul of every citizen hangs suspended, and can attend to nothing but his daily gain; mankind are ready to learn any branch of knowledge, and to follow any pursuit which tends to this end, and they laugh at every other:--that is one reason why a city will not be in earnest about such contests or any other good and honourable pursuit. But from an insatiable love of gold and silver, every man will stoop to any art or contrivance, seemly or unseemly, in the hope of becoming rich; and will make no objection to performing any action, holy, or unholy and utterly base, if only like a beast he have the power of eating and drinking all kinds of things, and procuring for himself in every sort of way the gratification of his lusts.

**CLEINIAS:** True.

**ATHENIAN:** Let this, then, be deemed one of the causes which prevent states from pursuing in an efficient manner the art of war, or any other noble aim, but makes the orderly and temperate part of mankind into merchants, and captains of ships, and servants, and converts the valiant sort into thieves and burglars and robbers of temples, and violent, tyrannical persons; many of whom are not without ability, but they are unfortunate.

**CLEINIAS:** What do you mean?

**ATHENIAN:** Must not they be truly unfortunate whose souls are compelled to pass through life always hungering?

**CLEINIAS:** Then that is one cause, Stranger; but you spoke of another.

**ATHENIAN:** Thank you for reminding me.

**CLEINIAS:** The insatiable lifelong love of wealth, as you were saying, is one clause which absorbs mankind, and prevents them from rightly practising the arts of war:--Granted; and now tell me, what is the other?

**ATHENIAN:** Do you imagine that I delay because I am in a perplexity?

**CLEINIAS:** No; but we think that you are too severe upon the money-loving temper, of which you seem in the present discussion to have a peculiar dislike.

**ATHENIAN:** That is a very fair rebuke, Cleinias; and I will now proceed to the second cause.

**CLEINIAS:** Proceed.

**ATHENIAN:** I say that governments are a cause--democracy, oligarchy, tyranny, concerning which I have often spoken in the previous discourse; or rather governments they are not, for none of them exercises a voluntary rule over voluntary subjects; but they may be truly called states of discord, in which while the government is voluntary, the subjects always obey against their will, and have to be coerced; and the ruler fears the subject, and will not, if he can help, allow him to become either noble, or rich, or strong, or valiant, or warlike at all. These two are the chief causes of almost all evils, and of the evils of which I have been speaking they are notably the causes. But our state has escaped both of them; for her citizens have the greatest leisure, and they are not subject to one another, and will, I think, be made by these laws the reverse of lovers of money. Such a constitution may be reasonably supposed to be the only one existing which will accept the education which we have described, and the martial pastimes which have been perfected according to our idea.

**CLEINIAS:** True.

**ATHENIAN:** Then next we must remember, about all gymnastic contests, that only the warlike sort of them are to be practised and to have prizes of victory; and those which are not military are to be given up. The military sort had better be completely described and established by law; and first, let us speak of running and swiftness.

**CLEINIAS:** Very good.

**ATHENIAN:** Certainly the most military of all qualities is general activity of body, whether of foot or hand. For escaping or for capturing an enemy, quickness of foot is required; but hand-to-hand conflict and combat need vigour and strength.

**CLEINIAS:** Very true.

**ATHENIAN:** Neither of them can attain their greatest efficiency without arms.

**CLEINIAS:** How can they?

**ATHENIAN:** Then our herald, in accordance with the prevailing practice, will first summon the runner;--he will appear armed, for to an unarmed competitor we will not give a prize. And he shall enter first who is to run the single course bearing arms; next, he who is to run the double course; third, he who is to run the horse-course; and fourthly, he who is to run the long course; the fifth whom we start, shall be the first sent forth in heavy armour, and shall run a course of sixty stadia to some temple of Ares--and we will send forth another, whom we will style the more heavily armed, to run over smoother ground. There remains the archer; and he shall run in the full equipments of an archer a distance of 100 stadia over mountains, and across every sort of country, to a temple of Apollo and Artemis; this shall be the order of the contest, and we will wait for them until they return, and will give a prize to the conqueror in each.

**CLEINIAS:** Very good.

**ATHENIAN:** Let us suppose that there are three kinds of contests,--one of boys, another of beardless youths, and a third of men. For the youths we will fix the length of the contest at two-thirds, and for the boys at half of the entire course, whether they contend as archers or as heavy-armed. Touching the women, let the girls who are not grown up compete naked in the stadium and the double course, and the horse-course and the long course, and let them run on the race-ground itself; those who are thirteen years of age and upwards until their marriage shall continue to share in contests if they are not more than twenty, and shall be compelled to run up to eighteen; and they shall descend into the arena in suitable dresses. Let these be the regulations about contests in running both for men and women.

Respecting contests of strength, instead of wrestling and similar contests of the heavier sort, we will institute conflicts in armour of one against one, and two against two, and so on up to ten against ten. As to what a man ought not to suffer or do, and to what extent, in order to gain the victory--as in wrestling, the masters of the art have laid down what is fair and what is not fair, so in fighting in armour--we ought to call in skilful persons, who shall judge for us and be our assessors in the work of legislation; they shall say who deserves to be victor in combats of this sort, and what he is not to do or have done to him, and in like manner what rule determines who is defeated; and let these ordinances apply to women until they are married as well as to men. The pancration shall have a counterpart in a combat of the light-armed; they shall contend with bows and with light shields and with javelins and in the throwing of stones by slings and by hand: and laws shall be made about it, and rewards and prizes given to him who best fulfils the ordinances of the law.

Next in order we shall have to legislate about the horse contests. Now we do not need many horses, for they cannot be of much use in a country like Crete, and hence we naturally do not take great pains about the rearing of them or about horse races. There is no one who keeps a chariot among us, and any rivalry in such matters would be altogether out of place; there would be no sense nor any shadow of sense in instituting contests which are not after the manner of our country. And therefore we give our prizes for single horses,--for colts who have not yet cast their teeth, and for those who are intermediate, and for the full-grown horses themselves; and thus our equestrian games will accord with the nature of the country. Let them have conflict and rivalry in these matters in accordance with the law, and let the colonels and generals of horse decide together about all courses and about the armed competitors in them. But we have nothing to say to the unarmed either in gymnastic exercises or in these contests. On the other hand, the Cretan bowman or javelin-man who fights in armour on horseback is useful, and therefore we may as well place a competition of this sort among our amusements. Women are not to be forced to compete by laws and ordinances; but if from previous training they have acquired the habit and are strong enough and like to take part, let them do so, girls as well as boys, and no blame to them.

Thus the competition in gymnastic and the mode of learning it have been described; and we have spoken also of the toils of the contest, and of daily exercises under the superintendence of masters. Likewise, what relates to music has been, for the most part, completed. But as to rhapsodes and the like, and the contests of choruses which are to perform at feasts, all this shall be arranged when the months and days and years have been appointed for Gods and demi-gods, whether every third year, or again every fifth year, or in whatever way or manner the Gods may put into men's minds the distribution and order of them. At the same time, we may expect that the musical contests will be celebrated in their turn by the command of the judges and the director of education and the guardians of the law meeting together for this purpose, and themselves becoming legislators of the times and nature and conditions of the choral contests and of dancing in general. What they ought severally to be in language and song, and in the admixture of harmony with rhythm and the dance, has been often declared by the original legislator; and his successors ought to follow him, making the games and sacrifices duly to correspond at fitting times, and appointing public festivals. It is not difficult to determine how these and the like matters may have a regular order; nor, again, will the alteration of them do any great good or harm to the state. There is, however, another matter of great importance and difficulty, concerning which God should legislate, if there were any possibility of obtaining from Him an ordinance about it. But seeing that divine aid is not to be had, there appears to be a need of some bold man who specially honours plainness of speech, and will say outright what he thinks best for the city and citizens,--ordaining what is good and convenient for the whole state amid the corruptions of human souls, opposing the mightiest lusts, and having no man his helper but himself standing alone and following reason only.

**CLEINIAS:** What is this, Stranger, that you are saying? For we do not as yet understand your meaning.

**ATHENIAN:** Very likely; I will endeavour to explain myself more clearly. When I came to the subject of education, I beheld young men and maidens holding friendly intercourse with one another. And there naturally arose in my mind a sort of apprehension--I could not help thinking how one is to deal with a city in which youths and maidens are well nurtured, and have nothing to do, and are not undergoing the excessive and servile toils which extinguish wantonness, and whose only cares during their whole life are sacrifices and festivals and dances. How, in such a state as this, will they abstain from desires which thrust many a man and woman into perdition; and from which reason, assuming the functions of law, commands them to abstain? The ordinances already made may possibly get the better of most of these desires; the prohibition of excessive wealth is a very considerable gain in the direction of temperance, and the whole education of our youth imposes a law of moderation on them; moreover, the eye of the rulers is required always to watch over the young, and never to lose sight of them; and these provisions do, as far as human means can effect anything, exercise a regulating influence upon the desires in general. But how can we take precautions against the unnatural loves of either sex, from which innumerable evils have come upon individuals and cities? How shall we devise a remedy and way of escape out of so great a danger? Truly, Cleinias, here is a difficulty. In many ways Crete and Lacedaemon furnish a great help to those who make peculiar laws; but in the matter of love, as we are alone, I must confess that they are quite against us. For if any one following nature should lay down the law which existed before the days of Laius, and denounce these lusts as contrary to nature, adducing the animals as a proof that such unions were monstrous, he might prove his point, but he would be wholly at variance with the custom of your states. Further, they are repugnant to a principle which we say that a legislator should always observe; for we are always enquiring which of our enactments tends to virtue and which not. And suppose we grant that these loves are accounted by law to be honourable, or at least not disgraceful, in what degree will they contribute to virtue? Will such passions implant in the soul of him who is seduced the habit of courage, or in the soul of the seducer the principle of temperance? Who will ever believe this?--or rather, who will not blame the effeminacy of him who yields to pleasures and is unable to hold out against them? Will not all men censure as womanly him who imitates the woman? And who would ever think of establishing such a practice by law? Certainly no one who had in his mind the image of true law. How can we prove that what I am saying is true? He who would rightly consider these matters must see the nature of friendship and desire, and of these so-called loves, for they are of two kinds, and out of the two arises a third kind, having the same name; and this similarity of name causes all the difficulty and obscurity.

**CLEINIAS:** How is that?

**ATHENIAN:** Dear is the like in virtue to the like, and the equal to the equal; dear also, though unlike, is he who has abundance to him who is in want. And when either of these friendships becomes excessive, we term the excess love.

**CLEINIAS:** Very true.

**ATHENIAN:** The friendship which arises from contraries is horrible and coarse, and has often no tie of communion; but that which arises from likeness is gentle, and has a tie of communion which lasts through life. As to the mixed sort which is made up of them both, there is, first of all, a difficulty in determining what he who is possessed by this third love desires; moreover, he is drawn different ways, and is in doubt between the two principles; the one exhorting him to enjoy the beauty of youth, and the other forbidding him. For the one is a lover of the body, and hungers after beauty, like ripe fruit, and would fain satisfy himself without any regard to the character of the beloved; the other holds the desire of the body to be a secondary matter, and looking rather than loving and with his soul desiring the soul of the other in a becoming manner, regards the satisfaction of the bodily love as wantonness; he reverences and respects temperance and courage and magnanimity and wisdom, and wishes to live chastely with the chaste object of his affection. Now the sort of love which is made up of the other two is that which we have described as the third. Seeing then that there are these three sorts of love, ought the law to prohibit and forbid them all to exist among us? Is it not rather clear that we should wish to have in the state the love which is of virtue and which desires the beloved youth to be the best possible; and the other two, if possible, we should hinder? What do you say, friend Megillus?

**MEGILLUS:** I think, Stranger, that you are perfectly right in what you have been now saying.

**ATHENIAN:** I knew well, my friend, that I should obtain your assent, which I accept, and therefore have no need to analyze your custom any further. Cleinias shall be prevailed upon to give me his assent at some other time. Enough of this; and now let us proceed to the laws.

**MEGILLUS:** Very good.

**ATHENIAN:** Upon reflection I see a way of imposing the law, which, in one respect, is easy, but, in another, is of the utmost difficulty.

**MEGILLUS:** What do you mean?

**ATHENIAN:** We are all aware that most men, in spite of their lawless natures, are very strictly and precisely restrained from intercourse with the fair, and this is not at all against their will, but entirely with their will.

**MEGILLUS:** When do you mean?

**ATHENIAN:** When any one has a brother or sister who is fair; and about a son or daughter the same unwritten law holds, and is a most perfect safeguard, so that no open or secret connexion ever takes place between them. Nor does the thought of such a thing ever enter at all into the minds of most of them.

**MEGILLUS:** Very true.

**ATHENIAN:** Does not a little word extinguish all pleasures of that sort?

**MEGILLUS:** What word?

**ATHENIAN:** The declaration that they are unholy, hated of God, and most infamous; and is not the reason of this that no one has ever said the opposite, but every one from his earliest childhood has heard men speaking in the same manner about them always and everywhere, whether in comedy or in the graver language of tragedy? When the poet introduces on the stage a Thyestes or an Oedipus, or a Macareus having secret intercourse with his sister, he represents him, when found out, ready to kill himself as the penalty of his sin.

**MEGILLUS:** You are very right in saying that tradition, if no breath of opposition ever assails it, has a marvellous power.

**ATHENIAN:** Am I not also right in saying that the legislator who wants to master any of the passions which master man may easily know how to subdue them? He will consecrate the tradition of their evil character among all, slaves and freemen, women and children, throughout the city:--that will be the surest foundation of the law which he can make.

**MEGILLUS:** Yes; but will he ever succeed in making all mankind use the same language about them?

**ATHENIAN:** A good objection; but was I not just now saying that I had a way to make men use natural love and abstain from unnatural, not intentionally destroying the seeds of human increase, or sowing them in stony places, in which they will take no root; and that I would command them to abstain too from any female field of increase in which that which is sown is not likely to grow? Now if a law to this effect could only be made perpetual, and gain an authority such as already prevents intercourse of parents and children--such a law, extending to other sensual desires, and conquering them, would be the source of ten thousand blessings. For, in the first place, moderation is the appointment of nature, and deters men from all frenzy and madness of love, and from all adulteries and immoderate use of meats and drinks, and makes them good friends to their own wives. And innumerable other benefits would result if such a could only be enforced. I can imagine some lusty youth who is standing by, and who, on hearing this enactment, declares in scurrilous terms that we are making foolish and impossible laws, and fills the world with his outcry. And therefore I said that I knew a way of enacting and perpetuating such a law, which was very easy in one respect, but in another most difficult. There is no difficulty in seeing that such a law is possible, and in what way; for, as I was saying, the ordinance once consecrated would master the soul of every man, and terrify him into obedience. But matters have now come to such a pass that even then the desired result seems as if it could not be attained, just as the continuance of an entire state in the practice of common meals is also deemed impossible. And although this latter is partly disproven by the fact of their existence among you, still even in your cities the common meals of women would be regarded as unnatural and impossible. I was thinking of the rebelliousness of the human heart when I said that the permanent establishment of these things is very difficult.

**MEGILLUS:** Very true.

**ATHENIAN:** Shall I try and find some sort of persuasive argument which will prove to you that such enactments are possible, and not beyond human nature?

**CLEINIAS:** By all means.

**ATHENIAN:** Is a man more likely to abstain from the pleasures of love and to do what he is bidden about them, when his body is in a good condition, or when he is in an ill condition, and out of training?

**CLEINIAS:** He will be far more temperate when he is in training.

**ATHENIAN:** And have we not heard of Iccus of Tarentum, who, with a view to the Olympic and other contests, in his zeal for his art, ind also because he was of a manly and temperate disposition, never had any connexion with a woman or a youth during the whole time of his training? And the same is said of Crison and Astylus and Diopompus and many others; and yet, Cleinias, they were far worse educated in their minds than your and my citizens, and in their bodies far more lusty.

**CLEINIAS:** No doubt this fact has been often affirmed positively by the ancients of these athletes.

**ATHENIAN:** And had they the courage to abstain from what is ordinarily deemed a pleasure for the sake of a victory in wrestling, running, and the like; and shall our young men be incapable of a similar endurance for the sake of a much nobler victory, which is the noblest of all, as from their youth upwards we will tell them, charming them, as we hope, into the belief of this by tales and sayings and songs?

**CLEINIAS:** Of what victory are you speaking?

**ATHENIAN:** Of the victory over pleasure, which if they win, they will live happily; or if they are conquered, the reverse of happily. And, further, may we not suppose that the fear of impiety will enable them to master that which other inferior people have mastered?

**CLEINIAS:** I dare say.

**ATHENIAN:** And since we have reached this point in our legislation, and have fallen into a difficulty by reason of the vices of mankind, I affirm that our ordinance should simply run in the following terms: Our citizens ought not to fall below the nature of birds and beasts in general, who are born in great multitudes, and yet remain until the age for procreation virgin and unmarried, but when they have reached the proper time of life are coupled, male and female, and lovingly pair together, and live the rest of their lives in holiness and innocence, abiding firmly in their original compact:--surely, we will say to them, you should be better than the animals. But if they are corrupted by the other Hellenes and the common practice of barbarians, and they see with their eyes and hear with their ears of the so-called free love everywhere prevailing among them, and they themselves are not able to get the better of the temptation, the guardians of the law, exercising the functions of lawgivers, shall devise a second law against them.

**CLEINIAS:** And what law would you advise them to pass if this one failed?

**ATHENIAN:** Clearly, Cleinias, the one which would naturally follow.

**CLEINIAS:** What is that?

**ATHENIAN:** Our citizens should not allow pleasures to strengthen with indulgence, but should by toil divert the aliment and exuberance of them into other parts of the body; and this will happen if no immodesty be allowed in the practice of love. Then they will be ashamed of frequent intercourse, and they will find pleasure, if seldom enjoyed, to be a less imperious mistress. They should not be found out doing anything of the sort. Concealment shall be honourable, and sanctioned by custom and made law by unwritten prescription; on the other hand, to be detected shall be esteemed dishonourable, but not, to abstain wholly. In this way there will be a second legal standard of honourable and dishonourable, involving a second notion of right. Three principles will comprehend all those corrupt natures whom we call inferior to themselves, and who form but one class, and will compel them not to transgress.

**CLEINIAS:** What are they?

**ATHENIAN:** The principle of piety, the love of honour, and the desire of beauty, not in the body but in the soul. These are, perhaps, romantic aspirations; but they are the noblest of aspirations, if they could only be realized in all states, and, God willing, in the matter of love we may be able to enforce one of two things--either that no one shall venture to touch any person of the freeborn or noble class except his wedded wife, or sow the unconsecrated and bastard seed among harlots, or in barren and unnatural lusts; or at least we may abolish altogether the connexion of men with men; and as to women, if any man has to do with any but those who come into his house duly married by sacred rites, whether they be bought or acquired in any other way, and he offends publicly in the face of all mankind, we shall be right in enacting that he be deprived of civic honours and privileges, and be deemed to be, as he truly is, a stranger. Let this law, then, whether it is one, or ought rather to be called two, be laid down respecting love in general, and the intercourse of the sexes which arises out of the desires, whether rightly or wrongly indulged.

**MEGILLUS:** I, for my part, Stranger, would gladly receive this law. Cleinias shall speak for himself, and tell you what is his opinion.

**CLEINIAS:** I will, Megillus, when an opportunity offers; at present, I think that we had better allow the Stranger to proceed with his laws.

**MEGILLUS:** Very good.

**ATHENIAN:** We had got about as far as the establishment of the common tables, which in most places would be difficult, but in Crete no one would think of introducing any other custom. There might arise a question about the manner of them--whether they shall be such as they are here in Crete, or such as they are in Lacedaemon,--or is there a third kind which may be better than either of them? The answer to this question might be easily discovered, but the discovery would do no great good, for at present they are very well ordered.

Leaving the common tables, we may therefore proceed to the means of providing food. Now, in cities the means of life are gained in many ways and from divers sources, and in general from two sources, whereas our city has only one. For most of the Hellenes obtain their food from sea and land, but our citizens from land only. And this makes the task of the legislator less difficult--half as many laws will be enough, and much less than half; and they will be of a kind better suited to free men. For he has nothing to do with laws about shipowners and merchants and retailers and innkeepers and tax collectors and mines and moneylending and compound interest and innumerable other things--bidding good-bye to these, he gives laws to husbandmen and shepherds and bee-keepers, and to the guardians and superintendents of their implements; and he has already legislated for greater matters, as for example, respecting marriage and the procreation and nurture of children, and for education, and the establishment of offices--and now he must direct his laws to those who provide food and labour in preparing it.

Let us first of all, then, have a class of laws which shall be called the laws of husbandmen. And let the first of them be the law of Zeus, the god of boundaries. Let no one shift the boundary line either of a fellow-citizen who is a neighbour, or, if he dwells at the extremity of the land, of any stranger who is conterminous with him, considering that this is truly 'to move the immovable,' and every one should be more willing to move the largest rock which is not a landmark, than the least stone which is the sworn mark of friendship and hatred between neighbours; for Zeus, the god of kindred, is the witness of the citizen, and Zeus, the god of strangers, of the stranger, and when aroused, terrible are the wars which they stir up. He who obeys the law will never know the fatal consequences of disobedience, but he who despises the law shall be liable to a double penalty, the first coming from the Gods, and the second from the law. For let no one wilfully remove the boundaries of his neighbour's land, and if any one does, let him who will inform the landowners, and let them bring him into court, and if he be convicted of re-dividing the land by stealth or by force, let the court determine what he ought to suffer or pay. In the next place, many small injuries done by neighbours to one another, through their multiplication, may cause a weight of enmity, and make neighbourhood a very disagreeable and bitter thing. Wherefore a man ought to be very careful of committing any offence against his neighbour, and especially of encroaching on his neighbour's land; for any man may easily do harm, but not every man can do good to another. He who encroaches on his neighbour's land,

and transgresses his boundaries, shall make good the damage, and, to cure him of his impudence and also of his meanness, he shall pay a double penalty to the injured party. Of these and the like matters the wardens of the country shall take cognizance, and be the judges of them and assessors of the damage; in the more important cases, as has been already said, the whole number of them belonging to any one of the twelve divisions shall decide, and in the lesser cases the commanders: or, again, if any one pastures his cattle on his neighbour's land, they shall see the injury, and adjudge the penalty. And if any one, by decoying the bees, gets possession of another's swarms, and draws them to himself by making noises, he shall pay the damage; or if any one sets fire to his own wood and takes no care of his neighbour's property, he shall be fined at the discretion of the magistrates. And if in planting he does not leave a fair distance between his own and his neighbour's land, he shall be punished, in accordance with the enactments of many lawgivers, which we may use, not deeming it necessary that the great legislator of our state should determine all the trifles which might be decided by any body; for example, husbandmen have had of old excellent laws about waters, and there is no reason why we should propose to divert their course: He who likes may draw water from the fountain-head of the common stream on to his own land, if he do not cut off the spring which clearly belongs to some other owner; and he may take the water in any direction which he pleases, except through a house or temple or sepulchre, but he must be careful to do no harm beyond the channel. And if there be in any place a natural dryness of the earth, which keeps in the rain from heaven, and causes a deficiency in the supply of water, let him dig down on his own land as far as the clay, and if at this depth he finds no water, let him obtain water from his neighbours, as much as is required for his servants' drinking, and if his neighbours, too, are limited in their supply, let him have a fixed measure, which shall be determined by the wardens of the country. This he shall receive each day, and on these terms have a share of his neighbours' water. If there be heavy rain, and one of those on the lower ground injures some tiller of the upper ground, or some one who has a common wall, by refusing to give them an outlet for water; or, again, if some one living on the higher ground recklessly lets off the water on his lower neighbour, and they cannot come to terms with one another, let him who will call in a warden of the city, if he be in the city, or if he be in the country, a warden of the country, and let him obtain a decision determining what each of them is to do. And he who will not abide by the decision shall suffer for his malignant and morose temper, and pay a fine to the injured party, equivalent to double the value of the injury, because he was unwilling to submit to the magistrates.

Now the participation of fruits shall be ordered on this wise. The goddess of Autumn has two gracious gifts: one, the joy of Dionysus which is not treasured up; the other, which nature intends to be stored. Let this be the law, then, concerning the fruits of autumn: He who tastes the common or storing fruits of autumn, whether grapes or figs, before the season of vintage which coincides with Arcturus, either on his own land or on that of others,--let him pay fifty drachmae, which shall be sacred to Dionysus, if he pluck them from his own land; and if from his neighbour's land, a mina, and if from any others', two-thirds of a mina. And he who would gather the 'choice' grapes or the 'choice' figs, as they are now termed, if he take them off his own land, let him pluck them how and when he likes; but if he take them from the ground of others without their leave, let him in that case be always punished in accordance with the law which ordains that he should not move what he has not laid down. And if a slave touches any fruit of this sort, without the consent of the owner of the land, he shall be beaten with as many blows as there are grapes on the bunch, or figs on the fig-tree. Let a metic purchase the 'choice' autumnal fruit, and then, if he pleases, he may gather it; but if a stranger is passing along the road, and desires to eat, let him take of the 'choice' grape for himself and a single follower without payment, as a tribute of hospitality. The law however forbids strangers from sharing in the sort which is not used for eating; and if any one, whether he be master or slave, takes of them in ignorance, let the slave be beaten, and the freeman dismissed with admonitions, and instructed to take of the other autumnal fruits which are unfit for making raisins and wine, or for laying by as dried figs. As to pears, and apples, and pomegranates, and similar fruits, there shall be no disgrace in taking them secretly; but he who is caught, if he be of less than thirty years of age, shall be struck and beaten off, but not wounded; and no freeman shall have any right of satisfaction for such blows. Of these fruits the stranger may partake, just as he may of the fruits of autumn. And if an elder, who is more than thirty years of age, eat of them on the spot, let him, like the stranger, be allowed to partake of all such fruits, but he must carry away nothing. If, however, he will not obey the law, let him run risk of failing in the competition of virtue, in case any one takes notice of his actions before the judges at the time.

Water is the greatest element of nutrition in gardens, but is easily polluted. You cannot poison the soil, or the sun, or the air, which are the other elements of nutrition in plants, or divert them, or steal them; but all these things may very likely happen in regard to water, which must therefore be protected by law. And let this be the law:--If any one intentionally pollutes the water of another, whether the water of a spring, or collected in reservoirs, either by poisonous substances, or by digging, or by theft, let the injured party bring the cause before the wardens of the city, and claim in writing the value of the loss; if the accused be found guilty of injuring the water by deleterious substances, let him not only pay damages, but purify the stream or the cistern which contains the water, in such manner as the laws of the interpreters order the purification to be made by the offender in each case.

With respect to the gathering in of the fruits of the soil, let a man, if he pleases, carry his own fruits through any place in which he either does no harm to any one, or himself gains three times as much as his neighbour loses. Now of these things the magistrates should be cognisant, as of all other things in which a man intentionally does injury to another or to the property of another, by fraud or force, in the use which he makes of his own property. All these matters a man should lay before the magistrates, and receive damages, supposing the injury to be not more than three minae; or if he have a charge against another which involves a larger amount, let him bring his suit into the public courts and have the evil-doer punished. But if any of the magistrates appear to adjudge the penalties which he imposes in an unjust spirit, let him be liable to pay double to the injured party. Any one may bring the offences of magistrates, in any particular case, before the public courts. There are innumerable little matters relating to the modes of punishment, and applications for suits, and summonses and the witnesses to summonses--for example, whether two witnesses should be required for a summons, or how many--and all such details, which cannot be omitted in legislation, but are beneath the wisdom of an aged legislator. These lesser matters, as they indeed are in comparison with the greater ones, let a younger generation regulate by law, after the patterns which have preceded, and according to their own experience of the usefulness and necessity of such laws; and when they are duly regulated let there be no alteration, but let the citizens live in the observance of them.

Now of artisans, let the regulations be as follows:--In the first place, let no citizen or servant of a citizen be occupied in handicraft arts; for he who is to secure and preserve the public order of the state, has an art which requires much study and many kinds of knowledge, and does not admit of being made a secondary occupation; and hardly any human being is capable of pursuing two professions or two arts rightly, or of practising one art himself, and superintending some one else who is practising another. Let this, then, be our first principle in the state:--No one who is a smith shall also be a carpenter, and if he be a carpenter, he shall not superintend the smith's art rather than his own, under the pretext that in superintending many servants who are working for him, he is likely to superintend them better, because more revenue will accrue to him from them than from his own art; but let every man in the state have one art, and get his living by that. Let the wardens of the city labour to maintain this law, and if any citizen incline to any other art than the study of virtue, let them punish him with disgrace and infamy, until they bring him back into his own right course; and if any stranger profess two arts, let them chastise him with bonds and money penalties, and expulsion from the state, until they compel him to be one only and not many.

But as touching payments for hire, and contracts of work, or in case any one does wrong to any of the citizens, or they do wrong to any other, up to fifty drachmae, let the wardens of the city decide the case; but if a greater amount be involved, then let the public courts decide according to law. Let no one pay any duty either on the importation or exportation of goods; and as to frankincense and similar perfumes, used in the service of the Gods, which come from abroad, and purple and other dyes which are not produced in the country, or the materials of any art which have to be imported, and which are not necessary--no one should import them; nor, again, should any one export anything which is wanted in the country. Of all these things let there be inspectors and superintendents, taken from the guardians of the law; and they shall be the twelve next in order to the five seniors. Concerning arms, and all implements which are required for military purposes, if there be need of introducing any art, or plant, or metal, or chains of any kind, or animals for use in war, let the commanders of the horse and the generals have authority over their importation and exportation; the city shall send them out and also receive them, and the guardians of the law shall make fit and proper laws about them. But let there be no retail trade for the sake of moneymaking, either in these or any other articles, in the city or country at all.

With respect to food and the distribution of the produce of the country, the right and proper way seems to be nearly that which is the custom of Crete; for all should be required to distribute the fruits of the soil into twelve parts, and in this way consume them. Let the twelfth portion of each (as for instance of wheat and barley, to which the rest of the fruits of the earth shall be added, as well as the animals which are for sale in each of the twelve divisions) be divided in due proportion into three parts; one part for freemen, another for their servants, and a third for craftsmen and in general for strangers, whether sojourners who may be dwelling in the city, and like other men must live, or those who come on some business which they have with the state, or with some individual. Let only this third part of all necessaries be required to be sold; out of the other two-thirds no one shall be compelled to sell. And how will they be best distributed? In the first place, we see clearly that the distribution will be of equals in one point of view, and in another point of view of unequals.

**CLEINIAS:** What do you mean?

**ATHENIAN:** I mean that the earth of necessity produces and nourishes the various articles of food, sometimes better and sometimes worse.

**CLEINIAS:** Of course.

**ATHENIAN:** Such being the case, let no one of the three portions be greater than either of the other two;--neither that which is assigned to masters or to slaves, nor again that of the stranger; but let the distribution to all be equal and alike, and let every citizen take his two portions and distribute them among slaves and freemen, he having power to determine the quantity and quality. And what remains he shall distribute by measure and number among the animals who have to be sustained from the earth, taking the whole number of them.

In the second place, our citizens should have separate houses duly ordered, and this will be the order proper for men like them. There shall be twelve hamlets, one in the middle of each twelfth portion, and in each hamlet they shall first set apart a market-place, and the temples of the Gods, and of their attendant demi-gods; and if there be any local deities of the Magnetes, or holy seats of other ancient deities, whose memory has been preserved, to these let them pay their ancient honours. But Hestia, and Zeus, and Athene will have temples everywhere together with the God who presides in each of the twelve districts. And the first erection of houses shall be around these temples, where the ground is highest, in order to provide the safest and most defensible place of retreat for the guards. All the rest of the country they shall settle in the following manner:-- They shall make thirteen divisions of the craftsmen; one of them they shall establish in the city, and this, again, they shall subdivide into twelve lesser divisions, among the twelve districts of the city, and the remainder shall be distributed in the country round about; and in each village they shall settle various classes of craftsmen, with a view to the convenience of the husbandmen. And the chief officers of the wardens of the country shall superintend all these matters, and see how many of them, and which class of them, each place requires; and fix them where they are likely to be least troublesome, and most useful to the husbandman. And the wardens of the city shall see to similar matters in the city.

Now the wardens of the agora ought to see to the details of the agora. Their first care, after the temples which are in the agora have been seen to, should be to prevent any one from doing any wrong in dealings between man and man; in the second place, as being inspectors of temperance and violence, they should chastise him who requires chastisement. Touching articles of sale, they should first see whether the articles which the citizens are under regulations to sell to strangers are sold to them, as the law ordains. And let the law be as follows:--On the first day of the month, the persons in charge, whoever they are, whether strangers or slaves, who have the charge on behalf of the citizens, shall produce to the strangers the portion which falls to them, in the first place, a twelfth portion of the corn;--the stranger shall purchase corn for the whole month, and other cereals, on the first market day; and on the tenth day of the month the one party shall sell, and the other buy, liquids sufficient to last during the whole month; and on the twenty-third day there shall be a sale of animals by those who are willing to sell to the people who want to buy, and of implements and other things which husbandmen sell (such as skins and all kinds of clothing, either woven or made of felt and other goods of the same sort,) and which strangers are compelled to buy and purchase of others. As to the retail trade in these things, whether of barley or wheat set apart for meal and flour, or any other kind of food, no one shall sell them to citizens or their slaves, nor shall any one buy of a citizen; but let the stranger sell them in the market of strangers, to artisans and their slaves, making an exchange of wine and food, which is commonly called retail trade. And butchers shall offer for sale parts of dismembered animals to the strangers, and artisans, and their servants. Let any stranger who likes buy fuel from day to day wholesale, from those who have the care of it in the country, and let him sell to the strangers as much he pleases and when he pleases. As to other goods and implements which are likely to be wanted, they shall sell them in the common market, at any place which the guardians of the law and the wardens of the market and city, choosing according to their judgment, shall determine; at such places they shall exchange money for goods, and goods for money, neither party giving credit to the other; and he who gives credit must be satisfied, whether he obtain his money not, for in such exchanges he will not be protected by law. But whenever property has been bought or sold, greater in quantity or value than is allowed by the law, which has determined within what limits a man may increase and diminish his possessions, let the excess be registered in the books of the guardians of the law; or in case of diminution, let there be an erasure made. And let the same rule be observed about the registration of the property of the metics. Any one who likes may come and be a metic on certain conditions; a foreigner, if he likes, and is able to settle, may dwell in the land, but he must practise an art, and not abide more than twenty years from the time at which he has registered himself; and he shall pay no sojourner's tax, however small, except good conduct, nor any other tax for buying and selling. But when the twenty years have expired, he shall take his property with him and depart. And if in the course of these years he should chance to distinguish himself by any considerable benefit which he confers on the state, and he thinks that he can persuade the council and assembly, either to grant him delay in leaving the country, or to allow him to remain for the whole of his life, let him go and persuade the city, and whatever they assent to at his instance shall take effect. For the children of the metics, being artisans, and of fifteen years of age, let the time of their sojourn commence after their fifteenth year; and let them remain for twenty years, and then go where they like; but any of them who wishes to remain, may do so, if he can persuade the council and assembly. And if he depart, let him erase all the entries which have been made by him in the register kept by the magistrates.

# BOOK IX.

Next to all the matters which have preceded in the natural order of legislation will come suits of law. Of suits those which relate to agriculture have been already described, but the more important have not been described. Having mentioned them severally under their usual names, we will proceed to say what punishments are to be inflicted for each offence, and who are to be the judges of them.

**CLEINIAS:** Very good.

**ATHENIAN:** There is a sense of disgrace in legislating, as we are about to do, for all the details of crime in a state which, as we say, is to be well regulated and will be perfectly adapted to the practice of virtue. To assume that in such a state there will arise some one who will be guilty of crimes as heinous as any which are ever perpetrated in other states, and that we must legislate for him by anticipation, and threaten and make laws against him if he should arise, in order to deter him, and punish his acts, under the idea that he will arise--this, as I was saying, is in a manner disgraceful. Yet seeing that we are not like the ancient legislators, who gave laws to heroes and sons of gods, being, according to the popular belief, themselves the offspring of the gods, and legislating for others, who were also the children of divine parents, but that we are only men who are legislating for the sons of men, there is no uncharitableness in apprehending that some one of our citizens may be like a seed which has touched the ox's horn, having a heart so hard that it cannot be softened any more than those seeds can be softened by fire. Among our citizens there may be those who cannot be subdued by all the strength of the laws; and for their sake, though an ungracious task, I will proclaim my first law about the robbing of temples, in case any one should dare to commit such a crime. I do not expect or imagine that any well-brought-up citizen will ever take the infection, but their servants, and strangers, and strangers' servants may be guilty of many impieties. And with a view to them especially, and yet not without a provident eye to the weakness of human nature generally, I will proclaim the law about robbers of temples and similar incurable, or almost incurable, criminals. Having already agreed that such enactments ought always to have a short prelude, we may speak to the criminal, whom some tormenting desire by night and by day tempts to go and rob a temple, the fewest possible words of admonition and exhortation: --O sir, we will say to him, the impulse which moves you to rob temples is not an ordinary human malady, nor yet a visitation of heaven, but a madness which is begotten in a man from ancient and unexpiated crimes of his race, an ever-recurring curse;--against this you must guard with all your might, and how you are to guard we will explain to you. When any such thought comes into your mind, go and perform expiations, go as a suppliant to the temples of the Gods who avert evils, go to the society of those who are called good men among you; hear them tell and yourself try to repeat after them, that every man should honour the noble and the just. Fly from the company of the wicked--fly and turn not back; and if your disorder is lightened by these remedies, well and good, but if not, then acknowledge death to be nobler than life, and depart hence.

Such are the preludes which we sing to all who have thoughts of unholy and treasonable actions, and to him who hearkens to them the law has nothing to say. But to him who is disobedient when the prelude is over, cry with a loud voice--He who is taken in the act of robbing temples, if he be a slave or stranger, shall have his evil deed engraven on his face and hands, and shall be beaten with as many stripes as may seem good to the judges, and be cast naked beyond the borders of the land. And if he suffers this punishment he will probably return to his right mind and be improved; for no penalty which the law inflicts is designed for evil, but always makes him who suffers either better or not so much worse as he would have been. But if any citizen be found guilty of any great or unmentionable wrong, either in relation to the gods, or his parents, or the state, let the judge deem him to be incurable, remembering that after receiving such an excellent education and training from youth upward, he has not abstained from the greatest of crimes. His punishment shall be death, which to him will be the least of evils; and his example will benefit others, if he perish ingloriously, and be cast beyond the borders of the land. But let his children and family, if they avoid the ways of their father, have glory, and let honourable mention be made of them, as having nobly and manfully escaped out of evil into good. None of them should have their goods confiscated to the state, for the lots of the citizens ought always to continue the same and equal.

Touching the exaction of penalties, when a man appears to have done anything which deserves a fine, he shall pay the fine, if he have anything in excess of the lot which is assigned to him; but more than that he shall not pay. And to secure exactness, let the guardians of the law refer to the registers, and inform the judges of the precise truth, in order that none of the lots may go uncultivated for want of money. But if any one seems to deserve a greater penalty, let him undergo a long and public imprisonment and be dishonoured, unless some of his friends are willing to be surety for him, and liberate him by assisting him to pay the fine. No criminal shall go unpunished, not even for a single offence, nor if he have fled the country; but let the penalty be according to his deserts,--death, or bonds, or blows, or degrading places of sitting or standing, or removal to some temple on the borders of the land; or let him pay fines, as we said before. In cases of death, let the judges be the guardians of the law, and a court selected by merit from the last year's magistrates. But how the causes are to be brought into court, how the summonses are to be served, the the like, these things may be left to the younger generation of legislators to determine; the manner of voting we must determine ourselves.

Let the vote be given openly; but before they come to the vote let the judges sit in order of seniority over against plaintiff and defendant, and let all the citizens who can spare time hear and take a serious interest in listening to such causes. First of all the plaintiff shall make one speech, and then the defendant shall make another; and after the speeches have been made the eldest judge shall begin to examine the parties, and proceed to make an adequate enquiry into what has been said; and after the oldest has spoken, the rest shall proceed in order to examine either party as to what he finds defective in the evidence, whether of statement or omission; and he who has nothing to ask shall hand over the examination to another. And on so much of what has been said as is to the purpose all the judges shall set their seals, and place the writings on the altar of Hestia. On the next day they shall meet again, and in like manner put their questions and go through the cause, and again set their seals upon the evidence; and when they have three times done this, and have had witnesses and evidence enough, they shall each of them give a holy vote, after promising by Hestia that they will decide justly and truly to the utmost of their power; and so they shall put an end to the suit.

Next, after what relates to the Gods, follows what relates to the dissolution of the state:--Whoever by promoting a man to power enslaves the laws, and subjects the city to factions, using violence and stirring up sedition contrary to law, him we will deem the greatest enemy of the whole state. But he who takes no part in such proceedings, and, being one of the chief magistrates of the state, has no knowledge of the treason, or, having knowledge of it, by reason of cowardice does not interfere on behalf of his country, such an one we must consider nearly as bad. Every man who is worth anything will inform the magistrates, and bring the conspirator to trial for making a violent and illegal attempt to change the government. The judges of such cases shall be the same as of the robbers of temples; and let the whole proceeding be carried on in the same way, and the vote of the majority condemn to death. But let there be a general rule, that the disgrace and punishment of the father is not to be visited on the children, except in the case of some one whose father, grandfather, and great- grandfather have successively undergone the penalty of death. Such persons the city shall send away with all their possessions to the city and country of their ancestors, retaining only and wholly their appointed lot. And out of the citizens who have more than one son of not less than ten years of age, they shall select ten whom their father or grandfather by the mother's or father's side shall appoint, and let them send to Delphi the names of those who are selected, and him whom the God chooses they shall establish as heir of the house which has failed; and may he have better fortune than his predecessors!

**CLEINIAS:** Very good.

**ATHENIAN:** Once more let there be a third general law respecting the judges who are to give judgment, and the manner of conducting suits against those who are tried on an accusation of treason; and as concerning the remaining or departure of their descendants,--there shall be one law for all three, for the traitor, and the robber of temples, and the subverter by violence of the laws of the state. For a thief, whether he steal much or little, let there be one law, and one punishment for all alike: in the first place, let him pay double the amount of the theft if he be convicted, and if he have so much over and above the allotment;--if he have not, he shall be bound until he pay the penalty, or persuade him who has obtained the sentence against him to forgive him. But if a person be convicted of a theft against the state, then if he can persuade the city, or if he will pay back twice the amount of the theft, he shall be set free from his bonds.

**CLEINIAS:** What makes you say, Stranger, that a theft is all one, whether the thief may have taken much or little, and either from sacred or secular places--and these are not the only differences in thefts:--seeing, then, that they are of many kinds, ought not the legislator to adapt himself to them, and impose upon them entirely different penalties?

**ATHENIAN:** Excellent. I was running on too fast, Cleinias, and you impinged upon me, and brought me to my senses, reminding me of what, indeed, had occurred to my mind already, that legislation was never yet rightly worked out, as I may say in passing.--Do you remember the image in which I likened the men for whom laws are now made to slaves who are doctored by slaves? For of this you may be very sure, that if one of those empirical physicians, who practise medicine without science, were to come upon the gentleman physician talking to his gentleman patient, and using the language almost of philosophy, beginning at the beginning of the disease and discoursing about the whole nature of the body, he would burst into a hearty laugh--he would say what most of those who are called doctors always have at their tongue's end:--Foolish fellow, he would say, you are not healing the sick man, but you are educating him; and he does not want to be made a doctor, but to get well.

**CLEINIAS:** And would he not be right?

**ATHENIAN:** Perhaps he would; and he might remark upon us, that he who discourses about laws, as we are now doing, is giving the citizens education and not laws; that would be rather a telling observation.

**CLEINIAS:** Very true.

**ATHENIAN:** But we are fortunate.

**CLEINIAS:** In what way?

**ATHENIAN:** Inasmuch as we are not compelled to give laws, but we may take into consideration every form of government, and ascertain what is best and what is most needful, and how they may both be carried into execution; and we may also, if we please, at this very moment choose what is best, or, if we prefer, what is most necessary--which shall we do?

**CLEINIAS:** There is something ridiculous, Stranger, in our proposing such an alternative, as if we were legislators, simply bound under some great necessity which cannot be deferred to the morrow. But we, as I may by the grace of Heaven affirm, like gatherers of stones or beginners of some composite work, may gather a heap of materials, and out of this, at our leisure, select what is suitable for our projected construction. Let us then suppose ourselves to be at leisure, not of necessity building, but rather like men who are partly providing materials, and partly putting them together. And we may truly say that some of our laws, like stones, are already fixed in their places, and others lie at hand.

**ATHENIAN:** Certainly, in that case, Cleinias, our view of law will be more in accordance with nature. For there is another matter affecting legislators, which I must earnestly entreat you to consider.

**CLEINIAS:** What is it?

**ATHENIAN:** There are many writings to be found in cities, and among them there are discourses composed by legislators as well as by other persons.

**CLEINIAS:** To be sure.

**ATHENIAN:** Shall we give heed rather to the writings of those others,--poets and the like, who either in metre or out of metre have recorded their advice about the conduct of life, and not to the writings of legislators? or shall we give heed to them above all?

**CLEINIAS:** Yes; to them far above all others.

**ATHENIAN:** And ought the legislator alone among writers to withhold his opinion about the beautiful, the good, and the just, and not to teach what they are, and how they are to be pursued by those who intend to be happy?

**CLEINIAS:** Certainly not.

**ATHENIAN:** And is it disgraceful for Homer and Tyrtaeus and other poets to lay down evil precepts in their writings respecting life and the pursuits of men, but not so disgraceful for Lycurgus and Solon and others who were legislators as well as writers? Is it not true that of all the writings to be found in cities, those which relate to laws, when you unfold and read them, ought to be by far the noblest and the best? and should not other writings either agree with them, or if they disagree, be deemed ridiculous? We should consider whether the laws of states ought not to have the character of loving and wise parents, rather than of tyrants and masters, who command and threaten, and, after writing their decrees on walls, go their ways; and whether, in discoursing of laws, we should not take the gentler view of them which may or may not be attainable,--at any rate, we will show our readiness to entertain such a view, and be prepared to undergo whatever may be the result. And may the result be good, and if God be gracious, it will be good!

**CLEINIAS:** Excellent; let us do as you say.

**ATHENIAN:** Then we will now consider accurately, as we proposed, what relates to robbers of temples, and all kinds of thefts, and offences in general; and we must not be annoyed if, in the course of legislation, we have enacted some things, and have not made up our minds about some others; for as yet we are not legislators, but we may soon be. Let us, if you please, consider these matters.

**CLEINIAS:** By all means.

**ATHENIAN:** Concerning all things honourable and just, let us then endeavour to ascertain how far we are consistent with ourselves, and how far we are inconsistent, and how far the many, from whom at any rate we should profess a desire to differ, agree and disagree among themselves.

**CLEINIAS:** What are the inconsistencies which you observe in us?

**ATHENIAN:** I will endeavour to explain. If I am not mistaken, we are all agreed that justice, and just men and things and actions, are all fair, and, if a person were to maintain that just men, even when they are deformed in body, are still perfectly beautiful in respect of the excellent justice of their minds, no one would say that there was any inconsistency in this.

**CLEINIAS:** They would be quite right.

**ATHENIAN:** Perhaps; but let us consider further, that if all things which are just are fair and honourable, in the term 'all' we must include just sufferings which are the correlatives of just actions.

**CLEINIAS:** And what is the inference?

**ATHENIAN:** The inference is, that a just action in partaking of the just partakes also in the same degree of the fair and honourable.

**CLEINIAS:** Certainly.

**ATHENIAN:** And must not a suffering which partakes of the just principle be admitted to be in the same degree fair and honourable, if the argument is consistently carried out?

**CLEINIAS:** True.

**ATHENIAN:** But then if we admit suffering to be just and yet dishonourable, and the term 'dishonourable' is applied to justice, will not the just and the honourable disagree?

**CLEINIAS:** What do you mean?

**ATHENIAN:** A thing not difficult to understand; the laws which have been already enacted would seem to announce principles directly opposed to what we are saying.

**CLEINIAS:** To what?

**ATHENIAN:** We had enacted, if I am not mistaken, that the robber of temples, and he who was the enemy of law and order, might justly be put to death, and we were proceeding to make divers other enactments of a similar nature. But we stopped short, because we saw that these sufferings are infinite in number and degree, and that they are, at once, the most just and also the most dishonourable of all sufferings. And if this be true, are not the just and the honourable at one time all the same, and at another time in the most diametrical opposition?

**CLEINIAS:** Such appears to be the case.

**ATHENIAN:** In this discordant and inconsistent fashion does the language of the many rend asunder the honourable and just.

**CLEINIAS:** Very true, Stranger.

**ATHENIAN:** Then now, Cleinias, let us see how far we ourselves are consistent about these matters.

**CLEINIAS:** Consistent in what?

**ATHENIAN:** I think that I have clearly stated in the former part of the discussion, but if I did not, let me now state--

**CLEINIAS:** What?

**ATHENIAN:** That all bad men are always involuntarily bad; and from this must proceed to draw a further inference.

**CLEINIAS:** What is it?

**ATHENIAN:** That the unjust man may be bad, but that he is bad against his will. Now that an action which is voluntary should be done involuntarily is a contradiction; wherefore he who maintains that injustice is involuntary will deem that the unjust does injustice involuntarily. I too admit that all men do injustice involuntarily, and if any contentious or disputatious person says that men are unjust against their will, and yet that many do injustice willingly, I do not agree with him. But, then, how can I avoid being inconsistent with myself, if you, Cleinias, and you, Megillus, say to me,--Well, Stranger, if all this be as you say, how about legislating for the city of the Magnetes--shall we legislate or not--what do you advise? Certainly we will, I should reply. Then will you determine for them what are voluntary and what are involuntary crimes, and shall we make the punishments greater of voluntary errors and crimes and less for the involuntary? or shall we make the punishment of all to be alike, under the idea that there is no such thing as voluntary crime?

**CLEINIAS:** Very good, Stranger; and what shall we say in answer to these objections?

**ATHENIAN:** That is a very fair question. In the first place, let us--

**CLEINIAS:** Do what?

**ATHENIAN:** Let us remember what has been well said by us already, that our ideas of justice are in the highest degree confused and contradictory. Bearing this in mind, let us proceed to ask ourselves once more whether we have discovered a way out of the difficulty. Have we ever determined in what respect these two classes of actions differ from one another? For in all states and by all legislators whatsoever, two kinds of actions have been distinguished--the one, voluntary, the other, involuntary; and they have legislated about them accordingly. But shall this new word of ours, like an oracle of God, be only spoken, and get away without giving any explanation or verification of itself? How can a word not understood be the basis of legislation? Impossible. Before proceeding to legislate, then, we must prove that they are two, and what is the difference between them, that when we impose the penalty upon either, every one may understand our proposal, and be able in some way to judge whether the penalty is fitly or unfitly inflicted.

**CLEINIAS:** I agree with you, Stranger; for one of two things is certain: either we must not say that all unjust acts are involuntary, or we must show the meaning and truth of this statement.

**ATHENIAN:** Of these two alternatives, the one is quite intolerable--not to speak what I believe to be the truth would be to me unlawful and unholy. But if acts of injustice cannot be divided into voluntary and involuntary, I must endeavour to find some other distinction between them.

**CLEINIAS:** Very true, Stranger; there cannot be two opinions among us upon that point.

**ATHENIAN:** Reflect, then; there are hurts of various kinds done by the citizens to one another in the intercourse of life, affording plentiful examples both of the voluntary and involuntary.

**CLEINIAS:** Certainly.

**ATHENIAN:** I would not have any one suppose that all these hurts are injuries, and that these injuries are of two kinds--one, voluntary, and the other, involuntary; for the involuntary hurts of all men are quite as many and as great as the voluntary. And please to consider whether I am right or quite wrong in what I am going to say; for I deny, Cleinias and Megillus, that he who harms another involuntarily does him an injury involuntarily, nor should I legislate about such an act under the idea that I am legislating for an involuntary injury. But I should rather say that such a hurt, whether great or small, is not an injury at all; and, on the other hand, if I am right, when a benefit is wrongly conferred, the author of the benefit may often be said to injure. For I maintain, O my friends, that the mere giving or taking away of anything is not to be described either as just or unjust; but the legislator has to consider whether mankind do good or harm to one another out of a just principle and intention. On the distinction between injustice and hurt he must fix his eye; and when there is hurt, he must, as far as he can, make the hurt good by law, and save that which is ruined, and raise up that which is fallen, and make that which is dead or wounded whole. And when compensation has been given for injustice, the law must always seek to win over the doers and sufferers of the several hurts from feelings of enmity to those of friendship.

**CLEINIAS:** Very good.

**ATHENIAN:** Then as to unjust hurts (and gains also, supposing the injustice to bring gain), of these we may heal as many as are capable of being healed, regarding them as diseases of the soul; and the cure of injustice will take the following direction.

**CLEINIAS:** What direction?

**ATHENIAN:** When any one commits any injustice, small or great, the law will admonish and compel him either never at all to do the like again, or never voluntarily, or at any rate in a far less degree; and he must in addition pay for the hurt. Whether the end is to be attained by word or action, with pleasure or pain, by giving or taking away privileges, by means of fines or gifts, or in whatsoever way the law shall proceed to make a man hate injustice, and love or not hate the nature of the just,--this is quite the noblest work of law. But if the legislator sees any one who is incurable, for him he will appoint a law and a penalty. He knows quite well that to such men themselves there is no profit in the continuance of their lives, and that they would do a double good to the rest of mankind if they would take their departure, inasmuch as they would be an example to other men not to offend, and they would relieve the city of bad citizens. In such cases, and in such cases only, the legislator ought to inflict death as the punishment of offences.

**CLEINIAS:** What you have said appears to me to be very reasonable, but will you favour me by stating a little more clearly the difference between hurt and injustice, and the various complications of the voluntary and involuntary which enter into them?

**ATHENIAN:** I will endeavour to do as you wish:--Concerning the soul, thus much would be generally said and allowed, that one element in her nature is passion, which may be described either as a state or a part of her, and is hard to be striven against and contended with, and by irrational force overturns many things.

**CLEINIAS:** Very true.

**ATHENIAN:** And pleasure is not the same with passion, but has an opposite power, working her will by persuasion and by the force of deceit in all things.

**CLEINIAS:** Quite true.

**ATHENIAN:** A man may truly say that ignorance is a third cause of crimes. Ignorance, however, may be conveniently divided by the legislator into two sorts: there is simple ignorance, which is the source of lighter offences, and double ignorance, which is accompanied by a conceit of wisdom; and he who is under the influence of the latter fancies that he knows all about matters of which he knows nothing. This second kind of ignorance, when possessed of power and strength, will be held by the legislator to be the source of great and monstrous times, but when attended with weakness, will only result in the errors of children and old men; and these he will treat as errors, and will make laws accordingly for those who commit them, which will be the mildest and most merciful of all laws.

**CLEINIAS:** You are perfectly right.

**ATHENIAN:** We all of us remark of one man that he is superior to pleasure and passion, and of another that he is inferior to them; and this is true.

**CLEINIAS:** Certainly.

**ATHENIAN:** But no one was ever yet heard to say that one of us is superior and another inferior to ignorance.

**CLEINIAS:** Very true.

**ATHENIAN:** We are speaking of motives which incite men to the fulfilment of their will; although an individual may be often drawn by them in opposite directions at the same time.

**CLEINIAS:** Yes, often.

**ATHENIAN:** And now I can define to you clearly, and without ambiguity, what I mean by the just and unjust, according to my notion of them:--When anger and fear, and pleasure and pain, and jealousies and desires, tyrannize over the soul, whether they do any harm or not,--I call all this injustice. But when the opinion of the best, in whatever part of human nature states or individuals may suppose that to dwell, has dominion in the soul and orders the life of every man, even if it be sometimes mistaken, yet what is done in accordance therewith, the principle in individuals which obeys this rule, and is best for the whole life of man, is to be called just; although the hurt done by mistake is thought by many to be involuntary injustice. Leaving the question of names, about which we are not going to quarrel, and having already delineated three sources of error, we may begin by recalling them somewhat more vividly to our memory:--One of them was of the painful sort, which we denominate anger and fear.

**CLEINIAS:** Quite right.

**ATHENIAN:** There was a second consisting of pleasures and desires, and a third of hopes, which aimed at true opinion about the best. The latter being subdivided into three, we now get five sources of actions, and for these five we will make laws of two kinds.

**CLEINIAS:** What are the two kinds?

**ATHENIAN:** There is one kind of actions done by violence and in the light of day, and another kind of actions which are done in darkness and with secret deceit, or sometimes both with violence and deceit; the laws concerning these last ought to have a character of severity.

**CLEINIAS:** Naturally.

**ATHENIAN:** And now let us return from this digression and complete the work of legislation. Laws have been already enacted by us concerning the robbers of the Gods, and concerning traitors, and also concerning those who corrupt the laws for the purpose of subverting the government. A man may very likely commit some of these crimes, either in a state of madness or when affected by disease, or under the influence of extreme old age, or in a fit of childish wantonness, himself no better than a child. And if this be made evident to the judges elected to try the cause, on the appeal of the criminal or his advocate, and he be judged to have been in this state when he committed the offence, he shall simply pay for the hurt which he may have done to another; but he shall be exempt from other penalties, unless he have slain some one, and have on his hands the stain of blood. And in that case he shall go to another land and country, and there dwell for a year; and if he return before the expiration of the time which the law appoints, or even set his foot at all on his native land, he shall be bound by the guardians of the law in the public prison for two years, and then go free.

Having begun to speak of homicide, let us endeavour to lay down laws concerning every different kind of homicide; and, first of all, concerning violent and involuntary homicides. If any one in an athletic contest, and at the public games, involuntarily kills a friend, and he dies either at the time or afterwards of the blows which he has received; or if the like misfortune happens to any one in war, or military exercises, or mimic contests of which the magistrates enjoin the practice, whether with or without arms, when he has been purified according to the law brought from Delphi relating to these matters, he shall be innocent. And so in the case of physicians: if their patient dies against their will, they shall be held guiltless by the law. And if one slay another with his own hand, but unintentionally, whether he be unarmed or have some instrument or dart in his hand; or if he kill him by administering food or drink, or by the application of fire or cold, or by suffocating him, whether he do the deed by his own hand, or by the agency of others, he shall be deemed the agent, and shall suffer one of the following penalties:--If he kill the slave of another in the belief that he is his own, he shall bear the master of the dead man harmless from loss, or shall pay a penalty of twice the value of the dead man, which the judges shall assess; but purifications must be used greater and more numerous than for those who committed homicide at the games;--what they are to be, the interpreters whom the God appoints shall be authorized to declare. And if a man kills his own slave, when he has been purified according to law, he shall be quit of the homicide. And if a man kills a freeman unintentionally, he shall undergo the same purification as he did who killed the slave. But let him not forget also a tale of olden time, which is to this effect:--He who has suffered a violent end, when newly dead, if he has had the soul of a freeman in life, is angry with the author of his death; and being himself full of fear and panic by reason of his violent end, when he sees his murderer walking about in his own accustomed haunts, he is stricken with terror and becomes disordered, and this disorder of his, aided by the guilty recollection of the other, is communicated by him with overwhelming force to the murderer and his deeds. Wherefore also the murderer must go out of the way of his victim for the entire period of a year, and not himself be found in any spot which was familiar to him throughout the country. And if the dead man be a stranger, the homicide shall be kept from the country of the stranger during a like period. If any one voluntarily obeys this law, the next of kin to the deceased, seeing all that has happened, shall take pity on him, and make peace with him, and show him all gentleness. But if any one is disobedient, either ventures to go to any of the temples and sacrifice unpurified, or will not continue in exile during the appointed time, the next of kin to the deceased shall proceed against him for murder; and if he be convicted, every part of his punishment shall be doubled. And if the next of kin do not proceed against the perpetrator of the crime, then the pollution shall be deemed to fall upon his own head;--the murdered man will fix the guilt upon his kinsman, and he who has a mind to proceed against him may compel him to be absent from his country during five years, according to law. If a stranger unintentionally kill a stranger who is dwelling in the city, he who likes shall prosecute the cause according to the same rules. If he be a metic, let him be absent for a year, or if he be an entire stranger, in addition to the purification, whether he have slain a stranger, or a metic, or a citizen, he shall be banished for life from the country which is in possession of our laws. And if he return contrary to law, let the guardians of the law punish him with death; and let them hand over his property, if he have any, to him who is next of kin to the sufferer. And if he be wrecked, and driven on the coast against his will, he shall take up his abode on the seashore, wetting his feet in the sea, and watching for an opportunity of sailing; but if he be brought by land, and is not his own master, let the magistrate whom he first comes across in the city, release him and send him unharmed over the border.

If any one slays a freeman with his own hand, and the deed be done in passion, in the case of such actions we must begin by making a distinction. For a deed is done from passion either when men suddenly, and without intention to kill, cause the death of another by blows and the like on a momentary impulse, and are sorry for the deed immediately afterwards; or again, when after having been insulted in deed or word, men pursue revenge, and kill a person intentionally, and are not sorry for the act. And, therefore, we must assume that these homicides are of two kinds, both of them arising from passion, which may be justly said to be in a mean between the voluntary and involuntary; at the same time, they are neither of them anything more than a likeness or shadow of either. He who treasures up his anger, and avenges himself, not immediately and at the moment, but with insidious design, and after an interval, is like the voluntary; but he who does not treasure up his anger, and takes vengeance on the instant, and without malice prepense, approaches to the involuntary; and yet even he is not altogether involuntary, but only the image or shadow of the involuntary; wherefore about homicides committed in hot blood, there is a difficulty in determining whether in legislating we shall reckon them as voluntary or as partly involuntary. The best and truest view is to regard them respectively as likenesses only of the voluntary and involuntary, and to distinguish them accordingly as they are done with or without premeditation. And we should make the penalties heavier for those who commit homicide with angry premeditation, and lighter for those who do not premeditate, but smite upon the instant; for that which is like a greater evil should be punished more severely, and that which is like a less evil should be punished less severely: this shall be the rule of our laws.

**CLEINIAS:** Certainly.

**ATHENIAN:** Let us proceed:--If any one slays a freeman with his own hand, and the deed be done in a moment of anger, and without premeditation, let the offender suffer in other respects as the involuntary homicide would have suffered, and also undergo an exile of two years, that he may learn to school his passions. But he who slays another from passion, yet with premeditation, shall in other respects suffer as the former; and to this shall be added an exile of three instead of two years,--his punishment is to be longer because his passion is greater. The manner of their return shall be on this wise: (and here the law has difficulty in determining exactly; for in some cases the murderer who is judged by the law to be the worse may really be the less cruel, and he who is judged the less cruel may be really the worse, and may have executed the murder in a more savage manner, whereas the other may have been gentler. But in general the degrees of guilt will be such as we have described them. Of all these things the guardians of the law must take cognizance):--When a homicide of either kind has completed his term of exile, the guardians shall send twelve judges to the borders of the land; these during the interval shall have informed themselves of the actions of the criminals, and they shall judge respecting their pardon and reception; and the homicides shall abide by their judgment. But if after they have returned home, any one of them in a moment of anger repeats the deed, let him be an exile, and return no more; or if he returns, let him suffer as the stranger was to suffer in a similar case. He who kills his own slave shall undergo a purification, but if he kills the slave of another in anger, he shall pay twice the amount of the loss to his owner. And if any homicide is disobedient to the law, and without purification pollutes the agora, or the games, or the temples, he who pleases may bring to trial the next of kin to the dead man for permitting him, and the murderer with him, and may compel the one to exact and the other to suffer a double amount of fines and purifications; and the accuser shall himself receive the fine in accordance with the law. If a slave in a fit of passion kills his master, the kindred of the deceased man may do with the murderer (provided only they do not spare his life) whatever they please, and they will be pure; or if he kills a freeman, who is not his master, the owner shall give up the slave to the relatives of the deceased, and they shall be under an obligation to put him to death, but this may be done in any manner which they please. And if (which is a rare occurrence, but does sometimes happen) a father or a mother in a moment of passion slays a son or daughter by blows, or some other violence, the slayer shall undergo the same purification as in other cases, and be exiled during three years; but when the exile returns the wife shall separate from the husband, and the husband from the wife, and they shall never afterwards beget children together, or live under the same roof, or partake of the same sacred rites with those whom they have deprived of a child or of a brother. And he who is impious and disobedient in such a case shall be brought to trial for impiety by any one who pleases. If in a fit of anger a husband kills his wedded wife, or the wife her husband, the slayer shall undergo the same purification, and the term of exile shall be three years. And when he who has committed any such crime returns, let him have no communication in sacred rites with his children, neither let him sit at the same table with them, and the father or son who disobeys shall be liable to be brought to trial for impiety by any one who pleases. If a brother or a sister in a fit of passion kills a brother or a sister, they shall undergo purification and exile, as was the case with parents who killed their offspring: they shall not come under the same roof, or share in the sacred rites of those whom they have deprived of their brethren, or of their children. And he who is disobedient shall be justly liable to the law concerning impiety, which relates to these matters. If any one is so violent in his passion against his parents, that in the madness of his anger he dares to kill one of them, if the murdered person before dying freely forgives the murderer, let him undergo the purification which is assigned to those who have been guilty of involuntary homicide, and do as they do, and he shall be pure. But if he be not acquitted, the perpetrator of such a deed shall be amenable to many laws;--he shall be amenable to the extreme punishments for assault, and impiety, and robbing of temples, for he has robbed his parent of life; and if a man could be slain more than once, most justly would he who in a fit of passion has slain father or mother, undergo many deaths. How can he, whom, alone of all men, even in defence of his life, and when about to suffer death at the hands of his parents, no law will allow to kill his father or his mother who are the authors of his being, and whom the legislator will command to endure any extremity rather than do this--how can he, I say, lawfully receive any other punishment? Let death then be the appointed punishment of him who in a fit of passion slays his father or his mother. But if brother kills brother in a civil broil, or under other like circumstances, if the other has begun, and he only defends himself, let him be free from guilt, as he would be if he had slain an enemy; and the same rule will apply if a citizen kill a citizen, or a stranger a stranger. Or if a stranger kill a citizen or a citizen a stranger in self-defence, let him be free from guilt in like manner; and so in the case of a slave who has killed a slave; but if a slave have killed a freeman in self-defence, let him be subject to the same law as he who has killed a father; and let the law about the remission of penalties in the case of parricide apply equally to every other remission. Whenever any sufferer of his own accord remits the guilt of homicide to another, under the idea that his act was involuntary, let the perpetrator of the deed undergo a purification and remain in exile for a year, according to law.

Enough has been said of murders violent and involuntary and committed in passion: we have now to speak of voluntary crimes done with injustice of every kind and with premeditation, through the influence of pleasures, and desires, and jealousies.

**CLEINIAS:** Very good.

**ATHENIAN:** Let us first speak, as far as we are able, of their various kinds. The greatest cause of them is lust, which gets the mastery of the soul maddened by desire; and this is most commonly found to exist where the passion reigns which is strongest and most prevalent among the mass of mankind: I mean where the power of wealth breeds endless desires of never- to-be-satisfied acquisition, originating in natural disposition, and a miserable want of education. Of this want of education, the false praise of wealth which is bruited about both among Hellenes and barbarians is the cause; they deem that to be the first of goods which in reality is only the third. And in this way they wrong both posterity and themselves, for nothing can be nobler and better than that the truth about wealth should be spoken in all states--namely, that riches are for the sake of the body, as the body is for the sake of the soul. They are good, and wealth is intended by nature to be for the sake of them, and is therefore inferior to them both, and third in order of excellence. This argument teaches us that he who would be happy ought not to seek to be rich, or rather he should seek to be rich justly and temperately, and then there would be no murders in states requiring to be purged away by other murders. But now, as I said at first, avarice is the chiefest cause and source of the worst trials for voluntary homicide. A second cause is ambition: this creates jealousies, which are troublesome companions, above all to the jealous man himself, and in a less degree to the chiefs of the state. And a third cause is cowardly and unjust fear, which has been the occasion of many murders. When a man is doing or has done something which he desires that no one should know him to be doing or to have done, he will take the life of those who are likely to inform of such things, if he have no other means of getting rid of them. Let this be said as a prelude concerning crimes of violence in general; and I must not omit to mention a tradition which is firmly believed by many, and has been received by them from those who are learned in the mysteries: they say that such deeds will be punished in the world below, and also that when the perpetrators return to this world they will pay the natural penalty which is due to the sufferer, and end their lives in like manner by the hand of another. If he who is about to commit murder believes this, and is made by the mere prelude to dread such a penalty, there is no need to proceed with the proclamation of the law. But if he will not listen, let the following law be declared and registered against him:--Whoever shall wrongfully and of design slay with his own hand any of his kinsmen, shall in the first place be deprived of legal privileges; and he shall not pollute the temples, or the agora, or the harbours, or any other place of meeting, whether he is forbidden of men or not; for the law, which represents the whole state, forbids him, and always is and will be in the attitude of forbidding him. And if a cousin or nearer relative of the deceased, whether on the male or female side, does not prosecute the homicide when he ought, and have him proclaimed an outlaw, he shall in the first place be involved in the pollution, and incur the hatred of the Gods, even as the curse of the law stirs up the voices of men against him; and in the second place he shall be liable to be prosecuted by any one who is willing to inflict retribution on behalf of the dead. And he who would avenge a murder shall observe all the precautionary ceremonies of lavation, and any others which the God commands in cases of this kind. Let him have proclamation made, and then go forth and compel the perpetrator to suffer the execution of justice according to the law. Now the legislator may easily show that these things must be accomplished by prayers and sacrifices to certain Gods, who are concerned with the prevention of murders in states. But who these Gods are, and what should be the true manner of instituting such trials with due regard to religion, the guardians of the law, aided by the interpreters, and the prophets, and the God, shall determine, and when they have determined let them carry on the prosecution at law. The cause shall have the same judges who are appointed to decide in the case of those who plunder temples. Let him who is convicted be punished with death, and let him not be buried in the country of the murdered man, for this would be shameless as well as impious. But if he fly and will not stand his trial, let him fly for ever; or, if he set foot anywhere on any part of the murdered man's country, let any relation of the deceased, or any other citizen who may first happen to meet with him, kill him with impunity, or bind and deliver him to those among the judges of the case who are magistrates, that they may put him to death. And let the prosecutor demand surety of him whom he prosecutes; three sureties sufficient in the opinion of the magistrates who try the cause shall be provided by him, and they shall undertake to produce him at the trial. But if he be unwilling or unable to provide sureties, then the magistrates shall take him and keep him in bonds, and produce him at the day of trial.

If a man do not commit a murder with his own hand, but contrives the death of another, and is the author of the deed in intention and design, and he continues to dwell in the city, having his soul not pure of the guilt of murder, let him be tried in the same way, except in what relates to the sureties; and also, if he be found guilty, his body after execution may have burial in his native land, but in all other respects his case shall be as the former; and whether a stranger shall kill a citizen, or a citizen a stranger, or a slave a slave, there shall be no difference as touching murder by one's own hand or by contrivance, except in the matter of sureties; and these, as has been said, shall be required of the actual murderer only, and he who brings the accusation shall bind them over at the time. If a slave be convicted of slaying a freeman voluntarily, either by his own hand or by contrivance, let the public executioner take him in the direction of the sepulchre, to a place whence he can see the tomb of the dead man, and inflict upon him as many stripes as the person who caught him orders, and if he survive, let him put him to death. And if any one kills a slave who has done no wrong, because he is afraid that he may inform of some base and evil deeds of his own, or for any similar reason, in such a case let him pay the penalty of murder, as he would have done if he had slain a citizen. There are things about which it is terrible and unpleasant to legislate, but impossible not to legislate. If, for example, there should be murders of kinsmen, either perpetrated by the hands of kinsmen, or by their contrivance, voluntary and purely malicious, which most often happen in ill-regulated and ill-educated states, and may perhaps occur even in a country where a man would not expect to find them, we must repeat once more the tale which we narrated a little while ago, in the hope that he who hears us will be the more disposed to abstain voluntarily on these grounds from murders which are utterly abominable. For the myth, or saying, or whatever we ought to call it, has been plainly set forth by priests of old; they have pronounced that the justice which guards and avenges the blood of kindred, follows the law of retaliation, and ordains that he who has done any murderous act should of necessity suffer that which he has done. He who has slain a father shall himself be slain at some time or other by his children,--if a mother, he shall of necessity take a woman's nature, and lose his life at the hands of his offspring in after ages; for where the blood of a family has been polluted there is no other purification, nor can the pollution be washed out until the homicidal soul which the deed has given life for life, and has propitiated and laid to sleep the wrath of the whole family. These are the retributions of Heaven, and by such punishments men should be deterred. But if they are not deterred, and any one should be incited by some fatality to deprive his father, or mother, or brethren, or children, of life voluntarily and of purpose, for him the earthly lawgiver legislates as follows:--There shall be the same proclamations about outlawry, and there shall be the same sureties which have been enacted in the former cases. But in his case, if he be convicted, the servants of the judges and the magistrates shall slay him at an appointed place without the city where three ways meet, and there expose his body naked, and each of the magistrates on behalf of the whole city shall take a stone and cast it upon the head of the dead man, and so deliver the city from pollution; after that, they shall bear him to the borders of the land, and cast him forth unburied, according to law. And what shall he suffer who slays him who of all men, as they say, is his own best friend? I mean the suicide, who deprives himself by violence of his appointed share of life, not because the law of the state requires him, nor yet under the compulsion of some painful and inevitable misfortune which has come upon him, nor because he has had to suffer from irremediable and intolerable shame, but who from sloth or want of manliness imposes upon himself an unjust penalty. For him, what ceremonies there are to be of purification and burial God knows, and about these the next of kin should enquire of the interpreters and of the laws thereto relating, and do according to their injunctions. They who meet their death in this way shall be buried alone, and none shall be laid by their side; they shall be buried ingloriously in the borders of the twelve portions of the land, in such places as are uncultivated and nameless, and no column or inscription shall mark the place of their interment. And if a beast of burden or other animal cause the death of any one, except in the case of anything of that kind happening to a competitor in the public contests, the kinsmen of the deceased shall prosecute the slayer for murder, and the wardens of the country, such, and so many as the kinsmen appoint, shall try the cause, and let the beast when condemned be slain by them, and let them cast it beyond the borders. And if any lifeless thing deprive a man of life, except in the case of a thunderbolt or other fatal dart sent from the Gods,--whether a man is killed by lifeless objects falling upon him, or by his falling upon them, the nearest of kin shall appoint the nearest neighbour to be a judge, and thereby acquit himself and the whole family of guilt. And he shall cast forth the guilty thing beyond the border, as has been said about the animals.

If a man is found dead, and his murderer be unknown, and after a diligent search cannot be detected, there shall be the same proclamation as in the previous cases, and the same interdict on the murderer; and having proceeded against him, they shall proclaim in the agora by a herald, that he who has slain such and such a person, and has been convicted of murder, shall not set his foot in the temples, nor at all in the country of the murdered man, and if he appears and is discovered, he shall die, and be cast forth unburied beyond the border. Let this one law then be laid down by us about murder; and let cases of this sort be so regarded.

And now let us say in what cases and under what circumstances the murderer is rightly free from guilt:--If a man catch a thief coming into his house by night to steal, and he take and kill him, or if he slay a footpad in self-defence, he shall be guiltless. And any one who does violence to a free woman or a youth, shall be slain with impunity by the injured person, or by his or her father or brothers or sons. If a man find his wife suffering violence, he may kill the violator, and be guiltless in the eye of the law; or if a person kill another in warding off death from his father or mother or children or brethren or wife who are doing no wrong, he shall assuredly be guiltless.

Thus much as to the nurture and education of the living soul of man, having which, he can, and without which, if he unfortunately be without them, he cannot live; and also concerning the punishments which are to be inflicted for violent deaths, let thus much be enacted. Of the nurture and education of the body we have spoken before, and next in order we have to speak of deeds of violence, voluntary and involuntary, which men do to one another; these we will now distinguish, as far as we are able, according to their nature and number, and determine what will be the suitable penalties of each, and so assign to them their proper place in the series of our enactments. The poorest legislator will have no difficulty in determining that wounds and mutilations arising out of wounds should follow next in order after deaths. Let wounds be divided as homicides were divided--into those which are involuntary, and which are given in passion or from fear, and those inflicted voluntarily and with premeditation. Concerning all this, we must make some such proclamation as the following:--Mankind must have laws, and conform to them, or their life would be as bad as that of the most savage beast. And the reason of this is that no man's nature is able to know what is best for human society; or knowing, always able and willing to do what is best. In the first place, there is a difficulty in apprehending that the true art of politics is concerned, not with private but with public good (for public good binds together states, but private only distracts them); and that both the public and private good as well of individuals as of states is greater when the state and not the individual is first considered. In the second place, although a person knows in the abstract that this is true, yet if he be possessed of absolute and irresponsible power, he will never remain firm in his principles or persist in regarding the public good as primary in the state, and the private good as secondary. Human nature will be always drawing him into avarice and selfishness, avoiding pain and pursuing pleasure without any reason, and will bring these to the front, obscuring the juster and better; and so working darkness in his soul will at last fill with evils both him and the whole city. For if a man were born so divinely gifted that he could naturally apprehend the truth, he would have no need of laws to rule over him; for there is no law or order which is above knowledge, nor can mind, without impiety, be deemed the subject or slave of any man, but rather the lord of all. I speak of mind, true and free, and in harmony with nature. But then there is no such mind anywhere, or at least not much; and therefore we must choose law and order, which are second best. These look at things as they exist for the most part only, and are unable to survey the whole of them. And therefore I have spoken as I have.

And now we will determine what penalty he ought to pay or suffer who has hurt or wounded another. Any one may easily imagine the questions which have to be asked in all such cases:--What did he wound, or whom, or how, or when? for there are innumerable particulars of this sort which greatly vary from one another. And to allow courts of law to determine all these things, or not to determine any of them, is alike impossible. There is one particular which they must determine in all cases--the question of fact. And then, again, that the legislator should not permit them to determine what punishment is to be inflicted in any of these cases, but should himself decide about all of them, small or great, is next to impossible.

**CLEINIAS:** Then what is to be the inference?

**ATHENIAN:** The inference is, that some things should be left to courts of law; others the legislator must decide for himself.

**CLEINIAS:** And what ought the legislator to decide, and what ought he to leave to courts of law?

**ATHENIAN:** I may reply, that in a state in which the courts are bad and mute, because the judges conceal their opinions and decide causes clandestinely; or what is worse, when they are disorderly and noisy, as in a theatre, clapping or hooting in turn this or that orator--I say that then there is a very serious evil, which affects the whole state. Unfortunate is the necessity of having to legislate for such courts, but where the necessity exists, the legislator should only allow them to ordain the penalties for the smallest offences; if the state for which he is legislating be of this character, he must take most matters into his own hands and speak distinctly. But when a state has good courts, and the judges are well trained and scrupulously tested, the determination of the penalties or punishments which shall be inflicted on the guilty may fairly and with advantage be left to them. And we are not to be blamed for not legislating concerning all that large class of matters which judges far worse educated than ours would be able to determine, assigning to each offence what is due both to the perpetrator and to the sufferer. We believe those for whom we are legislating to be best able to judge, and therefore to them the greater part may be left. At the same time, as I have often said, we should exhibit to the judges, as we have done, the outline and form of the punishments to be inflicted, and then they will not transgress the just rule. That was an excellent practice, which we observed before, and which now that we are resuming the work of legislation, may with advantage be repeated by us.

Let the enactment about wounding be in the following terms:--If any one has a purpose and intention to slay another who is not his enemy, and whom the law does not permit him to slay, and he wounds him, but is unable to kill him, he who had the intent and has wounded him is not to be pitied--he deserves no consideration, but should be regarded as a murderer and be tried for murder. Still having respect to the fortune which has in a manner favoured him, and to the providence which in pity to him and to the wounded man saved the one from a fatal blow, and the other from an accursed fate and calamity--as a thank-offering to this deity, and in order not to oppose his will--in such a case the law will remit the punishment of death, and only compel the offender to emigrate to a neighbouring city for the rest of his life, where he shall remain in the enjoyment of all his possessions. But if he have injured the wounded man, he shall make such compensation for the injury as the court deciding the cause shall assess, and the same judges shall decide who would have decided if the man had died of his wounds. And if a child intentionally wound his parents, or a servant his master, death shall be the penalty. And if a brother or a sister intentionally wound a brother or a sister, and is found guilty, death shall be the penalty. And if a husband wound a wife, or a wife a husband, with intent to kill, let him or her undergo perpetual exile; if they have sons or daughters who are still young, the guardians shall take care of their property, and have charge of the children as orphans. If their sons are grown up, they shall be under no obligation to support the exiled parent, but they shall possess the property themselves. And if he who meets with such a misfortune has no children, the kindred of the exiled man to the degree of sons of cousins, both on the male and female side, shall meet together, and after taking counsel with the guardians of the law and the priests, shall appoint a 5040th citizen to be the heir of the house, considering and reasoning that no house of all the 5040 belongs to the inhabitant or to the whole family, but is the public and private property of the state. Now the state should seek to have its houses as holy and happy as possible. And if any one of the houses be unfortunate, and stained with impiety, and the owner leave no posterity, but dies unmarried, or married and childless, having suffered death as the penalty of murder or some other crime committed against the Gods or against his fellow-citizens, of which death is the penalty distinctly laid down in the law; or if any of the citizens be in perpetual exile, and also childless, that house shall first of all be purified and undergo expiation according to law; and then let the kinsmen of the house, as we were just now saying, and the guardians of the law, meet and consider what family there is in the state which is of the highest repute for virtue and also for good fortune, in which there are a number of sons; from that family let them take one and introduce him to the father and forefathers of the dead man as their son, and, for the sake of the omen, let him be called so, that he may be the continuer of their family, the keeper of their hearth, and the minister of their sacred rites with better fortune than his father had; and when they have made this supplication, they shall make him heir according to law, and the offending person they shall leave nameless and childless and portionless when calamities such as these overtake him.

Now the boundaries of some things do not touch one another, but there is a borderland which comes in between, preventing them from touching. And we were saying that actions done from passion are of this nature, and come in between the voluntary and involuntary. If a person be convicted of having inflicted wounds in a passion, in the first place he shall pay twice the amount of the injury, if the wound be curable, or, if incurable, four times the amount of the injury; or if the wound be curable, and at the same time cause great and notable disgrace to the wounded person, he shall pay fourfold. And whenever any one in wounding another injures not only the sufferer, but also the city, and makes him incapable of defending his country against the enemy, he, besides the other penalties, shall pay a penalty for the loss which the state has incurred. And the penalty shall be, that in addition to his own times of service, he shall serve on behalf of the disabled person, and shall take his place in war; or, if he refuse, he shall be liable to be convicted by law of refusal to serve. The compensation for the injury, whether to be twofold or threefold or fourfold, shall be fixed by the judges who convict him. And if, in like manner, a brother wounds a brother, the parents and kindred of either sex, including the children of cousins, whether on the male or female side, shall meet, and when they have judged the cause, they shall entrust the assessment of damages to the parents, as is natural; and if the estimate be disputed, then the kinsmen on the male side shall make the estimate, or if they cannot, they shall commit the matter to the guardians of the law. And when similar charges of wounding are brought by children against their parents, those who are more than sixty years of age, having children of their own, not adopted, shall be required to decide; and if any one is convicted, they shall determine whether he or she ought to die, or suffer some other punishment either greater than death, or, at any rate, not much less. A kinsman of the offender shall not be allowed to judge the cause, not even if he be of the age which is prescribed by the law. If a slave in a fit of anger wound a freeman, the owner of the slave shall give him up to the wounded man, who may do as he pleases with him, and if be not give him up he shall himself make good the injury. And if any one says that the slave and the wounded man are conspiring together, let him argue the point, and if he is cast, he shall pay for the wrong three times over, but if he gains his case, the freeman who conspired with the slave shall be liable to an action for kidnapping. And if any one unintentionally wounds another he shall simply pay for the harm, for no legislator is able to control chance. In such a case the judges shall be the same as those who are appointed in the case of children suing their parents; and they shall estimate the amount of the injury.

All the preceding injuries and every kind of assault are deeds of violence; and every man, woman, or child ought to consider that the elder has the precedence of the younger in honour, both among the Gods and also among men who would live in security and happiness. Wherefore it is a foul thing and hateful to the Gods to see an elder man assaulted by a younger in the city; and it is reasonable that a young man when struck by an elder should lightly endure his anger, laying up in store for himself a like honour when he is old. Let this be the law:--Every one shall reverence his elder in word and deed; he shall respect any one who is twenty years older than himself, whether male or female, regarding him or her as his father or mother; and he shall abstain from laying hands on any one who is of an age to have been his father or his mother, out of reverence to the Gods who preside over birth; similarly he shall keep his hands from a stranger, whether he be an old inhabitant or newly arrived; he shall not venture to correct such an one by blows, either as the aggressor or in self-defence. If he thinks that some stranger has struck him out of wantonness or insolence, and ought to be punished, he shall take him to the wardens of the city, but let him not strike him, that the stranger may be kept far away from the possibility of lifting up his hand against a citizen, and let the wardens of the city take the offender and examine him, not forgetting their duty to the God of Strangers, and in case the stranger appears to have struck the citizen unjustly, let them inflict upon him as many blows with the scourge as he has himself inflicted, and quell his presumption. But if he be innocent, they shall threaten and rebuke the man who arrested him, and let them both go. If a person strikes another of the same age or somewhat older than himself, who has no children, whether he be an old man who strikes an old man or a young man who strikes a young man, let the person struck defend himself in the natural way without a weapon and with his hands only. He who, being more than forty years of age, dares to fight with another, whether he be the aggressor or in self-defence, shall be regarded as rude and ill-mannered and slavish;--this will be a disgraceful punishment, and therefore suitable to him. The obedient nature will readily yield to such exhortations, but the disobedient, who heeds not the prelude, shall have the law ready for him:--If any man smite another who is older than himself, either by twenty or by more years, in the first place, he who is at hand, not being younger than the combatants, nor their equal in age, shall separate them, or be disgraced according to law; but if he be the equal in age of the person who is struck or younger, he shall defend the person injured as he would a brother or father or still older relative. Further, let him who dares to smite an elder be tried for assault, as I have said, and if he be found guilty, let him be imprisoned for a period of not less than a year, or if the judges approve of a longer period, their decision shall be final. But if a stranger or metic smite one who is older by twenty years or more, the same law shall hold about the bystanders assisting, and he who is found guilty in such a suit, if he be a stranger but not resident, shall be imprisoned during a period of two years; and a metic who disobeys the laws shall be imprisoned for three years, unless the court assign him a longer term. And let him who was present in any of these cases and did not assist according to law be punished, if he be of the highest class, by paying a fine of a mina; or if he be of the second class, of fifty drachmas; or if of the third class, by a fine of thirty drachmas; or if he be of the fourth class, by a fine of twenty drachmas; and the generals and taxiarchs and phylarchs and hipparchs shall form the court in such cases.

Laws are partly framed for the sake of good men, in order to instruct them how they thay live on friendly terms with one another, and partly for the sake of those who refuse to be instructed, whose spirit cannot be subdued, or softened, or hindered from plunging into evil. These are the persons who cause the word to be spoken which I am about to utter; for them the legislator legislates of necessity, and in the hope that there may be no need of his laws. He who shall dare to lay violent hands upon his father or mother, or any still older relative, having no fear either of the wrath of the Gods above, or of the punishments that are spoken of in the world below, but transgresses in contempt of ancient and universal traditions as though he were too wise to believe in them, requires some extreme measure of prevention. Now death is not the worst that can happen to men; far worse are the punishments which are said to pursue them in the world below. But although they are most true tales, they work on such souls no prevention; for if they had any effect there would be no slayers of mothers, or impious hands lifted up against parents; and therefore the punishments of this world which are inflicted during life ought not in such cases to fall short, if possible, of the terrors of the world below. Let our enactment then be as follows:--If a man dare to strike his father or his mother, or their fathers or mothers, he being at the time of sound mind, then let any one who is at hand come to the rescue as has been already said, and the metic or stranger who comes to the rescue shall be called to the first place in the games; but if he do not come he shall suffer the punishment of perpetual exile. He who is not a metic, if he comes to the rescue, shall have praise, and if he do not come, blame. And if a slave come to the rescue, let him be made free, but if he do not come the rescue, let him receive 100 strokes of the whip, by order of the wardens of the agora, if the occurrence take place in the agora; or if somewhere in the city beyond the limits of the agora, any warden of the city who is in residence shall punish him; or if in the country, then the commanders of the wardens of the country. If those who are near at the time be inhabitants of the same place, whether they be youths, or men, or women, let them come to the rescue and denounce him as the impious one; and he who does not come to the rescue shall fall under the curse of Zeus, the God of kindred and of ancestors, according to law. And if any one is found guilty of assaulting a parent, let him in the first place be for ever banished from the city into the country, and let him abstain from the temples; and if he do not abstain, the wardens of the country shall punish him with blows, or in any way which they please, and if he return he shall be put to death. And if any freeman eat or drink, or have any other sort of intercourse with him, or only meeting him have voluntarily touched him, he shall not enter into any temple, nor into the agora, nor into the city, until he is purified; for he should consider that he has become tainted by a curse. And if he disobeys the law, and pollutes the city and the temples contrary to law, and one of the magistrates sees him and does not indict him, when he gives in his account this omission shall be a most serious charge.

If a slave strike a freeman, whether a stranger or a citizen, let any one who is present come to the rescue, or pay the penalty already mentioned; and let the bystanders bind him, and deliver him up to the injured person, and he receiving him shall put him in chains, and inflict on him as many stripes as he pleases; but having punished him he must surrender him to his master according to law, and not deprive him of his property. Let the law be as follows:--The slave who strikes a freeman, not at the command of the magistrates, his owner shall receive bound from the man whom he has stricken, and not release him until the slave has persuaded the man whom he has stricken that he ought to be released. And let there be the same laws about women in relation to women, and about men and women in relation to one another.

# BOOK X.

And now having spoken of assaults, let us sum up all acts of violence under a single law, which shall be as follows:--No one shall take or carry away any of his neighbour's goods, neither shall he use anything which is his neighbour's without the consent of the owner; for these are the offences which are and have been, and will ever be, the source of all the aforesaid evils. The greatest of them are excesses and insolences of youth, and are offences against the greatest when they are done against religion; and especially great when in violation of public and holy rites, or of the partly-common rites in which tribes and phratries share; and in the second degree great when they are committed against private rites and sepulchres, and in the third degree (not to repeat the acts formerly mentioned), when insults are offered to parents; the fourth kind of violence is when any one, regardless of the authority of the rulers, takes or carries away or makes use of anything which belongs to them, not having their consent; and the fifth kind is when the violation of the civil rights of an individual demands reparation. There should be a common law embracing all these cases. For we have already said in general terms what shall be the punishment of sacrilege, whether fraudulent or violent, and now we have to determine what is to be the punishment of those who speak or act insolently toward the Gods. But first we must give them an admonition which may be in the following terms:--No one who in obedience to the laws believed that there were Gods, ever intentionally did any unholy act, or uttered any unlawful word; but he who did must have supposed one of three things,-- either that they did not exist,--which is the first possibility, or secondly, that, if they did, they took no care of man, or thirdly, that they were easily appeased and turned aside from their purpose by sacrifices and prayers.

**CLEINIAS:** What shall we say or do to these persons?

**ATHENIAN:** My good friend, let us first hear the jests which I suspect that they in their superiority will utter against us.

**CLEINIAS:** What jests?

**ATHENIAN:** They will make some irreverent speech of this sort:--'O inhabitants of Athens, and Sparta, and Cnosus,' they will reply, 'in that you speak truly; for some of us deny the very existence of the Gods, while others, as you say, are of opinion that they do not care about us; and others that they are turned from their course by gifts. Now we have a right to claim, as you yourself allowed, in the matter of laws, that before you are hard upon us and threaten us, you should argue with us and convince us--you should first attempt to teach and persuade us that there are Gods by reasonable evidences, and also that they are too good to be unrighteous, or to be propitiated, or turned from their course by gifts. For when we hear such things said of them by those who are esteemed to be the best of poets, and orators, and prophets, and priests, and by innumerable others, the thoughts of most of us are not set upon abstaining from unrighteous acts, but upon doing them and atoning for them. When lawgivers profess that they are gentle and not stern, we think that they should first of all use persuasion to us, and show us the existence of Gods, if not in a better manner than other men, at any rate in a truer; and who knows but that we shall hearken to you? If then our request is a fair one, please to accept our challenge.'

**CLEINIAS:** But is there any difficulty in proving the existence of the Gods?

**ATHENIAN:** How would you prove it?

**CLEINIAS:** How? In the first place, the earth and the sun, and the stars and the universe, and the fair order of the seasons, and the division of them into years and months, furnish proofs of their existence; and also there is the fact that all Hellenes and barbarians believe in them.

**ATHENIAN:** I fear, my sweet friend, though I will not say that I much regard, the contempt with which the profane will be likely to assail us. For you do not understand the nature of their complaint, and you fancy that they rush into impiety only from a love of sensual pleasure.

**CLEINIAS:** Why, Stranger, what other reason is there?

**ATHENIAN:** One which you who live in a different atmosphere would never guess.

**CLEINIAS:** What is it?

**ATHENIAN:** A very grievous sort of ignorance which is imagined to be the greatest wisdom.

**CLEINIAS:** What do you mean?

**ATHENIAN:** At Athens there are tales preserved in writing which the virtue of your state, as I am informed, refuses to admit. They speak of the Gods in prose as well as verse, and the oldest of them tell of the origin of the heavens and of the world, and not far from the beginning of their story they proceed to narrate the birth of the Gods, and how after they were born they behaved to one another. Whether these stories have in other ways a good or a bad influence, I should not like to be severe upon them, because they are ancient; but, looking at them with reference to the duties of children to their parents, I cannot praise them, or think that they are useful, or at all true. Of the words of the ancients I have nothing more to say; and I should wish to say of them only what is pleasing to the Gods. But as to our younger generation and their wisdom, I cannot let them off when they do mischief. For do but mark the effect of their words: when you and I argue for the existence of the Gods, and produce the sun, moon, stars, and earth, claiming for them a divine being, if we would listen to the aforesaid philosophers we should say that they are earth and stones only, which can have no care at all of human affairs, and that all religion is a cooking up of words and a make-believe.

**CLEINIAS:** One such teacher, O Stranger, would be bad enough, and you imply that there are many of them, which is worse.

**ATHENIAN:** Well, then; what shall we say or do?--Shall we assume that some one is accusing us among unholy men, who are trying to escape from the effect of our legislation; and that they say of us--How dreadful that you should legislate on the supposition that there are Gods! Shall we make a defence of ourselves? or shall we leave them and return to our laws, lest the prelude should become longer than the law? For the discourse will certainly extend to great length, if we are to treat the impiously disposed as they desire, partly demonstrating to them at some length the things of which they demand an explanation, partly making them afraid or dissatisfied, and then proceed to the requisite enactments.

**CLEINIAS:** Yes, Stranger; but then how often have we repeated already that on the present occasion there is no reason why brevity should be preferred to length; for who is 'at our heels?'--as the saying goes, and it would be paltry and ridiculous to prefer the shorter to the better. It is a matter of no small consequence, in some way or other to prove that there are Gods, and that they are good, and regard justice more than men do. The demonstration of this would be the best and noblest prelude of all our laws. And therefore, without impatience, and without hurry, let us unreservedly consider the whole matter, summoning up all the power of persuasion which we possess.

**ATHENIAN:** Seeing you thus in earnest, I would fain offer up a prayer that I may succeed:--but I must proceed at once. Who can be calm when he is called upon to prove the existence of the Gods? Who can avoid hating and abhorring the men who are and have been the cause of this argument; I speak of those who will not believe the tales which they have heard as babes and sucklings from their mothers and nurses, repeated by them both in jest and earnest, like charms, who have also heard them in the sacrificial prayers, and seen sights accompanying them--sights and sounds delightful to children,--and their parents during the sacrifices showing an intense earnestness on behalf of their children and of themselves, and with eager interest talking to the Gods, and beseeching them, as though they were firmly convinced of their existence; who likewise see and hear the prostrations and invocations which are made by Hellenes and barbarians at the rising and setting of the sun and moon, in all the vicissitudes of life, not as if they thought that there were no Gods, but as if there could be no doubt of their existence, and no suspicion of their non-existence; when men, knowing all these things, despise them on no real grounds, as would be admitted by all who have any particle of intelligence, and when they force us to say what we are now saying, how can any one in gentle terms remonstrate with the like of them, when he has to begin by proving to them the very existence of the Gods? Yet the attempt must be made; for it would be unseemly that one half of mankind should go mad in their lust of pleasure, and the other half in their indignation at such persons. Our address to these lost and perverted natures should not be spoken in passion; let us suppose ourselves to select some one of them, and gently reason with him, smothering our anger:--O my son, we will say to him, you are young, and the advance of time will make you reverse may of the opinions which you now hold. Wait awhile, and do not attempt to judge at present of the highest things; and that is the highest of which you now think nothing--to know the Gods rightly and to live accordingly. And in the first place let me indicate to you one point which is of great importance, and about which I cannot be deceived:--You and your friends are not the first who have held this opinion about the Gods. There have always been persons more or less numerous who have had the same disorder. I have known many of them, and can tell you, that no one who had taken up in youth this opinion, that the Gods do not exist, ever continued in the same until he was old; the two other notions certainly do continue in some cases, but not in many; the notion, I mean, that the Gods exist, but take no heed of human things, and the other notion that they do take heed of them, but are easily propitiated with sacrifices and prayers. As to the opinion about the Gods which may some day become clear to you, I advise you to wait and consider if it be true or not; ask of others, and above all of the legislator. In the meantime take care that you do not offend against the Gods. For the duty of the legislator is and always will be to teach you the truth of these matters.

**CLEINIAS:** Our address, Stranger, thus far, is excellent.

**ATHENIAN:** Quite true, Megillus and Cleinias, but I am afraid that we have unconsciously lighted on a strange doctrine.

**CLEINIAS:** What doctrine do you mean?

**ATHENIAN:** The wisest of all doctrines, in the opinion of many.

**CLEINIAS:** I wish that you would speak plainer.

**ATHENIAN:** The doctrine that all things do become, have become, and will become, some by nature, some by art, and some by chance.

**CLEINIAS:** Is not that true?

**ATHENIAN:** Well, philosophers are probably right; at any rate we may as well follow in their track, and examine what is the meaning of them and their disciples.

**CLEINIAS:** By all means.

**ATHENIAN:** They say that the greatest and fairest things are the work of nature and of chance, the lesser of art, which, receiving from nature the greater and primeval creations, moulds and fashions all those lesser works which are generally termed artificial.

**CLEINIAS:** How is that?

**ATHENIAN:** I will explain my meaning still more clearly. They say that fire and water, and earth and air, all exist by nature and chance, and none of them by art, and that as to the bodies which come next in order,--earth, and sun, and moon, and stars,--they have been created by means of these absolutely inanimate existences. The elements are severally moved by chance and some inherent force according to certain affinities among them-- of hot with cold, or of dry with moist, or of soft with hard, and according to all the other accidental admixtures of opposites which have been formed by necessity. After this fashion and in this manner the whole heaven has been created, and all that is in the heaven, as well as animals and all plants, and all the seasons come from these elements, not by the action of mind, as they say, or of any God, or from art, but as I was saying, by nature and chance only. Art sprang up afterwards and out of these, mortal and of mortal birth, and produced in play certain images and very partial imitations of the truth, having an affinity to one another, such as music and painting create and their companion arts. And there are other arts which have a serious purpose, and these co-operate with nature, such, for example, as medicine, and husbandry, and gymnastic. And they say that politics cooperate with nature, but in a less degree, and have more of art; also that legislation is entirely a work of art, and is based on assumptions which are not true.

**CLEINIAS:** How do you mean?

**ATHENIAN:** In the first place, my dear friend, these people would say that the Gods exist not by nature, but by art, and by the laws of states, which are different in different places, according to the agreement of those who make them; and that the honourable is one thing by nature and another thing by law, and that the principles of justice have no existence at all in nature, but that mankind are always disputing about them and altering them; and that the alterations which are made by art and by law have no basis in nature, but are of authority for the moment and at the time at which they are made.--These, my friends, are the sayings of wise men, poets and prose writers, which find a way into the minds of youth. They are told by them that the highest right is might, and in this way the young fall into impieties, under the idea that the

Gods are not such as the law bids them imagine; and hence arise factions, these philosophers inviting them to lead a true life according to nature, that is, to live in real dominion over others, and not in legal subjection to them.

**CLEINIAS:** What a dreadful picture, Stranger, have you given, and how great is the injury which is thus inflicted on young men to the ruin both of states and families!

**ATHENIAN:** True, Cleinias; but then what should the lawgiver do when this evil is of long standing? should he only rise up in the state and threaten all mankind, proclaiming that if they will not say and think that the Gods are such as the law ordains (and this may be extended generally to the honourable, the just, and to all the highest things, and to all that relates to virtue and vice), and if they will not make their actions conform to the copy which the law gives them, then he who refuses to obey the law shall die, or suffer stripes and bonds, or privation of citizenship, or in some cases be punished by loss of property and exile? Should he not rather, when he is making laws for men, at the same time infuse the spirit of persuasion into his words, and mitigate the severity of them as far as he can?

**CLEINIAS:** Why, Stranger, if such persuasion be at all possible, then a legislator who has anything in him ought never to weary of persuading men; he ought to leave nothing unsaid in support of the ancient opinion that there are Gods, and of all those other truths which you were just now mentioning; he ought to support the law and also art, and acknowledge that both alike exist by nature, and no less than nature, if they are the creations of mind in accordance with right reason, as you appear to me to maintain, and I am disposed to agree with you in thinking.

**ATHENIAN:** Yes, my enthusiastic Cleinias; but are not these things when spoken to a multitude hard to be understood, not to mention that they take up a dismal length of time?

**CLEINIAS:** Why, Stranger, shall we, whose patience failed not when drinking or music were the themes of discourse, weary now of discoursing about the Gods, and about divine things? And the greatest help to rational legislation is that the laws when once written down are always at rest; they can be put to the test at any future time, and therefore, if on first hearing they seem difficult, there is no reason for apprehension about them, because any man however dull can go over them and consider them again and again; nor if they are tedious but useful, is there any reason or religion, as it seems to me, in any man refusing to maintain the principles of them to the utmost of his power.

**MEGILLUS:** Stranger, I like what Cleinias is saying.

**ATHENIAN:** Yes, Megillus, and we should do as he proposes; for if impious discourses were not scattered, as I may say, throughout the world, there would have been no need for any vindication of the existence of the Gods-- but seeing that they are spread far and wide, such arguments are needed; and who should come to the rescue of the greatest laws, when they are being undermined by bad men, but the legislator himself?

**MEGILLUS:** There is no more proper champion of them.

**ATHENIAN:** Well, then, tell me, Cleinias--for I must ask you to be my partner,--does not he who talks in this way conceive fire and water and earth and air to be the first elements of all things? these he calls nature, and out of these he supposes the soul to be formed afterwards; and this is not a mere conjecture of ours about his meaning, but is what he really means.

**CLEINIAS:** Very true.

**ATHENIAN:** Then, by Heaven, we have discovered the source of this vain opinion of all those physical investigators; and I would have you examine their arguments with the utmost care, for their impiety is a very serious matter; they not only make a bad and mistaken use of argument, but they lead away the minds of others: that is my opinion of them.

**CLEINIAS:** You are right; but I should like to know how this happens.

**ATHENIAN:** I fear that the argument may seem singular.

**CLEINIAS:** Do not hesitate, Stranger; I see that you are afraid of such a discussion carrying you beyond the limits of legislation. But if there be no other way of showing our agreement in the belief that there are Gods, of whom the law is said now to approve, let us take this way, my good sir.

**ATHENIAN:** Then I suppose that I must repeat the singular argument of those who manufacture the soul according to their own impious notions; they affirm that which is the first cause of the generation and destruction of all things, to be not first, but last, and that which is last to be first, and hence they have fallen into error about the true nature of the Gods.

**CLEINIAS:** Still I do not understand you.

**ATHENIAN:** Nearly all of them, my friends, seem to be ignorant of the nature and power of the soul, especially in what relates to her origin: they do not know that she is among the first of things, and before all bodies, and is the chief author of their changes and transpositions. And if this is true, and if the soul is older than the body, must not the things which are of the soul's kindred be of necessity prior to those which appertain to the body?

**CLEINIAS:** Certainly.

**ATHENIAN:** Then thought and attention and mind and art and law will be prior to that which is hard and soft and heavy and light; and the great and primitive works and actions will be works of art; they will be the first, and after them will come nature and works of nature, which however is a wrong term for men to apply to them; these will follow, and will be under the government of art and mind.

**CLEINIAS:** But why is the word 'nature' wrong?

**ATHENIAN:** Because those who use the term mean to say that nature is the first creative power; but if the soul turn out to be the primeval element, and not fire or air, then in the truest sense and beyond other things the soul may be said to exist by nature; and this would be true if you proved that the soul is older than the body, but not otherwise.

**CLEINIAS:** You are quite right.

**ATHENIAN:** Shall we, then, take this as the next point to which our attention should be directed?

**CLEINIAS:** By all means.

**ATHENIAN:** Let us be on our guard lest this most deceptive argument with its youthful looks, beguiling us old men, give us the slip and make a laughing-stock of us. Who knows but we may be aiming at the greater, and fail of attaining the lesser? Suppose that we three have to pass a rapid river, and I, being the youngest of the three and experienced in rivers, take upon me the duty of making the attempt first by myself; leaving you in safety on the bank, I am to examine whether the river is passable by older men like yourselves, and if such appears to be the case then I shall invite you to follow, and my experience will help to convey you across; but if the river is impassable by you, then there will have been no danger to anybody but myself,--would not that seem to be a very fair proposal? I mean to say that the argument in prospect is likely to be too much for you, out of your depth and beyond your strength, and I should be afraid that the stream of my questions might create in you who are not in the habit of answering, giddiness and confusion of mind, and hence a feeling of unpleasantness and unsuitableness might arise. I think therefore that I had better first ask the questions and then answer them myself while you listen in safety; in that way I can carry on the argument until I have completed the proof that the soul is prior to the body.

**CLEINIAS:** Excellent, Stranger, and I hope that you will do as you propose.

**ATHENIAN:** Come, then, and if ever we are to call upon the Gods, let us call upon them now in all seriousness to come to the demonstration of their own existence. And so holding fast to the rope we will venture upon the depths of the argument. When questions of this sort are asked of me, my safest answer would appear to be as follows:--Some one says to me, 'O Stranger, are all things at rest and nothing in motion, or is the exact opposite of this true, or are some things in motion and others at rest?'-- To this I shall reply that some things are in motion and others at rest. 'And do not things which move in a place, and are not the things which are at rest at rest in a place?' Certainly. 'And some move or rest in one place and some in more places than one?' You mean to say, we shall rejoin, that those things which rest at the centre move in one place, just as the circumference goes round of globes which are said to be at rest? 'Yes.' And we observe that, in the revolution, the motion which carries round the larger and the lesser circle at the same time is proportionally distributed to greater and smaller, and is greater and smaller in a certain proportion. Here is a wonder which might be thought an impossibility, that the same motion should impart swiftness and slowness in due proportion to larger and lesser circles. 'Very true.' And when you speak of bodies moving in many places, you seem to me to mean those which move from one place to another, and sometimes have one centre of motion and sometimes more than one because they turn upon their axis; and whenever they meet anything, if it be stationary, they are divided by it; but if they get in the midst between bodies which are approaching and moving towards the same spot from opposite directions, they unite with them. 'I admit the truth of what you are saying.' Also when they unite they grow, and when they are divided they waste away,--that is, supposing the constitution of each to remain, or if that fails, then there is a second reason of their dissolution. 'And when are all things created and how?' Clearly, they are created when the first principle receives increase and attains to the second dimension, and from this arrives at the one which is neighbour to this, and after reaching the third becomes perceptible to sense. Everything which is thus changing and moving is in process of generation; only when at rest has it real existence, but when passing into another state it is destroyed utterly. Have we not mentioned all motions that there are, and comprehended them under their kinds and numbered them with the exception, my friends, of two?

**CLEINIAS:** Which are they?

**ATHENIAN:** Just the two, with which our present enquiry is concerned.

**CLEINIAS:** Speak plainer.

**ATHENIAN:** I suppose that our enquiry has reference to the soul?

**CLEINIAS:** Very true.

**ATHENIAN:** Let us assume that there is a motion able to move other things, but not to move itself;--that is one kind; and there is another kind which can move itself as well as other things, working in composition and decomposition, by increase and diminution and generation and destruction,-- that is also one of the many kinds of motion.

**CLEINIAS:** Granted.

**ATHENIAN:** And we will assume that which moves other, and is changed by other, to be the ninth, and that which changes itself and others, and is co-incident with every action and every passion, and is the true principle of change and motion in all that is,--that we shall be inclined to call the tenth.

**CLEINIAS:** Certainly.

**ATHENIAN:** And which of these ten motions ought we to prefer as being the mightiest and most efficient?

**CLEINIAS:** I must say that the motion which is able to move itself is ten thousand times superior to all the others.

**ATHENIAN:** Very good; but may I make one or two corrections in what I have been saying?

**CLEINIAS:** What are they?

**ATHENIAN:** When I spoke of the tenth sort of motion, that was not quite correct.

**CLEINIAS:** What was the error?

**ATHENIAN:** According to the true order, the tenth was really the first in generation and power; then follows the second, which was strangely enough termed the ninth by us.

**CLEINIAS:** What do you mean?

**ATHENIAN:** I mean this: when one thing changes another, and that another, of such will there be any primary changing element? How can a thing which is moved by another ever be the beginning of change? Impossible. But when the self-moved changes other, and that again other, and thus thousands upon tens of thousands of bodies are set in motion, must not the beginning of all this motion be the change of the self-moving principle?

**CLEINIAS:** Very true, and I quite agree.

**ATHENIAN:** Or, to put the question in another way, making answer to ourselves:--If, as most of these philosophers have the audacity to affirm, all things were at rest in one mass, which of the above-mentioned principles of motion would first spring up among them?

**CLEINIAS:** Clearly the self-moving; for there could be no change in them arising out of any external cause; the change must first take place in themselves.

**ATHENIAN:** Then we must say that self-motion being the origin of all motions, and the first which arises among things at rest as wel as among things in motion, is the eldest and mightiest principle of change, and that which is changed by another and yet moves other is second.

**CLEINIAS:** Quite true.

**ATHENIAN:** At this stage of the argument let us put a question.

**CLEINIAS:** What question?

**ATHENIAN:** If we were to see this power existing in any earthy, watery, or fiery substance, simple or compound--how should we describe it?

**CLEINIAS:** You mean to ask whether we should call such a self-moving power life?

**ATHENIAN:** I do.

**CLEINIAS:** Certainly we should.

**ATHENIAN:** And when we see soul in anything, must we not do the same--must we not admit that this is life?

**CLEINIAS:** We must.

**ATHENIAN:** And now, I beseech you, reflect;--you would admit that we have a threefold knowledge of things?

**CLEINIAS:** What do you mean?

**ATHENIAN:** I mean that we know the essence, and that we know the definition of the essence, and the name,--these are the three; and there are two questions which may be raised about anything.

**CLEINIAS:** How two?

**ATHENIAN:** Sometimes a person may give the name and ask the definition; or he may give the definition and ask the name. I may illustrate what I mean in this way.

**CLEINIAS:** How?

**ATHENIAN:** Number like some other things is capable of being divided into equal parts; when thus divided, number is named 'even,' and the definition of the name 'even' is 'number divisible into two equal parts'?

**CLEINIAS:** True.

**ATHENIAN:** I mean, that when we are asked about the definition and give the name, or when we are asked about the name and give the definition--in either case, whether we give name or definition, we speak of the same thing, calling 'even' the number which is divided into two equal parts.

**CLEINIAS:** Quite true.

**ATHENIAN:** And what is the definition of that which is named 'soul'? Can we conceive of any other than that which has been already given--the motion which can move itself?

**CLEINIAS:** You mean to say that the essence which is defined as the self- moved is the same with that which has the name soul?

**ATHENIAN:** Yes; and if this is true, do we still maintain that there is anything wanting in the proof that the soul is the first origin and moving power of all that is, or has become, or will be, and their contraries, when she has been clearly shown to be the source of change and motion in all things?

**CLEINIAS:** Certainly not; the soul as being the source of motion, has been most satisfactorily shown to be the oldest of all things.

**ATHENIAN:** And is not that motion which is produced in another, by reason of another, but never has any self-moving power at all, being in truth the change of an inanimate body, to be reckoned second, or by any lower number which you may prefer?

**CLEINIAS:** Exactly.

**ATHENIAN:** Then we are right, and speak the most perfect and absolute truth, when we say that the soul is prior to the body, and that the body is second and comes afterwards, and is born to obey the soul, which is the ruler?

**CLEINIAS:** Nothing can be more true.

**ATHENIAN:** Do you remember our old admission, that if the soul was prior to the body the things of the soul were also prior to those of the body?

**CLEINIAS:** Certainly.

**ATHENIAN:** Then characters and manners, and wishes and reasonings, and true opinions, and reflections, and recollections are prior to length and breadth and depth and strength of bodies, if the soul is prior to the body.

**CLEINIAS:** To be sure.

**ATHENIAN:** In the next place, must we not of necessity admit that the soul is the cause of good and evil, base and honourable, just and unjust, and of all other opposites, if we suppose her to be the cause of all things?

**CLEINIAS:** We must.

**ATHENIAN:** And as the soul orders and inhabits all things that move, however moving, must we not say that she orders also the heavens?

**CLEINIAS:** Of course.

**ATHENIAN:** One soul or more? More than one--I will answer for you; at any rate, we must not suppose that there are less than two--one the author of good, and the other of evil.

**CLEINIAS:** Very true.

**ATHENIAN:** Yes, very true; the soul then directs all things in heaven, and earth, and sea by her movements, and these are described by the terms-- will, consideration, attention, deliberation, opinion true and false, joy and sorrow, confidence, fear, hatred, love, and other primary motions akin to these; which again receive the secondary motions of corporeal substances, and guide all things to growth and decay, to composition and decomposition, and to the qualities which accompany them, such as heat and cold, heaviness and lightness, hardness and softness, blackness and whiteness, bitterness and sweetness, and all those other qualities which the soul uses, herself a goddess, when truly receiving the divine mind she disciplines all things rightly to their happiness; but when she is the companion of folly, she does the very contrary of all this. Shall we assume so much, or do we still entertain doubts?

**CLEINIAS:** There is no room at all for doubt.

**ATHENIAN:** Shall we say then that it is the soul which controls heaven and earth, and the whole world?--that it is a principle of wisdom and virtue, or a principle which has neither wisdom nor virtue? Suppose that we make answer as follows:--

**CLEINIAS:** How would you answer?

**ATHENIAN:** If, my friend, we say that the whole path and movement of heaven, and of all that is therein, is by nature akin to the movement and revolution and calculation of mind, and proceeds by kindred laws, then, as is plain, we must say that the best soul takes care of the world and guides it along the good path.

**CLEINIAS:** True.

**ATHENIAN:** But if the world moves wildly and irregularly, then the evil soul guides it.

**CLEINIAS:** True again.

**ATHENIAN:** Of what nature is the movement of mind?--To this question it is not easy to give an intelligent answer; and therefore I ought to assist you in framing one.

**CLEINIAS:** Very good.

**ATHENIAN:** Then let us not answer as if we would look straight at the sun, making ourselves darkness at midday--I mean as if we were under the impression that we could see with mortal eyes, or know adequately the nature of mind;--it will be safer to look at the image only.

**CLEINIAS:** What do you mean?

**ATHENIAN:** Let us select of the ten motions the one which mind chiefly resembles; this I will bring to your recollection, and will then make the answer on behalf of us all.

**CLEINIAS:** That will be excellent.

**ATHENIAN:** You will surely remember our saying that all things were either at rest or in motion?

**CLEINIAS:** I do.

**ATHENIAN:** And that of things in motion some were moving in one place, and others in more than one?

**CLEINIAS:** Yes.

**ATHENIAN:** Of these two kinds of motion, that which moves in one place must move about a centre like globes made in a lathe, and is most entirely akin and similar to the circular movement of mind.

**CLEINIAS:** What do you mean?

**ATHENIAN:** In saying that both mind and the motion which is in one place move in the same and like manner, in and about the same, and in relation to the same, and according to one proportion and order, and are like the motion of a globe, we invented a fair image, which does no discredit to our ingenuity.

**CLEINIAS:** It does us great credit.

**ATHENIAN:** And the motion of the other sort which is not after the same manner, nor in the same, nor about the same, nor in relation to the same, nor in one place, nor in order, nor according to any rule or proportion, may be said to be akin to senselessness and folly?

**CLEINIAS:** That is most true.

**ATHENIAN:** Then, after what has been said, there is no difficulty in distinctly stating, that since soul carries all things round, either the best soul or the contrary must of necessity carry round and order and arrange the revolution of the heaven.

**CLEINIAS:** And judging from what has been said, Stranger, there would be impiety in asserting that any but the most perfect soul or souls carries round the heavens.

**ATHENIAN:** You have understood my meaning right well, Cleinias, and now let me ask you another question.

**CLEINIAS:** What are you going to ask?

**ATHENIAN:** If the soul carries round the sun and moon, and the other stars, does she not carry round each individual of them?

**CLEINIAS:** Certainly.

**ATHENIAN:** Then of one of them let us speak, and the same argument will apply to all.

**CLEINIAS:** Which will you take?

**ATHENIAN:** Every one sees the body of the sun, but no one sees his soul, nor the soul of any other body living or dead; and yet there is great reason to believe that this nature, unperceived by any of our senses, is circumfused around them all, but is perceived by mind; and therefore by mind and reflection only let us apprehend the following point.

**CLEINIAS:** What is that?

**ATHENIAN:** If the soul carries round the sun, we shall not be far wrong in supposing one of three alternatives.

**CLEINIAS:** What are they?

**ATHENIAN:** Either the soul which moves the sun this way and that, resides within the circular and visible body, like the soul which carries us about every way; or the soul provides herself with an external body of fire or air, as some affirm, and violently propels body by body; or thirdly, she is without such a body, but guides the sun by some extraordinary and wonderful power.

**CLEINIAS:** Yes, certainly; the soul can only order all things in one of these three ways.

**ATHENIAN:** And this soul of the sun, which is therefore better than the sun, whether taking the sun about in a chariot to give light to men, or acting from without, or in whatever way, ought by every man to be deemed a God.

**CLEINIAS:** Yes, by every man who has the least particle of sense.

**ATHENIAN:** And of the stars too, and of the moon, and of the years and months and seasons, must we not say in like manner, that since a soul or souls having every sort of excellence are the causes of all of them, those souls are Gods, whether they are living beings and reside in bodies, and in this way order the whole heaven, or whatever be the place and mode of their existence;--and will any one who admits all this venture to deny that all things are full of Gods?

**CLEINIAS:** No one, Stranger, would be such a madman.

**ATHENIAN:** And now, Megillus and Cleinias, let us offer terms to him who has hitherto denied the existence of the Gods, and leave him.

**CLEINIAS:** What terms?

**ATHENIAN:** Either he shall teach us that we were wrong in saying that the soul is the original of all things, and arguing accordingly; or, if he be not able to say anything better, then he must yield to us and live for the remainder of his life in the belief that there are Gods.--Let us see, then, whether we have said enough or not enough to those who deny that there are Gods.

**CLEINIAS:** Certainly,--quite enough, Stranger.

**ATHENIAN:** Then to them we will say no more. And now we are to address him who, believing that there are Gods, believes also that they take no heed of human affairs: To him we say,--O thou best of men, in believing that there are Gods you are led by some affinity to them, which attracts you towards your kindred and makes you honour and believe in them. But the fortunes of evil and unrighteous men in private as well as public life, which, though not really happy, are wrongly counted happy in the judgment of men, and are celebrated both by poets and prose writers--these draw you aside from your natural piety. Perhaps you have seen impious men growing old and leaving their children's children in high offices, and their prosperity shakes your faith--you have known or heard or been yourself an eyewitness of many monstrous impieties, and have beheld men by such criminal means from small beginnings attaining to sovereignty and the pinnacle of greatness; and considering all these things you do not like to accuse the Gods of them, because they are your relatives; and so from some want of reasoning power, and also from an unwillingness to find fault with them, you have come to believe that they exist indeed, but have no thought or care of human things. Now, that your present evil opinion may not grow to still greater impiety, and that we may if possible use arguments which may conjure away the evil before it arrives, we will add another argument to that originally addressed to him who utterly denied the existence of the Gods. And do you, Megillus and Cleinias, answer for the young man as you did before; and if any impediment comes in our way, I will take the word out of your mouths, and carry you over the river as I did just now.

**CLEINIAS:** Very good; do as you say, and we will help you as well as we can.

**ATHENIAN:** There will probably be no difficulty in proving to him that the Gods care about the small as well as about the great. For he was present and heard what was said, that they are perfectly good, and that the care of all things is most entirely natural to them.

**CLEINIAS:** No doubt he heard that.

**ATHENIAN:** Let us consider together in the next place what we mean by this virtue which we ascribe to them. Surely we should say that to be temperate and to possess mind belongs to virtue, and the contrary to vice?

**CLEINIAS:** Certainly.

**ATHENIAN:** Yes; and courage is a part of virtue, and cowardice of vice?

**CLEINIAS:** True.

**ATHENIAN:** And the one is honourable, and the other dishonourable?

**CLEINIAS:** To be sure.

**ATHENIAN:** And the one, like other meaner things, is a human quality, but the Gods have no part in anything of the sort?

**CLEINIAS:** That again is what everybody will admit.

**ATHENIAN:** But do we imagine carelessness and idleness and luxury to be virtues? What do you think?

**CLEINIAS:** Decidedly not.

**ATHENIAN:** They rank under the opposite class?

**CLEINIAS:** Yes.

**ATHENIAN:** And their opposites, therefore, would fall under the opposite class?

**CLEINIAS:** Yes.

**ATHENIAN:** But are we to suppose that one who possesses all these good qualities will be luxurious and heedless and idle, like those whom the poet compares to stingless drones?

**CLEINIAS:** And the comparison is a most just one.

**ATHENIAN:** Surely God must not be supposed to have a nature which He Himself hates?--he who dares to say this sort of thing must not be tolerated for a moment.

**CLEINIAS:** Of course not. How could He have?

**ATHENIAN:** Should we not on any principle be entirely mistaken in praising any one who has some special business entrusted to him, if he have a mind which takes care of great matters and no care of small ones? Reflect; he who acts in this way, whether he be God or man, must act from one of two principles.

**CLEINIAS:** What are they?

**ATHENIAN:** Either he must think that the neglect of the small matters is of no consequence to the whole, or if he knows that they are of consequence, and he neglects them, his neglect must be attributed to carelessness and indolence. Is there any other way in which his neglect can be explained? For surely, when it is impossible for him to take care of all, he is not negligent if he fails to attend to these things great or small, which a God or some inferior being might be wanting in strength or capacity to manage?

**CLEINIAS:** Certainly not.

**ATHENIAN:** Now, then, let us examine the offenders, who both alike confess that there are Gods, but with a difference,--the one saying that they may be appeased, and the other that they have no care of small matters: there are three of us and two of them, and we will say to them,--In the first place, you both acknowledge that the Gods hear and see and know all things, and that nothing can escape them which is matter of sense and knowledge:-- do you admit this?

**CLEINIAS:** Yes.

**ATHENIAN:** And do you admit also that they have all power which mortals and immortals can have?

**CLEINIAS:** They will, of course, admit this also.

**ATHENIAN:** And surely we three and they two--five in all--have acknowledged that they are good and perfect?

**CLEINIAS:** Assuredly.

**ATHENIAN:** But, if they are such as we conceive them to be, can we possibly suppose that they ever act in the spirit of carelessness and indolence? For in us inactivity is the child of cowardice, and carelessness of inactivity and indolence.

**CLEINIAS:** Most true.

**ATHENIAN:** Then not from inactivity and carelessness is any God ever negligent; for there is no cowardice in them.

**CLEINIAS:** That is very true.

**ATHENIAN:** Then the alternative which remains is, that if the Gods neglect the lighter and lesser concerns of the universe, they neglect them because they know that they ought not to care about such matters--what other alternative is there but the opposite of their knowing?

**CLEINIAS:** There is none.

**ATHENIAN:** And, O most excellent and best of men, do I understand you to mean that they are careless because they are ignorant, and do not know that they ought to take care, or that they know, and yet like the meanest sort of men, knowing the better, choose the worse because they are overcome by pleasures and pains?

**CLEINIAS:** Impossible.

**ATHENIAN:** Do not all human things partake of the nature of soul? And is not man the most religious of all animals?

**CLEINIAS:** That is not to be denied.

**ATHENIAN:** And we acknowledge that all mortal creatures are the property of the Gods, to whom also the whole of heaven belongs?

**CLEINIAS:** Certainly.

**ATHENIAN:** And, therefore, whether a person says that these things are to the Gods great or small--in either case it would not be natural for the Gods who own us, and who are the most careful and the best of owners, to neglect us.--There is also a further consideration.

**CLEINIAS:** What is it?

**ATHENIAN:** Sensation and power are in an inverse ratio to each other in respect to their ease and difficulty.

**CLEINIAS:** What do you mean?

**ATHENIAN:** I mean that there is greater difficulty in seeing and hearing the small than the great, but more facility in moving and controlling and taking care of small and unimportant things than of their opposites.

**CLEINIAS:** Far more.

**ATHENIAN:** Suppose the case of a physician who is willing and able to cure some living thing as a whole,--how will the whole fare at his hands if he takes care only of the greater and neglects the parts which are lesser?

**CLEINIAS:** Decidedly not well.

**ATHENIAN:** No better would be the result with pilots or generals, or householders or statesmen, or any other such class, if they neglected the small and regarded only the great;--as the builders say, the larger stones do not lie well without the lesser.

**CLEINIAS:** Of course not.

**ATHENIAN:** Let us not, then, deem God inferior to human workmen, who, in proportion to their skill, finish and perfect their works, small as well as great, by one and the same art; or that God, the wisest of beings, who is both willing and able to take care, is like a lazy good-for-nothing, or a coward, who turns his back upon labour and gives no thought to smaller and easier matters, but to the greater only.

**CLEINIAS:** Never, Stranger, let us admit a supposition about the Gods which is both impious and false.

**ATHENIAN:** I think that we have now argued enough with him who delights to accuse the Gods of neglect.

**CLEINIAS:** Yes.

**ATHENIAN:** He has been forced to acknowledge that he is in error, but he still seems to me to need some words of consolation.

**CLEINIAS:** What consolation will you offer him?

**ATHENIAN:** Let us say to the youth:--The ruler of the universe has ordered all things with a view to the excellence and preservation of the whole, and each part, as far as may be, has an action and passion appropriate to it. Over these, down to the least fraction of them, ministers have been appointed to preside, who have wrought out their perfection with infinitesimal exactness. And one of these portions of the universe is thine own, unhappy man, which, however little, contributes to the whole; and you do not seem to be aware that this and every other creation is for the sake of the whole, and in order that the life of the whole may be blessed; and that you are created for the sake of the whole, and not the whole for the sake of you. For every physician and every skilled artist does all things for the sake of the whole, directing his effort towards the common good, executing the part for the sake of the whole, and not the whole for the sake of the part. And you are annoyed because you are ignorant how what is best for you happens to you and to the universe, as far as the laws of the common creation admit. Now, as the soul combining first with one body and then with another undergoes all sorts of changes, either of herself, or through the influence of another soul, all that remains to the player of the game is that he should shift the pieces; sending the better nature to the better place, and the worse to the worse, and so assigning to them their proper portion.

**CLEINIAS:** In what way do you mean?

**ATHENIAN:** In a way which may be supposed to make the care of all things easy to the Gods. If any one were to form or fashion all things without any regard to the whole,--if, for example, he formed a living element of water out of fire, instead of forming many things out of one or one out of many in regular order attaining to a first or second or third birth, the transmutation would have been infinite; but now the ruler of the world has a wonderfully easy task.

**CLEINIAS:** How so?

**ATHENIAN:** I will explain:--When the king saw that our actions had life, and that there was much virtue in them and much vice, and that the soul and body, although not, like the Gods of popular opinion, eternal, yet having once come into existence, were indestructible (for if either of them had been destroyed, there would have been no generation of living beings); and when he observed that the good of the soul was ever by nature designed to profit men, and the evil to harm them--he, seeing all this, contrived so to place each of the parts that their position might in the easiest and best manner procure the victory of good and the defeat of evil in the whole. And he contrived a general plan by which a thing of a certain nature found a certain seat and room. But the formation of qualities he left to the wills of individuals. For every one of us is made pretty much what he is by the bent of his desires and the nature of his soul.

**CLEINIAS:** Yes, that is probably true.

**ATHENIAN:** Then all things which have a soul change, and possess in themselves a principle of change, and in changing move according to law and to the order of destiny: natures which have undergone a lesser change move less and on the earth's surface, but those which have suffered more change and have become more criminal sink into the abyss, that is to say, into Hades and other places in the world below, of which the very names terrify men, and which they picture to themselves as in a dream, both while alive and when released from the body. And whenever the soul receives more of good or evil from her own energy and the strong influence of others--when she has communion with divine virtue and becomes divine, she is carried into another and better place, which is perfect in holiness; but when she has communion with evil, then she also changes the place of her life.

*'This is the justice of the Gods who inhabit Olympus.' (Homer Odyss.)*

O youth or young man, who fancy that you are neglected by the Gods, know that if you become worse you shall go to the worse souls, or if better to the better, and in every succession of life and death you will do and suffer what like may fitly suffer at the hands of like. This is the justice of heaven, which neither you nor any other unfortunate will ever glory in escaping, and which the ordaining powers have specially ordained; take good heed thereof, for it will be sure to take heed of you. If you say:--I am small and will creep into the depths of the earth, or I am high and will fly up to heaven, you are not so small or so high but that you shall pay the fitting penalty, either here or in the world below or in some still more savage place whither you shall be conveyed. This is also the explanation of the fate of those whom you saw, who had done unholy and evil deeds, and from small beginnings had grown great, and you fancied that from being miserable they had become happy; and in their actions, as in a mirror, you seemed to see the universal neglect of the Gods, not knowing how they make all things work together and contribute to the great whole. And thinkest thou, bold man, that thou needest not to know this?--he who knows it not can never form any true idea of the happiness or unhappiness of life or hold any rational discourse respecting either. If Cleinias and this our reverend company succeed in proving to you that you know not what you say of the Gods, then will God help you; but should you desire to hear more, listen to what we say to the third opponent, if you have any understanding whatsoever. For I think that we have sufficiently proved the existence of the Gods, and that they care for men:--The other notion that they are appeased by the wicked, and take gifts, is what we must not concede to any one, and what every man should disprove to the utmost of his power.

**CLEINIAS:** Very good; let us do as you say.

**ATHENIAN:** Well, then, by the Gods themselves I conjure you to tell me,--if they are to be propitiated, how are they to be propitiated? Who are they, and what is their nature? Must they not be at least rulers who have to order unceasingly the whole heaven?

**CLEINIAS:** True.

**ATHENIAN:** And to what earthly rulers can they be compared, or who to them? How in the less can we find an image of the greater? Are they charioteers of contending pairs of steeds, or pilots of vessels? Perhaps they might be compared to the generals of armies, or they might be likened to physicians providing against the diseases which make war upon the body, or to husbandmen observing anxiously the effects of the seasons on the growth of plants; or perhaps to shepherds of flocks. For as we acknowledge the world to be full of many goods and also of evils, and of more evils than goods, there is, as we affirm, an immortal conflict going on among us, which requires marvellous watchfulness; and in that conflict the Gods and demigods are our allies, and we are their property. Injustice and insolence and folly are the destruction of us, and justice and temperance and wisdom are our salvation; and the place of these latter is in the life of the Gods, although some vestige of them may occasionally be discerned among mankind. But upon this earth we know that there dwell souls possessing an unjust spirit, who may be compared to brute animals, which fawn upon their keepers, whether dogs or shepherds, or the best and most perfect masters; for they in like manner, as the voices of the wicked declare, prevail by flattery and prayers and incantations, and are allowed to make their gains with impunity. And this sin, which is termed dishonesty, is an evil of the same kind as what is termed disease in living bodies or pestilence in years or seasons of the year, and in cities and governments has another name, which is injustice.

**CLEINIAS:** Quite true.

**ATHENIAN:** What else can he say who declares that the Gods are always lenient to the doers of unjust acts, if they divide the spoil with them? As if wolves were to toss a portion of their prey to the dogs, and they, mollified by the gift, suffered them to tear the flocks. Must not he who maintains that the Gods can be propitiated argue thus?

**CLEINIAS:** Precisely so.

**ATHENIAN:** And to which of the above-mentioned classes of guardians would any man compare the Gods without absurdity? Will he say that they are like pilots, who are themselves turned away from their duty by 'libations of wine and the savour of fat,' and at last overturn both ship and sailors?

**CLEINIAS:** Assuredly not.

**ATHENIAN:** And surely they are not like charioteers who are bribed to give up the victory to other chariots?

**CLEINIAS:** That would be a fearful image of the Gods.

**ATHENIAN:** Nor are they like generals, or physicians, or husbandmen, or shepherds; and no one would compare them to dogs who have been silenced by wolves.

**CLEINIAS:** A thing not to be spoken of.

**ATHENIAN:** And are not all the Gods the chiefest of all guardians, and do they not guard our highest interests?

**CLEINIAS:** Yes; the chiefest.

**ATHENIAN:** And shall we say that those who guard our noblest interests, and are the best of guardians, are inferior in virtue to dogs, and to men even of moderate excellence, who would never betray justice for the sake of gifts which unjust men impiously offer them?

**CLEINIAS:** Certainly not: nor is such a notion to be endured, and he who holds this opinion may be fairly singled out and characterized as of all impious men the wickedest and most impious.

**ATHENIAN:** Then are the three assertions--that the Gods exist, and that they take care of men, and that they can never be persuaded to do injustice, now sufficiently demonstrated? May we say that they are?

**CLEINIAS:** You have our entire assent to your words.

**ATHENIAN:** I have spoken with vehemence because I am zealous against evil men; and I will tell dear Cleinias, why I am so. I would not have the wicked think that, having the superiority in argument, they may do as they please and act according to their various imaginations about the Gods; and this zeal has led me to speak too vehemently; but if we have at all succeeded in persuading the men to hate themselves and love their opposites, the prelude of our laws about impiety will not have been spoken in vain.

**CLEINIAS:** So let us hope; and even if we have failed, the style of our argument will not discredit the lawgiver.

**ATHENIAN:** After the prelude shall follow a discourse, which will be the interpreter of the law; this shall proclaim to all impious persons that they must depart from their ways and go over to the pious. And to those who disobey, let the law about impiety be as follows:--If a man is guilty of any impiety in word or deed, any one who happens to be present shall give information to the magistrates, in aid of the law; and let the magistrates who first receive the information bring him before the appointed court according to the law; and if a magistrate, after receiving information, refuses to act, he shall be tried for impiety at the instance of any one who is willing to vindicate the laws; and if any one be cast, the court shall estimate the punishment of each act of impiety; and let all such criminals be imprisoned. There shall be three prisons in the state: the first of them is to be the common prison in the neighbourhood of the agora for the safe-keeping of the generality of offenders; another is to be in the neighbourhood of the nocturnal council, and is to be called the 'House of Reformation'; another, to be situated in some wild and desolate region in the centre of the country, shall be called by some name expressive of retribution. Now, men fall into impiety from three causes, which have been already mentioned, and from each of these causes arise two sorts of impiety, in all six, which are worth distinguishing, and should not all have the same punishment. For he who does not believe in the Gods, and yet has a righteous nature, hates the wicked and dislikes and refuses to do injustice, and avoids unrighteous men, and loves the righteous. But they who besides believing that the world is devoid of Gods are intemperate, and have at the same time good memories and quick wits, are worse; although both of them are unbelievers, much less injury is done by the one than by the other. The one may talk loosely about the Gods and about sacrifices and oaths, and perhaps by laughing at other men he may make them like himself, if he be not punished. But the other who holds the same opinions and is called a clever man, is full of stratagem and deceit--men of this class deal in prophecy and jugglery of all kinds, and out of their ranks sometimes come tyrants and demagogues and generals and hierophants of private mysteries and the Sophists, as they are termed, with their ingenious devices. There are many kinds of unbelievers, but two only for whom legislation is required; one the hypocritical sort, whose crime is deserving of death many times over, while the other needs only bonds and admonition. In like manner also the notion that the Gods take no thought of men produces two other sorts of crimes, and the notion that they may be propitiated produces two more. Assuming these divisions, let those who have been made what they are only from want of understanding, and not from malice or an evil nature, be placed by the judge in the House of Reformation, and ordered to suffer imprisonment during a period of not less than five years. And in the meantime let them have no intercourse with the other citizens, except with members of the nocturnal council, and with them let them converse with a view to the improvement of their soul's health. And when the time of their imprisonment has expired, if any of them be of sound mind let him be restored to sane company, but if not, and if he be condemned a second time, let him be punished with death. As to that class of monstrous natures who not only believe that there are no Gods, or that they are negligent, or to be propitiated, but in contempt of mankind conjure the souls of the living and say that they can conjure the dead and promise to charm the Gods with sacrifices and prayers, and will utterly overthrow individuals and whole houses and states for the sake of money--let him who is guilty of any of these things be condemned by the court to be bound according to law in the prison which is in the centre of the land, and let no freeman ever approach him, but let him receive the rations of food appointed by the guardians of the law from the hands of the public slaves; and when he is dead let him be cast beyond the borders unburied, and if any freeman assist in burying him, let him pay the penalty of impiety to any one who is willing to bring a suit against him. But if he leaves behind him children who are fit to be citizens, let the guardians of orphans take care of them, just as they would of any other orphans, from the day on which their father is convicted.

In all these cases there should be one law, which will make men in general less liable to transgress in word or deed, and less foolish, because they will not be allowed to practise religious rites contrary to law. And let this be the simple form of the law:--No man shall have sacred rites in a private house. When he would sacrifice, let him go to the temples and hand over his offerings to the priests and priestesses, who see to the sanctity of such things, and let him pray himself, and let any one who pleases join with him in prayer. The reason of this is as follows:--Gods and temples are not easily instituted, and to establish them rightly is the work of a mighty intellect. And women especially, and men too, when they are sick or in danger, or in any sort of difficulty, or again on their receiving any good fortune, have a way of consecrating the occasion, vowing sacrifices, and promising shrines to Gods, demigods, and sons of Gods; and when they are awakened by terrible apparitions and dreams or remember visions, they find in altars and temples the remedies of them, and will fill every house and village with them, placing them in the open air, or wherever they may have had such visions; and with a view to all these cases we should obey the law. The law has also regard to the impious, and would not have them fancy that by the secret performance of these actions--by raising temples and by building altars in private houses, they can propitiate the God secretly with sacrifices and prayers, while they are really multiplying their crimes infinitely, bringing guilt from heaven upon themselves, and also upon those who permit them, and who are better men than they are; and the consequence is that the whole state reaps the fruit of their impiety, which, in a certain sense, is deserved. Assuredly God will not blame the legislator, who will enact the following law:--No one shall possess shrines of the Gods in private houses, and he who is found to possess them, and perform any sacred rites not publicly authorized,--supposing the offender to be some man or woman who is not guilty of any other great and impious crime,--shall be informed against by him who is acquainted with the fact, which shall be announced by him to the guardians of the law; and let them issue orders that he or she shall carry away their private rites to the public temples, and if they do not persuade them, let them inflict a penalty on them until they comply. And if a person be proven guilty of impiety, not merely from childish levity, but such as grown-up men may be guilty of, whether he have sacrificed publicly or privately to any Gods, let him be punished with death, for his sacrifice is impure. Whether the deed has been done in earnest, or only from childish levity, let the guardians of the law determine, before they bring the matter into court and prosecute the offender for impiety.

# BOOK XI.

In the next place, dealings between man and man require to be suitably regulated. The principle of them is very simple:--Thou shalt not, if thou canst help, touch that which is mine, or remove the least thing which belongs to me without my consent; and may I be of a sound mind, and do to others as I would that they should do to me. First, let us speak of treasure-trove:--May I never pray the Gods to find the hidden treasure, which another has laid up for himself and his family, he not being one of my ancestors, nor lift, if I should find, such a treasure. And may I never have any dealings with those who are called diviners, and who in any way or manner counsel me to take up the deposit entrusted to the earth, for I should not gain so much in the increase of my possessions, if I take up the prize, as I should grow in justice and virtue of soul, if I abstain; and this will be a better possession to me than the other in a better part of myself; for the possession of justice in the soul is preferable to the possession of wealth. And of many things it is well said,--'Move not the immovables,' and this may be regarded as one of them. And we shall do well to believe the common tradition which says, that such deeds prevent a man from having a family. Now as to him who is careless about having children and regardless of the legislator, taking up that which neither he deposited, nor any ancestor of his, without the consent of the depositor, violating the simplest and noblest of laws which was the enactment of no mean man:--'Take not up that which was not laid down by thee,'--of him, I say, who despises these two legislators, and takes up, not some small matter which he has not deposited, but perhaps a great heap of treasure, what he ought to suffer at the hands of the Gods, God only knows; but I would have the first person who sees him go and tell the wardens of the city, if the occurrence has taken place in the city, or if the occurrence has taken place in the agora he shall tell the wardens of the agora, or if in the country he shall tell the wardens of the country and their commanders. When information has been received the city shall send to Delphi, and, whatever the God answers about the money and the remover of the money, that the city shall do in obedience to the oracle; the informer, if he be a freeman, shall have the honour of doing rightly, and he who informs not, the dishonour of doing wrongly; and if he be a slave who gives information, let him be freed, as he ought to be, by the state, which shall give his master the price of him; but if he do not inform he shall be punished with death. Next in order shall follow a similar law, which shall apply equally to matters great and small:--If a man happens to leave behind him some part of his property, whether intentionally or unintentionally, let him who may come upon the left property suffer it to remain, reflecting that such things are under the protection of the Goddess of ways, and are dedicated to her by the law. But if any one defies the law, and takes the property home with him, let him, if the thing is of little worth, and the man who takes it a slave, be beaten with many stripes by him, being a person of not less than thirty years of age. Or if he be a freeman, in addition to being thought a mean person and a despiser of the laws, let him pay ten times the value of the treasure which he has moved to the leaver. And if some one accuses another of having anything which belongs to him, whether little or much, and the other admits that he has this thing, but denies that the property in dispute belongs to the other, if the property be registered with the magistrates according to law, the claimant shall summon the possessor, who shall bring it before the magistrates; and when it is brought into court, if it be registered in the public registers, to which of the litigants it belonged, let him take it and go his way. Or if the property be registered as belonging to some one who is not present, whoever will offer sufficient surety on behalf of the absent person that he will give it up to him, shall take it away as the representative of the other. But if the property which is deposited be not registered with the magistrates, let it remain until the time of trial with three of the eldest of the magistrates; and if it be an animal which is deposited, then he who loses the suit shall pay the magistrates for its keep, and they shall determine the cause within three days.

Any one who is of sound mind may arrest his own slave, and do with him whatever he will of such things as are lawful; and he may arrest the runaway slave of any of his friends or kindred with a view to his safe-keeping. And if any one takes away him who is being carried off as a slave, intending to liberate him, he who is carrying him off shall let him go; but he who takes him away shall give three sufficient sureties; and if he give them, and not without giving them, he may take him away, but if he take him away after any other manner he shall be deemed guilty of violence, and being convicted shall pay as a penalty double the amount of the damages claimed to him who has been deprived of the slave. Any man may also carry off a freedman, if he do not pay respect or sufficient respect to him who freed him. Now the respect shall be, that the freedman go three times in the month to the hearth of the person who freed him, and offer to do whatever he ought, so far as he can; and he shall agree to make such a marriage as his former master approves. He shall not be permitted to have more property than he who gave him liberty, and what more he has shall belong to his master. The freedman shall not remain in the state more than twenty years, but like other foreigners shall go away, taking his entire property with him, unless he has the consent of the magistrates and of his former master to remain. If a freedman or any other stranger has a property greater than the census of the third class, at the expiration of thirty days from the day on which this comes to pass, he shall take that which is his and go his way, and in this case he shall not be allowed to remain any longer by the magistrates. And if any one disobeys this regulation, and is brought into court and convicted, he shall be punished with death, his property shall be confiscated. Suits about these matters shall take place before the tribes, unless the plaintiff and defendant have got rid of the accusation either before their neighbours or before judges chosen by them. If a man lay claim to any animal or anything else which he declares to be his, let the possessor refer to the seller or to some honest and trustworthy person, who has given, or in some legitimate way made over the property to him; if he be a citizen or a metic, sojourning in the city, within thirty days, or, if the property have been delivered to him by a stranger, within five months, of which the middle month shall include the summer solstice. When goods are exchanged by selling and buying, a man shall deliver them, and receive the price of them, at a fixed place in the agora, and have done with the matter; but he shall not buy or sell anywhere else, nor give credit. And if in any other manner or in any other place there be an exchange of one thing for another, and the seller give credit to the man who buys from him, he must do this on the understanding that the law gives no protection in cases of things sold not in accordance with these regulations. Again, as to contributions, any man who likes may go about collecting contributions as a friend among friends, but if any difference arises about the collection, he is to act on the understanding that the law gives no protection in such cases. He who sells anything above the value of fifty drachmas shall be required to remain in the city for ten days, and the purchaser shall be informed of the house of the seller, with a view to the sort of charges which are apt to arise in such cases, and the restitutions which the law allows. And let legal restitution be on this wise:--If a man sells a slave who is in a consumption, or who has the disease of the stone, or of strangury, or epilepsy, or some other tedious and incurable disorder of body or mind, which is not discernible to the ordinary man, if the purchaser be a physician or trainer, he shall have no right of restitution; nor shall there be any right of restitution if the seller has told the truth beforehand to the buyer. But if a skilled person sells to another who is not skilled, let the buyer appeal for restitution within six months, except in the case of epilepsy, and then the appeal may be made within a year. The cause shall be determined by such physicians as the parties may agree to choose; and the defendant, if he lose the suit, shall pay double the price at which he sold. If a private person sell to another private person, he shall have the right of restitution, and the decision shall be given as before, but the defendant, if he be cast, shall only pay back the price of the slave. If a person sells a homicide to another, and they both know of the fact, let there be no restitution in such a case, but if he do not know of the fact, there shall be a right of restitution, whenever the buyer makes the discovery; and the decision shall rest with the five youngest guardians of the law, and if the decision be that the seller was cognisant of the fact, he shall purify the house of the purchaser, according to the law of the interpreters, and shall pay back three times the purchase-money.

If man exchanges either money for money, or anything whatever for anything else, either with or without life, let him give and receive them genuine and unadulterated, in accordance with the law. And let us have a prelude about all this sort of roguery, like the preludes of our other laws. Every man should regard adulteration as of one and the same class with falsehood and deceit, concerning which the many are too fond of saying that at proper times and places the practice may often be right. But they leave the occasion, and the when, and the where, undefined and unsettled, and from this want of definiteness in their language they do a great deal of harm to themselves and to others. Now a legislator ought not to leave the matter undetermined; he ought to prescribe some limit, either greater or less. Let this be the rule prescribed:--No one shall call the Gods to witness, when he says or does anything false or deceitful or dishonest, unless he would be the most hateful of mankind to them. And he is most hateful to them who takes a false oath, and pays no heed to the Gods; and in the next degree, he who tells a falsehood in the presence of his superiors. Now better men are the superiors of worse men, and in general elders are the superiors of the young; wherefore also parents are the superiors of their offspring, and men of women and children, and rulers of their subjects; for all men ought to reverence any one who is in any position of authority, and especially those who are in state offices. And this is the reason why I have spoken of these matters. For every one who is guilty of adulteration in the agora tells a falsehood, and deceives, and when he invokes the Gods, according to the customs and cautions of the wardens of the agora, he does but swear without any respect for God or man. Certainly, it is an excellent rule not lightly to defile the names of the Gods, after the fashion of men in general, who care little about piety and purity in their religious actions. But if a man will not conform to this rule, let the law be as follows:--He who sells anything in the agora shall not ask two prices for that which he sells, but he shall ask one price, and if he do not obtain this, he shall take away his goods; and on that day he shall not value them either at more or less; and there shall be no praising of any goods, or oath taken about them. If a person disobeys this command, any citizen who is present, not being less than thirty years of age, may with impunity chastise and beat the swearer, but if instead of obeying the laws he takes no heed, he shall be liable to the charge of having betrayed them. If a man sells any adulterated goods and will not obey these regulations, he who knows and can prove the fact, and does prove it in the presence of the magistrates, if he be a slave or a metic, shall have the adulterated goods; but if he be a citizen, and do not pursue the charge, he shall be called a rogue, and deemed to have robbed the Gods of the agora; or if he proves the charge, he shall dedicate the goods to the Gods of the agora. He who is proved to have sold any adulterated goods, in addition to losing the goods themselves, shall be beaten with stripes,--a stripe for a drachma, according to the price of the goods; and the herald shall proclaim in the agora the offence for which he is going to be beaten. The wardens of the agora and the guardians of the law shall obtain information from experienced persons about the rogueries and adulterations of the sellers, and shall write up what the seller ought and ought not to do in each case; and let them inscribe their laws on a column in front of the court of the wardens of the agora, that they may be clear instructors of those who have business in the agora. Enough has been said in what has preceded about the wardens of the city, and if anything seems to be wanting, let them communicate with the guardians of the law, and write down the omission, and place on a column in the court of the wardens of the city the primary and secondary regulations which are laid down for them about their office.

After the practices of adulteration naturally follow the practices of retail trade. Concerning these, we will first of all give a word of counsel and reason, and the law shall come afterwards. Retail trade in a city is not by nature intended to do any harm, but quite the contrary; for is not he a benefactor who reduces the inequalities and incommensurabilities of goods to equality and common measure? And this is what the power of money accomplishes, and the merchant may be said to be appointed for this purpose. The hireling and the tavern-keeper, and many other occupations, some of them more and others less seemly--all alike have this object;--they seek to satisfy our needs and equalize our possessions. Let us then endeavour to see what has brought retail trade into ill-odour, and wherein lies the dishonour and unseemliness of it, in order that if not entirely, we may yet partially, cure the evil by legislation. To effect this is no easy matter, and requires a great deal of virtue.

**CLEINIAS:** What do you mean?

**ATHENIAN:** Dear Cleinias, the class of men is small--they must have been rarely gifted by nature, and trained by education,--who, when assailed by wants and desires, are able to hold out and observe moderation, and when they might make a great deal of money are sober in their wishes, and prefer a moderate to a large gain. But the mass of mankind are the very opposite: their desires are unbounded, and when they might gain in moderation they prefer gains without limit; wherefore all that relates to retail trade, and merchandise, and the keeping of taverns, is denounced and numbered among dishonourable things. For if what I trust may never be and will not be, we were to compel, if I may venture to say a ridiculous thing, the best men everywhere to keep taverns for a time, or carry on retail trade, or do anything of that sort; or if, in consequence of some fate or necessity, the best women were compelled to follow similar callings, then we should know how agreeable and pleasant all these things are; and if all such occupations were managed on incorrupt principles, they would be honoured as we honour a mother or a nurse. But now that a man goes to desert places and builds houses which can only be reached by long journeys, for the sake of retail trade, and receives strangers who are in need at the welcome resting-place, and gives them peace and calm when they are tossed by the storm, or cool shade in the heat; and then instead of behaving to them as friends, and showing the duties of hospitality to his guests, treats them as enemies and captives who are at his mercy, and will not release them until they have paid the most unjust, abominable, and extortionate ransom, --these are the sort of practices, and foul evils they are, which cast a reproach upon the succour of adversity. And the legislator ought always to be devising a remedy for evils of this nature. There is an ancient saying, which is also a true one--'To fight against two opponents is a difficult thing,' as is seen in diseases and in many other cases. And in this case also the war is against two enemies--wealth and poverty; one of whom corrupts the soul of man with luxury, while the other drives him by pain into utter shamelessness. What remedy can a city of sense find against this disease? In the first place, they must have as few retail traders as possible; and in the second place, they must assign the occupation to that class of men whose corruption will be the least injury to the state; and in the third place, they must devise some way whereby the followers of these occupations themselves will not readily fall into habits of unbridled shamelessness and meanness.

After this preface let our law run as follows, and may fortune favour us:- - No landowner among the Magnetes, whose city the God is restoring and resettling--no one, that is, of the 5040 families, shall become a retail trader either voluntarily or involuntarily; neither shall he be a merchant, or do any service for private persons unless they equally serve him, except for his father or his mother, and their fathers and mothers; and in general for his elders who are freemen, and whom he serves as a freeman. Now it is difficult to determine accurately the things which are worthy or unworthy of a freeman, but let those who have obtained the prize of virtue give judgment about them in accordance with their feelings of right and wrong. He who in any way shares in the illiberality of retail trades may be indicted for dishonouring his race by any one who likes, before those who have been judged to be the first in virtue; and if he appear to throw dirt upon his father's house by an unworthy occupation, let him be imprisoned for a year and abstain from that sort of thing; and if he repeat the offence, for two years; and every time that he is convicted let the length of his imprisonment be doubled. This shall be the second law:--He who engages in retail trade must be either a metic or a stranger. And a third law shall be:--In order that the retail trader who dwells in our city may be as good or as little bad as possible, the guardians of the law shall remember that they are not only guardians of those who may be easily watched and prevented from becoming lawless or bad, because they are well- born and bred; but still more should they have a watch over those who are of another sort, and follow pursuits which have a very strong tendency to make men bad. And, therefore, in respect of the multifarious occupations of retail trade, that is to say, in respect of such of them as are allowed to remain, because they seem to be quite necessary in a state,--about these the guardians of the law should meet and take counsel with those who have experience of the several kinds of retail trade, as we before commanded concerning adulteration (which is a matter akin to this), and when they meet they shall consider what amount of receipts, after deducting expenses, will produce a moderate gain to the retail trades, and they shall fix in writing and strictly maintain what they find to be the right percentage of profit; this shall be seen to by the wardens of the agora, and by the wardens of the city, and by the wardens of the country. And so retail trade will benefit every one, and do the least possible injury to those in the state who practise it.

When a man makes an agreement which he does not fulfil, unless the agreement be of a nature which the law or a vote of the assembly does not allow, or which he has made under the influence of some unjust compulsion, or which he is prevented from fulfilling against his will by some unexpected chance, the other party may go to law with him in the courts of the tribes, for not having completed his agreement, if the parties are not able previously to come to terms before arbiters or before their neighbours. The class of craftsmen who have furnished human life with the arts is dedicated to Hephaestus and Athene; and there is a class of craftsmen who preserve the works of all craftsmen by arts of defence, the votaries of Ares and Athene, to which divinities they too are rightly dedicated. All these continue through life serving the country and the people; some of them are leaders in battle; others make for hire implements and works, and they ought not to deceive in such matters, out of respect to the Gods who are their ancestors. If any craftsman through indolence omit to execute his work in a given time, not reverencing the God who gives him the means of life, but considering, foolish fellow, that he is his own God and will let him off easily, in the first place, he shall suffer at the hands of the God, and in the second place, the law shall follow in a similar spirit. He shall owe to him who contracted with him the price of the works which he has failed in performing, and he shall begin again and execute them gratis in the given time. When a man undertakes a work, the law gives him the same advice which was given to the seller, that he should not attempt to raise the price, but simply ask the value; this the law enjoins also on the contractor; for the craftsman assuredly knows the value of his work. Wherefore, in free states the man of art ought not to attempt to impose upon private individuals by the help of his art, which is by nature a true thing; and he who is wronged in a matter of this sort, shall have a right of action against the party who has wronged him. And if any one lets out work to a craftsman, and does not pay him duly according to the lawful agreement, disregarding Zeus the guardian of the city and Athene, who are the partners of the state, and overthrows the foundations of society for the sake of a little gain, in his case let the law and the Gods maintain the common bonds of the state. And let him who, having already received the work in exchange, does not pay the price in the time agreed, pay double the price; and if a year has elapsed, although interest is not to be taken on loans, yet for every drachma which he owes to the contractor let him pay a monthly interest of an obol. Suits about these matters are to be decided by the courts of the tribes; and by the way, since we have mentioned craftsmen at all, we must not forget that other craft of war, in which generals and tacticians are the craftsmen, who undertake voluntarily or involuntarily the work of our safety, as other craftsmen undertake other public works;--if they execute their work well the law will never tire of praising him who gives them those honours which are the just rewards of the soldier; but if any one, having already received the benefit of any noble service in war, does not make the due return of honour, the law will blame him. Let this then be the law, having an ingredient of praise, not compelling but advising the great body of the citizens to honour the brave men who are the saviours of the whole state, whether by their courage or by their military skill;--they should honour them, I say, in the second place; for the first and highest tribute of respect is to be given to those who are able above other men to honour the words of good legislators.

The greater part of the dealings between man and man have been now regulated by us with the exception of those that relate to orphans and the supervision of orphans by their guardians. These follow next in order, and must be regulated in some way. But to arrive at them we must begin with the testamentary wishes of the dying and the case of those who may have happened to die intestate. When I said, Cleinias, that we must regulate them, I had in my mind the difficulty and perplexity in which all such matters are involved. You cannot leave them unregulated, for individuals would make regulations at variance with one another, and repugnant to the laws and habits of the living and to their own previous habits, if a person were simply allowed to make any will which he pleased, and this were to take effect in whatever state he may have been at the end of his life; for most of us lose our senses in a manner, and feel crushed when we think that we are about to die.

**CLEINIAS:** What do you mean, Stranger?

**ATHENIAN:** O Cleinias, a man when he is about to die is an intractable creature, and is apt to use language which causes a great deal of anxiety and trouble to the legislator.

**CLEINIAS:** In what way?

**ATHENIAN:** He wants to have the entire control of all his property, and will use angry words.

**CLEINIAS:** Such as what?

**ATHENIAN:** O ye Gods, he will say, how monstrous that I am not allowed to give, or not to give, my own to whom I will--less to him who has been bad to me, and more to him who has been good to me, and whose badness and goodness have been tested by me in time of sickness or in old age and in every other sort of fortune!

**CLEINIAS:** Well Stranger, and may he not very fairly say so?

**ATHENIAN:** In my opinion, Cleinias, the ancient legislators were too good- natured, and made laws without sufficient observation or consideration of human things.

**CLEINIAS:** What do you mean?

**ATHENIAN:** I mean, my friend, that they were afraid of the testator's reproaches, and so they passed a law to the effect that a man should be allowed to dispose of his property in all respects as he liked; but you and I, if I am not mistaken, will have something better to say to our departing citizens.

**CLEINIAS:** What?

**ATHENIAN:** O my friends, we will say to them, hard is it for you, who are creatures of a day, to know what is yours,--hard too, as the Delphic oracle says, to know yourselves at this hour. Now I, as the legislator, regard you and your possessions, not as belonging to yourselves, but as belonging to your whole family, both past and future, and yet more do I regard both family and possessions as belonging to the state; wherefore, if some one steals upon you with flattery, when you are tossed on the sea of disease or old age, and persuades you to dispose of your property in a way that is not for the best, I will not, if I can help, allow this; but I will legislate with a view to the whole, considering what is best both for the state and for the family, esteeming as I ought the feelings of an individual at a lower rate; and I hope that you will depart in peace and kindness towards us, as you are going the way of all mankind; and we will impartially take care of all your concerns, not neglecting any of them, if we can possibly help. Let this be our prelude and consolation to the living and dying, Cleinias, and let the law be as follows:--He who makes a disposition in a testament, if he be the father of a family, shall first of all inscribe as his heir any one of his sons whom he may think fit; and if he gives any of his children to be adopted by another citizen, let the adoption be inscribed. And if he has a son remaining over and above who has not been adopted upon any lot, and who may be expected to be sent out to a colony according to law, to him his father may give as much as he pleases of the rest of his property, with the exception of the paternal lot and the fixtures on the lot. And if there are other sons, let him distribute among them what there is more than the lot in such portions as he pleases. And if one of the sons has already a house of his own, he shall not give him of the money, nor shall he give money to a daughter who has been betrothed, but if she is not betrothed he may give her money. And if any of the sons or daughters shall be found to have another lot of land in the country, which has accrued after the testament has been made, they shall leave the lot which they have inherited to the heir of the man who has made the will. If the testator has no sons, but only daughters, let him choose the husband of any one of his daughters whom he pleases, and leave and inscribe him as his son and heir. And if a man have lost his son, when he was a child, and before he could be reckoned among grown-up men, whether his own or an adopted son, let the testator make mention of the circumstance and inscribe whom he will to be his second son in hope of better fortune. If the testator has no children at all, he may select and give to any one whom he pleases the tenth part of the property which he has acquired; but let him not be blamed if he gives all the rest to his adopted son, and makes a friend of him according to the law. If the sons of a man require guardians, and the father when he dies leaves a will appointing guardians, those who have been named by him, whoever they are and whatever their number be, if they are able and willing to take charge of the children, shall be recognized according to the provisions of the will. But if he dies and has made no will, or a will in which he has appointed no guardians, then the next of kin, two on the father's and two on the mother's side, and one of the friends of the deceased, shall have the authority of guardians, whom the guardians of the law shall appoint when the orphans require guardians. And the fifteen eldest guardians of the law shall have the whole care and charge of the orphans, divided into threes according to seniority,--a body of three for one year, and then another body of three for the next year, until the cycle of the five periods is complete; and this, as far as possible, is to continue always. If a man dies, having made no will at all, and leaves sons who require the care of guardians, they shall share in the protection which is afforded by these laws. And if a man dying by some unexpected fate leaves daughters behind him, let him pardon the legislator if he gives them in marriage, he have a regard only to two out of three conditions,--nearness of kin and the preservation of the lot, and omits the third condition, which a father would naturally consider, for he would choose out of all the citizens a son for himself, and a husband for his daughter, with a view to his character and disposition--the father, say, shall forgive the legislator if he disregards this, which to him is an impossible consideration. Let the law about these matters where practicable be as follows:--If a man dies without making a will, and leaves behind him daughters, let his brother, being the son of the same father or of the same mother, having no lot, marry the daughter and have the lot of the dead man. And if he have no brother, but only a brother's son, in like manner let them marry, if they be of a suitable age; and if there be not even a brother's son, but only the son of a sister, let them do likewise, and so in the fourth degree, if there be only the testator's father's brother, or in the fifth degree, his father's brother's son, or in the sixth degree, the child of his father's sister. Let kindred be always reckoned in this way: if a person leaves daughters the relationship shall proceed upwards through brothers and sisters, and brothers' and sisters' children, and first the males shall come, and after them the females in the same family. The judge shall consider and determine the suitableness or unsuitableness of age in marriage; he shall make an inspection of the males naked, and of the women naked down to the navel. And if there be a lack of kinsmen in a family extending to grandchildren of a brother, or to the grandchildren of a grandfather's children, the maiden may choose with the consent of her guardians any one of the citizens who is willing and whom she wills, and he shall be the heir of the dead man, and the husband of his daughter. Circumstances vary, and there may sometimes be a still greater lack of relations within the limits of the state; and if any maiden has no kindred living in the city, and there is some one who has been sent out to a colony, and she is disposed to make him the heir of her father's possessions, if he be indeed of her kindred, let him proceed to take the lot according to the regulation of the law; but if he be not of her kindred, she having no kinsmen within the city, and he be chosen by the daughter of the dead man, and empowered to marry by the guardians, let him return home and take the lot of him who died intestate. And if a man has no children, either male or female, and dies without making a will, let the previous law in general hold; and let a man and a woman go forth from the family and share the deserted house, and let the lot belong absolutely to them; and let the heiress in the first degree be a sister, and in a second degree a daughter of a brother, and in the third, a daughter of a sister, in the fourth degree the sister of a father, and in the fifth degree the daughter of a father's brother, and in a sixth degree of a father's sister; and these shall dwell with their male kinsmen, according to the degree of relationship and right, as we enacted before. Now we must not conceal from ourselves that such laws are apt to be oppressive and that there may sometimes be a hardship in the lawgiver commanding the kinsman of the dead man to marry his relation; he may be thought not to have considered the innumerable hindrances which may arise among men in the execution of such ordinances; for there may be cases in which the parties refuse to obey, and are ready to do anything rather than marry, when there is some bodily or mental malady or defect among those who are bidden to marry or be married. Persons may fancy that the legislator never thought of this, but they are mistaken; wherefore let us make a common prelude on behalf of the lawgiver and of his subjects, the law begging the latter to forgive the legislator, in that he, having to take care of the common weal, cannot order at the same time the various circumstances of individuals, and begging him to pardon them if naturally they are sometimes unable to fulfil the act which he in his ignorance imposes upon them.

**CLEINIAS:** And how, Stranger, can we act most fairly under the circumstances?

**ATHENIAN:** There must be arbiters chosen to deal with such laws and the subjects of them.

**CLEINIAS:** What do you mean?

**ATHENIAN:** I mean to say, that a case may occur in which the nephew, having a rich father, will be unwilling to marry the daughter of his uncle; he will have a feeling of pride, and he will wish to look higher. And there are cases in which the legislator will be imposing upon him the greatest calamity, and he will be compelled to disobey the law, if he is required, for example, to take a wife who is mad, or has some other terrible malady of soul or body, such as makes life intolerable to the sufferer. Then let what we are saying concerning these cases be embodied in a law:--If any one finds fault with the established laws respecting testaments, both as to other matters and especially in what relates to marriage, and asserts that the legislator, if he were alive and present, would not compel him to obey, --that is to say, would not compel those who are by our law required to marry or be given in marriage, to do either,--and some kinsman or guardian dispute this, the reply is that the legislator left fifteen of the guardians of the law to be arbiters and fathers of orphans, male or female, and to them let the disputants have recourse, and by their aid determine any matters of the kind, admitting their decision to be final. But if any one thinks that too great power is thus given to the guardians of the law, let him bring his adversaries into the court of the select judges, and there have the points in dispute determined. And he who loses the cause shall have censure and blame from the legislator, which, by a man of sense, is felt to be a penalty far heavier than a great loss of money.

Thus will orphan children have a second birth. After their first birth we spoke of their nurture and education, and after their second birth, when they have lost their parents, we ought to take measures that the misfortune of orphanhood may be as little sad to them as possible. In the first place, we say that the guardians of the law are lawgivers and fathers to them, not inferior to their natural fathers. Moreover, they shall take charge of them year by year as of their own kindred; and we have given both to them and to the children's own guardians a suitable admonition concerning the nurture of orphans. And we seem to have spoken opportunely in our former discourse, when we said that the souls of the dead have the power after death of taking an interest in human affairs, about which there are many tales and traditions, long indeed, but true; and seeing that they are so many and so ancient, we must believe them, and we must also believe the lawgivers, who tell us that these things are true, if they are not to be regarded as utter fools. But if these things are really so, in the first place men should have a fear of the Gods above, who regard the loneliness of the orphans; and in the second place of the souls of the departed, who by nature incline to take an especial care of their own children, and are friendly to those who honour, and unfriendly to those who dishonour them. Men should also fear the souls of the living who are aged and high in honour; wherever a city is well ordered and prosperous, their descendants cherish them, and so live happily; old persons are quick to see and hear all that relates to them, and are propitious to those who are just in the fulfilment of such duties, and they punish those who wrong the orphan and the desolate, considering that they are the greatest and most sacred of trusts. To all which matters the guardian and magistrate ought to apply his mind, if he has any, and take heed of the nurture and education of the orphans, seeking in every possible way to do them good, for he is making a contribution to his own good and that of his children. He who obeys the tale which precedes the law, and does no wrong to an orphan, will never experience the wrath of the legislator. But he who is disobedient, and wrongs any one who is bereft of father or mother, shall pay twice the penalty which he would have paid if he had wronged one whose parents had been alive. As touching other legislation concerning guardians in their relation to orphans, or concerning magistrates and their superintendence of the guardians, if they did not possess examples of the manner in which children of freemen should be brought up in the bringing up of their own children, and of the care of their property in the care of their own, or if they had not just laws fairly stated about these very things,--there would have been reason in making laws for them, under the idea that they were a peculiar class, and we might distinguish and make separate rules for the life of those who are orphans and of those who are not orphans. But as the case stands, the condition of orphans with us is not different from the case of those who have father, though in regard to honour and dishonour, and the attention given to them, the two are not usually placed upon a level. Wherefore, touching the legislation about orphans, the law speaks in serious accents, both of persuasion and threatening, and such a threat as the following will be by no means out of place:--He who is the guardian of an orphan of either sex, and he among the guardians of the law to whom the superintendence of this guardian has been assigned, shall love the unfortunate orphan as though he were his own child, and he shall be as careful and diligent in the management of his possessions as he would be if they were his own, or even more careful and diligent. Let every one who has the care of an orphan observe this law. But any one who acts contrary to the law on these matters, if he be a guardian of the child, may be fined by a magistrate, or, if he be himself a magistrate, the guardian may bring him before the court of select judges, and punish him, if convicted, by exacting a fine of double the amount of that inflicted by the court. And if a guardian appears to the relations of the orphan, or to any other citizen, to act negligently or dishonestly, let them bring him before the same court, and whatever damages are given against him, let him pay fourfold, and let half belong to the orphan and half to him who procured the conviction. If any orphan arrives at years of discretion, and thinks that he has been ill-used by his guardians, let him within five years of the expiration of the guardianship be allowed to bring them to trial; and if any of them be convicted, the court shall determine what he shall pay or suffer. And if a magistrate shall appear to have wronged the orphan by neglect, and he be convicted, let the court determine what he shall suffer or pay to the orphan, and if there be dishonesty in addition to neglect, besides paying the fine, let him be deposed from his office of guardian of the law, and let the state appoint another guardian of the law for the city and for the country in his room.

Greater differences than there ought to be sometimes arise between fathers and sons, on the part either of fathers who will be of opinion that the legislator should enact that they may, if they wish, lawfully renounce their son by the proclamation of a herald in the face of the world, or of sons who think that they should be allowed to indict their fathers on the charge of imbecility when they are disabled by disease or old age. These things only happen, as a matter of fact, where the natures of men are utterly bad; for where only half is bad, as, for example, if the father be not bad, but the son be bad, or conversely, no great calamity is the result of such an amount of hatred as this. In another state, a son disowned by his father would not of necessity cease to be a citizen, but in our state, of which these are to be the laws, the disinherited must necessarily emigrate into another country, for no addition can be made even of a single family to the 5040 households; and, therefore, he who deserves to suffer these things must be renounced not only by his father, who is a single person, but by the whole family, and what is done in these cases must be regulated by some such law as the following:--He who in the sad disorder of his soul has a mind, justly or unjustly, to expel from his family a son whom he has begotten and brought up, shall not lightly or at once execute his purpose; but first of all he shall collect together his own kinsmen, extending to cousins, and in like manner his son's kinsmen by the mother's side, and in their presence he shall accuse his son, setting forth that he deserves at the hands of them all to be dismissed from the family; and the son shall be allowed to address them in a similar manner, and show that he does not deserve to suffer any of these things. And if the father persuades them, and obtains the suffrages of more than half of his kindred, exclusive of the father and mother and the offender himself--I say, if he obtains more than half the suffrages of all the other grown-up members of the family, of both sexes, the father shall be permitted to put away his son, but not otherwise. And if any other citizen is willing to adopt the son who is put away, no law shall hinder him; for the characters of young men are subject to many changes in the course of their lives. And if he has been put away, and in a period of ten years no one is willing to adopt him, let those who have the care of the superabundant population which is sent out into colonies, see to him, in order that he may be suitably provided for in the colony. And if disease or age or harshness of temper, or all these together, makes a man to be more out of his mind than the rest of the world are,--but this is not observable, except to those who live with him,--and he, being master of his property, is the ruin of the house, and his son doubts and hesitates about indicting his father for insanity, let the law in that case ordain that he shall first of all go to the eldest guardians of the law and tell them of his father's misfortune, and they shall duly look into the matter, and take counsel as to whether he shall indict him or not. And if they advise him to proceed, they shall be both his witnesses and his advocates; and if the father is cast, he shall henceforth be incapable of ordering the least particular of his life; let him be as a child dwelling in the house for the remainder of his days. And if a man and his wife have an unfortunate incompatibility of temper, ten of the guardians of the law, who are impartial (or, 'who are intermediate in age':--i.e. who are neither the youngest nor the oldest guardians of the law), and ten of the women who regulate marriages, shall look to the matter, and if they are able to reconcile them they shall be formally reconciled; but if their souls are too much tossed with passion, they shall endeavour to find other partners. Now they are not likely to have very gentle tempers; and, therefore, we must endeavour to associate with them deeper and softer natures. Those who have no children, or only a few, at the time of their separation, should choose their new partners with a view to the procreation of children; but those who have a sufficient number of children should separate and marry again in order that they may have some one to grow old with and that the pair may take care of one another in age. If a woman dies, leaving children, male or female, the law will advise rather than compel the husband to bring up the children without introducing into the house a stepmother. But if he have no children, then he shall be compelled to marry until he has begotten a sufficient number of sons to his family and to the state. And if a man dies leaving a sufficient number of children, the mother of his children shall remain with them and bring them up. But if she appears to be too young to live virtuously without a husband, let her relations communicate with the women who superintend marriage, and let both together do what they think best in these matters; if there is a lack of children, let the choice be made with a view to having them; two children, one of either sex, shall be deemed sufficient in the eye of the law. When a child is admitted to be the offspring of certain parents and is acknowledged by them, but there is need of a decision as to which parent the child is to follow,--in case a female slave have intercourse with a male slave, or with a freeman or freedman, the offspring shall always belong to the master of the female slave. Again, if a free woman have intercourse with a male slave, the offspring shall belong to the master of the slave; but if a child be born either of a slave by her master, or of his mistress by a slave--and this be proven--the offspring of the woman and its father shall be sent away by the women who superintend marriage into another country, and the guardians of the law shall send away the offspring of the man and its mother.

Neither God, nor a man who has understanding, will ever advise any one to neglect his parents. To a discourse concerning the honour and dishonour of parents, a prelude such as the following, about the service of the Gods, will be a suitable introduction:--There are ancient customs about the Gods which are universal, and they are of two kinds: some of the Gods we see with our eyes and we honour them, of others we honour the images, raising statues of them which we adore; and though they are lifeless, yet we imagine that the living Gods have a good will and gratitude to us on this account. Now, if a man has a father or mother, or their fathers or mothers treasured up in his house stricken in years, let him consider that no statue can be more potent to grant his requests than they are, who are sitting at his hearth, if only he knows how to show true service to them.

**CLEINIAS:** And what do you call the true mode of service?

**ATHENIAN:** I will tell you, O my friend, for such things are worth listening to.

**CLEINIAS:** Proceed.

**ATHENIAN:** Oedipus, as tradition says, when dishonoured by his sons, invoked on them curses which every one declares to have been heard and ratified by the Gods, and Amyntor in his wrath invoked curses on his son Phoenix, and Theseus upon Hippolytus, and innumerable others have also called down wrath upon their children, whence it is clear that the Gods listen to the imprecations of parents; for the curses of parents are, as they ought to be, mighty against their children as no others are. And shall we suppose that the prayers of a father or mother who is specially dishonoured by his or her children, are heard by the Gods in accordance with nature; and that if a parent is honoured by them, and in the gladness of his heart earnestly entreats the Gods in his prayers to do them good, he is not equally heard, and that they do not minister to his request? If not, they would be very unjust ministers of good, and that we affirm to be contrary to their nature.

**CLEINIAS:** Certainly.

**ATHENIAN:** May we not think, as I was saying just now, that we can possess no image which is more honoured by the Gods, than that of a father or grandfather, or of a mother stricken in years? whom when a man honours, the heart of the God rejoices, and he is ready to answer their prayers. And, truly, the figure of an ancestor is a wonderful thing, far higher than that of a lifeless image. For the living, when they are honoured by us, join in our prayers, and when they are dishonoured, they utter imprecations against us; but lifeless objects do neither. And therefore, if a man makes a right use of his father and grandfather and other aged relations, he will have images which above all others will win him the favour of the Gods.

**CLEINIAS:** Excellent.

**ATHENIAN:** Every man of any understanding fears and respects the prayers of parents, knowing well that many times and to many persons they have been accomplished. Now these things being thus ordered by nature, good men think it a blessing from heaven if their parents live to old age and reach the utmost limit of human life, or if taken away before their time they are deeply regretted by them; but to bad men parents are always a cause of terror. Wherefore let every man honour with every sort of lawful honour his own parents, agreeably to what has now been said. But if this prelude be an unmeaning sound in the ears of any one, let the law follow, which may be rightly imposed in these terms:--If any one in this city be not sufficiently careful of his parents, and do not regard and gratify in every respect their wishes more than those of his sons and of his other offspring or of himself,--let him who experiences this sort of treatment either come himself, or send some one to inform the three eldest guardians of the law, and three of the women who have the care of marriages; and let them look to the matter and punish youthful evil-doers with stripes and bonds if they are under thirty years of age, that is to say, if they be men, or if they be women, let them undergo the same punishment up to forty years of age. But if, when they are still more advanced in years, they continue the same neglect of their parents, and do any hurt to any of them, let them be brought before a court in which every single one of the eldest citizens shall be the judges, and if the offender be convicted, let the court determine what he ought to pay or suffer, and any penalty may be imposed on him which a man can pay or suffer. If the person who has been wronged be unable to inform the magistrates, let any freeman who hears of his case inform, and if he do not, he shall be deemed base, and shall be liable to have a suit for damage brought against him by any one who likes. And if a slave inform, he shall receive freedom; and if he be the slave of the injurer or injured party, he shall be set free by the magistrates, or if he belong to any other citizen, the public shall pay a price on his behalf to the owner; and let the magistrates take heed that no one wrongs him out of revenge, because he has given information.

Cases in which one man injures another by poisons, and which prove fatal, have been already discussed (i.e. they are cases of murder); but about other cases in which a person intentionally and of malice harms another with meats, or drinks, or ointments, nothing has as yet been determined. For there are two kinds of poisons used among men, which cannot clearly be distinguished. There is the kind just now explicitly mentioned, which injures bodies by the use of other bodies according to a natural law; there is also another kind which persuades the more daring class that they can do injury by sorceries, and incantations, and magic knots, as they are termed, and makes others believe that they above all persons are injured by the powers of the magician. Now it is not easy to know the nature of all these things; nor if a man do know can he readily persuade others to believe him. And when men are disturbed in their minds at the sight of waxen images fixed either at their doors, or in a place where three ways meet, or on the sepulchres of parents, there is no use in trying to persuade them that they should despise all such things because they have no certain knowledge about them. But we must have a law in two parts, concerning poisoning, in whichever of the two ways the attempt is made, and we must entreat, and exhort, and advise men not to have recourse to such practices, by which they scare the multitude out of their wits, as if they were children, compelling the legislator and the judge to heal the fears which the sorcerer arouses, and to tell them in the first place, that he who attempts to poison or enchant others knows not what he is doing, either as regards the body (unless he has a knowledge of medicine), or as regards his enchantments (unless he happens to be a prophet or diviner). Let the law, then, run as follows about poisoning or witchcraft:--He who employs poison to do any injury, not fatal, to a man himself, or to his servants, or any injury, whether fatal or not, to his cattle or his bees, if he be a physician, and be convicted of poisoning, shall be punished with death; or if he be a private person, the court shall determine what he is to pay or suffer. But he who seems to be the sort of man who injures others by magic knots, or enchantments, or incantations, or any of the like practices, if he be a prophet or diviner, let him die; and if, not being a prophet, he be convicted of witchcraft, as in the previous case, let the court fix what he ought to pay or suffer.

When a man does another any injury by theft or violence, for the greater injury let him pay greater damages to the injured man, and less for the smaller injury; but in all cases, whatever the injury may have been, as much as will compensate the loss. And besides the compensation of the wrong, let a man pay a further penalty for the chastisement of his offence: he who has done the wrong instigated by the folly of another, through the lightheartedness of youth or the like, shall pay a lighter penalty; but he who has injured another through his own folly, when overcome by pleasure or pain, in cowardly fear, or lust, or envy, or implacable anger, shall endure a heavier punishment. Not that he is punished because he did wrong, for that which is done can never be undone, but in order that in future times, he, and those who see him corrected, may utterly hate injustice, or at any rate abate much of their evil-doing. Having an eye to all these things, the law, like a good archer, should aim at the right measure of punishment, and in all cases at the deserved punishment. In the attainment of this the judge shall be a fellow-worker with the legislator, whenever the law leaves to him to determine what the offender shall suffer or pay; and the legislator, like a painter, shall give a rough sketch of the cases in which the law is to be applied. This is what we must do, Megillus and Cleinias, in the best and fairest manner that we can, saying what the punishments are to be of all actions of theft and violence, and giving laws of such a kind as the Gods and sons of Gods would have us give.

If a man is mad he shall not be at large in the city, but his relations shall keep him at home in any way which they can; or if not, let them pay a penalty,--he who is of the highest class shall pay a penalty of one hundred drachmas, whether he be a slave or a freeman whom he neglects; and he of the second class shall pay four-fifths of a mina; and he of the third class three-fifths; and he of the fourth class two-fifths. Now there are many sorts of madness, some arising out of disease, which we have already mentioned; and there are other kinds, which originate in an evil and passionate temperament, and are increased by bad education; out of a slight quarrel this class of madmen will often raise a storm of abuse against one another, and nothing of that sort ought to be allowed to occur in a well- ordered state. Let this, then, be the law about abuse, which shall relate to all cases:--No one shall speak evil of another; and when a man disputes with another he shall teach and learn of the disputant and the company, but he shall abstain from evil-speaking; for out of the imprecations which men utter against one another, and the feminine habit of casting aspersions on one another, and using foul names, out of words light as air, in very deed the greatest enmities and hatreds spring up. For the speaker gratifies his anger, which is an ungracious element of his nature; and nursing up his wrath by the entertainment of evil thoughts, and exacerbating that part of his soul which was formerly civilized by education, he lives in a state of savageness and moroseness, and pays a bitter penalty for his anger. And in such cases almost all men take to saying something ridiculous about their opponent, and there is no man who is in the habit of laughing at another who does not miss virtue and earnestness altogether, or lose the better half of greatness. Wherefore let no one utter any taunting word at a temple, or at the public sacrifices, or at the games, or in the agora, or in a court of justice, or in any public assembly. And let the magistrate who presides on these occasions chastise an offender, and he shall be blameless; but if he fails in doing so, he shall not claim the prize of virtue; for he is one who heeds not the laws, and does not do what the legislator commands. And if in any other place any one indulges in these sort of revilings, whether he has begun the quarrel or is only retaliating, let any elder who is present support the law, and control with blows those who indulge in passion, which is another great evil; and if he do not, let him be liable to pay the appointed penalty. And we say now, that he who deals in reproaches against others cannot reproach them without attempting to ridicule them; and this, when done in a moment of anger, is what we make matter of reproach against him. But then, do we admit into our state the comic writers who are so fond of making mankind ridiculous, if they attempt in a good-natured manner to turn the laugh against our citizens? or do we draw the distinction of jest and earnest, and allow a man to make use of ridicule in jest and without anger about any thing or person; though as we were saying, not if he be angry have a set purpose? We forbid earnest--that is unalterably fixed; but we have still to say who are to be sanctioned or not to be sanctioned by the law in the employment of innocent humour. A comic poet, or maker of iambic or satirical lyric verse, shall not be permitted to ridicule any of the citizens, either by word or likeness, either in anger or without anger. And if any one is disobedient, the judges shall either at once expel him from the country, or he shall pay a fine of three minae, which shall be dedicated to the God who presides over the contests. Those only who have received permission shall be allowed to write verses at one another, but they shall be without anger and in jest; in anger and in serious earnest they shall not be allowed. The decision of this matter shall be left to the superintendent of the general education of the young, and whatever he may license, the writer shall be allowed to produce, and whatever he rejects let not the poet himself exhibit, or ever teach anybody else, slave or freeman, under the penalty of being dishonoured, and held disobedient to the laws.

Now he is not to be pitied who is hungry, or who suffers any bodily pain, but he who is temperate, or has some other virtue, or part of a virtue, and at the same time suffers from misfortune; it would be an extraordinary thing if such an one, whether slave or freeman, were utterly forsaken and fell into the extremes of poverty in any tolerably well-ordered city or government. Wherefore the legislator may safely make a law applicable to such cases in the following terms:--Let there be no beggars in our state; and if anybody begs, seeking to pick up a livelihood by unavailing prayers, let the wardens of the agora turn him out of the agora, and the wardens of the city out of the city, and the wardens of the country send him out of any other parts of the and across the border, in order that the land may be cleared of this sort of animal.

If a slave of either sex injure anything, which is not his or her own, through inexperience, or some improper practice, and the person who suffers damage be not himself in part to blame, the master of the slave who has done the harm shall either make full satisfaction, or give up the slave who has done the injury. But if master argue that the charge has arisen by collusion between the injured party and the injurer, with the view of obtaining the slave, let him sue the person, who says that he has been injured, for malpractices. And if he gain a conviction, let him receive double the value which the court fixes as the price of the slave; and if he lose his suit, let him make amends for the injury, and give up the slave. And if a beast of burden, or horse, or dog, or any other animal, injure the property of a neighbour, the owner shall in like manner pay for the injury.

If any man refuses to be a witness, he who wants him shall summon him, and he who is summoned shall come to the trial; and if he knows and is willing to bear witness, let him bear witness, but if he says he does not know let him swear by the three divinities Zeus, and Apollo, and Themis, that he does not, and have no more to do with the cause. And he who is summoned to give witness and does not answer to his summoner, shall be liable for the harm which ensues according to law. And if a person calls up as a witness any one who is acting as a judge, let him give his witness, but he shall not afterwards vote in the cause. A free woman may give her witness and plead, if she be more than forty years of age, and may bring an action if she have no husband; but if her husband be alive she shall only be allowed to bear witness. A slave of either sex and a child shall be allowed to give evidence and to plead, but only in cases of murder; and they must produce sufficient sureties that they will certainly remain until the trial, in case they should be charged with false witness. And either of the parties in a cause may bring an accusation of perjury against witnesses, touching their evidence in whole or in part, if he asserts that such evidence has been given; but the accusation must be brought previous to the final decision of the cause. The magistrates shall preserve the accusations of false witness, and have them kept under the seal of both parties, and produce them on the day when the trial for false witness takes place. If a man be twice convicted of false witness, he shall not be required, and if thrice, he shall not be allowed to bear witness; and if he dare to witness after he has been convicted three times, let any one who pleases inform against him to the magistrates, and let the magistrates hand him over to the court, and if he be convicted he shall be punished with death. And in any case in which the evidence is rightly found to be false, and yet to have given the victory to him who wins the suit, and more than half the witnesses are condemned, the decision which was gained by these means shall be rescinded, and there shall be a discussion and a decision as to whether the suit was determined by that false evidence or not; and in whichever way the decision may be given, the previous suit shall be determined accordingly.

There are many noble things in human life, but to most of them attach evils which are fated to corrupt and spoil them. Is not justice noble, which has been the civilizer of humanity? How then can the advocate of justice be other than noble? And yet upon this profession which is presented to us under the fair name of art has come an evil reputation (the text is probably corrupt). In the first place, we are told that by ingenious pleas and the help of an advocate the law enables a man to win a particular cause, whether just or unjust; and that both the art, and the power of speech which is thereby imparted, are at the service of him who is willing to pay for them. Now in our state this so-called art, whether really an art or only an experience and practice destitute of any art, ought if possible never to come into existence, or if existing among us should listen to the request of the legislator and go away into another land, and not speak contrary to justice. If the offenders obey we say no more; but for those who disobey, the voice of the law is as follows:--If any one thinks that he will pervert the power of justice in the minds of the judges, and unseasonably litigate or advocate, let any one who likes indict him for malpractices of law and dishonest advocacy, and let him be judged in the court of select judges; and if he be convicted, let the court determine whether he may be supposed to act from a love of money or from contentiousness. And if he is supposed to act from contentiousness, the court shall fix a time during which he shall not be allowed to institute or plead a cause; and if he is supposed to act as he does from love of money, in case he be a stranger, he shall leave the country, and never return under penalty of death; but if he be a citizen, he shall die, because he is a lover of money, in whatever manner gained; and equally, if he be judged to have acted more than once from contentiousness, he shall die.

# BOOK XII.

If a herald or an ambassador carry a false message from our city to any other, or bring back a false message from the city to which he is sent, or be proved to have brought back, whether from friends or enemies, in his capacity of herald or ambassador, what they have never said, let him be indicted for having violated, contrary to the law, the commands and duties imposed upon him by Hermes and Zeus, and let there be a penalty fixed, which he shall suffer or pay if he be convicted.

Theft is a mean, and robbery a shameless thing; and none of the sons of Zeus delight in fraud and violence, or ever practised either. Wherefore let no one be deluded by poets or mythologers into a mistaken belief of such things, nor let him suppose, when he thieves or is guilty of violence, that he is doing nothing base, but only what the Gods themselves do. For such tales are untrue and improbable; and he who steals or robs contrary to the law, is never either a God or the son of a God; of this the legislator ought to be better informed than all the poets put together. Happy is he and may he be forever happy, who is persuaded and listens to our words; but he who disobeys shall have to contend against the following law:--If a man steal anything belonging to the public, whether that which he steals be much or little, he shall have the same punishment. For he who steals a little steals with the same wish as he who steals much, but with less power, and he who takes up a greater amount, not having deposited it, is wholly unjust. Wherefore the law is not disposed to inflict a less penalty on the one than on the other because his theft is less, but on the ground that the thief may possibly be in one case still curable, and may in another case be incurable. If any one convict in a court of law a stranger or a slave of a theft of public property, let the court determine what punishment he shall suffer, or what penalty he shall pay, bearing in mind that he is probably not incurable. But the citizen who has been brought up as our citizens will have been, if he be found guilty of robbing his country by fraud or violence, whether he be caught in the act or not, shall be punished with death; for he is incurable.

Now for expeditions of war much consideration and many laws are required; the great principle of all is that no one of either sex should be without a commander; nor should the mind of any one be accustomed to do anything, either in jest or earnest, of his own motion, but in war and in peace he should look to and follow his leader, even in the least things being under his guidance; for example, he should stand or move, or exercise, or wash, or take his meals, or get up in the night to keep guard and deliver messages when he is bidden; and in the hour of danger he should not pursue and not retreat except by order of his superior; and in a word, not teach the soul or accustom her to know or understand how to do anything apart from others. Of all soldiers the life should be always and in all things as far as possible in common and together; there neither is nor ever will be a higher, or better, or more scientific principle than this for the attainment of salvation and victory in war. And we ought in time of peace from youth upwards to practise this habit of commanding others, and of being commanded by others; anarchy should have no place in the life of man or of the beasts who are subject to man. I may add that all dances ought to be performed with a view to military excellence; and agility and ease should be cultivated for the same object, and also endurance of the want of meats and drinks, and of winter cold and summer heat, and of hard couches; and, above all, care should be taken not to destroy the peculiar qualities of the head and the feet by surrounding them with extraneous coverings, and so hindering their natural growth of hair and soles. For these are the extremities, and of all the parts of the body, whether they are preserved or not is of the greatest consequence; the one is the servant of the whole body, and the other the master, in whom all the ruling senses are by nature set. Let the young man imagine that he hears in what has preceded the praises of the military life; the law shall be as follows:--He shall serve in war who is on the roll or appointed to some special service, and if any one is absent from cowardice, and without the leave of the generals; he shall be indicted before the military commanders for failure of service when the army comes home; and the soldiers shall be his judges; the heavy- armed, and the cavalry, and the other arms of the service shall form separate courts; and they shall bring the heavy-armed before the heavy- armed, and the horsemen before the horsemen, and the others in like manner before their peers; and he who is found guilty shall never be allowed to compete for any prize of valour, or indict another for not serving on an expedition, or be an accuser at all in any military matters. Moreover, the court shall further determine what punishment he shall suffer, or what penalty he shall pay. When the suits for failure of service are completed, the leaders of the several kinds of troops shall again hold an assembly, and they shall adjudge the prizes of valour; and he who likes shall give judgment in his own branch of the service, saying nothing about any former expedition, nor producing any proof or witnesses to confirm his statement, but speaking only of the present occasion. The crown of victory shall be an olive wreath which the victor shall offer up the temple of any war-god whom he likes, adding an inscription for a testimony to last during life, that such an one has received the first, the second, or the third prize. If any one goes on an expedition, and returns home before the appointed time, when the generals have not withdrawn the army, be shall be indicted for desertion before the same persons who took cognizance of failure of service, and if he be found guilty, the same punishment shall be inflicted on him.

Now every man who is engaged in any suit ought to be very careful of bringing false witness against any one, either intentionally or unintentionally, if he can help; for justice is truly said to be an honourable maiden, and falsehood is naturally repugnant to honour and justice. A witness ought to be very careful not to sin against justice, as for example in what relates to the throwing away of arms--he must distinguish the throwing them away when necessary, and not make that a reproach, or bring in action against some innocent person on that account. To make the distinction may be difficult; but still the law must attempt to define the different kinds in some way. Let me endeavour to explain my meaning by an ancient tale:--If Patroclus had been brought to the tent still alive but without his arms (and this has happened to innumerable persons), the original arms, which the poet says were presented to Peleus by the Gods as a nuptial gift when he married Thetis, remaining in the hands of Hector, then the base spirits of that day might have reproached the son of Menoetius with having cast away his arms. Again, there is the case of those who have been thrown down precipices and lost their arms; and of those who at sea, and in stormy places, have been suddenly overwhelmed by floods of water; and there are numberless things of this kind which one might adduce by way of extenuation, and with the view of justifying a misfortune which is easily misrepresented. We must, therefore, endeavour to divide to the best of our power the greater and more serious evil from the lesser. And a distinction may be drawn in the use of terms of reproach. A man does not always deserve to be called the thrower away of his shield; he may be only the loser of his arms. For there is a great or rather absolute difference between him who is deprived of his arms by a sufficient force, and him who voluntarily lets his shield go. Let the law then be as follows:--If a person having arms is overtaken by the enemy and does not turn round and defend himself, but lets them go voluntarily or throws them away, choosing a base life and a swift escape rather than a courageous and noble and blessed death--in such a case of the throwing away of arms let justice be done, but the judge need take no note of the case just now mentioned; for the bad man ought always to be punished, in the hope that he may be improved, but not the unfortunate, for there is no advantage in that. And what shall be the punishment suited to him who has thrown away his weapons of defence? Tradition says that Caeneus, the Thessalian, was changed by a God from a woman into a man; but the converse miracle cannot now be wrought, or no punishment would be more proper than that the man who throws away his shield should be changed into a woman. This however is impossible, and therefore let us make a law as nearly like this as we can--that he who loves his life too well shall be in no danger for the remainder of his days, but shall live for ever under the stigma of cowardice. And let the law be in the following terms:--When a man is found guilty of disgracefully throwing away his arms in war, no general or military officer shall allow him to serve as a soldier, or give him any place at all in the ranks of soldiers; and the officer who gives the coward any place, shall suffer a penalty which the public examiner shall exact of him; and if he be of the highest class, he shall pay a thousand drachmae; or if he be of the second class, five minae; or if he be of the third, three minae; or if he be of the fourth class, one mina. And he who is found guilty of cowardice, shall not only be dismissed from manly dangers, which is a disgrace appropriate to his nature, but he shall pay a thousand drachmae, if he be of the highest class, and five minae if he be of the second class, and three if he be of the third class, and a mina, like the preceding, if he be of the fourth class.

What regulations will be proper about examiners, seeing that some of our magistrates are elected by lot, and for a year, and some for a longer time and from selected persons? Of such magistrates, who will be a sufficient censor or examiner, if any of them, weighed down by the pressure of office or his own inability to support the dignity of his office, be guilty of any crooked practice? It is by no means easy to find a magistrate who excels other magistrates in virtue, but still we must endeavour to discover some censor or examiner who is more than man. For the truth is, that there are many elements of dissolution in a state, as there are also in a ship, or in an animal; they all have their cords, and girders, and sinews,--one nature diffused in many places, and called by many names; and the office of examiner is a most important element in the preservation and dissolution of states. For if the examiners are better than the magistrates, and their duty is fulfilled justly and without blame, then the whole state and country flourishes and is happy; but if the examination of the magistrates is carried on in a wrong way, then, by the relaxation of that justice which is the uniting principle of all constitutions, every power in the state is rent asunder from every other; they no longer incline in the same direction, but fill the city with faction, and make many cities out of one, and soon bring all to destruction. Wherefore the examiners ought to be admirable in every sort of virtue. Let us invent a mode of creating them, which shall be as follows:--Every year, after the summer solstice, the whole city shall meet in the common precincts of Helios and Apollo, and shall present to the God three men out of their own number in the manner following:--Each citizen shall select, not himself, but some other citizen whom he deems in every way the best, and who is not less than fifty years of age. And out of the selected persons who have the greatest number of votes, they shall make a further selection until they reduce them to one-half, if they are an even number; but if they are not an even number, they shall subtract the one who has the smallest number of votes, and make them an even number, and then leave the half which have the greater number of votes. And if two persons have an equal number of votes, and thus increase the number beyond one-half, they shall withdraw the younger of the two and do away with the excess; and then including all the rest they shall again vote, until there are left three having an unequal number of votes. But if all the three, or two out of the three, have equal votes, let them commit the election to good fate and fortune, and separate off by lot the first, and the second, and the third; these they shall crown with an olive wreath and give them the prize of excellence, at the same time proclaiming to all the world that the city of the Magnetes, by providence of the Gods, is again preserved, and presents to the Sun and to Apollo her three best men as first-fruits, to be a common offering to them, according to the ancient law, as long as their lives answer to the judgment formed of them. And these shall appoint in their first year twelve examiners, to continue until each has completed seventy-five years, to whom three shall afterwards be added yearly; and let these divide all the magistracies into twelve parts, and prove the holders of them by every sort of test to which a freeman may be subjected; and let them live while they hold office in the precinct of Helios and Apollo, in which they were chosen, and let each one form a judgment of some things individually, and of others in company with his colleagues; and let him place a writing in the agora about each magistracy, and what the magistrate ought to suffer or pay, according to the decision of the examiners. And if a magistrate does not admit that he has been justly judged, let him bring the examiners before the select judges, and if he be acquitted by their decision, let him, if he will, accuse the examiners themselves; if, however, he be convicted, and have been condemned to death by the examiners, let him die (and of course he can only die once):--but any other penalties which admit of being doubled let him suffer twice over.

And now let us pass under review the examiners themselves; what will their examination be, and how conducted? During the life of these men, whom the whole state counts worthy of the rewards of virtue, they shall have the first seat at all public assemblies, and at all Hellenic sacrifices and sacred missions, and other public and holy ceremonies in which they share. The chiefs of each sacred mission shall be selected from them, and they only of all the citizens shall be adorned with a crown of laurel; they shall all be priests of Apollo and Helios; and one of them, who is judged first of the priests created in that year, shall be high priest; and they shall write up his name in each year to be a measure of time as long as the city lasts; and after their death they shall be laid out and carried to the grave and entombed in a manner different from the other citizens. They shall be decked in a robe all of white, and there shall be no crying or lamentation over them; but a chorus of fifteen maidens, and another of boys, shall stand around the bier on either side, hymning the praises of the departed priests in alternate responses, declaring their blessedness in song all day long; and at dawn a hundred of the youths who practise gymnastic exercises, and whom the relations of the departed shall choose, shall carry the bier to the sepulchre, the young men marching first, dressed in the garb of warriors,--the cavalry with their horses, the heavy- armed with their arms, and the others in like manner. And boys near the bier and in front of it shall sing their national hymn, and maidens shall follow behind, and with them the women who have passed the age of child- bearing; next, although they are interdicted from other burials, let priests and priestesses follow, unless the Pythian oracle forbid them; for this burial is free from pollution. The place of burial shall be an oblong vaulted chamber underground, constructed of tufa, which will last for ever, having stone couches placed side by side. And here they will lay the blessed person, and cover the sepulchre with a circular mound of earth and plant a grove of trees around on every side but one; and on that side the sepulchre shall be allowed to extend for ever, and a new mound will not be required. Every year they shall have contests in music and gymnastics, and in horsemanship, in honour of the dead. These are the honours which shall be given to those who at the examination are found blameless; but if any of them, trusting to the scrutiny being over, should, after the judgment has been given, manifest the wickedness of human nature, let the law ordain that he who pleases shall indict him, and let the cause be tried in the following manner. In the first place, the court shall be composed of the guardians of the law, and to them the surviving examiners shall be added, as well as the court of select judges; and let the pursuer lay his indictment in this form--he shall say that so-and-so is unworthy of the prize of virtue and of his office; and if the defendant be convicted let him be deprived of his office, and of the burial, and of the other honours given him. But if the prosecutor do not obtain the fifth part of the votes, let him, if he be of the first class, pay twelve minae, and eight if he be of the second class, and six if he be of the third class, and two minae if he be of the fourth class.

The so-called decision of Rhadamanthus is worthy of all admiration. He knew that the men of his own time believed and had no doubt that there were Gods, which was a reasonable belief in those days, because most men were the sons of Gods, and according to tradition he was one himself. He appears to have thought that he ought to commit judgment to no man, but to the Gods only, and in this way suits were simply and speedily decided by him. For he made the two parties take an oath respecting the points in dispute, and so got rid of the matter speedily and safely. But now that a certain portion of mankind do not believe at all in the existence of the Gods, and others imagine that they have no care of us, and the opinion of most men, and of the worst men, is that in return for a small sacrifice and a few flattering words they will be their accomplices in purloining large sums and save them from many terrible punishments, the way of Rhadamanthus is no longer suited to the needs of justice; for as the opinions of men about the Gods are changed, the laws should also be changed;--in the granting of suits a rational legislation ought to do away with the oaths of the parties on either side--he who obtains leave to bring an action should write down the charges, but should not add an oath; and the defendant in like manner should give his denial to the magistrates in writing, and not swear; for it is a dreadful thing to know, when many lawsuits are going on in a state, that almost half the people who meet one another quite unconcernedly at the public meals and in other companies and relations of private life are perjured. Let the law, then, be as follows: --A judge who is about to give judgment shall take an oath, and he who is choosing magistrates for the state shall either vote on oath or with a voting tablet which he brings from a temple; so too the judge of dances and of all music, and the superintendents and umpires of gymnastic and equestrian contests, and any matters in which, as far as men can judge, there is nothing to be gained by a false oath; but all cases in which a denial confirmed by an oath clearly results in a great advantage to the taker of the oath, shall be decided without the oath of the parties to the suit, and the presiding judges shall not permit either of them to use an oath for the sake of persuading, nor to call down curses on himself and his race, nor to use unseemly supplications or womanish laments. But they shall ever be teaching and learning what is just in auspicious words; and he who does otherwise shall be supposed to speak beside the point, and the judges shall again bring him back to the question at issue. On the other hand, strangers in their dealings with strangers shall as at present have power to give and receive oaths, for they will not often grow old in the city or leave a fry of young ones like themselves to be the sons and heirs of the land.

As to the initiation of private suits, let the manner of deciding causes between all citizens be the same as in cases in which any freeman is disobedient to the state in minor matters, of which the penalty is not stripes, imprisonment, or death. But as regards attendance at choruses or processions or other shows, and as regards public services, whether the celebration of sacrifice in peace, or the payment of contributions in war-- in all these cases, first comes the necessity of providing a remedy for the loss; and by those who will not obey, there shall be security given to the officers whom the city and the law empower to exact the sum due; and if they forfeit their security, let the goods which they have pledged be sold and the money given to the city; but if they ought to pay a larger sum, the several magistrates shall impose upon the disobedient a suitable penalty, and bring them before the court, until they are willing to do what they are ordered.

Now a state which makes money from the cultivation of the soil only, and has no foreign trade, must consider what it will do about the emigration of its own people to other countries, and the reception of strangers from elsewhere. About these matters the legislator has to consider, and he will begin by trying to persuade men as far as he can. The intercourse of cities with one another is apt to create a confusion of manners; strangers are always suggesting novelties to strangers. When states are well governed by good laws the mixture causes the greatest possible injury; but seeing that most cities are the reverse of well-ordered, the confusion which arises in them from the reception of strangers, and from the citizens themselves rushing off into other cities, when any one either young or old desires to travel anywhere abroad at whatever time, is of no consequence. On the other hand, the refusal of states to receive others, and for their own citizens never to go to other places, is an utter impossibility, and to the rest of the world is likely to appear ruthless and uncivilized; it is a practise adopted by people who use harsh words, such as xenelasia or banishment of strangers, and who have harsh and morose ways, as men think. And to be thought or not to be thought well of by the rest of the world is no light matter; for the many are not so far wrong in their judgment of who are bad and who are good, as they are removed from the nature of virtue in themselves. Even bad men have a divine instinct which guesses rightly, and very many who are utterly depraved form correct notions and judgments of the differences between the good and bad. And the generality of cities are quite right in exhorting us to value a good reputation in the world, for there is no truth greater and more important than this--that he who is really good (I am speaking of the man who would be perfect) seeks for reputation with, but not without, the reality of goodness. And our Cretan colony ought also to acquire the fairest and noblest reputation for virtue from other men; and there is every reason to expect that, if the reality answers to the idea, she will be one of the few well-ordered cities which the sun and the other Gods behold. Wherefore, in the matter of journeys to other countries and the reception of strangers, we enact as follows:--In the first place, let no one be allowed to go anywhere at all into a foreign country who is less than forty years of age; and no one shall go in a private capacity, but only in some public one, as a herald, or on an embassy; or on a sacred mission. Going abroad on an expedition or in war is not to be included among travels of the class authorized by the state. To Apollo at Delphi and to Zeus at Olympia and to Nemea and to the Isthmus, citizens should be sent to take part in the sacrifices and games there dedicated to the Gods; and they should send as many as possible, and the best and fairest that can be found, and they will make the city renowned at holy meetings in time of peace, procuring a glory which shall be the converse of that which is gained in war; and when they come home they shall teach the young that the institutions of other states are inferior to their own. And they shall send spectators of another sort, if they have the consent of the guardians, being such citizens as desire to look a little more at leisure at the doings of other men; and these no law shall hinder. For a city which has no experience of good and bad men or intercourse with them, can never be thoroughly and perfectly civilized, nor, again, can the citizens of a city properly observe the laws by habit only, and without an intelligent understanding of them. And there always are in the world a few inspired men whose acquaintance is beyond price, and who spring up quite as much in ill-ordered as in well-ordered cities. These are they whom the citizens of a well-ordered city should be ever seeking out, going forth over sea and over land to find him who is incorruptible-- that he may establish more firmly institutions in his own state which are good already; and amend what is deficient; for without this examination and enquiry a city will never continue perfect any more than if the examination is ill-conducted.

**CLEINIAS:** How can we have an examination and also a good one?

**ATHENIAN:** In this way:--In the first place, our spectator shall be of not less than fifty years of age; he must be a man of reputation, especially in war, if he is to exhibit to other cities a model of the guardians of the law, but when he is more than sixty years of age he shall no longer continue in his office of spectator. And when he has carried on his inspection during as many out of the ten years of his office as he pleases, on his return home let him go to the assembly of those who review the laws. This shall be a mixed body of young and old men, who shall be required to meet daily between the hour of dawn and the rising of the sun. They shall consist, in the first place, of the priests who have obtained the rewards of virtue; and in the second place, of guardians of the law, the ten eldest being chosen; the general superintendent of education shall also be a member, as well the last appointed as those who have been released from the office; and each of them shall take with him as his companion a young man, whomsoever he chooses, between the ages of thirty and forty. These shall be always holding conversation and discourse about the laws of their own city or about any specially good ones which they may hear to be existing elsewhere; also about kinds of knowledge which may appear to be of use and will throw light upon the examination, or of which the want will make the subject of laws dark and uncertain to them. Any knowledge of this sort which the elders approve, the younger men shall learn with all diligence; and if any one of those who have been invited appear to be unworthy, the whole assembly shall blame him who invited him. The rest of the city shall watch over those among the young men who distinguish themselves, having an eye upon them, and especially honouring them if they succeed, but dishonouring them above the rest if they turn out to be inferior. This is the assembly to which he who has visited the institutions of other men, on his return home shall straightway go, and if he have discovered any one who has anything to say about the enactment of laws or education or nurture, or if he have himself made any observations, let him communicate his discoveries to the whole assembly. And if he be seen to have come home neither better nor worse, let him be praised at any rate for his enthusiasm; and if he be much better, let him be praised so much the more; and not only while he lives but after his death let the assembly honour him with fitting honours. But if on his return home he appear to have been corrupted, pretending to be wise when he is not, let him hold no communication with any one, whether young or old; and if he will hearken to the rulers, then he shall be permitted to live as a private individual; but if he will not, let him die, if he be convicted in a court of law of interfering about education and the laws. And if he deserve to be indicted, and none of the magistrates indict him, let that be counted as a disgrace to them when the rewards of virtue are decided.

Let such be the character of the person who goes abroad, and let him go abroad under these conditions. In the next place, the stranger who comes from abroad should be received in a friendly spirit. Now there are four kinds of strangers, of whom we must make some mention--the first is he who comes and stays throughout the summer; this class are like birds of passage, taking wing in pursuit of commerce, and flying over the sea to other cities, while the season lasts; he shall be received in market-places and harbours and public buildings, near the city but outside, by those magistrates who are appointed to superintend these matters; and they shall take care that a stranger, whoever he be, duly receives justice; but he shall not be allowed to make any innovation. They shall hold the intercourse with him which is necessary, and this shall be as little as possible. The second kind is just a spectator who comes to see with his eyes and hear with his ears the festivals of the Muses; such ought to have entertainment provided them at the temples by hospitable persons, and the priests and ministers of the temples should see and attend to them. But they should not remain more than a reasonable time; let them see and hear that for the sake of which they came, and then go away, neither having suffered nor done any harm. The priests shall be their judges, if any of them receive or do any wrong up to the sum of fifty drachmae, but if any greater charge be brought, in such cases the suit shall come before the wardens of the agora. The third kind of stranger is he who comes on some public business from another land, and is to be received with public honours. He is to be received only by the generals and commanders of horse and foot, and the host by whom he is entertained, in conjunction with the Prytanes, shall have the sole charge of what concerns him. There is a fourth class of persons answering to our spectators, who come from another land to look at ours. In the first place, such visits will be rare, and the visitor should be at least fifty years of age; he may possibly be wanting to see something that is rich and rare in other states, or himself to show something in like manner to another city. Let such an one, then, go unbidden to the doors of the wise and rich, being one of them himself: let him go, for example, to the house of the superintendent of education, confident that he is a fitting guest of such a host, or let him go to the house of some of those who have gained the prize of virtue and hold discourse with them, both learning from them, and also teaching them; and when he has seen and heard all, he shall depart, as a friend taking leave of friends, and be honoured by them with gifts and suitable tributes of respect. These are the customs, according to which our city should receive all strangers of either sex who come from other countries, and should send forth her own citizens, showing respect to Zeus, the God of hospitality, not forbidding strangers at meals and sacrifices, as is the manner which prevails among the children of the Nile, nor driving them away by savage proclamations.

When a man becomes surety, let him give the security in a distinct form, acknowledging the whole transaction in a written document, and in the presence of not less than three witnesses if the sum be under a thousand drachmae, and of not less than five witnesses if the sum be above a thousand drachmae. The agent of a dishonest or untrustworthy seller shall himself be responsible; both the agent and the principal shall be equally liable. If a person wishes to find anything in the house of another, he shall enter naked, or wearing only a short tunic and without a girdle, having first taken an oath by the customary Gods that he expects to find it there; he shall then make his search, and the other shall throw open his house and allow him to search things both sealed and unsealed. And if a person will not allow the searcher to make his search, he who is prevented shall go to law with him, estimating the value of the goods after which he is searching, and if the other be convicted he shall pay twice the value of the article. If the master be absent from home, the dwellers in the house shall let him search the unsealed property, and on the sealed property the searcher shall set another seal, and shall appoint any one whom he likes to guard them during five days; and if the master of the house be absent during a longer time, he shall take with him the wardens of the city, and so make his search, opening the sealed property as well as the unsealed, and then, together with the members of the family and the wardens of the city, he shall seal them up again as they were before. There shall be a limit of time in the case of disputed things, and he who has had possession of them during a certain time shall no longer be liable to be disturbed. As to houses and lands there can be no dispute in this state of ours; but if a man has any other possessions which he has used and openly shown in the city and in the agora and in the temples, and no one has put in a claim to them, and some one says that he was looking for them during this time, and the possessor is proved to have made no concealment, if they have continued for a year, the one having the goods and the other looking for them, the claim of the seeker shall not be allowed after the expiration of the year; or if he does not use or show the lost property in the market or in the city, but only in the country, and no one offers himself as the owner during five years, at the expiration of the five years the claim shall be barred for ever after; or if he uses them in the city but within the house, then the appointed time of claiming the goods shall be three years, or ten years if he has them in the country in private. And if he has them in another land, there shall be no limit of time or prescription, but whenever the owner finds them he may claim them.

If any one prevents another by force from being present at a trial, whether a principal party or his witnesses; if the person prevented be a slave, whether his own or belonging to another, the suit shall be incomplete and invalid; but if he who is prevented be a freeman, besides the suit being incomplete, the other who has prevented him shall be imprisoned for a year, and shall be prosecuted for kidnapping by any one who pleases. And if any one hinders by force a rival competitor in gymnastic or music, or any other sort of contest, from being present at the contest, let him who has a mind inform the presiding judges, and they shall liberate him who is desirous of competing; and if they are not able, and he who hinders the other from competing wins the prize, then they shall give the prize of victory to him who is prevented, and inscribe him as the conqueror in any temples which he pleases; and he who hinders the other shall not be permitted to make any offering or inscription having reference to that contest, and in any case he shall be liable for damages, whether he be defeated or whether he conquer.

If any one knowingly receives anything which has been stolen, he shall undergo the same punishment as the thief, and if a man receives an exile he shall be punished with death. Every man should regard the friend and enemy of the state as his own friend and enemy; and if any one makes peace or war with another on his own account, and without the authority of the state, he, like the receiver of the exile, shall undergo the penalty of death. And if any fraction of the city declare war or peace against any, the generals shall indict the authors of this proceeding, and if they are convicted death shall be the penalty. Those who serve their country ought to serve without receiving gifts, and there ought to be no excusing or approving the saying, 'Men should receive gifts as the reward of good, but not of evil deeds'; for to know which we are doing, and to stand fast by our knowledge, is no easy matter. The safest course is to obey the law which says, 'Do no service for a bribe,' and let him who disobeys, if he be convicted, simply die. With a view to taxation, for various reasons, every man ought to have had his property valued: and the tribesmen should likewise bring a register of the yearly produce to the wardens of the country, that in this way there may be two valuations; and the public officers may use annually whichever on consideration they deem the best, whether they prefer to take a certain portion of the whole value, or of the annual revenue, after subtracting what is paid to the common tables.

Touching offerings to the Gods, a moderate man should observe moderation in what he offers. Now the land and the hearth of the house of all men is sacred to all Gods; wherefore let no man dedicate them a second time to the Gods. Gold and silver, whether possessed by private persons or in temples, are in other cities provocative of envy, and ivory, the product of a dead body, is not a proper offering; brass and iron, again, are instruments of war; but of wood let a man bring what offering he likes, provided it be a single block, and in like manner of stone, to the public temples; of woven work let him not offer more than one woman can execute in a month. White is a colour suitable to the Gods, especially in woven works, but dyes should only be used for the adornments of war. The most divine of gifts are birds and images, and they should be such as one painter can execute in a single day. And let all other offerings follow a similar rule.

Now that the whole city has been divided into parts of which the nature and number have been described, and laws have been given about all the most important contracts as far as this was possible, the next thing will be to have justice done. The first of the courts shall consist of elected judges, who shall be chosen by the plaintiff and the defendant in common: these shall be called arbiters rather than judges. And in the second court there shall be judges of the villages and tribes corresponding to the twelvefold division of the land, and before these the litigants shall go to contend for greater damages, if the suit be not decided before the first judges; the defendant, if he be defeated the second time, shall pay a fifth more than the damages mentioned in the indictment; and if he find fault with his judges and would try a third time, let him carry the suit before the select judges, and if he be again defeated, let him pay the whole of the damages and half as much again. And the plaintiff, if when defeated before the first judges he persist in going on to the second, shall if he wins receive in addition to the damages a fifth part more, and if defeated he shall pay a like sum; but if he is not satisfied with the previous decision, and will insist on proceeding to a third court, then if he win he shall receive from the defendant the amount of the damages and, as I said before, half as much again, and the plaintiff, if he lose, shall pay half of the damages claimed. Now the assignment by lot of judges to courts and the completion of the number of them, and the appointment of servants to the different magistrates, and the times at which the several causes should be heard, and the votings and delays, and all the things that necessarily concern suits, and the order of causes, and the time in which answers have to be put in and parties are to appear--of these and other things akin to these we have indeed already spoken, but there is no harm in repeating what is right twice or thrice:--All lesser and easier matters which the elder legislator has omitted may be supplied by the younger one. Private courts will be sufficiently regulated in this way, and the public and state courts, and those which the magistrates must use in the administration of their several offices, exist in many other states. Many very respectable institutions of this sort have been framed by good men, and from them the guardians of the law may by reflection derive what is necessary for the order of our new state, considering and correcting them, and bringing them to the test of experience, until every detail appears to be satisfactorily determined; and then putting the final seal upon them, and making them irreversible, they shall use them for ever afterwards. As to what relates to the silence of judges and the abstinence from words of evil omen and the reverse, and the different notions of the just and good and honourable which exist in our own as compared with other states, they have been partly mentioned already, and another part of them will be mentioned hereafter as we draw near the end. To all these matters he who would be an equal judge shall justly look, and he shall possess writings about them that he may learn them. For of all kinds of knowledge the knowledge of good laws has the greatest power of improving the learner; otherwise there would be no meaning the divine and admirable law possessing a name akin to mind (nous, nomos). And of all other words, such as the praises and censures of individuals which occur in poetry and also in prose, whether written down or uttered in daily conversation, whether men dispute about them in the spirit of contention or weakly assent to them, as is often the case--of all these the one sure test is the writings of the legislator, which the righteous judge ought to have in his mind as the antidote of all other words, and thus make himself and the city stand upright, procuring for the good the continuance and increase of justice, and for the bad, on the other hand, a conversion from ignorance and intemperance, and in general from all unrighteousness, as far as their evil minds can be healed, but to those whose web of life is in reality finished, giving death, which is the only remedy for souls in their condition, as I may say truly again and again. And such judges and chiefs of judges will be worthy of receiving praise from the whole city.

When the suits of the year are completed the following laws shall regulate their execution:--In the first place, the judge shall assign to the party who wins the suit the whole property of him who loses, with the exception of mere necessaries, and the assignment shall be made through the herald immediately after each decision in the hearing of the judges; and when the month arrives following the month in which the courts are sitting, (unless the gainer of the suit has been previously satisfied,) the court shall follow up the case, and hand over to the winner the goods of the loser; but if they find that he has not the means of paying, and the sum deficient is not less than a drachma, the insolvent person shall not have any right of going to law with any other man until he have satisfied the debt of the winning party; but other persons shall still have the right of bringing suits against him. And if any one after he is condemned refuses to acknowledge the authority which condemned him, let the magistrates who are thus deprived of their authority bring him before the court of the guardians of the law, and if he be cast, let him be punished with death, as a subverter of the whole state and of the laws.

Thus a man is born and brought up, and after this manner he begets and brings up his own children, and has his share of dealings with other men, and suffers if he has done wrong to any one, and receives satisfaction if he has been wronged, and so at length in due time he grows old under the protection of the laws, and his end comes in the order of nature. Concerning the dead of either sex, the religious ceremonies which may fittingly be performed, whether appertaining to the Gods of the under-world or of this, shall be decided by the interpreters with absolute authority. Their sepulchres are not to be in places which are fit for cultivation, and there shall be no monuments in such spots, either large or small, but they shall occupy that part of the country which is naturally adapted for receiving and concealing the bodies of the dead with as little hurt as possible to the living. No man, living or dead, shall deprive the living of the sustenance which the earth, their foster-parent, is naturally inclined to provide for them. And let not the mound be piled higher than would be the work of five men completed in five days; nor shall the stone which is placed over the spot be larger than would be sufficient to receive the praises of the dead included in four heroic lines. Nor shall the laying out of the dead in the house continue for a longer time than is sufficient to distinguish between him who is in a trance only and him who is really dead, and speaking generally, the third day after death will be a fair time for carrying out the body to the sepulchre. Now we must believe the legislator when he tells us that the soul is in all respects superior to the body, and that even in life what makes each one us to be what we are is only the soul; and that the body follows us about in the likeness of each of us, and therefore, when we are dead, the bodies of the dead are quite rightly said to be our shades or images; for the true and immortal being of each one of us which is called the soul goes on her way to other Gods, before them to give an account--which is an inspiring hope to the good, but very terrible to the bad, as the laws of our fathers tell us; and they also say that not much can be done in the way of helping a man after he is dead. But the living--he should be helped by all his kindred, that while in life he may be the holiest and justest of men, and after death may have no great sins to be punished in the world below. If this be true, a man ought not to waste his substance under the idea that all this lifeless mass of flesh which is in process of burial is connected with him; he should consider that the son, or brother, or the beloved one, whoever he may be, whom he thinks he is laying in the earth, has gone away to complete and fulfil his own destiny, and that his duty is rightly to order the present, and to spend moderately on the lifeless altar of the Gods below. But the legis ator does not intend moderation to be taken in the sense of meanness. Let the law, then, be as follows:--The expenditure on the entire funeral of him who is of the highest class, shall not exceed five minae; and for him who is of the second class, three minae, and for him who is of the third class, two minae, and for him who is of the fourth class, one mina, will be a fair limit of expense. The guardians of the law ought to take especial care of the different ages of life, whether childhood, or manhood, or any other age. And at the end of all, let there be some one guardian of the law presiding, who shall be chosen by the friends of the deceased to superintend, and let it be glory to him to manage with fairness and moderation what relates to the dead, and a discredit to him if they are not well managed. Let the laying out and other ceremonies be in accordance with custom, but to the statesman who adopts custom as his law we must give way in certain particulars. It would be monstrous for example that he should command any man to weep or abstain from weeping over the dead; but he may forbid cries of lamentation, and not allow the voice of the mourner to be heard outside the house; also, he may forbid the bringing of the dead body into the open streets, or the processions of mourners in the streets, and may require that before daybreak they should be outside the city. Let these, then, be our laws relating to such matters, and let him who obeys be free from penalty; but he who disobeys even a single guardian of the law shall be punished by them all with a fitting penalty. Other modes of burial, or again the denial of burial, which is to be refused in the case of robbers of temples and parricides and the like, have been devised and are embodied in the preceding laws, so that now our work of legislation is pretty nearly at an end; but in all cases the end does not consist in doing something or acquiring something or establishing something,--the end will be attained and finally accomplished, when we have provided for the perfect and lasting continuance of our institutions; until then our creation is incomplete.

**CLEINIAS:** That is very good Stranger; but I wish you would tell me more clearly what you mean.

**ATHENIAN:** O Cleinias, many things of old time were well said and sung; and the saying about the Fates was one of them.

**CLEINIAS:** What is it?

**ATHENIAN:** The saying that Lachesis or the giver of the lots is the first of them, and that Clotho or the spinster is the second of them, and that Atropos or the unchanging one is the third of them; and that she is the preserver of the things which we have spoken, and which have been compared in a figure to things woven by fire, they both (i.e. Atropos and the fire) producing the quality of unchangeableness. I am speaking of the things which in a state and government give not only health and salvation to the body, but law, or rather preservation of the law, in the soul; and, if I am not mistaken, this seems to be still wanting in our laws: we have still to see how we can implant in them this irreversible nature.

**CLEINIAS:** It will be no small matter if we can only discover how such a nature can be implanted in anything.

**ATHENIAN:** But it certainly can be; so much I clearly see.

**CLEINIAS:** Then let us not think of desisting until we have imparted this quality to our laws; for it is ridiculous, after a great deal of labour has been spent, to place a thing at last on an insecure foundation.

**MEGILLUS:** I approve of your suggestion, and am quite of the same mind with you.

**CLEINIAS:** Very good: And now what, according to you, is to be the salvation of our government and of our laws, and how is it to be effected?

**ATHENIAN:** Were we not saying that there must be in our city a council which was to be of this sort:--The ten oldest guardians of the law, and all those who have obtained prizes of virtue, were to meet in the same assembly, and the council was also to include those who had visited foreign countries in the hope of hearing something that might be of use in the preservation of the laws, and who, having come safely home, and having been tested in these same matters, had proved themselves to be worthy to take part in the assembly;--each of the members was to select some young man of not less than thirty years of age, he himself judging in the first instance whether the young man was worthy by nature and education, and then suggesting him to the others, and if he seemed to them also to be worthy they were to adopt him; but if not, the decision at which they arrived was to be kept a secret from the citizens at large; and, more especially, from the rejected candidate. The meeting of the council was to be held early in the morning, when everybody was most at leisure from all other business, whether public or private--was not something of this sort said by us before?

**CLEINIAS:** True.

**ATHENIAN:** Then, returning to the council, I would say further, that if we let it down to be the anchor of the state, our city, having everything which is suitable to her, will preserve all that we wish to preserve.

**CLEINIAS:** What do you mean?

**ATHENIAN:** Now is the time for me to speak the truth in all earnestness.

**CLEINIAS:** Well said, and I hope that you will fulfil your intention.

**ATHENIAN:** Know, Cleinias, that everything, in all that it does, has a natural saviour, as of an animal the soul and the head are the chief saviours.

**CLEINIAS:** Once more, what do you mean?

**ATHENIAN:** The well-being of those two is obviously the preservation of every living thing.

**CLEINIAS:** How is that?

**ATHENIAN:** The soul, besides other things, contains mind, and the head, besides other things, contains sight and hearing; and the mind, mingling with the noblest of the senses, and becoming one with them, may be truly called the salvation of all.

**CLEINIAS:** Yes, quite so.

**ATHENIAN:** Yes, indeed; but with what is that intellect concerned which, mingling with the senses, is the salvation of ships in storms as well as in fair weather? In a ship, when the pilot and the sailors unite their perceptions with the piloting mind, do they not save both themselves and their craft?

**CLEINIAS:** Very true.

**ATHENIAN:** We do not want many illustrations about such matters:--What aim would the general of an army, or what aim would a physician propose to himself, if he were seeking to attain salvation?

**CLEINIAS:** Very good.

**ATHENIAN:** Does not the general aim at victory and superiority in war, and do not the physician and his assistants aim at producing health in the body?

**CLEINIAS:** Certainly.

**ATHENIAN:** And a physician who is ignorant about the body, that is to say, who knows not that which we just now called health, or a general who knows not victory, or any others who are ignorant of the particulars of the arts which we mentioned, cannot be said to have understanding about any of these matters.

**CLEINIAS:** They cannot.

**ATHENIAN:** And what would you say of the state? If a person proves to be ignorant of the aim to which the statesman should look, ought he, in the first place, to be called a ruler at all; further, will he ever be able to preserve that of which he does not even know the aim?

**CLEINIAS:** Impossible.

**ATHENIAN:** And therefore, if our settlement of the country is to be perfect, we ought to have some institution, which, as I was saying, will tell what is the aim of the state, and will inform us how we are to attain this, and what law or what man will advise us to that end. Any state which has no such institution is likely to be devoid of mind and sense, and in all her actions will proceed by mere chance.

**CLEINIAS:** Very true.

**ATHENIAN:** In which, then, of the parts or institutions of the state is any such guardian power to be found? Can we say?

**CLEINIAS:** I am not quite certain, Stranger; but I have a suspicion that you are referring to the assembly which you just now said was to meet at night.

**ATHENIAN:** You understand me perfectly, Cleinias; and we must assume, as the argument implies, that this council possesses all virtue; and the beginning of virtue is not to make mistakes by guessing many things, but to look steadily at one thing, and on this to fix all our aims.

**CLEINIAS:** Quite true.

**ATHENIAN:** Then now we shall see why there is nothing wonderful in states going astray--the reason is that their legislators have such different aims; nor is there anything wonderful in some laying down as their rule of justice, that certain individuals should bear rule in the state, whether they be good or bad, and others that the citizens should be rich, not caring whether they are the slaves of other men or not. The tendency of others, again, is towards freedom; and some legislate with a view to two things at once,--they want to be at the same time free and the lords of other states; but the wisest men, as they deem themselves to be, look to all these and similar aims, and there is no one of them which they exclusively honour, and to which they would have all things look.

**CLEINIAS:** Then, Stranger, our former assertion will hold, for we were saying that laws generally should look to one thing only; and this, as we admitted, was rightly said to be virtue.

**ATHENIAN:** Yes.

**CLEINIAS:** And we said that virtue was of four kinds?

**ATHENIAN:** Quite true.

**CLEINIAS:** And that mind was the leader of the four, and that to her the three other virtues and all other things ought to have regard?

**ATHENIAN:** You follow me capitally, Cleinias, and I would ask you to follow me to the end, for we have already said that the mind of the pilot, the mind of the physician and of the general look to that one thing to which they ought to look; and now we may turn to mind political, of which, as of a human creature, we will ask a question:--O wonderful being, and to what are you looking? The physician is able to tell his single aim in life, but you, the superior, as you declare yourself to be, of all intelligent beings, when you are asked are not able to tell. Can you, Megillus, and you, Cleinias, say distinctly what is the aim of mind political, in return for the many explanations of things which I have given you?

**CLEINIAS:** We cannot, Stranger.

**ATHENIAN:** Well, but ought we not to desire to see it, and to see where it is to be found?

**CLEINIAS:** For example, where?

**ATHENIAN:** For example, we were saying that there are four kinds of virtue, and as there are four of them, each of them must be one.

**CLEINIAS:** Certainly.

**ATHENIAN:** And further, all four of them we call one; for we say that courage is virtue, and that prudence is virtue, and the same of the two others, as if they were in reality not many but one, that is, virtue.

**CLEINIAS:** Quite so.

**ATHENIAN:** There is no difficulty in seeing in what way the two differ from one another, and have received two names, and so of the rest. But there is more difficulty in explaining why we call these two and the rest of them by the single name of virtue.

**CLEINIAS:** How do you mean?

**ATHENIAN:** I have no difficulty in explaining what I mean. Let us distribute the subject into questions and answers.

**CLEINIAS:** Once more, what do you mean?

**ATHENIAN:** Ask me what is that one thing which call virtue, and then again speak of as two, one part being courage and the other wisdom. I will tell you how that occurs:--One of them has to do with fear; in this the beasts also participate, and quite young children,--I mean courage; for a courageous temper is a gift of nature and not of reason. But without reason there never has been, or is, or will be a wise and understanding soul; it is of a different nature.

**CLEINIAS:** That is true.

**ATHENIAN:** I have now told you in what way the two are different, and do you in return tell me in what way they are one and the same. Suppose that I ask you in what way the four are one, and when you have answered me, you will have a right to ask of me in return in what way they are four; and then let us proceed to enquire whether in the case of things which have a name and also a definition to them, true knowledge consists in knowing the name only and not the definition. Can he who is good for anything be ignorant of all this without discredit where great and glorious truths are concerned?

**CLEINIAS:** I suppose not.

**ATHENIAN:** And is there anything greater to the legislator and the guardian of the law, and to him who thinks that he excels all other men in virtue, and has won the palm of excellence, than these very qualities of which we are now speaking,--courage, temperance, wisdom, justice?

**CLEINIAS:** How can there be anything greater?

**ATHENIAN:** And ought not the interpreters, the teachers, the lawgivers, the guardians of the other citizens, to excel the rest of mankind, and perfectly to show him who desires to learn and know or whose evil actions require to be punished and reproved, what is the nature of virtue and vice? Or shall some poet who has found his way into the city, or some chance person who pretends to be an instructor of youth, show himself to be better than him who has won the prize for every virtue? And can we wonder that when the guardians are not adequate in speech or action, and have no adequate knowledge of virtue, the city being unguarded should experience the common fate of cities in our day?

**CLEINIAS:** Wonder! no.

**ATHENIAN:** Well, then, must we do as we said? Or can we give our guardians a more precise knowledge of virtue in speech and action than the many have? or is there any way in which our city can be made to resemble the head and senses of rational beings because possessing such a guardian power?

**CLEINIAS:** What, Stranger, is the drift of your comparison?

**ATHENIAN:** Do we not see that the city is the trunk, and are not the younger guardians, who are chosen for their natural gifts, placed in the head of the state, having their souls all full of eyes, with which they look about the whole city? They keep watch and hand over their perceptions to the memory, and inform the elders of all that happens in the city; and those whom we compared to the mind, because they have many wise thoughts-- that is to say, the old men--take counsel, and making use of the younger men as their ministers, and advising with them,--in this way both together truly preserve the whole state:--Shall this or some other be the order of our state? Are all our citizens to be equal in acquirements, or shall there be special persons among them who have received a more careful training and education?

**CLEINIAS:** That they should be equal, my good sir, is impossible.

**ATHENIAN:** Then we ought to proceed to some more exact training than any which has preceded.

**CLEINIAS:** Certainly.

**ATHENIAN:** And must not that of which we are in need be the one to which we were just now alluding?

**CLEINIAS:** Very true.

**ATHENIAN:** Did we not say that the workman or guardian, if he be perfect in every respect, ought not only to be able to see the many aims, but he should press onward to the one? this he should know, and knowing, order all things with a view to it.

**CLEINIAS:** True.

**ATHENIAN:** And can any one have a more exact way of considering or contemplating anything, than the being able to look at one idea gathered from many different things?

**CLEINIAS:** Perhaps not.

**ATHENIAN:** Not 'Perhaps not,' but 'Certainly not,' my good sir, is the right answer. There never has been a truer method than this discovered by any man.

**CLEINIAS:** I bow to your authority, Stranger; let us proceed in the way which you propose.

**ATHENIAN:** Then, as would appear, we must compel the guardians of our divine state to perceive, in the first place, what that principle is which is the same in all the four--the same, as we affirm, in courage and in temperance, and in justice and in prudence, and which, being one, we call as we ought, by the single name of virtue. To this, my friends, we will, if you please, hold fast, and not let go until we have sufficiently explained what that is to which we are to look, whether to be regarded as one, or as a whole, or as both, or in whatever way. Are we likely ever to be in a virtuous condition, if we cannot tell whether virtue is many, or four, or one? Certainly, if we take counsel among ourselves, we shall in some way contrive that this principle has a place amongst us; but if you have made up your mind that we should let the matter alone, we will.

**CLEINIAS:** We must not, Stranger, by the God of strangers I swear that we must not, for in our opinion you speak most truly; but we should like to know how you will accomplish your purpose.

**ATHENIAN:** Wait a little before you ask; and let us, first of all, be quite agreed with one another that the purpose has to be accomplished.

**CLEINIAS:** Certainly, it ought to be, if it can be.

**ATHENIAN:** Well, and about the good and the honourable, are we to take the same view? Are our guardians only to know that each of them is many, or also how and in what way they are one?

**CLEINIAS:** They must consider also in what sense they are one.

**ATHENIAN:** And are they to consider only, and to be unable to set forth what they think?

**CLEINIAS:** Certainly not; that would be the state of a slave.

**ATHENIAN:** And may not the same be said of all good things--that the true guardians of the laws ought to know the truth about them, and to be able to interpret them in words, and carry them out in action, judging of what is and what is not well, according to nature?

**CLEINIAS:** Certainly.

**ATHENIAN:** Is not the knowledge of the Gods which we have set forth with so much zeal one of the noblest sorts of knowledge;--to know that they are, and know how great is their power, as far as in man lies? We do indeed excuse the mass of the citizens, who only follow the voice of the laws, but we refuse to admit as guardians any who do not labour to obtain every possible evidence that there is respecting the Gods; our city is forbidden and not allowed to choose as a guardian of the law, or to place in the select order of virtue, him who is not an inspired man, and has not laboured at these things.

**CLEINIAS:** It is certainly just, as you say, that he who is indolent about such matters or incapable should be rejected, and that things honourable should be put away from him.

**ATHENIAN:** Are we assured that there are two things which lead men to believe in the Gods, as we have already stated?

**CLEINIAS:** What are they?

**ATHENIAN:** One is the argument about the soul, which has been already mentioned--that it is the eldest, and most divine of all things, to which motion attaining generation gives perpetual existence; the other was an argument from the order of the motion of the stars, and of all things under the dominion of the mind which ordered the universe. If a man look upon the world not lightly or ignorantly, there was never any one so godless who did not experience an effect opposite to that which the many imagine. For they think that those who handle these matters by the help of astronomy, and the accompanying arts of demonstration, may become godless, because they see, as far as they can see, things happening by necessity, and not by an intelligent will accomplishing good.

**CLEINIAS:** But what is the fact?

**ATHENIAN:** Just the opposite, as I said, of the opinion which once prevailed among men, that the sun and stars are without soul. Even in those days men wondered about them, and that which is now ascertained was then conjectured by some who had a more exact knowledge of them--that if they had been things without soul, and had no mind, they could never have moved with numerical exactness so wonderful; and even at that time some ventured to hazard the conjecture that mind was the orderer of the universe. But these same persons again mistaking the nature of the soul, which they conceived to be younger and not older than the body, once more overturned the world, or rather, I should say, themselves; for the bodies which they saw moving in heaven all appeared to be full of stones, and earth, and many other lifeless substances, and to these they assigned the causes of all things. Such studies gave rise to much atheism and perplexity, and the poets took occasion to be abusive,--comparing the philosophers to she-dogs uttering vain howlings, and talking other nonsense of the same sort. But now, as I said, the case is reversed.

**CLEINIAS:** How so?

**ATHENIAN:** No man can be a true worshipper of the Gods who does not know these two principles--that the soul is the eldest of all things which are born, and is immortal and rules over all bodies; moreover, as I have now said several times, he who has not contemplated the mind of nature which is said to exist in the stars, and gone through the previous training, and seen the connexion of music with these things, and harmonized them all with laws and institutions, is not able to give a reason of such things as have a reason. And he who is unable to acquire this in addition to the ordinary virtues of a citizen, can hardly be a good ruler of a whole state; but he should be the subordinate of other rulers. Wherefore, Cleinias and Megillus, let us consider whether we may not add to all the other laws which we have discussed this further one,--that the nocturnal assembly of the magistrates, which has also shared in the whole scheme of education proposed by us, shall be a guard set according to law for the salvation of the state. Shall we propose this?

**CLEINIAS:** Certainly, my good friend, we will if the thing is in any degree possible.

**ATHENIAN:** Let us make a common effort to gain such an object; for I too will gladly share in the attempt. Of these matters I have had much experience, and have often considered them, and I dare say that I shall be able to find others who will also help.

**CLEINIAS:** I agree, Stranger, that we should proceed along the road in which God is guiding us; and how we can proceed rightly has now to be investigated and explained.

**ATHENIAN:** O Megillus and Cleinias, about these matters we cannot legislate further until the council is constituted; when that is done, then we will determine what authority they shall have of their own; but the explanation of how this is all to be ordered would only be given rightly in a long discourse.

**CLEINIAS:** What do you mean, and what new thing is this?

**ATHENIAN:** In the first place, a list would have to be made out of those who by their ages and studies and dispositions and habits are well fitted for the duty of a guardian. In the next place, it will not be easy for them to discover themselves what they ought to learn, or become the disciple of one who has already made the discovery. Furthermore, to write down the times at which, and during which, they ought to receive the several kinds of instruction, would be a vain thing; for the learners themselves do not know what is learned to advantage until the knowledge which is the result of learning has found a place in the soul of each. And so these details, although they could not be truly said to be secret, might be said to be incapable of being stated beforehand, because when stated they would have no meaning.

**CLEINIAS:** What then are we to do, Stranger, under these circumstances?

**ATHENIAN:** As the proverb says, the answer is no secret, but open to all of us:--We must risk the whole on the chance of throwing, as they say, thrice six or thrice ace, and I am willing to share with you the danger by stating and explaining to you my views about education and nurture, which is the question coming to the surface again. The danger is not a slight or ordinary one, and I would advise you, Cleinias, in particular, to see to the matter; for if you order rightly the city of the Magnetes, or whatever name God may give it, you will obtain the greatest glory; or at any rate you will be thought the most courageous of men in the estimation of posterity. Dear companions, if this our divine assembly can only be established, to them we will hand over the city;

none of the present company of legislators, as I may call them, would hesitate about that. And the state will be perfected and become a waking reality, which a little while ago we attempted to create as a dream and in idea only, mingling together reason and mind in one image, in the hope that our citizens might be duly mingled and rightly educated; and being educated, and dwelling in the citadel of the land, might become perfect guardians, such as we have never seen in all our previous life, by reason of the saving virtue which is in them.

**MEGILLUS:** Dear Cleinias, after all that has been said, either we must detain the Stranger, and by supplications and in all manner of ways make him share in the foundation of the city, or we must give up the undertaking.

**CLEINIAS:** Very true, Megillus; and you must join with me in detaining him.

**MEGILLUS:** I will.

Made in the USA
Monee, IL
04 November 2026

67384066R00167